GENIUS, POWER AND MAGIC

A Cultural History of Germany
from Goethe to Wagner

RODERICK CAVALIERO

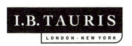

I.B.TAURIS
LONDON · NEW YORK

Published in 2013 by I.B. Tauris & Co Ltd
6 Salem Road, London W2 4BU
175 Fifth Avenue, New York NY 10010
www.ibtauris.com

Distributed in the United States and Canada Exclusively by Palgrave Macmillan
175 Fifth Avenue, New York NY 10010

ISBN: 978 1 78076 400 9

A full CIP record for this book is available from the British Library
A full CIP record is available from the Library of Congress

Library of Congress Catalog Card Number: available

Every attempt has been made to gain permission for the use of the images in this book.
Any omissions will be rectified in future editions.

Typeset in Perpetua by 4word Ltd, Bristol

Printed and bound in Britain by T.J. International, Padstow, Cornwall

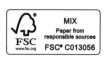

MIX
Paper from
responsible sources
FSC® C013056

Contents

List of Illustrations		vi
	Introduction	1
1.	Fitzboodle in Pumpernickel	13
2.	A German Panorama	23
3.	Genius: Germans in Search of God	43
4.	Genius: Germans in Search of Man (1)	55
5.	Genius: Germans in Search of Man (2)	69
6.	Potentates and Patrons (1)	87
7.	Potentates and Patrons (2)	103
8.	The Catholic South	119
9.	Magic: Musical Germany	127
10.	Pumpernickel Discovered	147
11.	Revolution Across the Rhine	163
12.	The Return of 'Pumpernickel'	183
13.	Romance on the Rhine	207
14.	The Tales of the Hoffmen	225
15.	Harmony and Dissonance	247
16.	Butterflies or Maggots	271
17.	'Pumpernickel' by Binoculars	289
18.	Power over Genius and Magic	313
Chronological Data		329
Notes		335
Bibliography		365
Index		371

Illustrations

1. Caspar David Friedrich, *The Stages of Life* (1830). Museum der bildenden Künste, Leipzig.
2. Dominikus Zimmermann (1685–1766), Wies Pilgrimage Church, Steingaden (1750s).
3. King Ludwig II, as a general in the Bavarian army, in coronation robes in 1865, aged 20. Bayerische Staatsgemäldesammlungen, Munich.
4. Richard Wagner, 1882, a portrait by Pierre-Auguste Renoir, from the Musée d'Orsay, Paris.
5. Karl Friedrich Schinkel (1781–1841), arch-Romantic and polymath, *A Gothic Temple by Water* (1823). Nationalgalerie, Berlin, Staatlichen Museen Preussischer Kulturbesitz.
6. Karl Friedrich Schinkel, *A Riverbank in Streslau* (1817). Nationalgalerie, Berlin, Staatlichen Museen Preussischer Kulturbesitz.
7. Schloss Solitude, the city imitation of Versailles that Duke Charles Eugene of Württemberg built in Stuttgart between 1763 and 1767. Staatsgalerie, Stuttgart.
8. *Tannhäuser in the Venusberg*, a painting by John Collier (1901). Atkinson Art Gallery, Southport, Lancashire.
9. A musical party given in a cartoon by Thomas Rowlandson (1736–1827). Musicians' Union. Private collection.
10. The real Baron (Freiherr) Karl Friedrich Münchhausen according to Gustave Doré. Public domain.
11. A pencil sketch of Hoffmann, third from right, carrying his hat, by Johann Peter Lyser in 1833. André Meyer collection, Paris in H. C. Robbins-Landon, *Beethoven*.
12. *La ballade de Lénore* by Horace Vernet (1849). Musée de Beaux-Arts, Nantes, France.
13. The Rhine-maidens in *Das Rheingold*. Arthur Rackham, *The Rainbow Bridge into Valhalla*, from *The Rhinegold and the Valkyrie*, William Heinemann, London, 1912.
14. Lola Montez in 1847, from a portrait by Joseph Karl Stieler. Schonheitenberg Gallerie (Gallery of Beauties), Munich.

Genius, Power and Magic

A Land of Pumpernickel, Philosophy and Poetry

Providence has given to the French the empire of the land, to the
English that of the sea, and to the Germans that of – the air.
(Attributed by Thomas Carlyle to Johann Paul Richter [1763–1825])

There is an imperative which commands certain conduct
immediately … This imperative is Categorical …
This imperative may be called that of Morality.
(Immanuel Kant, *Fundamental Principles of the Metaphysics of Ethics*, 1785)

Thy bread Westphalia, thy brown bread I sing,
Bread which might make the dinner of a king;
Though one of those whom Englishmen call dogs,
One whose nice palate has been us'd to frogs,
Could not, forsooth, digest a stuff so coarse,
But call'd it good provision for his horse.
(James Boswell, *On the Grand Tour*, 20 October 1764)

*T*HE AIR TO which Germany was given the empire, in the words
of Johann Paul Richter, was that numinous, vaporous mist of
metaphysical complexity. Some of this was interpreted as genius, much as
magic. Power it was not, since the Germany that entered the eighteenth
century was a loose conglomeration of variously sovereign principalities,
nurtured on deep thought, fine music and hard rye bread which, in terms
of power, seemed an essential futility. Some were sustained by memories
of a past as inheritors of the power and prestige of the Roman Empire,

as a bulwark against the menace from the east, as myrmidons of Imperial greatness, as champions of Martin Luther and reformed Christianity. Others were still in the vanguard of Latinity, in their devotion to Rome, sandwiched as they were between Rome's two protectors, the empires of Austria and France. The first was the titular legatee of the Holy Roman Empire, the second heir to Louis XIV's Carolingian hubris, and both were locked in almost permanent rivalry for land, power and influence. As a result there were few visitors to a land that consisted largely of forest, unless they were the armies that pillaged and sacked their way across territory not their own, in struggles that left a trail of desolation for those who had no lord strong enough to protect them.

Some of that past had been glorious. Germans had defended Europe from the Mongol, and the Slav and, for those who wanted to be free of him, had defied the Pope. But during a 30-year war, which finally ended in virtual stalemate in 1648, their country had been torn to pieces by religious strife, trampled over by polyglot Imperial armies, Swedes and French. Her Imperial grandeur now belonged to Austria, her German-speaking but hardly German neighbour to the south, who had, in that war, employed mercenary armies to achieve religious conformity and dynastic ambition. By the beginning of the eighteenth century that other menace to peace and prosperity, Louis XIV's vain ambitions, had been thwarted by the genius of the Duke of Marlborough. But a brittle glamour from across the Rhine still dazzled German potentates with dreams that they might too if they pressed hard enough on their citizenry and kept out of serious trouble, be *rois soleils*, living in grand palaces and indulging their royal whims. The princes collected soldiers, less for defence than for show and as a source of income, lending them out to more powerful monarchs. Their principal use, otherwise, was to play war games, sometimes, weather permitting, in the vast palaces themselves. They also formed the nucleus of orchestras for which many of the princes had a passion. The princesses largely stocked nurseries, for Germany was known for her plentiful supply of consorts to be found among her philoprogenitive royalty. By an accident of marriage and dynastic history, Great Britain had found her king there. That gave the electorate of Hanover prestige for its ruler as a king, if not a German king, but little else.

It was hard for ordinary mortals to appreciate what was happening in Germany. The language was largely incomprehensible, and though she was virtually a cultural colony of France, she was no France. Nor, despite her forests and mountains, her medieval cities and Gothic cathedrals, was she Italy. Such Romance as she had was that of the fairy story, and her fairy stories were pretty gruesome. During the long eighteenth and nineteenth centuries between the end of the War of Spanish Succession (1701–14) and the coronation of a Prussian overlord as *Kaiser* (1871), Germany was understood to be a land of Pumpernickel, Philosophers and Poets. All three were largely indigestible to foreigners and not to them alone, but in that time Germany experienced a renaissance in many ways as epoch-making as that of their fellow 'geographical expression', Italy. The collective, idiosyncratic description of the principalities of pre-Imperial Germany as 'Pumpernickel' states derives from Thackeray's excursions into the pocket handkerchief-size Grand-Duchy of Kalbsbraten-Pumpernickel in *The Fitzboodle Papers* and *Vanity Fair*. Pumpernickel was one of the components of that air, wind rather, of abstractions and eccentricities of which in Johann Paul Richter's words Germany had the empire. Thackeray's lofty detachment from their grand ducal triviality was worthy of the Punch editorial table, and was intended to cast a comic light on the ferment of intellectual energy many of them were experiencing, but Thackeray was too lofty to perceive that this ferment was questioning the position of God, of man, of nature and sensibility, drinking deep of the elixir of Romance that was beginning to sweep across Europe at the time. The German princes may have been as essentially powerless in the face of their final destiny, as were their Italian counterparts, but their Romantic Renaissance was to be every bit as profound.

European Romanticism was fuelled by British empiricism, French rationalism and German mysticism. The emergence of British world power was attributed to their sense of enquiry linked to a lust for adventure, which gave them the empire of the sea. Britain's was not *une mission civilisatrice;* they were in pursuit of markets and pelth. France on the other hand, apart from empire of the land, was also the so-far unchallenged conquistador of an intellectual empire. The Germans, in response to both, sought to establish a claim to a culture, however insubstantial, which acknowledged her past and defined her future, and in this they evoked, if they did not entirely accept, the rational enlightenment of both France and England.

These essays attempt, not to define that German culture, which continues to defy simple prescription, but to chart how under prevailing Romantic influences it limped from the empire of the 'insubstantial air' to an intellectual power that could rival the fascination of France, and challenge the pragmatic certainties of England. France had traditionally seen Austria as her main European rival and France's cultural colonies, the German states, as uncertain allies and fair-weather friends. England saw the German states mainly as a source of mercenaries and of that other kind of mercenary, royal spouses. When one of the French intellectual conquistadors, Madame de Staël, was exiled by Napoleon, she made her home in French, not German-speaking Switzerland, but she saw in Germany, not Austria, a potential challenge to French intellectual supremacy.

In England, transmogrified into Great Britain, only philologists were interested in their Germanic roots; even Dr Johnson was more at home in the classical and Romance texts. German might be a language spoken by Baltic traders, but diplomatists and other visitors used French. The British royal family may have been German but by 1760 the monarch, George III, claimed that he was first and foremost a Briton. Over the century three things were to promote an interest in Germany; the Anglophilia of her foremost savant and poet, Goethe; the earth-shaking discovery by German writers of William Shakespeare; and Prussia's defiance of Louis XV and final participation, despite years of defeat and retribution, in the defeat of Napoleon, rolling back France to the west bank of the Rhine. A minor contributory factor was the decline in the popularity of Italy with post-war tourists, now looking, like Jos Sedley in *Vanity Fair*, for cheap and comfortable vacations for their sisters, their cousins and their aunts, more exotic, and less costly, than Bath with which they had had to be satisfied through the long years of the French wars. In Scotland the eyes of the Athens of the North turned across the latitude to other northern states. After all, Germany's foremost philosopher, Immanuel Kant, had Scottish forbears, and the Scottish tongue bore, Walter Scott thought, a family resemblance to low German.

The German King of England, also elector of Hanover, founded a university in his territories, at Göttingen in 1737, to be as enlightened as a university could be, free from royal and religious pressure. Thither

Coleridge, 60 years later, went to learn German, write a life of Lessing and immerse himself in the German empire of the air: in its ideas, philosophy and poetry. It inspired him with an ambition to enrich English drama by German models, in themselves enriched by Shakespeare, and he returned to England determined to translate Schiller and understand, and help his fellow countrymen understand, Immanuel Kant. Carlyle, translating Goethe and Schiller in the 1820s, and rejecting Coleridge's Kantian claims, finding his increasingly drug-induced person vague and incomprehensible, as he found Kant himself, became his St Paul in the mission to convert the British to appreciation of their nearest cousins in Germany. Though never going to Weimar himself until after Goethe's death, he had early become a distant acolyte of Goethe and champion of his poetry and prose, and then persuaded himself to translate poetry into power as he fell under the thrall of Frederick the Great of Prussia.

For all Carlyle's enthusiasm, the English never fell under the spell of Goethe's zeitgeist novel, *The Sorrows of Young Werther* (1774), which infected Europeans with a Romantic bohemianism. Unlike Casanova who was fornicating his way round some of the princely states at much the same time, Goethe seemed to suggest that unconsummated love was a suitable, even a preferable recipe for Romantic life and, frequently, early death. Casanova's memoirs of his amatory travels, on the other hand, published posthumously between 1826 and 1838, while Carlyle was writing the life and opinions of Professor Teufelsdröckh in *Sartor Resartus*, were perhaps a truer picture of the Germany of the lesser courts, before they were overtaken by Goethe's moral earnestness, and Romantic idealism. Coleridge, for his part, fell in love with thinkers as transcendentally vague as he. Carlyle, who in his Romantic, secular agnosticism accepted the existence of a God but also His relegation to the broom cupboard, came to believe that Germany had become a nursery for lesser deities. They were not gods but they determined the destiny of human affairs, and were to be designated as heroes.

Despite and often because of the sceptical light shed on knowledge by Scotland's Hume and France's *philosophes*, all was not bathed in clear sunshine. There was throughout Europe an anti-intellectual, anti-enlightenment element in contemporary, even radical, thought, and Carlyle recognised it, was even its prophet. Deep in the German soul, as in his own, there was a predilection for the mysterious, opaque, arcane and even sinister – indeed for magic. Germany was still in search of the philosopher's stone, or a simulacrum of power. Alchemists were more common than chemists and language was magically bent to imply, if not assert meaning, manifest in the literary lucubration of Herder and the philosophic conundra of Fichte.[1]

The leaps in the thought of Kant seemed like verbal gymnastics. It all appealed mightily to Coleridge, who sought, in its effusions, answers to the deepest problems of human existence. It had its origins in the cult of a pre-historic Germany of forests, sylvan gods and devils; it was nourished by legends of German defiance of a Rome attempting to pierce these sacred spaces with a rationality of arms; it confounded the Latin version of reasonable religion with the confusions of Pietism, and it countered the idealism of Hellenism and the southern Renaissance with mystagogues, like Eckhart, Paracelsus and Böhme. It revelled in the obscurities of Kant and Fichte and of the *Illuministe* members of lodges of irrationalism; it invented the 'shudder novel' of inexplicable horrors that stalked the corridors of peaceful homes. Even in Goethe's exaltation of 'Nature' lurked the deity Pandaemon, not the clock-maker god of the 'enlightened'. Carlyle was accused of promoting a new paganism or 'goetheism', which was to replace the scepticism of the eighteenth century.[2] Spirits of malevolence, caprice and cruelty even haunted Germany's nurseries, as starkly chronicled by the brothers Grimm. Presiding over this was an aristocracy for the most part semi-literate, boorish and gluttonous, with passions modelled on what was conceived as the lifestyle of the Bourbon kings of France for hunting wildlife and women. Coleridge and Carlyle in their different ways found the whole mix intoxicating.

German, however, did not come easy to the English tongue, despite its Germanic roots, and the poets, dramatists and theologians of Germany, inspired by English (and Scottish) poets and thinkers, wrapped their thought in a language which concealed hidden beauties and profound truths from the uninitiated. This was attractive to the writer who was to call herself George Eliot, but language and the ideas it concealed were not among Germany's more accessible glories. These were Germany's baroque and rococo palaces and churches in which its musical life was to rival that of both France and Italy. The roll call of composers, from the

Bachs and Handel to Liszt and Wagner, was witness to the growing passion of little courts, starved often of visitors and intelligent conversation, for some entertainment higher than that provided by hunting and feasting, warring and whoring. When Dr Charles Burney in 1773 went to sample the sophisticated musical culture of the German-speaking world, he felt even then he was talking to titans, and Mozart, Haydn and Beethoven were not among them. Haydn had been for the last dozen years quietly tucked away in the Esterházy palace in Slovakian Hungary, Mozart was still a teenager and Beethoven was only three years old. Of three British visitors to eighteenth century Germany, Charles Burney and Boswell found it an uncomfortable country to visit but, like John Moore, making a tour of little courts in 1772, they were attracted by its easy going hedonism, and by its music, performed by musicians many of whom were barely a cut above country bumpkins.

The Napoleonic interlude badly dented the general admiration for the supremacy of French civilisation. Even such a formidable prince as Frederick the Great had shown his ability as an enlightened ruler and ruthless war leader, in French. Berlin, in his reign, followed French models. The palace of Sanssouci, his favourite retreat, his prolific if traditional musical compositions, his collection of savants which for a time numbered Voltaire, were all devices to create a court in Potsdam as brilliant as that presided over in Paris by La Pompadour, (even if he commemorated that lady satirically on the cupola of his new palace as one of the three naked graces, along with his other foes, the Austrian Empress, Maria Theresa, and Catherine the Great of Russia). The post-Frederickian defeats in the wars that followed, the humiliation of Prussia by Napoleon in 1806, the unhappy subservience of so many German polities to French control, which culminated in the kingdom of Westphalia under Napoleon's youngest brother, all combined to promote, if not a sense of political unity, a sense of German cultural identity, which wanted to owe little to France. The Battle of Waterloo, which for the humiliated Prussians was a Prussian victory, sealed the flight from French and initiated a new compact with Britain, France's oldest foe and the German's latter-day ally.

Goethe had managed to keep himself from the Napoleonic embrace, politely hearing but not heeding the Emperor's invitation to go to Paris and write a proper novel. He found Mme de Staël opinionated and superficial, but he would have agreed with her belief that German culture might replace French, now, in her view, in terminal decline. While he did not hope for a super-king or hero to lead a united Germany, he thought that Germanic culture was advanced enough to achieve the unity of which Germans were beginning to dream. Despite the enthusiasm of Coleridge and Carlyle, however, it was not the search for that cultural renaissance which brought Byron sailing down the Rhine; he was en route to the mountains and the Romantic freedom they gave to Switzerland. Even Walter Scott, who was enthusiastic enough to translate Goethe's first novel and who would have liked to visit Weimar and meet the author himself, attempted no German novel. His imagination brought him near, when, fascinated by the later Middle Ages and the emergence of the Swiss as the nemesis of Charles the Bold of Burgundy, the richest and most powerful prince at the time in Europe, he wrote *Anne of Geierstein* (1829). Part of it was set in the Rhineland. For both Childe Harold in 1816 and Walter Scott 12 years later, the Rhine was the great waterway defining Europe; to the west was France, to the south Austria and to the east a no-man's land of forests and fairy tale phantoms and philosophers, flea-bite principalities and fleas.

It was Disraeli who broke this clouded window into a new world. Venturing east in his first novel, *Vivian Grey* (1826), he described a young man's romantic adventures in a petty German principality, which he himself had never visited, and was entirely fictional. Thackeray did go further east still but he did so with a sneer at the almost buffoonish seriousness of such societies, concluding that all was burlesque and pretence. Even as late as the 1870s, when George Meredith wrote *The Adventures of Harry Richmond*, the German principality in which most of the action takes place, remains, like those visited by Vivian Grey and George Fitzboodle (1842), a sinister but also absurd place of Romantic make-believe. At the end of the century, this make-believe finally lingered on the air in Anthony Hope's creation of Ruritania (*Prisoner of Zenda,* 1894). 'Pumpernickel' despite the growing power of Prussia seemed immortal.

Flattered by German worship of Shakespeare, which had never been a strong point with the French, the British showed a growing interest in the Romantic ambiguities of the Germans. Coleridge translated two of Schiller's historical plays; Carlyle wrote his life, and Schubert's settings of romantic poems brought ecstatic German romantic love and melody to British drawing rooms. The marriage of a half-German queen to a 'Pumpernickel' prince, impeccable in manners, constitutional integrity and universally good taste, quickened that interest. Victoria and Albert between them emerged as model 'Pumpernickel' monarchs. The grandfather of Felix Mendelssohn may have begun as a poor rabbi's scribe and ended as the German Socrates, yet Frederick the Great took pains never to meet him. Before his musical grandson, the Queen of England knelt to pick up the music that had fallen to the floor. The prince presided over the creation of a cultural centre in London, almost rivalling the embellishment of Munich and Berlin by their respective monarchs and, using the decoration of the newly built Houses of Parliament as the catalyst, tried to animate a school of English art just as Ludwig I of Bavaria (*regnavit* 1825–48) had done for German in Munich before his infatuation for the Irish adventuress, Lola Montes.

If Johann Sebastian Bach, after 100 years, emerged under Mendelssohn's baton as the authentic voice of God, (who remained, when He was allowed to remain at all, a retiring deity), Richard Wagner became, for his royal admirer, Ludwig's grandson in Munich, almost God himself. For Carlyle, as for many Germans, Goethe's was the voice of God's replacement, Nature, and Schiller was a German Shakespeare. Disraeli, Meredith and Anthony Hope by allowing their heroes to play with German princesses, unimportant beyond their Pumpernickel capsules, created a home for Romantic fiction. Schiller's *Ode to Joy*, which had soared over Europe in the final movement of Beethoven's apotheosis symphony (composers may write thereafter more than nine symphonies, but none for over a century was prepared to call any of them his tenth), was within 50 years to usher in a new and less joyous Germany.

One state in Germany, the kingdom of Prussia, had emerged as a result of Napoleon's wars as the largest and most significant German state after the Austrian Empire. Her territorial acquisitions on the Rhine during the peace after 1815 converted her, in due course, from an Eastern to an industrialised Western European power. The reforms that followed the debacle of 1806, when the ensigns of Frederick the Great went down before the French Eagles, so improved general literacy that, by 1850, levels exceeded that of Great Britain. Serious reforms in the universities turned the student body from duelling and wassailing to serious study, and their staff from metaphysical alchemy to intensive enquiry into experimental science and research. Berlin, from being a military cantonment, emerged as the cultural capital of the north, filching that accolade from Saxony's Dresden and Goethe's Weimar. Imperial grandeur inspired Friedrich Schinkel to create a new city, as Nash had done for London, and Haussmann was to do for Paris.

Goethe may have invented the German novel with *The Sorrows of Young Werther*, but the coterie of Berlin writers, Kleist, Hoffmann and La Motte Fouqué, gave Germany her short story. These were internationalist in scope, welding together Romantic fantasy, psychological intensity and mystery, which also characterised the stories of Edgar Allan Poe. Hoffmann, was by way of being a polymath, writer, painter, composer and critic; Kleist was a suicidal depressive, and La Motte Fouqué, a failed soldier who was obsessed by Prussia's military past which had saved her more than once from extinction. The spirit of discipline bequeathed by Frederick William I and his son, Frederick the Great, despite this efflorescence of literary creation, still remained the guiding spirit of the State. Frederick William III and his son, fourth of that name, tried to rule as autocrats until forced to concede a constitution in the 1848–9 Year of Revolutions. The ethos of the State, however, which had emerged from the sandy wastes of Brandenburg and the spiritual desolation of Pomerania, so marked in the work of Caspar David Friedrich, from the French effusions of Frederick the Great and from the Romantic importance of being Ernest Theodore 'Amadeus' Hoffmann, remained Junkerdom, and this was, in the end, to be the nemesis of 'Pumpernickel'. 'Elizabeth' von Arnim's gentle references to her Man of Wrath and her Pomeranian German garden (1898) could not conceal the dim beat of war drums.

The little courts of Germany, like those of Italy, had been for different reasons incubators of a renaissance in philosophy, poetry and music. None of these, aspiring to the 'empire of the air', threatened the political status quo. Even Goethe, no more than Clemenz Metternich, wanted a dangerous ebullition of nationalism. For him, cultural rather than political unity would be enough, until the German states had spent another century evolving towards nationhood. Like that other fragmented nation, Italy, the little courts of Germany were to receive their quietus at the hands of the north, the bare bodkin being wielded, for the Italians by the more efficient (and Frenchified) Piedmontese, and for the Germans by military-mad Prussian dynasts, whose ambitions embraced national greatness. Pumpernickel bowed before their glory, lamented only by those who feared that poetry would be suffocated in the swirling clouds of military incense, and its delectable music be drowned by the brass of big bands. Sadly they had reason to fear.

In the use of German names in the main text, I have adopted a compromise. I use the normal English rendering of Frederick the Great (not Friedrich) and Johann Sebastian (not John Sebastian) Bach, Charles instead of Karl, except where it is more appropriate to use Karl (as in Marx), but Johann, not John, Wolfgang von Goethe. Two people have read this book in its preparation and I am grateful to Linda Kelly and to Glen Cavaliero for perceptive comments; its shortcomings are entirely mine. I dedicate it to a kinder, gentler, more eccentric but essentially more civilised German Republic that, today, has replaced that of the Men of Wrath.

Fitzboodle in Pumpernickel

Thackeray goes to Learn German

> The prince did not inhabit his capital but imitating in every
> respect the ceremonial of the court of Versailles, built himself
> a magnificent palace and a superb aristocratic town, inhabited
> entirely by his nobles and the officers of his sumptuous court.
> (W. M. Thackeray, *Barry Lyndon*, chapter x)

> Pray fag at your German. If you have enjoyment of old ways,
> habits, customs and ceremonies, look to court life.
> (George Meredith, *The Adventures of Harry Richmond*, chapter 22)

*I*T WAS SOME years after the Battle of Waterloo that a small party, made
up of Major Dobbin, Amelia Osborne, née Sedley, young George
Osborne then in his teens and his uncle, Joseph Sedley, the ex-Collector of
Bogglywallah, India, set out for a tour of Europe. The Channel packet was
full of rosy children, nursemaids and pink-bonneted ladies and gentlemen
in travelling caps and linen suits, for this was the annual invasion of the
watering places of Europe. They were bound for Rotterdam, after which
the party transferred to a steamer that took them down the Rhine to
Cologne. They luxuriated in the pleasant Rhenish gardens, among the
purple-clad, castle-crested mountains, the old towns and their quaint,
protective ramparts, listening to the jingling bells of the lowing cattle
returning from sweet pastures. The ex-Collector was gratified that in
the daily gazette he had been promoted to Herr Graf Lord von Sedley.
Everything was idyllic.

During their journey, they went often,

to those, snug, unassuming dear old operas in the German towns, where the noblesse sits and cries and knits stockings on the one side, over against the bourgeoisie on the other, and His Transparency the Duke and his Transparent family, all very fat and good-natured ... occupy the great box in the middle and the pit is full of the most elegant, slim-waisted officers with straw-coloured mustachios.

At last they reached a comfortable little town, the seat of the Duke of Pumpernickel. It had a good hotel and a better table where the young George Osborne tucked into lavish quantities of 'schinken and braten and kartoffeln, cranberry jam and salad and pudding and roast meats and sweetmeats'.[1]

They were in the realm of His Transparency Duke Victor Aurelius XVII, sovereign of a dukedom some ten miles in breadth, bordered on one side by Prussia and on the other by the river Pump and the territory of the Prince of Potzenthal. The Duchy of Pumpernickel had its own army, with a rich and numerous staff of officers and few men, who spent much of their time 'marching in Turkish dresses with rouge on and wooden scimitars, or as Roman warriors with ophicleides[2] and trombones, or playing to the café society in the Aurelius Platz'. The Duchy had diplomatic representatives from both France and Britain; the latter, the British *chargé d'affaires*, Lord Tapeworm, succeeded in persuading the party to linger some months in such a delightful spot. Joseph (Jos) Sedley, having persuaded Major Dobbin to bring his ceremonial uniform, donned his East India Company court dress for the inevitable honour of being presented to His Transparency, after which all the court ladies called on the Sedley caravan. An earlier duke, 'a perfect wonder of licentious elegance'[3] had attempted to build his Versailles but ran out of money; the gardens however had impressive fountains which spouted water and made dreadful groans from their lead Tritons – on feast days only – to which all were invited. To pay for the palace and gardens, everyone had been ennobled for a fee. Pumpernickel was the very model of a modern state. It had a constitution and a Chamber that may have been elected or it may not, but it did not matter as it never met. The theatre, however, was open twice a week, and there were receptions and salons practically every other night so that a man's life was a perfect round of pleasure.

Great power rivalry provided a certain spice to quiet and unpretending Pumpernickel, the *chargés* of France and Britain championing one or other of the divas of the opera. Tapeworm espoused the sweet little Mme Lederlung, his rival the greater singing range of Mme Strumpff, who had three more notes. But she was middle aged and so stout that in Bellini's *La Sonnambula* she had difficulty in sleepwalking out of her window across a narrow mill plank, which creaked and trembled under her weight. Mr Titmarsh, visiting at the same time as the Sedleys, thought that the hero was lucky not to be suffocated by *La Sonnambula*'s final embrace but, then, partisan politics were no judges of voice.

A royal wedding took place during the stay of the Sedleys, between the Hereditary Prince of Pumpernickel and the Princess Amelia of Humbourg-Schlippenschlop, to which all the neighbouring princes and grandees were invited. Bushels of each prince's noble orders of chivalry were exchanged, the French *chargé* appearing covered in ribbons like a prize carthorse – at which sight Lord Tapeworm was grateful for the royal edict that members of the British diplomatic corps might not accept any foreign chivalric decorations without their sovereign's express licence.[4] The fountains ran with sour wine or beer, there were contests for sausages suspended from slippery poles, and gaming booths were erected for all those ready to lose money, in which the amiable Jos was to cover the bets of a domino-masked Becky Sharp.

* * *

William Makepeace Thackeray, alias Mr Titmarsh, actually arrived in Weimar in September 1830, with the intention of learning some German in case he decided to become a member of the foreign service. At the same time, George Savage Fitzboodle of the estate of Boodle, held in the Boodle family since the reign of King Henry II, arrived in his travels through Germany at the Grand Duchy of Kalbsbraten-Pumpernickel. George Fitzboodle, despite his boasted heritage, was an indigent second son, who had flunked out of Cambridge, been persuaded to resign his commission in the army, and was now in need of an affluent wife. He had an eye for pretty if buxom girls but his appetite for tobacco had so far successfully nauseated any likely spouses. The Grand Duke himself had been present – indeed accidentally knocked down – in the haste of Fitzboodle's escape from the reception that was to announce the fulfilment of his vow to give up tobacco for six months, whereafter his affianced bride-to-be, Mary McAlister, would announce their betrothal. The reception had ended dramatically with the discovery that Fitzboodle had smoked a cheroot that very morning.

The Grand Duke's father had, as Grand Duke of Kalbsbraten-Pumpernickel, married his cousin the Princess of Saxe-Pumpernickel, so that Duke Philibert Sigismund Emanuel Maria now ruled a city of 2,000 people from a palace which would accommodate twice that number, with an army headed by a General, two major-Generals and 64 officers, all Knights Grand Cross of the ancient Order of the Potato (*Kartoffel*) (as indeed was almost everyone else in his dominions.) Most of the foot soldiers had been cut to pieces at Waterloo.

George Fitzboodle could not resist the pleasures of a court where the Grand Duchess numbered so many beauties among her maids of honour. He fell wildly in love with two in rapid succession, first the daughter of the Herr Oberhof und Bau-Inspector of the Duchy, and second the muse, the Corinne of Kalbsbraten-Pumpernickel, Ottilia von Schlippenschlop. Neither beauty was either slender or ethereal, this not being a physical characteristic of the Pumpernickel ladies. Dorothea, the daughter of the Herr Bau-Inspector was 'of the earth earthy and must have weighed ten stone four or five pounds if she weighed an ounce'. The first fell from grace at a ball while dancing the waltz with Fitzboodle, collapsing in a heap of arms legs and bountiful flesh to the fury of her parents and the amusement of the men who thought Fitzboodle far too pleased with himself. His physical and Platonic attraction for Ottilia was dimmed first by the gradual conviction that she ate far too much and was finally killed by her eating at least nine oysters that were clearly 'off'. She also proposed to eat Fitzboodle's share of the contaminated delicacy, sent by the free city of Hamburg to Grand Duke Philibert to mark the signature of a commercial treaty between them.[5]

* * *

Thackeray was visiting Europe under licence from his mother, having left Trinity College, Cambridge, early without taking a degree. He had only a vague idea of what he wanted to do in life but was 19, dilettante, devoted to the theatre, probably sexually experienced, and heir to comfortable expectations. So he decided to go to Germany to learn German, and to hone his journalistic skills by producing a German sketchbook – which he never did, unlike his *Irish* and *Paris Sketchbooks* and his *From Cornhill to Grand Cairo*. The sardonic memories of his time in Germany were however to surface in *The Fitzboodle Papers*, in *Barry Lyndon*, in *Vanity Fair*, and in *The Rose and the Ring*.

By chance, Thackeray met an old acquaintance in Weimar studying German for the Foreign Office, and was persuaded to prolong what would otherwise have been a fleeting visit to immerse himself in the life of the tiny state which extended 20 miles from Jena to Erfurt, and which had survived the Napoleonic wars as one of the 33 (now reduced by 1830 to 32) states which made up the German Confederation. Actually its great days were over. Grand Duke Charles-Augustus, who had patronised music and letters and numbered not only Goethe, but Schiller, Herder and August von Kotzebue among the State luminaries, had died a year earlier. Weimar's army was slightly larger than that of Grand Duke Philibert of Kalbsbraten-Pumpernickel, numbering 100 men under arms. Its magnificent theatre had put on the best of German classical and contemporary drama and it had as many bookshops and concert halls as Bath. Its greatest attraction by far was Goethe, still alive and only too willing to show off his knowledge of the work of Scott and Byron to the 20 or so English studying German in Weimar. The last he thought undoubtedly the greatest genius of the century, the one true representative of the modern poetical era.[6]

Thackeray found he had an easy entrée to the social life of Weimar, to its balls and parties, cutting a dash with his great height (six feet, three inches) in the uniform of the Devon Yeomanry of which he asked his mother to buy him a commission and a uniform. Despite his reception by Goethe in a very 'kindly and rather in a more distingué manner than he used to the other Englishmen', Thackeray was not impressed by the encounter. Goethe might be 'a noble poet and an interesting old man to speak to ... but I believe he is little better than an old rogue', for Goethe was not held in England to be the great man he was considered elsewhere in Europe.[7] His not wholly sentimental passions for otherwise married young women, the sorrows of Werther whose remains his chaste *innamorata* had watched, 'borne before her on a shutter, (when) like a well conducted person (she) went on cutting bread and butter'; all inspired a cool contempt for so self-celebrating a literary lion.

The Fitzboodle Papers appeared in *Fraser's Magazine* in 1842–3, but Thackeray's opinion had softened by 1855 when he wrote to George Lewes, contributing his mite to Lewes's monumental life of Goethe. He then recorded that his reception by the great man had been kindly and his daughter-in-law's tea table was always spread for English visitors. Goethe and he passed hour after hour together, according to Thackeray that is, reading over novels and poems in English, in French as well as in German. He recollected that the 'Great Man's' glittering eyes unnerved him as a young visitor for they resembled those of Melmoth the Wanderer who had made his bargain with a *Certain Person*. Their talk was always of 'Art and Letters'. All in all, from the generosity and kindness of the Grand Duchess, to the respect and veneration in which Weimar held its foremost citizen, Thackeray thought he had never 'seen a society more simple, charitable, courteous and gentlemanlike than the dear little Saxon city where the good Schiller and the great Goethe lived and lie buried'.[8]

This good feeling extended retrospectively to his relations with Ottilie, Goethe's widowed daughter-in-law, who, for all Thackeray's good memories of her, is the inspiration for George Fitzboodle's Ottlilia von Schlippenschlopp, the Muse of Karlsbraten-Pumpernickel, 'an historian, a poet, a blue of the ultramarinest sort'.[9] This avatar of Lady Jane of Gilbert's *Patience* was

> pale and delicate, ... wore her glistening black hair in bands, and dressed in vapoury white muslin ... She sang her own words to her harp ... suffered some inexpressible and mysterious heart pangs ... and might look for a premature interment. [10]

Ottilia's ballades all had sad ends, either consumptive or suicidal. Thackeray's unflattering portraits of the Weimar beauties were not wholly without substance. *The Fitzboodle Papers* owe everything to Thackeray's experiences in Weimar, but whether they created or merely supported the mordant view of feminine achievement which he showed in his novels is debatable. Ottilie von Goethe welcomed visiting writers – in 1854 they included George Lewes and George Eliot – and she was always ready to talk about her father-in-law but, in Thackeray's satirical portrait, she contributed to the creation of Pumpernickel.

* * *

Thackeray's growing nostalgia for the Germany he had visited at 19 never eradicated his general belief that there was something absurd about the country, with its 33 sovereign courts, its dull but copious meals and its picture book history. The passion for things medieval and Gothic which Walter Scott had inspired struck him as harmless but basically comic, and inspired his pastiche of a German Romantic *Legend of the Rhine,* with its silly names, and chronological absurdities. The poem is set at the time of the Crusades but men nevertheless drank coffee and smoked cigars, and ate meals they might expect at one of the sophisticated chop shops of Jermyn Street. Ruined and haunted castles with ghosts of former castellans, clearly forerunners of the denizens of Gilbert's *Ruddigore* and of J. K. Rowling's Hogwarts, while the awful Count Rowski of Donnerblitz steps straight into Monty Python. The troop of peasants 'chanting Rhine-songs and leading in their ox-drawn carts the peach-cheeked girls from the vinelands' belong to the world of *Euryanthe* and other German Romantic operas. Nor is Thackeray above the onomatopoeic 'whizz! crash! clang! bang! whang!' of Dennis the Menace and children's comics. At one point, to make doubly sure his readers know that he is guying the concept of chivalry, he refers his readers to *Ivanhoe.* There is a lot of swearing by local saints and feats of prodigious skill, terminating in a happy marriage between the hero, a dispossessed prince in mufti and a peachy princess, well within the class structure. Thackeray was stepping out of Pumpernickel into *The Ingoldsby Legends.*

* * *

Few people before the end of the Napoleonic wars visited Germany. Some might have sailed down the Rhine on their way to Italy, others like the indomitable Dr Burney, Fanny's father, might have gone in pursuit of music or, like Boswell, in search of courtly pleasures. Some were mercenaries, like Boswell's old patron, Lord Keith, or diplomatists, like Lord Tapeworm, caught up in the trivial pursuits of the normal Pumpernickel courts. Travel in Germany was not undertaken lightly without one's own conveyance. All who were without any found the experience atrocious.

Comfort-loving James Boswell did his best to laugh away the transport and the inns. The post was 'a barbarity of manners, just a large cart, mounted upon very high wheels which jolt prodigiously and had three or four deal boards laid across to serve for seats'. Nor was the resting place at the end of the day a model of cleanliness or decorum. In the Prussian territory of Vellinghausen, in the county of Mark in the Rhineland, the traveller had to do with a table spread with straw as a bed. 'Thus was I,' wrote Boswell, 'just in the situation of a bold officer. Thus did I endure the very hardship of a German campaign which I used to tremble at the thought of when at Auchinleck.' A few days later he had to lay in a stable, on the straw-covered floor, under a sheet, with cows on one side, horses on the other and cocks which crowed all night. 'I admired the wisdom of the Sybarites who slew all those noisy birds.' In north Germany he made straight for the stable to secure a comfortable billet of straw, despite the risk of being robbed or trampled on. As he travelled south the inns improved.[11]

After a journey of 75 miles in 1772, Dr Burney was 'roasted alive and jumbled to death'. He felt he had 'been rather kicked than carried from one place to another.'[12] John Moore, travelling with an English duke in 1786 had a slightly better experience. At Frankfurt he found inns that for cleanliness, convenience and number of apartments were superior to any other he had met with on the continent and on a par with the most magnificent establishments in England.[13] But that was anything but the experience of William and Dorothy Wordsworth who travelled with Coleridge in 1798. The Wordsworths were not impressed, the streets of Hamburg were ill-paved and stinking from sewage and abandoned rubbish. The inn was dirty, the food served crudely, and everyone seemed to be intent on cheating them. Perhaps there were honest people in Hamburg but William and Dorothy lacked the skill, or the will, to find them.

The crowded carriage that took them on to their next destination was like a dung cart, and the wretched inns at which the Wordsworths stayed were each one more strange and miserable than the last. Dorothy suffered in her bowels from the jolting of the dung cart on the horrible roads. They finally came to rest in Goslar, in Lower Saxony, with no German and a total misanthropic view of the German people, a wretched race of grocers and linen drapers, a selfish race intent upon gain. The brother and sister declined to cultivate the society of this humdrum, sleepy little town. It was somewhere they wished to forget, except that in the solitude of this hotel Wordsworth wrote Book I of *The Prelude*, and the three Lucy poems. Was it for this that they had left Grasmere?[14] Coleridge meanwhile, having come to learn German, had left them for a pastor's family in Stettin and then the University of Göttingen, at both of which he was supremely happy.

The emergence of Prussia as a major power in Germany, and the replacement of what had been electors, dukes and margraves by kings, meant that the diplomatic service wanted German speakers, hence the large number, at least a score, of young Englishmen whom Thackeray met learning the language in Weimar, where Saxon, fast becoming the received pronunciation in Germany, was spoken. With the purest German, the extensive mountains, lakes and forests, providing a Lake District of immense size in which to pedestrianise, with its castle eyries, great cathedrals and palaces, with the sausage, potatoes, beer and pumpernickel which produced a placid and contented citizenry, Saxony was about to provide a Victorian Grand Tour attraction to rival Tuscany in Italy.

ᴬ German Panorama

A Panoply of Princes

It is reported that a Frenchman on being served
with it (pumpernickel) remarked '*qu'il était bon
pour Nickel*,' which was the name of his horse.
(Thomas Nugent, *The Grand Tour*, 1756, vol ii, p. 80)

To God I speak Spanish, to women Italian, to
men French, and to my horse – German.
(Charles V, 1509–58, according to Lord Chesterfield's letter to his son)

GERMANY TOOK A long time to recover from the Thirty Years War, which had ended in a peace of exhaustion in 1648. It had devastated her like a hurricane, exhausted her economy, decimated her population, and reduced her peasants in certain places to a state of savagery.[1] It had drained her energies, stultified her intellectual growth and dulled her religious enthusiasm. Survival and resuscitation were her principal concerns, peace from the depredation of marauding armies, and authority she could trust were the extremes of political ambition. The political map of old Europe had largely survived and the medieval mosaic of sovereignties, owning a phantom allegiance to a mystical head, the elected dignitary who held the position of Holy Roman Emperor, was the structure that it was hoped would provide, peace, prosperity and pumpernickel for all. The peace of Westphalia had accepted the division of Europe into Catholic and Protestant areas in which the principle that the head of State determined what should be the religious loyalty of his people. At the same time, these states having survived the crucible of war, their princes laid claim to an absolutism, that established despotisms, some benevolent, some not, in their search for a power that was beginning to accrue to the more developed polities in Cromwell's England, Richelieu's France and Imperial Austria. It was not accompanied by any sense of a German national identity. In their way they could have stated, as did the head of one of these more modern states, that *l'Etat, c'est moi*.

The megalomania of Louis XIV which nearly reduced western Germany to ruin similar to that which it suffered from the earlier war, and its recovery after 1714 was the work, not of peaceful, industrious citizens but of absolute rulers. These engrossed power and wealth into their own hands while they 'civilised' their people by the construction of courts that emulated the glory of the tyrant in France from whom the wars that had been fought had intended to 'liberate' them.

German-speaking central Europe was composed of over 300 sovereign principalities, secular and ecclesiastical, kingdoms, electorates, dukedoms, margravates, counties, free cities and church estates. Some were ancient sovereignties reaching back to the Middle Ages, some owed their existence to a decision of the Holy Roman Emperor, and some were the creation of disputed inheritance split among princely scions, or the result of war.[2] The Holy Roman Empire was a largely toothless tiger but still, in emotional and juridical terms, a tiger. Technically that dignitary had owed his election since 1692 to nine electors, the rulers of the five comparatively large electorates, Bohemia, Brandenburg-Prussia, Saxony, Bavaria and Hanover (in 1692 the Duke of Brunswick-Luneburg was elevated to Elector), the three princely archbishoprics of Mainz, Cologne and Trier, and the Elector Palatine. The Holy Roman Emperor had, since 1438, with few breaks, been the Habsburg Archduke of Austria (who as sovereign of Bohemia was also an Elector). Loyalty, or not, to the Emperor, even of pocket handkerchief-size clerical states and fragments like the County of Lippe, the smallest secular state, was dictated by self-interest. The empire was guided collectively by a Council of Electors, by a Council of Princes, which comprised the lesser rulers, the 34 ecclesiastical and 60 secular princes, and two collectives, one representing monasteries and religious houses, and the other the hundred or so Imperial counts, and finally by a Council of the 51 Free Cities of which some were major commercial centres and others barely villages.[3] These councils were a bureaucratic constellation of individual representatives who communicated with each other in writing but seldom, if ever, met. Throughout the second half of the seventeenth and most of the eighteenth centuries, princes, electors and free cities were all concerned to revive their individual states by economic activity, to defend their ancient privileges and to stay out of fratricidal conflict, but they were seldom able to override Imperial traditional law and custom. As their principal desire was to prevent the Imperial power from becoming too prepotent or interventionist while leaving them free to acquire territory for themselves within the existing mosaic of sovereignties, concerted action, except in comparatively trivial matters, was uncommon. The constituent members, however, could not ignore the apparatus of Imperial power.

In individual states political activism was discouraged, and intellectuals looked outside of Germany for stimulus. Despite the often wanton and disproportionate damage the armies of Louis XIV did to Germany, as they fought over her territory with a careless ferocity in their seventeenth- and eighteenth-century wars, hatred of Frenchmen did not lead to a rejection of the cultural dominance of France. Even in so advanced a state as Frederick II's Prussia [Frederick Hohenzollern, King Elector of Brandenburg-Prussia and Duke of Magdeburg, (*regnavit* 1740– 86)], French was the language of the court, Frenchmen were invited to serve the state as savants and administrators, and the natives were left to grumble but accept, so strong was the prestige of the ruler. To demonstrate a not entirely slavish dependence, the challenge of new ideas from England was beginning to be felt but devotion, even subservience, to the ruling prince was the rule, and society, under the influence of both French and English, or more often Scottish, ideas, became increasingly secular. Worldly Prince-Bishops and philosophic Lutheran clerics replaced the Church Militant as arbiters of behaviour. Some princes changed their religious faith to conform to that of the majority of their subjects, and thus assist the homogenisation of their state; others came to a *modus vivendi* with a majority that did not share their faith, all with the intention to secure greater temporal and spiritual powers. Provided these powers were not directly challenged, the aim for intellectuals, being lesser mortals, was to imitate the investigative questing of the English. For the princes, it was mainly a court on the French model, increasingly hedonistic, even barbaric, in its pursuit of pleasure.

All of them, whatever their private beliefs, shared one rule of State: that he who held the sovereignty determined the overt political, religious and economic duties of its citizens. Government was by single unchallenged authority, protected by a combination of naked power, backed by Imperial support, international treaty, or, sometimes, the will of (some of) the people. The old institutions of popular separation from the sovereign had faded, weakening any checks on the will of the ruler.[4] The law in this *olla podrida* of divided sovereignties always provided work for lawyers, harnessed to sustaining the power of the prevailing autocrats.

Theology, especially in the Protestant states, increasingly concentrated on producing obedient priests for an obedient faithful. It constituted the principal intellectual study at the many universities, thrusting into second place the philology and culture of ancient Greece and Rome. The study of Lutheranism and the classical world provided the principal vehicles through which the north German people participated in a common culture, without disturbing the prevailing rule of the prince. That there were 50 university establishments throughout Germany did not mean a disinterested love of learning; rather they were the preferred nurseries of administrative support to princely rule, inculcating judicial and economic administrative competence, philosophic and theological quiet, and pedagogic authority.

Germany was divided between the three main Christian confessions, Roman Catholic, Lutheran and Calvinist. The faithful did not always follow the profession of the ruler – there were more Protestant subjects throughout the empire though a greater number of Catholic princes – but the ruler did prescribe whatever limitations there were on dissidence: on who could hold office, what feasts they observed, what was taught in schools and universities. Expulsion rather than outright persecution was used to achieve conformity, and there was considerable movement from one principality to another. The dislike of one Christian belief for another and polemical wars of words, often spilling over into violence, still racked communities, but the common culture was one where obedience to the secular ruler was the sovereign requirement. What religion you professed should be optional.

This was the considered view of those students of the ancient world of Greece and Rome. Lutheran pastors could see the advantages of the general acceptance of toleration, as it left them free to explore theological conundra on the purpose of human life without fear of losing their posts. Dr Burney, travelling Germany to study its musical culture, was surprised to find women singing and Protestants worshipping in the devoutly Roman Catholic church of St Bartholomew in Frankfurt, whose tower was in the keeping of the Lutherans who appeared not to object to the arrangement.[5] Rulers by the middle of the eighteenth century had learned the commercial advantages which religious toleration often brought with it, to the point that a rationalist like Frederick the Great could declare that all religions were equal and good and that if Turks and heathens wanted to settle in Prussia he would build them places of worship.[6]

Not all rulers were as enlightened as Frederick, and despite Prussia's welcome in 1685 to some 14,000 Huguenot refugees after the revocation of the Edict of Nantes, his father, Frederick William I, felt impelled to dismiss Christian Wolff from the University of Halle, at the instance of the Pietist establishment, for his views on religion and reason. The Pietists in the early eighteenth century were trying to put religion back into daily life, since it seemed to have been banished to Sunday, and Halle was a centre of the new piety. Because Pietism preached order and discipline, especially in the army, it was popular with the king, who saw it as an essential prop to his theory of how to run a state, and Pietism became in effect the state religion of the absolutist Prussian state.

Religion was in all the principalities of Germany generally supportive of the notion that the ruler's word was law, whatever faith one espoused. The servility of that faith was ensured by government patronage and provision, so that in the words of Goethe the religion its clerics preached 'was merely a sort of dry morality' appealing neither to the soul or the heart.[7] The State was steadily replacing the Church as the supreme authority in German life. With few exceptions, the smaller the absolutist princes the less they could claim to have the true interests of their principalities at heart or to have deserved their power by their performance in war or in peace. Their effulgence was lighted by pomp and circumstance, accompanied by dancing masters, mistresses and opera singers and, where the Church professed to be independent, a complaisant Bishop or Abbot.

* * *

Lutheran church music provided an acceptable and generally uncontentious presentation of the divine, freeing the soul from more extreme doctrines of salvation. Devoted to praise of the Almighty and His works, it became the humaniser of an often bleak theology, while secular music represented in the fantasies of the opera the cultural international language devoted to the myths of the ancient world. Almost every German prince kept an orchestra and some were musical enough to perform with selected musicians in a court concert. Opera in Germany began in the Imperial court at Vienna, where members of the royal family were not above taking roles. The fashion soon spread. The free city of Hamburg was the first home to a public opera house; Munich had its own in 1689, enthusiastically supported by the Duke who imposed a tax on playing cards. Berlin followed suit in 1703 and Dresden about 1717. The main language of opera was Italian, as were also the singers and dancers, but the instrumental music was played largely by Germans, performing in private orchestras. The churches promoted choral music. Despite the domination of models from Italy and France, compositional confidence grew in the courts of these petty powers and became the seedbed to the reawakening of the German mind.

The musical world was bold, cosmopolitan and international, whereas literary activity, when not theological, at the beginning of the eighteenth century threatened to be a dangerous activity. What might begin as a republic of letters might follow the Dutch or English example and become a larger and more extensive republic, both anti-religious and anti-monarchical. Writing uncensored material could encourage both heresy and immorality. Yet in this semi-arid desert of the mind there was to be, in the years that followed the new century, an astonishing growth of intellectual activity. It was more remarkable because, since Martin Luther's day, the German language had almost atrophied, 'and left but the miserable bickering of theological camp-sutlers to quarrel over the stripping of the slain'.[8] All educated persons looked for their models first to France and later to England, as the two intellectually most advanced societies, as well as the principal contestants for world power. Because the clumsy and guttural High German was a linguistic hobbledehoy, French and Latin were the preferred vehicles of thought.

In Carlyle's words, French 'lay like a baleful incubus over the far nobler mind of Germany; and all true nationality vanished from its literature or was heard only in faint tones ... but could not reach ... the ears of foreigners'.[9] France dominated language, clothes, cuisine, furnishings, dance, music and even illnesses. In the palaces that each little prince had aimed to build like Louis XIV, life was to be as like a French court as possible, even though in its essential grossness and provincialism it might retain the features of an older Germany. Voltaire in 1759, when he wrote *Candide*, was not impressed by The Castle of Thunder-ten-Tronck, where his hero was born. To display the baron's greatness, the castle had a great gate and, marvel of marvels, windows of glass, and its hall was hung with tapestries. There was a pack of hounds that ran wild in the farm and could be mustered for hunting. The baroness weighed about 25 stone and everyone behaved as if the Baron Thunder-ten-Tronck *was* somebody.[10] Richer princes would employ French instructors in the kitchen, the garden and the stables, to ensure that noble life approximated to what went on in Versailles. A growing child might utter his first words in French, and from then on he would only hear German used to address soldiers and horses.

As all the princely courts achieved, more or less, a state of absolutist rule, following Louis's example, their absolutism became tempered by the practical problems of exercising it. Despotism was certainly the preferred Pumpernickel model but not often enlightenment. Charles Frederick, Margrave of Baden (*regnavit* 1738–1811) did abolish torture (1767) and serfdom (1783), remitted many feudal dues, imposed a tax on land and practised religious toleration, but he was the exception.[11] More often it was the size of the princely domain that inhibited reform as few rulers wanted to curtail the size of their revenues. For some, the most lucrative way of making money was to hire out their soldiers as mercenaries. The disciplined, drawing room armies of Pumpernickel thus went off to fight colonial wars in America and South Asia for the British and the Dutch, or were enlisted in the service of Austria and France to fight in their interminable conflicts. One of the episcopal Electors of Mainz, Emmerich Joseph (*regnavit* 1763–74), a scion of the Briedbach clan of Imperial Free Knights who had sunk their talons into ecclesiastical preferment, so controlled the revenues and behaviour of his electoral diocese as almost to become a Pope in his electorate, and provided models for the Josephan ecclesiastical reforms in the empire towards the end of the century.

* * *

If Carlyle represented the common profile of German rulers 'as wrapt up in ceremonial stateliness avoiding the most gifted man of a lower station, ... (an) ancient, thirsty, thick-headed, sixteen-quartered Baron', he was not entirely fair to do so, since in many cases the social life of German princes embraced savants, preachers, writers, actors, musicians, even, as with Casanova and Cagliostro, international charlatans.[12] There was, however, a marked degree of eccentricity, even madness among these Pumpernickel courts, induced sometimes by in-breeding, more often by the delusions bred of absolute power and by the strain of living up to a standard of civilisation they could not sustain, sometimes even from the fermented rye in pumpernickel. 'Germany swarms with princes, and dukes', wrote one observer, 'of whom three quarters aren't quite right in the head.'[13] Indeed in some states the princelings were not 'competent to rule chickens'.[14]

In most of the states, the ruling prince alone had money. Agriculture was largely subsistence only and the ruler took his tithe of it all; taxation concentrated wealth on the palace enabling princes to patronise architects and decorators, musicians and actors, so that the court provided the main source both of employment and entertainment for the citizens. The four Electors of Brandenburg (a kingdom since the beginning of the eighteenth century), Bavaria, Saxony and Hanover, ruling large states, had incomes greatly superior to the smaller principalities, but the Landgrave of the comparatively small state of Hesse-Kassel was among the richest and most powerful of them all.[15] Excessive wealth, lack of education and total autocracy induced habits of gluttony and drunkenness, of cruelty or neglect among many of the rulers. Wantonness on the part of both princely husband and wife was often more openly gross, as there were fewer people to observe it, than similar practices behind the civilised screens of Versailles. Augustus of Saxony (Elector of Saxony, 1694–1733, and twice King of Poland from 1697–1704 and 1709–33), and Margrave

Wilhelm of Baden (*regnavit* 1677–1707) exercised their seraglios in open court rather than discreetly in a *Pac des Cerfs*. A Prince of Brunswick got through two casks of Tokay each day, drinking it, feeding it to his parrots with bread soaked in it, and then bathing in it. Above all a competitive vanity often led them to outdo their neighbours. Life among the people however, as Casanova observed in 1752, was through enforced indigence economically chaste and rather dull.[16]

Dr Burney, visiting Germany in 1772, was convinced that the 'most shining parts of a German court, are usually its military, its music and its hunt'. Vast forests were kept intact to provide the second, while the people lived in beggary.[17] The German attachment to its forests had been noticed by Tacitus, who called them the *silves horrida* and when, in the eighteenth century the first forest histories appeared, it was their size, antiquity and Germanness that marked the peculiar distinction of Germany.[18] They had become one of the marks of princedom. Frederick II Hohenzollern thought that there was no cadet of a princely line that did not think he should behave like Louis XIV. According to Moore, he hunted insatiably, 'he builds his Versailles, he has mistresses, he keeps an army ... God have pity on a country afflicted with such a prince.'[19] Frederick in his time conformed to the type: he built his palace at Potsdam, and he provided entertainments free in the royal theatre. His indulgence, however, was the army. His father had created and nursed it carefully by keeping it out of wars, while Frederick's intention for its use was to wage successful aggressive and defensive wars. Prussia under Frederick William I had been run on tight military lines. Its nobles had one function: to be immaculate military officers; the pastimes of the king and his sons were military drills. Frederick continued the tradition. Even the music of the day was military, and only in the evening would the court relax at a concert, though Dr Burney found the programmes dull and old-fashioned.[20]

The full horrors of the Prussian military under Frederick II were tellingly described by Thackeray in his picaresque novel, *Barry Lyndon* (1844), under his Fitzboodle pen-name. It was the year in which Carlyle began his 14 years researching and writing the life and times of Frederick, some of the object of which was to rehabilitate his hero from Thackeray's obvious distaste for the man and his regime. Redmond Barry (*Lyndon*), the hero in flight from possible arrest in Ireland for murder, is kidnapped to serve in the Prussian army during the Seven Year War. As an unwilling trooper he graphically experiences the beatings and malevolence of Prussian officers until he is able to escape with his rapscallion uncle to engage in an alternative career, of chicanery and fraud, outside Prussia.

The two Barrys, Redmond and his uncle, the self-styled Chevalier de Balibari, are two Irish adventurers who survive by native wit and card-sharping. But the treatment of common soldiers in Frederick's service, the most notable part of the novel, was in Fitzboodle's description both barbaric and sadistic. Frederick ran a sort of Stasi-like information and spying service to bind the men to their officers and officers to their king, intended to discourage desertion but, in Barry's case, creating a resolve to defeat it.[21] Though Redmond Barry was a murderer and a deserter, his panache, his boasts that invariably ended in misfortune and his incurable self-confidence created an anti-hero among the 'scum of the earth enlisted for drink'. Thackeray did not find military service ennobling; Frederick did not consider it anything else.

Frederick shared his passion with other Pumpernickel princes for what were virtually private armies, but theirs were mainly for hire. The Duke of Württemberg kept, according to Burney, never less than 6,000 men under arms in time of peace, 'so that nothing can be seen in the streets except officers', in black whiskers, white peruques, with curls at the sides, six deep; their blue coats, patched and mended with great ingenuity and diligence. As there was little occupation for the sons of the nobility they opted for a military career as soldiers of fortune, often in the service of other potentates, like Maurice de Saxe (1696–1750), the most illustrious of the many bastards of Augustus the Strong of Saxony and Poland, who started his career as a hired officer at the age of 12. Most of these armies were for decoration. The Landgrave of Hesse-Kassel in 1786 used his wealth to keep 16,000 men in time of peace, drilling them in the Prussian manner, in whose army he held the rank of Field Marshal. When the weather was wet, 200 to 300 grenadiers performed immaculate manoeuvres in the dining hall of his palace.[22]

Because the prince was usually the only man in the State who could afford extravagance, a much-travelled man like Casanova in the 1750s found German towns were places of innocence and peace. Patriarchal manners dictated a simple and monotonous way of life, quiet and calm in its pleasures, where sensuality was extinct.[23] The smaller the principality the greater the pride of caste. Service at court conferred rank if not necessarily nobility, but a title was usually purchased, or granted, to go with what was otherwise a sinecure. Goethe at the court of Saxe-Weimar was addressed as Herr Baron, but his nobility carried no more than the label. Nobles who had been, however undistinguished, noble for generations preserved their sense of distinction. One provincial aristocrat hoped that at the last judgment he would not have to appear with his inferiors, while another reprimanded the priest for baptising his child using the same holy water with which he had also baptised the children of commoners.[24] Frederick II, liberal in many other respects, preferred to have his nobles as army officers, on the grounds that they might be incompetent but they had a sense of honour they were determined to uphold.

As part of the mock panoply of power there was a proliferation of titles. Some were often sold to boost the revenue of smaller and more impecunious states, but others were lavished on courtiers, frequently in default of salaries. The court of the prince of Hildburg, a state of a bare 12 square kilometres, boasted a Court Marshal, a Grand Master of Stables, a Grand Master of the Hunt and a Grand Master of Forests. So prolific had become the spawn of minor nobles that the Knights of Malta insisted on 16 quarterings on the family coat of arms before admission of knights to the German Tongue of the Order. This proliferation of offices was paid for by the heavy oppression of helpless subjects, by pensions from France or Austria in return for neutrality or alliance in the case of war, and by the fees for providing mercenaries.

* * *

The ordinary Prussian soldier seemed to one observer, to live in terror. 'For the least fault', Boswell observed in Berlin, 'they were beat like dogs.'[25] New recruits were caned with increasing ferocity until they mastered their firelocks, like a British schoolboy stumbling over his parsing. Steadiness under arms was inculcated by rigid discipline and it was barely possible for a soldier to escape punishment for some infraction or other. Frederick II presided over this regime with the attention of a true martinet; even when dying he was wheeled to his sickbay window to watch the drilling of his troops. It was made peculiarly difficult to desert from the ranks and a deserter was pursued like a beast of prey, peasants being rewarded for turning them in and savagely punished for not. [26] John Moore thought that 'the common state of slavery in Asia or that to which people of civil professions in the most despotic countries are subject, is as freedom in comparison of this kind of military slavery.' [27]

As well as a court of idle officials, a prince was expected to boast a mistress, or as in the case of Augustus the Strong, Elector of Saxony and King of Poland, two mistresses, one for each principality. To be *maîtresse en titre* carried with it rewards in cash and often preferment for the husband, another drain upon the state, for a mistress, as opposed to a concubine, expected to be received at court and at the court of neighbouring princes, suitably bedizened by diamonds. The greatest enemy of royalty, especially the monarch of a Pumpernickel state, was boredom. Boswell saw 'a certain joy in the faces of courtiers when strangers are announced'. [28] An egregious and facile conversationalist like Casanova found a last refuge from 1785 to 1798 as librarian to the Bohemian Count von Waldstein, but despite Boswell's belief that strangers were welcomed as bearers of interesting intelligence, conversation was not held in particularly high regard in the smaller courts of Pumpernickel. Affairs of State were usually off limits, and affairs of international politics were too remote, so that affairs of the heart, of the bed, of the table and of the chase tended to fill the hours that were not spent eating or drinking, or in masquerades. 'Being so much harassed with ceremony and form and cramped by the distance which birth throws between people', wrote John Moore in 1786, 'they are glad to seize every opportunity of assuming the mask and domino, that they may taste the pleasure of familiar conversation and social mirth.' [29] French observers found social conditions not far removed from savagery and they resolved to export French taste and culture as their 'civilising mission'. They found a warm reception among the German princes. Being civilised gave them something interesting to do.

Most European princes had a passion for hunting whether actively pursued or as spectator sport, and in addition to their palaces they also erected hunting lodges adorned with all modern conveniences and Baroque finishings in or near their extensive forests. One duke, of Württemberg, established a chivalric order, named after St Hubert, the patron saint of hunting, complete with its own banqueting hall and chapel, in which were enrolled most of his palace servants. One monarch, however, thought that hunting may have done something for the body but little for the mind, and Frederick II of Prussia demonstrated his disapproval by showing that the battlefield of Rossbach (in 1757 at the beginning of the Seven Years War) had not been won on the hunting fields of Pomerania.

Some princes claimed to share Frederick's contempt for frivolity and patronised savants and employed alchemists. Germany had long been, since the days of Paracelsus (1493–1541) and the Emperor Rudolph II (1552–1612), a Tom Tiddler's ground for quacks and mountebanks and in the eighteenth century was home to thousands of experimenters of doubtful competence. Some of them were genuine scientists, like Johann Friedrich Böttger in Saxony, who discovered the secret of the Chinese in the manufacture of porcelain, but more were plausible charlatans, like Cagliostro.[30]

∗   ∗   ∗

The predominant power in Germany was the Archduchy of Austria, whose Archduke had been elected Holy Roman Emperor pretty consistently for two centuries. German might be the language of this empire but apart from the actual archduchy itself, Austria was defined by its Habsburg rulers, and much of its ruling class, particularly its civil service, was drawn from other linguistic groups, Hungarians, Bohemians, Croatians, Serbs, Italians, Flemings, representing its component parts.[31] The Habsburgs had for two centuries been the principal bulwark against Ottoman expansion into Europe and now were pushing the eastern borders back into the upper reaches of the Balkans. The other vital frontier was with France, whose ambitions to extend her territorial boundaries east were frustrated by the cluster of Germanic principalities along the Rhine, who were bound together in a survival alliance with the Habsburg rulers of the empire.

Though Austria had not achieved her principal ambitions in the War of the Spanish Succession (1701–14), she had prevented a union of the French and Spanish crowns. With the help of the Duke of Marlborough and her own French-born soldier of fortune, Prince Eugène de Savoie-Carignan, she had frustrated Louis XIV's northern ambitions and expelled the French from Italy. For much of the eighteenth century Vienna's efforts were twofold: to sustain the alliance with buffer states to France, and to push the Ottoman further down the Danube, while ensuring that Russian power was increased more at the expense of the Ottomans than of Christian states on her borders. German affairs were regulated by the Imperial Diet, where Austria ensured her voice was dominant.

Frederick II's perfidious seizure of Silesia in 1756 that sparked off The Seven Years War led to the most damaging conflict for nearly 100 years. It was the first challenge to Austria's Imperial power from within Germany since The Thirty Years War and, in defending his aggression successfully in three wars, Frederick demonstrated that the Holy Roman Empire might be a carcase ready for picking. Before then, however, Prussia, Saxony, Bohemia, the Rhineland and the empire of Maria Theresa were visited by the four outriders of the Horses of the Apocalypse: devastation, looting, requisition and taxation. Recovery afterwards was Austria's first priority, hastened by a combination of social reform, limiting the extension of church lands, and by appropriation of the suppressed Society of Jesus. With the death of the Empress Maria Theresa, in 1780, her son Joseph II pressed on with the reformation of his sprawling empire. Enforcement of frugality became his watchword; he himself wore a simple army uniform and his court was run more on military lines than was deemed appropriate for so august a monarch. Student enrolment at the four permitted universities, of Vienna, Budapest, Louvain in the Low Countries and Pavia in Italy, was limited to the estimate of the number of government places that were waiting for them. Though Joseph's reforms mainly had to be undone in the face of opposition and unrest by the brother who succeeded him as Leopold II in 1790, and though the antipodes of the empire in Italy and the Low Countries were to be lost in the next century, the Imperial lands of middle Europe remained part of the Austrian, if not the Holy Roman, Empire until after the 1914–18 war.

* * *

The Imperial family was also musical in the tradition of Pumpernickel princes. Leopold I (Holy Roman Emperor from 1658–1705) was an accomplished musician, and often composed for his court orchestra;

his granddaughter, the Empress Maria Theresa (*regnavit* 1740–80), had a fine voice and as Archduchess, aged 22, had performed publicly with the foremost *castrato* singer of the day, Franceso Bernardi Senesino, in Florence.[32] Her voice was passed on to her daughters. Four of them were to perform Gluck's *Il Parnasso Confuso* in the Schönbrunn Palace while their brother, the Grand Duke of Tuscany, the future Emperor Leopold II, accompanied them on the harpsichord.[33] But Vienna was not then the musical mecca it later became. When Dr Burney visited in 1773, Gluck towered over the musical scene; otherwise, for such a prominent city of such a powerful state, he found Vienna a curious combination of grandeur and squalor, and getting there by coach and raft was not a journey to be lightly undertaken. Few English, apart from the diplomatists, had made the effort to go there before Dr Burney. Even after his visit, which had tried to put Vienna on the musical map, Imperial patronage was severely limited. Mozart, whose music pleased the Emperor, even to the extent that he would perform his piano music for his own delectation, waited for the offer of an Imperial post in vain, and Haydn depended after 1761 on the Hungarian Esterhazy family for his bed and board.

Burney had arrived by the fastest yet most primitive vehicle, a raft on the Danube. This could cover 70 or 80 miles a day on the rapid river waters but was otherwise poorly provided for food or shelter, and Burney hoped he would never have to travel that way again.[34] The raft was a kind of permanent ferry but its passenger quarters were leaky and ill-covered, and Burney travelled from Munich through lands which despite sumptuous palaces and grandiose monasteries were ill-provided with sources of food and drink. The streets of Vienna were narrow and badly-lit and appeared to be lined with palaces, with shops on the ground floor and the owners on the top floor, for the Emperor could lay claim to the provision of accommodation for court employees on the first floor. Actual purchases were not made from shops but from itinerant hawkers who made the rounds to sell at the door and make what price they could. It was all so very different from London. Burney was shocked by the public spectacles advertised, when the Viennese public, like blood-thirsty Imperial Romans, were regaled with baiting of animals by dogs, which would tear their victims to pieces. The spectacle might be concluded by a ferocious, half-starved bear attacking and devouring a wild Hungarian bull, assisted if necessary by a wolf. [35]

* * *

With the Hanoverian succession England's inarticulate monarch was the centre of patronage and courtly life more in the German tradition of Pumpernickel. The Elector had become king, by courtesy of his mother, the Duchess Sophia, daughter of the unhappy Elector Palatine, Winter King of Bohemia, and of Elizabeth Stuart, youngest sister of the equally unhappy Charles I of England and Scotland. Sophia, the Countess Palatine (1630–1714), perhaps the most sensible of the Stuarts, knew that about all she had in her wedding trousseau was a claim to the thrones of England and Scotland, but as this was uncertain, while Queen Anne survived childless through her 17 pregnancies, she rode her wanton, gourmandising husband, the Hanoverian Elector Ernest Augustus (1629–1698), with careful indulgence, and allowed him to play at dynastic politics with mercenary skill. She gave him seven children among them George Louis, the future Elector of Hanover and King of England.

The German Electors had the shadowy power to elect the Holy Roman Emperor. Otherwise, as Thackeray, writing in *The Cornhill* in 1861 with mordant memories of his travels in Germany, described George Louis's Hanoverian inheritance:

> the landscape (was) awful – wretched wastes, beggarly and plundered, half-burned cottages and trembling peasants gathering piteous harvest, gangs of such tramping along with bayonets behind them, and corporals with canes and cats-of-nine tails to flog them to barracks. [36]

Manpower was the main resource of German princes. George Louis's father had sold 6,000 as mercenaries to Venice, most of whom perished in Venetian wars with the Ottomans in the Greek Morea. George Louis himself headed a force of 10,000 in the service of the Emperor against the Turks; he helped to defend Vienna during its classic siege, and later fought against the French in Italy and on the Rhine, prudently despatching Hanoverian troops to fight with Marlborough at Blenheim. He divorced his wife for adultery and kept her immured in a castle until her death, before he became Elector of Hanover in 1698. He had all the pretensions and none of the joviality of his father, and was a cold, silent man saying little in German, as he would say nothing in English. But he was not unpopular with his Hanoverian subjects whom he ruled prudently and economically. His son, George II of England, spent as much tine as he could in Hanover, and while there laid aside all the pomp and circumstance of being King of England, where he was a figure of fun for his fondness for sauerkraut and sausages. He appeared on one occasion in Turkish dress at a fancy dress ball and, according to Thackeray, capered about for 20 years, 'a strutting Turkey cock of Herrenhausen, a naughty little Mahomet'.[37]

His father, George I of England, had never known for how long he would enjoy his new kingdom. But he saw to it that his Germans did as well as they could expect from his good fortune – he had the example of Dutch William III to learn from – and decided that he would let the English look after the affairs of England, and he would look after Hanover. England had given him a tepid reception; its ways were not his, and he was sensible enough not to try to change them.

In the German principalities, the rulers had built their mini-palaces of Versailles discreetly sheltered from their people by woods and gardens. 'One sees', wrote Lady Mary Wortley Montagu from Hanover to the Countess of Bristol in 1716, 'none of those fine seats of noblemen that are common among us, nor anything like a country gentleman's house. The whole people are divided into absolute sovereignties where all the riches and magnificence are at court or communities of merchants.'[38]

States with poor trade and worse agriculture kept their sovereigns in a pale version of French splendour and their populations polite but poor. Thackeray had no illusions; Versailles was the cynosure for all Pumpernickel German sovereignties,

Round all that royal Splendour lies a nation enslaved and ruined; there are people robbed of their rights – communities laid waste – faith, justice, commerce trampled upon and well-nigh destroyed – nay in the very centre of Royalty itself, what horrible stains and meanness, crimes and shame! It is to but a silly harlot that some of the noblest gentlemen and some of the proudest women in the world are bowing down; it is the price of a miserable province that the king ties in diamonds round his mistress's white neck. [39]

To build big bassoons, and play on them from trap-ladders; to do hunting, build opera houses, give court shows; what else, if they do not care to serve in foreign armies, is well possible for them?[40]

Carlyle's judgment on the ancestors of Queen Victoria's husband was not dissonant from Thackeray's. Prinz Albrecht Franz August Karl Emanuel von Sachsen-Coburg-Gotha had a name redolent of Pumpernickel but he was lucky to find himself as Prince Consort of Great Britain, at the hub of a serious monarchy.

* * *

George of Hanover, when he moved to London, was not accompanied by his librarian, the universal intellect of the day, Gottfried Wilhelm Leibniz, mathematician, inventor, jurist, diplomatist, philosopher, theologian and courtier. Leibniz was in correspondence on his mathematical theories widely with the savants throughout Europe and was considered the most learned man in Europe. But slow progress on the history of the House of Brunswick, to which he owed his position, and which was more important to George I than having an intellectual prodigy in his employment, persuaded the Elector to leave Leibniz behind in Germany. Though at his death in 1716 Leibniz had only reached the first millennium of the Brunswick history – the work lay in the Hanover archives until disinterred and published in 1843 – it epitomised the preoccupation of Pumpernickel.

George Louis of Hanover needed no more learned men in England; there were already more than enough to tell him what to do, but in Germany royal patronage of learning and music depended on the continuing prosperity and/or importance, both dynastic and honorific, of the princes, and these in turn depended on their having men of learning and talent adorning their courts to tell the world about them. It had become a royal fashion to create learned Academies and Royal Societies. Leibniz had created that of Prussia. He was its first president, and drew up the plans for an Academy in St Petersburg for Peter the Great, while only Jesuit opposition prevented his founding an Academy of Science in Vienna. Other princes built laboratories and libraries and some like the Dukes of Weimar collected savants as other rulers collected animals for their zoos and specimens for their botanical gardens. These tokens of a princely passion for distinction helped to secure learned men in princely if relatively modest pay (often supplemented by priestly stipends), and at the opening of the eighteenth century Germany embarked on its cultural and intellectual renaissance.[41] Leibniz had worried himself into accepting that the world was basically rational and that if one realised this, developed one's own intellect, and accepted one's own place in the order of things, as directed by the prince himself, then all would be for the best. The mind was then free to consider the problems of free will, the existence of God and of ethics without disturbing the social order.

∗ ∗ ∗

When did Romanticism rather than Romance embrace Pumpernickel? George I was by no means either romantic or a Romantic. Germany was not yet tinctured by the Spirit of Romance, which was to envelop it in the next century with the music of Weber, Hoffman, Schumann, Mendelssohn and Wagner. The prevailing intellectual ambition at the end of the seventeenth century, exhausted by the apostolic blows and knocks of the Thirty Years War, was to explore the example of that nation which had escaped involvement in the European holocaust and had, following a relatively bloodless – even if the blood shed was royal – civil war, and an almost wholly bloodless 'Glorious Revolution', changed its dynasty for one of the more mediocre of Pumpernickels.

The foundation in London of The Royal Society for Improving Natural Knowledge in 1660 followed by its royal charter two years later, had given an establishment imprimatur to experiment and empirical philosophy. The world was both expanding and shrinking. The discovery of new lands and the improvement of nautical skills expanded the world while they also shrank it by the speed with which new knowledge spread and ideas flourished. In 1690, after the savage strife of so-called civilised Europe, John Locke was confident enough to state categorically that 'reason is natural revelation whereby the eternal Father of light, and fountain of all knowledge communicates to mankind that portion of truth which he has laid within the reach of their natural faculties.' Facts were established by observation, and observation appeared to reveal that only the state of nature guaranteed humanity of peace, good will, mutual assistance and preservation, thus confirming that 'reason must be our last judge and guide in everything.'[42] Goethe in the next century was rather back-handedly to echo this view. 'Man's art is in all situations rather to fortify himself against Nature, to avoid her thousandfold ills and only to enjoy his measure of the good.' Confining all his true and factitious wants in a palace, 'he grows ever weaker, takes to "joys of the soul" and his powers melt away into – *horresco referens* – "Virtue, Benevolence, Sensibility"'.[43]

The 'state of nature' and 'natural law' were, however, easier to pronounce as actual and eternal than to define. Isaac Newton believed that natural law could be discerned in the laws of mathematics, a rational activity, and man by following his natural reason could find happiness and contentment. Reason and experiment were the sole paths to reliable knowledge, as he had demonstrated in his mathematical thesis on gravitational force in *Principia Mathematica* (1687). David Hume set the seal on this conviction in his *Treatise on Human Understanding* (1719), in which he dethroned traditional rules of life based on religion and other non-scientific principles, which could not be demonstrated as true by experiment and experience. The British philosophers had presented the Germans with conundra that they could spend their leisure trying to elucidate, an activity, on the whole, too abstruse to worry their rulers.

CHAPTER THREE

Genius: Germans in Search of God

Leibniz to Kant

Nihil est sine ratione. (There is nothing without a reason.)
(Leibniz, 1671)

If God were to hold out in his right hand all Truth, and in his left
just the active search for it, I should humbly take the left hand.
(Gotthold Lessing, 1778)[1]

*T*HE STIPENDS OF learned men at universities derived from princely support. Leibniz (1646–1716) was a tireless gatherer of information, but as a princely servant, he was the epitome of Pumpernickel in the person and philosophy of Dr Pangloss. He was also the great compromiser; in his world there were no absolute rights, no absolute wrongs. Religion could be reconciled with rationalism, authority with freedom, all were subsumed into a Platonic mysticism in which concepts as abstruse as monads, the world, souls, persons, God even, floated in a cosmic soup of benevolence. The brutally practical Voltaire was unimpressed. One thing was clear: this was not the best of all possible worlds, in which the apparently divisive aims of monads were mysteriously reconciled.

The debate on what sort of world it really was constituted the stuff of the *Aufklarung*. The word was invented by Immanuel Kant and translated a century later as 'enlightenment'.[2] Its German origins were in Brandenburg-Prussia, where one of the founders of the University of Halle, Christian Thomasius (1655–1728), invented the term 'natural reason'.[3] His study of human behaviour in a social context was based on observation. Authority and what was believed to be reason could not account solely for the way human beings behaved. The English interest in the eccentricities of human behaviour, which inspired most of the novels of the day, inspired his empirical method, which demonstrated that the ruling determinant of human behaviour ought to be common sense.

Thomasius's non-systematic approach was consistent with the accounts of peoples in different stages of civilisation, which appeared to prove that people were not autonomous, endowed like Frankenstein's (Mary Shelley's) monster with a desire to learn and improve, but irrational beings guided by their cultural values, which held them suspended at a certain stage of development. Thomasius had a limited following. Literacy had not much improved over two centuries and one reason for this may have been that the principal reading material was the Bible (which like the Koran among some Muslims today was considered all that it was necessary to read) and devotional glosses upon it. Thomasius founded periodicals, both cheap and improving, to impart behavioural and moral advice, based more on practical experience than on codes of behaviour dictated by established authority.

The way was set for 'popular philosophy' to enthuse the middle, educated and commercial, class. They read that moral action was determined by a combination of reason and unreason, of social pressure and of divine precept. The search for explanations and definitions was to occupy the best minds of the century. If Leibniz's thinking appeared to these popular philosophers opaque and sometimes muddled, it was given almost clarity at the hands of Christian Wolff (1679–1754). Wolff had studied mathematics and physics at Jena University but to such studies, being necessarily theoretical, he added philosophy. After an encounter with the universal but cloudy mind of Leibniz, he resolved to make all clear, and when he moved to Halle to teach mathematics, he soon enlarged his horizons to include the teaching of theoretical science and speculative thought.

He aimed to embrace all knowledge like his master, but also hoped to use mathematics to reduce it all to a system, producing a stream of books to support his theories. His reading of Newton and Locke suggested that the dominant force, which determined right human behaviour was natural law, and natural law guided reason. His writings, however, alarmed the Pietist theological establishment of Halle, no friends of learned theologising, for his attempt to provide a mathematical and thus reasonable basis for theological truth struck them as agnosticism, even atheism. They represented to King Frederick William I that Wolff was teaching that human behaviour was due less to free will than to natural determinants, and that any soldier who deserted could claim that outside forces beyond his control had determined him to do so. The monarchical martinet was horrified at such an idea and dismissed Wolff from all his posts. On laying down office, Wolff delivered a lecture on Confucius who, he argued, had arrived at moral truth by rational enquiry without divine influence of any kind.

Wolff accepted a post in Marbourg in the territory of the Margrave of Hesse-Kassel, and buoyed up by popular sympathy he became Germany's intellectual idol, inspiring a school of 'Wolffians' until invited back to Halle by Frederick II on the death of Frederick William I (1740). He believed that, by applying a rational series of judgments to truth, he had proved the existence of God and the immortality of the soul, but his ideas appeared to consign the deity to nullity. To Wolff human perfection in whatever world in which he lived was possible, if guided by natural law, and where he differed from Dr Pangloss was in suggesting that it was not reasonable to believe that this was the best of all possible worlds.

Wolff's mind was reductive not original and he appeared to espouse both the idea of popular sovereignty and that of total submission to the ruler. But his teaching on economics and administration was essentially practical and in pursuit of the common good, so that he established both as academic subjects worthy of study and the basis of advice to governments. Though his ideas may have contributed to the articulation of the American declaration of independence, in Germany they were discussed in a way that leeched from them any challenge to the established authority of state and Church. The advantage of this was no one wished to suppress the exchange of ideas since they obviously posed no threat to either. German thinkers were not, like their French precursors, seeking arguments to abolish belief in God and subvert religion; rather by stripping both of mythical accretions they sought to restore both to primacy in hearth and home. Most of Wolff's followers were clergy or sons of clergy, and their rationalism owed more to metaphysics than physics.

* * *

Wolff was too much of a rationalist to spend time reconciling what he perceived as natural law with the ontological questions it raised about the place of God, revelation, salvation, morality, and the afterlife. But if man was not to become a moral automaton, these had to be confronted. The confrontation was to come from a Prussian city on the Baltic coast. Königsberg was a very Pumpernickel town; formerly a stronghold of the Teutonic Knights and a member of the Hanseatic league, it had been the capital of the Duchy of Prussia, which had given it a university in 1544, and when the electoral duke became a king and moved his capital to Brandenburg, it became the second city of the kingdom. Königsberg by the seventeenth century had come strongly under the influence of Pietism, for it had received many Huguenot refugees expelled from Salzburg, and despite its university it was as quiet and regulated as discipline-loving King Frederick William I could have wanted. The Pietists emphasised personal faith and believed that the faithful should ignore all the intellectual fads and theories that afflicted theologians at the end of the seventeenth century. Union with God was achieved not by book learning but by a rigorous and regular examination of conscience and by simple faith and prayer. The humiliation of the self then allowed divine grace to enter.[4] Within this torpid and conformist regime an intellectual revolution was, however, gestating. The 16-year-old son of a saddler, called Immanuel Kant (1724–1804), was supporting himself at the university by giving private lessons to dimmer but richer fellow students and by supplementing what he earned there by playing billiards, at which he excelled, since he treated the game as a mathematical puzzle.

German philosophy, usually taught in Latin, was still scholastic and rigid, but coming increasingly under the influence of English thought. Wolff actually used German for his students and Latin to communicate his ideas to an international readership. His followers taught that the laws of nature could be discovered by rational enquiry, and that conclusions could be drawn from the operation of cause upon effect. More extreme thinkers, then, in seeking to emphasise their liberation from the fetters of rationality, believed that there were no laws of nature, in the sense of being controlling edicts; otherwise they reduced human behaviour to the inevitability of a mathematical equation. Moderate new thinking held that if natural law had anything like a legal imperative, it was to live according to its simple precepts and, in this sense, it was God. But this according to more conservative thinkers led inevitably to atheism, anarchy, rampant individualism and crime. Its followers were in danger of being lost in a wilderness of misdirected thought which could lead to suicide.

It was to be the mission of Immanuel Kant otherwise part-time teacher and billiards ace, to try to reconcile the traditional concept of a God with the new critiques posed by mathematics, empiricism and reason, which threatened to remove Him from human affairs. After lecturing to ever-increasing audiences in Königsberg, he became in 1770 professor of logic and metaphysics. He never married, never travelled except in his mind, and, it was said, lived so routinely organised a life that neighbours set their watches by his movements. Under the influence of David Hume's empirical and sceptical approach he was to bring about a revolution in thinking. Kant held that all Hume's conclusions could not be accepted as empirically observed fact, only assumptions. To resolve the conundra of human behaviour, Kant embarked on a lifetime's enquiry into the theory of knowledge, putting metaphysics, ethics and aesthetics under the microscope.

His thinking was abstruse and dense, and it was not expressed in French, more's the pity, as being the usual language of ideas it prized clarity and concision. Hume and Locke had written with both to prove that any notion of human behaviour being subject to anything timeless and innate could not be proved. Kant in the 1780s found this difficult to accept and wrote three *Critiques* exploring how the human mind arrived at judgments that were stated as fact, like the proposition that man had an immortal soul (which Hume thought was a statement basically without foundation), and that there were such things as time and space, with which knowledge we were born. Though the existence of both could not be proven, it was essential to believe that they existed, as they ordered the whole of human life, so the human mind had created them as concepts. In short, knowledge was the result of experience humanly interpreted, not given. What, he wondered, would prevail after human reason could explore no further? What was the 'true' nature of 'truth'? He accepted that this was, as Hume held, not capable of proof, but he held that in all human behaviour there was a right way to behave because there was a 'categorical imperative', a sort of DNA, a human instinct or blueprint of what was expected of him. 'Freedom – the ability of rational beings to initiate events and not be determined in their actions by extraneous causes – could not be shown not to exist.'[5]

47

So did it exist? Reason was conditioned by certain innate ideas and conduct was influenced by moral imperatives. Cloudier English thinkers, like Coleridge, who felt that the Hume/Locke school was too dispiriting, leaving no room for imagination and emotion, latched onto what they could understand of Kant's thinking. The 'perennial philosophers', like Plato and Thomas Aquinas, had started on the assumption that there was a reality existing outside us, whereas Kant held that man might study the existential mysteries, but his capacity to penetrate them was limited. The existence of the three great commonly held 'realities', of God, Freedom and Immortality, was beyond absolute certainty. Kant had to deny knowledge in order to make room for faith.[6] As one could not prove the existence of God, one could not verify revelation in Scripture. His existence depended on a quest in the human mind that strove to prove it. Philosophy could discard the crutches of dogma and belief.

Kant adorned his study with a portrait of Rousseau, but he did not accept Rousseau's thesis of Man's native goodness. There was too much evidence against it. But man could acquire the quality of goodness by intention. To act according to one's duty could be to act contrary to one's wilful nature and rise above it. Recent history may have shown that acting according to one's duty can also suppress one's better nature, but Kant's 'categorical imperatives' suggested that if everyone acted on them, then they would constitute natural law and would limit man's freedom as much as Rousseau's 'general will', however that was defined. Kant developed his concept of freedom to act free of unprovable laws into a categorical imperative to act in accordance with duty or in the pursuit of the ideal. In that notion there lay a directive for the 'collective subconscious of Europe'.[7] Some, as Carlyle put it, thought that 'the pious and peaceful sage of Königsberg passes for a sort of Necromancer and Black-artist in Metaphysics.'[8] Real life was actually governed by storm and stress, *sturm und drang*.

✳ ✳ ✳

By the end of the eighteenth century 'Kantians' predominated in the German universities. Goethe, who was advised not to get involved in studying his philosophy, felt impelled to line himself up with the sage of Königsberg and claim that they thought alike on certain things.[9] The very abstruseness of Kant's ideas meant that they were not revolutionary in politics but only in the manner of thinking, not acting. Goethe thought, indeed, that they exalted the dignity of mind while appearing to restrict it. Carlyle, who never really understood them, summed up the phenomenon in one lapidary sentence:

> The air of mysticism connected with [his] doctrines was attractive to the German mind, with which the vague and the vast are always pleasing qualities; the dreadful array of first principles, the forest huge of terminology and definitions where the panting intellect of weaker men … wanders as in pathless thickets oppressed with fatigue and suffocated with scholastic miasma, seemed sublime rather than appalling to the Germans.[10]

He understood enough to know that they applied the limitations of human experience to such universal subjects as morality, and reconciled empiricism on Hume's model to such philosophic abstracts as God, the soul and truth generally, and questioned whether ethics and morals were rationally acquired or intrinsic to human nature, thus to natural law. Carlyle wearily invoked the master spirit of the age who said that the Kantian scheme would 'have its day, as all things have'.[11]

Optimists were quick to see in Kantian arguments an antidote to the dark antinomian theory of human behaviour that could emerge from extreme Protestant, Pietistic thought, which counselled submission to God's will. They read into them evidence that real life was not a rational, ordered system but unfair, capricious, irrational and unequal, full indeed of storm and stress.[12] Its proponents, the *sturmers und drangers,* were mainly young men studying at universities, born in the 1740s and now nearly 20-years-old, for whom the world was not a coach-service following a well-planned timetable, but an anarchic free-for-all. Within this anarchy, freedom was exciting. They rejected the statutory powdered wig, preferring their own hair uncovered, and 'returned to nature' as Rousseau bid. Their 'nature' was unpredictable and followed rules of its own. They called on human creativity not to look for design but chaos, to see grandeur in cataclysms and storms, and to read in them that man was engaged in a constant struggle to assert his limited independence.

Kant viewed the revolt against superstition in England and France as a certain clearing up of truth. More exactly, it was a questioning of what had hitherto remained acceptable without question. There were no specific answers to the questions – they had after all been asked centuries before and the replies were even then a matter for argument. Up to the middle of the century, artists and men of letters looked for models first to France, and then increasingly to England. French cultural hegemony was under challenge as English society seemed to spawn political, scientific and philosophical ideas which threw a new light on, and promised a new way of viewing, the world. So far the principal export of the German principalities had not been ideas but dynasties, irrigating the blood bank of Europe. Now Germany felt a stirring in its literary genes, awakened by a clumsy translation of Milton by a Swiss Calvinist pastor who was then involved in an intense literary debate on whether poetry should be based on classic formulae or be more free-ranging. It was a debate as old as poetry itself, waged between traditionalists and innovators.

* * *

As there was little German poetry to be modelled on either, it sparked a creative surge. Gotthold Lessing (1729–81) was a Saxon. The son of a poor pastor, he had gravitated to work as a journalist in Prussia, first at Breslau and later Berlin. He then moved, with two important works behind him, to be director of the theatre at Hamburg. Never a Francophile, he had a correct respect for the French but felt that this should not be slavish.[13] Lessing's reputation rested on *Laoköon* (1766), an essay on Greek sculpture, which Winckelmann had chosen in his *History of the Art of Antiquity* (*Geschichte der Kunst des Alterthums*, 1764) as the model of antique proportion and restraint. Periclean Athens was held to mark the high peak of Hellenic thought and art, and Winckelmann, the son of a cobbler, saw in the sculpture of that time the expression of an ideal, carved in a climate of political freedom. It was the archetype of true beauty. Had the sculptor of the Laoköon statue in the Vatican, according to Winckelmann, revealed the agony and contortion of the life struggle with the serpent, this would have diminished the perfection and timelessness of the whole ensemble. Laoköon is portrayed in noble simplicity and calm grandeur; as he wrestles with the serpent he does not shriek out; he suffers the agony with total fortitude.[14] Lessing took issue with the dogmatism of the Master; he argued that, on the contrary, what was missing from the group was the distress and despair which the real life situation would have exhibited.

Real life emotions, not respect for the classic rules, should be the stuff of art. In Hamburg he was in a position to affect public choice and he chose to unseat the pedantry of French classical models by unlocking the imagination of German. He had discovered Shakespeare and hailed him as a greater poet than the twin demi-gods of German, indeed European, classicism, Corneille and Racine. This championing of Shakespeare seemed like a bolt of enlightenment when Lessing went on to claim that the Swan of Avon was the true heir of Sophocles. Winckelmann, so far the supreme arbiter of classicism, had stated that Greek art and letters were the unassailable pinnacles of human achievement. Now Lessing gave the Shakespearian raging of the human heart a kind of imprimatur. Lyric poetry of the imagination was liberated and often soared into unclassical excess. Carlyle thought that Lessing was the non-pareil, pervaded by 'a genial fire, a wit, a heartiness, a general richness and fineness of nature to which most logicians are strangers', and to which Englishmen should respond with readiest affection.[15]

Lessing's experiments in drama were the prompt to his religious doubts, expressed on the stage. He never abandoned Christianity as a general rule of life but felt that it had no need to be based on supernatural sanctions. It possessed the same truth as most religions but its special characteristics, the divinity and resurrection of Christ, were unprovable. Jesus was a traditional Jew; a nationalist who believed his destiny was to lead his nation to self-rule as the Messiah, but also a sublime moral teacher. A hypostatic union was, however, contrary to reason and to nature. The gospels were a stage on the enlightenment of humanity, which would govern itself not in the expectation of supernatural rewards but by the exercise of right thinking. All that one had to hold on to in Christianity was ultimately love.[16] When the Duke of Brunswick withdrew Lessing's licence to print his increasingly controversial ideas, he expressed them in 1779 in the form of a drama, Nathan the Wise.

Set in Jerusalem at the time of Saladin it is a poetic discussion on the nature of religion, and of the three Abrahamic faiths, between the Sultan, Nathan, a Jewish merchant, and an anonymous Templar. The core of the story is a magic ring, an heirloom, promised by Nathan unwisely to all three of his daughters. To meet his promise he has two replicas made so that each child should receive what she believed was the real heirloom. As the ring had special power to render its wearer pleasant to man and to God, an inevitable dispute broke out as to which was the real one. It was decided by a wise judgment that the real ring would be identified by the character of its wearer. The story was an old morality tale, used by Boccaccio in the *Decamerone*, and in the tripartite discussion round its meaning, Lessing pleaded tolerance between men, emphasised friendship, and repudiated any supernatural 'proofs' of the rightness of any one religion, dispensing with the need for miracles and denying that God had any preference in the matter. Needless to say, the play was not performed in Lessing's lifetime, but its inspiration lingered on in the subconscious of Walter Scott and Benjamin Disraeli who explored the same territory in *The Talisman* and in *Tancred*.

Lessing had a remarkable friend and fellow sceptic in the race of Disraeli. Moses Mendelssohn (1729–86), the grandfather of Felix, was born in Dessau in Prussia of a poor Jewish copyist, employed in producing scrolls for the synagogue. From birth he had a physical deformity of the spine, but being, so to speak, in the synagogual family, he received a conventional Rabbinic education in Biblical studies and the Talmud. When his teacher went to Berlin, Mendelssohn followed him on foot, his entrance to Berlin through the Rosenthaler gate being noted in the record: 'Today there passed through six oxen, seven swine and one Jew.'[17]

Despite being as poor as a synagogue mouse, he pursued his studies of the medieval Jewish master, Moses Maimonides. Mendelssohn had a voracious appetite for knowledge and an encyclopaedic memory. He taught himself to read and write in lucid German – his mother tongues were the colloquial Jewish dialect and Hebrew – and with the help of like-minded friends in the synagogue he mastered both the mathematics of the day and Latin. In this he read, with the aid of a dictionary, *The Essay Concerning Human Understanding* of David Hume. To read the English and French philosophers in the original he taught himself both languages, eventually securing for himself a job as tutor in a Jewish family, becoming eventually his employer's business partner.

In 1754 Mendelssohn was introduced to Lessing over a chessboard, similar to the one over which Lessing's Nathan the Wise and Saladin were later to meet. Lessing had recently produced a play, in which he tried to prove, unlike his hero Shakespeare that Jews were not all Shylocks, but could show nobility of character. Mendelssohn seemed to prove him right. The two became fast friends and Lessing set about revealing the remarkable talents of the Jew to his public, by publishing Mendelssohn's defence of Leibniz from the neglect, even contempt in which he was currently held. From that moment Mendelssohn enjoyed a reputation, remarkable at that time for a Jew, as a brilliant and original thinker, corresponding with thinkers from all over Europe. The laws concerning the rights of Jews, despite Frederick II's general toleration, were not liberal, but even the King had to admit that Mendelssohn was a new Moses (Maimonides rather than the Jewish author of the ten commandments) and, though he never met him personally – something he had many opportunities of doing, but managed to avoid – he made him a Protected Jew, free to live and work in Berlin.

Mendelssohn's method of applying mathematics to metaphysics was very much in line with modern thinking, and the prize he was given by Leibniz's Academy of Sciences (it was that for the runner up, as the first prize was taken by Immanuel Kant) did not worry Frederick, who did not believe in metaphysics and could not see in mathematics any practical threat to his way of running a state. Mendelssohn became the cynosure of Berlin intellectual society, though Frederick still refrained from a personal encounter,[18] and was emboldened to write *Phaidon* (1767), a thesis on the immortality of the soul based loosely on the Socratic dialogue on the soul, Plato's *Phaedo,* and employing the same discursive manner of exposition. It was a bestseller and translated at once, even into English.

For educated Jews he became a third Moses, by Germans he was hailed as the German Socrates. It was also suspected that he might be a closet Christian. He was prepared to believe that Jesus was a great moral teacher and had Jesus stayed within the limitations of Orthodox Judaism, Mendelssohn could follow Him. He would go no further. In a public declaration he refused to accept that he had no philosophic or rational reason for not converting to Christianity. He could honour Confucius without becoming a Confucian, so he could honour Jesus without becoming a Christian.

The publicity accorded to the debate on whether Judaism could stand up to the proofs of Christianity affected Mendelssohn's health. The rest of his life was spent in an attempt to improve the situation of Jews generally, and his co-religionists particularly. He ran foul of the rabbinate when he tried to prove that even Christian Jews were bound by Jewish lore, not however as interpreted and enforced by rabbinic teaching but by the application of reason. In an attempt to write a life of his friend Lessing, of whose ideas he approved, he became involved in a damaging controversy on whether Lessing, and so he himself, were essentially pantheists, which to the Jew as well as Christian meant an atheist. He died in 1786, in dispute with men who had once been his friends. Of his six children only two retained their Jewish faith. Joseph, who did, founded the Mendelssohn banking house. Abraham, who did not, was the father of Felix and Fanny. His daughter Recha, who did, became the mother-in-law of the brother of Giacomo Meyerbeer. Rich, successful Jews might be accepted by the literary and musical establishment, and Frederick II might invite Mendelssohn to his palace to meet a visiting savant, but he took care not be present himself.

* * *

Despite Frederick's penchant for French philosophers and administrators, and his imposition of the French language at court, Berlin became the powerhouse of the Germanic revival. Weimar may have enjoyed a literary golden age, being the home of Goethe and Schiller, but from the wintry shores of the Baltic the voice of religious debate found a tolerant and generally acquiescent forum in the agnostic court of Frederick. Theologians might dispute the nature of God, and the respect due to His laws, as long as they did not raise doubts about the respect due to the King of Prussia. The tide of events in Europe was sweeping away chivalry and replacing it, in the words of Edmund Burke, by one of 'sophisters, oeconomists and calculators', but there was bound to be a reaction.[19] Nature and nature's laws once revealed as ineluctable began to return to night and unpredictability. Kant was to be seen as 'a frozen-up old pedant who understood nothing worth understanding.' The mechanistic universe was too unsubtle to explain the wayward behaviour of man, and how what was deemed to be rationally inevitable had a way of being anything but either inevitable or rational.[20] Having relegated God to the broom cupboard, what was the role and destiny of Man? This was to become the study of the Romantics.

CHAPTER FOUR

Genius: Germans in Search of Man (1)

The Ascendancy of Goethe

I call classic what is healthy, and romantic what is sick.
(Goethe, *Conversations with Eckermann*, 2 April 1829)

I asked my fair one happy day what I should call her in my lay,
By what sweet name from Rome or Greece,
Lalage, Neæra, Chloris, Sappo,
Lesbia or Doris, Arethusa or Lucrece?
'Ah' replied my gentle fair, 'beloved, what are names but air?
Choose thou whatever suits the line,
Call me Sappho, call me Chloris, call me Lalage or Doris,
Only, only call me thine.
(Samuel Taylor Coleridge translating Lessing)

Whether the Is, from being actual fact, is more important than
the vague Might Be, or the Might Be, from taking wider scope,
is for that reason greater than the Is: and lastly how the Is and
Might Be stand compared with the inevitable Must.
(W. S. Gilbert, *Princess Ida*, act 1)

RESIDENT IN ONE of the smallest states of Pumpernickel was the man whose giant presence looms over the whole Germanic world like some brooding spirit, a polymath of letters, philosophy, science and poetry against whom everyone was to be measured. Wolfgang von Goethe had been born in Frankfurt in 1749 of affluent parents, who represented 'old German minds and old German manners'.[1] As a teenager he had experienced the French occupation of the city, and the billeting on his family of an officer who took him to the theatre company the occupying force had imported as part of its civilising mission in the Seven Years War. After the war was over he went to Leipzig University where he was bored by the traditional scholasticism of its teaching, so he attended art classes at the Academy.

When sent home seriously ill, he decided that he would educate himself, and as he recovered he threw himself into an intense study of philosophy, alchemy and astrology. His family had intended him for the law and he was sent to Strasbourg to complete his studies. Strasbourg was a wholly Germanic town under French rule and the sight of its minster impressed the young Goethe as a masterpiece of Germanic art that could hold its own, pitting its irregular, unfinished state against the best of classic taste. His devotion to things French began to evaporate under the sense that here was a symbol of *germanismus* for which he must find a voice. His love for an Alsatian pastor's daughter inspired love lyrics of mature beauty and his friendship with a slightly older Lutheran pastor, Gottfried Herder (1744–1803), who published his essay on the cathedral, introduced him to the work of Shakespeare. Under their joint influences he wrote a drama enacting the memory of the old robber barons of the Rhine, who were endowed, in the author's youthful enthusiasm, with a lofty notion of right and wrong.

Literature was now to be Goethe's life, and work began to pour from his pen on many subjects reflecting his encyclopaedic interests, until in 1775 he accepted the invitation of the 18-year-old heir apparent to the little duchy of Saxe-Weimar in the Saxon circle, Charles-Augustus (1757–1828), to come and live in an enlightened principality. There he threw himself into the affairs of the tiny state, becoming the soul of its government, falling repeatedly in love, pouring out love lyrics and literary criticism, and becoming the *nonpareil* of German letters. There he was to stay for the rest of his life, which ended only in 1832, surviving his great friend, the Grand-Duke, by only four years.[2] And like a bright candle in a naughty world he became an attraction to other poets and thinkers to join him in Weimar to form a new republic of letters.

Saxe-Weimar was no competitor for German supremacy, except in the rarefied stratosphere of thought and poetry. The ruling house was not rich, but it had the usual if slightly less extravagant taste for palace building, and kept an excessive administration for a population of 600 to 700 households. 'More like a village bordering a park than a capital with a court with all courtly environments', was how George Lewes, who was visiting in 1854 with his consort, Marian Evans (George Eliot), described it, and it had changed little in 100 years. When Goethe arrived, it was still surrounded by city walls, closed at night at its gates by portcullises, with chains pulled across the streets leading to the church on Sundays to discourage the driving of carriages during divine service.[3] Its future ruler had the Germanic taste for hunting and a bucolic love of earthy and practical jokes. The little town had no manufactories, and indeed nothing to suggest that it was soon to become the cynosure of German intellectuals, but it was in the heartland of the German reformation. Its most celebrated visitor so far had been Martin Luther, but when the 26-year-old Goethe arrived he trailed clouds of glory, woven by *Götz of Berlichingen* (1773) and *The Sorrows of Young Werther* (1774). In his stay there for nearly 60 years he was to transform Weimar from obscurity to the pride of Pumpernickel.

For Pumpernickel it most certainly was. The tiny Duchy had the usual plethora of ministers, chamberlains, pages and sycophants. There was a standing army of 600 men, with cavalry of 50 hussars 'managed by a War Department, with war minister, secretary and clerk'.[4] Goethe shortly after Charles-Augustus's accession was to join the government as a councillor, and for a time was war minister, a role he took very seriously. His promotion initially attracted criticism that he had not progressed through the system like everyone else, but then Charles-Augustus had taken a fancy to this golden youth, already a bestselling author, a scientist of wide knowledge, a poet and philosopher and an enquirer into Art, of all of which Weimar, unlike its larger neighbour in Dresden, was short.

Moreover Goethe was not a studious prig but a good companion, not above a good practical joke, a good dinner and a good rough walk into the delectable countryside, expounding the beauties of nature with a ducal bathe at the end of it in the limpid waters of the river Ilm, running freshly cold from the Thuringian highlands. He introduced skating on the stream's frozen waters, made the Duchess proficient at it, and let fresh air into the otherwise tobacco smoke-ridden rooms of the ducal palace. The

Dowager Duchess Amalia, niece of Frederick the Great, was enchanted. 'I believe the Godlike creature will remain longer with us than he intended, and if Weimar *can* do anything his presence will accomplish it.'[5]

Charles-Augustus, once Duke, was resolved to make something of his Duchy and for that he was dependent on Goethe, for whom he developed something approaching a passion, fired not by homosexual longing but by the same idol worship that possessed King Ludwig of Bavaria for Wagner.[6] Charles-Augustus, moreover, had no pretensions to being a surrogate Frenchman; he was a good pupil of Gotthold Lessing and admired Shakespeare; and shared Goethe's interest in the purified German of Saxony. His Duchess was not as accomplished a musician as her uncle, Frederick the Great, but she was gifted enough to set some of Goethe's poems to music, and had learned enough Greek to read Aristophanes and undertake the education of her children. Schiller thought her intellect limited, but he may have been jealous of her devotion to Goethe. Between them, under Goethe's abiding presence, the Duke and Duchess accepted that Weimar should be a literary, indeed spiritual, Mecca.

Weimar, it was jokingly said, had 10,000 poets and few inhabitants.[7] Indeed it was to number among its residents four of the luminaries of the German revival: Christof Wieland who had come to Weimar as Charles-Augustus's tutor, Gottfried Herder, who had come at Goethe's invitation to overhaul education in the Duchy and at the University of Jena, Goethe himself and, in 1784, Friedrich Schiller. With Goethe's arrival Weimar was immediately infected by the curious spasm that had overtaken Europe on the appearance of *The Sorrows of Young Werther;* Wertherism became a cult. Goethe himself, a veritable Bunthorne, wore a blue coat, brass buttons, top-boots and leather breeches, and the powdered hair and pigtail of his sentimental hero, and this was soon the established dress of those who wished to indicate that they were both tender and romantic. Werther had struck a chord among the restless minds of a generation itching for change. Political change it was not, but Werther in the unconsummated passion for his friend's wife elevated romance above the classic restraints of bloodless, still largely arranged marriage. The conventions of Lutheran morality may have prevailed but they could only be defied, if a man were true to his own essential morality, by self-destruction. Dante may have consigned Paolo Malatestsa and Francesca da Rimini to the shadowless perimeter of Hell for a chaste kiss; Goethe cast no judgment on a very human predicament. Not everyone was obliged to die for love but self-immolation to avoid a dishonourable action, prescribed a new morality and was heroic. Goethe was a poet not a hero and the apostle of Wertherism sustained the passion of love-sick maidens in plenty, mostly chastely married ladies, one of whom wished that she 'could lie on thy [Goethe's] breast in Sabbath holy evening stillness – oh, thou Angel'. 'This kind of rhodomontade went all round', sniffed his English biographer. 'They wept and were wept on.'[8]

Goethe himself contracted a liaison with his servant, eventually marrying her. He was the prophet not the paladin of the new spirit he had unleashed: of art and culture, of poetry and love of nature, essentially pacific and free from power and passion, evoking even in so tempestuous a character as Napoleon Bonaparte devotion to a world he believed lay at the end of his Imperial mission. As Carlyle put it:

> in reading Goethe's poetry we are reading the poetry of our own day and generation ... No demands are made on our credulity. The light, the science, the scepticism of our age are not hid from us. He does not deal in antiquated mythologies ... There are no supernal no infernal influences.[9]

Perhaps it was that which led Napoleon to bestow an honour on Goethe and, in recognition of it, Goethe to accept it.

Goethe was a conscientious councillor but the affairs of State barely kept him busy and Charles-Augustus eventually relieved him of the War Department and Presidency of the Council, giving him a largely honorific title of Councillor of State, with no defined brief. He wrote steadily, held soirées and dances and produced theatricals at the court and it was not long before Weimar too had its theatre, which was soon to be enriched by the presence of Schiller. Hitherto amateur productions were performed by the princely family and courtiers and attended by a subdued and respectful audience. Now there was a new theatre and Goethe its director, rather more fearsome than the prince as he tamed noisy audiences or uncooperative actors with imprecations in a bull-like bellow. Though the theatre was not a popular venue, it was innovative, for many of its productions were highly cerebral, particularly Schiller's later plays like the *Wallenstein* trilogy and *Don Carlos*, which were written rather to be declaimed than acted. Goethe never wrote *Faust* for the stage, which he directed and on which it would have made too many demands.[10]

A high moral and thoughtful tone was preserved throughout, by the artistic director of Weimar, the *Geheimrath* von Goethe, who in addition to the theatre acquired direction of the museums and other institutions of learning. Goethe was the star of continental Europe, the polymath whom everyone wanted to meet, though Goethe sometimes did not always relish these encounters, when he did not unfold the intricacies of his mind and would only discuss banalities and trivia. Napoleon made time to receive him; he tried not to meet Germaine de Stäel and, when he did, refused to take her seriously. Walter Scott would have visited him but was too ill; Thackeray made a point of it, when *he* refused to take Goethe seriously, and Carlyle dreamed of visiting his 'spiritual father', sending him translations of his work with humble dedications to the man who led him from darkness into light.

Goethe accompanied his duke on the campaign that his uncle, the Duke of Brunswick, led into France in 1791 to rescue Louis XVI from thraldom to the revolution. Charles-Augustus like all Pumpernickel princes was very attentive to and protective of his little army, but Goethe went because he felt obliged to accompany his prince, though he believed that the army would have been better protected by keeping it in barracks. His experience on that campaign converted him from any residual interest in military action left over from his time as Minister of War. He disliked the destructiveness of revolution but, if that was selective, attacking things of the mind, war was indiscriminate, for not only did the supposedly guilty suffer but so did the demonstrably innocent. His questing spirit, which sought to understand the corruptible nature of man that could lead to such follies, was to result in 1808 in the first part of *Faust*.[11]

Faust baffled Coleridge (Coleridge died in 1834 before he could be even more baffled by Part Two). He found its scenes 'mere magic lantern pictures', and Charles Lamb thought it a 'vulgar melodrama'.[12] For Goethe wanted to use the medieval legend of Dr Faustus and his calamitous pact with the Devil to show the danger that seemed always to mark the schism in the German soul: the belief that the pursuit of power and pleasure was more seductive than that of knowledge. Despite its capacity for pure speculative thought aimed at embracing the truths of God and Nature, Germany was yet mired in irrationalism, a world of supernatural speculation, leading inexorably to the determination of Mephistopheles to exact his due from the infernal pact. This was the price for falling to temptation, 'the blindness to consequences caused by the imperiousness of desire; the recklessness with which inevitable and terrible results are braved in perfect consciousness of their being inevitable, provided that a temporary pleasure can be obtained'.[13]

Criticised in 1813 for not rising to the reawakening spirit of Germany by writing patriotic rather than more love poetry, Goethe was spurred to respond. He was not indifferent, he said, to the ideas of freedom, fatherland and people, but in comparing Germans with other people he had found them honourable as individuals, but miserable as a whole. He had taken refuge in art and science, which were beyond the limits of nationality. Germany had a future as a nation but not yet. Were the people sufficiently awakened? Did they know what they wanted? The German sleep had been so deep that mere shaking would not awaken them. 'Freedom, you say, but perhaps it would be more correct to call it a setting free – not, however, a setting free from the yokes of foreigners, but from foreign yoke.'[14]

The president of this burgeoning republic of letters towered over it like some overweening public monument, which he became when, in 1826, a resolution was passed in the German Diet that the final edition of his works should be guaranteed against commercial injury anywhere in any member state.[15] Yet he belonged to no homeland, and has been called a chameleon, a man of many colours.[16] He vowed, after meeting Sir William Hamilton in Naples in 1786, that he would make the natural world his special study and threw himself into the world of geology, anatomy and optics, following the English theology of experiment as the source of knowledge.

> In his concept of the universe he could not separate God from it, placing Him above it, beyond (it), as the philosophers did who represented God whirling the universe round his fingers. He animated the universe with God; he animated fact with divine life; he saw in reality the incarnation of the ideal; he saw in morality the high and harmonious action of all human tendencies; he saw in Art the highest representation of Life.[17]

His many intellectual interests, however, outstripped the time he had to give to those interests. He made credible and creative hypotheses in the study of anatomy and botany, but his attempt to disprove Newton's theory of light showed his limitations as a scientist.[18]

He also aspired to being a universal critic, translating the French philosopher Diderot, Byron and the Italian memoirs of Benvenuto Cellini. He was also a poet, conversationalist, playwright and novelist, and while he may have been with Herder one of the founding fathers of the literary movement known as *sturm und drang* (storm and stress), he lived through but did not become slave to any literary movements. His first novel, written in 1773 under the influence of Herder, *Götz of Berlichingen*, was the stormy tale set contemporaneously with Luther's reformation of the Church, of a knight at odds with his time, redeemed by his love of liberty. Despite his enrolment in the generic role of robber baron, Götz is an honest, virtuous man surrounded by men less honest and more ruthless than himself. Goethe himself wrote of it that 'the figure of a rude well-meaning self-helper, in wild anarchic time excited my deepest sympathy.' His second novel, *The Sorrows of Young Werther* (1774), was in Carlyle's words 'a poetic (and prophetic) utterance of the World's Despair,' about a self-absorbed young man in love with love.[19] It became an international bestseller and by the end of the century it was available in translation in nearly every European language. This was not only because of the intensity of Werther's hopeless love for Lotte for, despite the protests of those who found its denouement shocking and its apotheosis of irrational behaviour offensive, it was also a hymn to ordinary human decency. More mordant critics saw it also as an invitation to 'a set of men who made the first commandment of genius to consist of loving your neighbours and your neighbour's wife'.[20]

There are no villains, no people with more than ordinary human failings, and these, of course, may in Carlyle's view amount to the despair of the world.[21] Lotte is faithfully married, her husband is Werther's friend and only mildly irritated by his friend's passion for his wife, and Lotte's own weakness before Werther's tempestuous final leave-taking is no more than a kind of tormented act of sympathy. The novel is set in autobiographical, epistolary style, charting, in the manner of Richardson's *Clarissa,* Werther's growing obsession with Lotte. Throughout there is a moral rejection, both on Lotte's and on Werther's part, of any chance to consummate this love, and this rejection leads to Werther's suicide. His was a frail nature, easily jarred and cracked. Jane Austen's young lovers, even the most afflicted with sensibility, Marianne Dashwood, would never have loved against the conventions of the day. Likewise Werther had no prospect of going against them, or even any resolve to do so. As he was not going to upset morality, the only consummation of his passion was to be in death. For Carlyle, however, just as *Götz* 'directed man's mind to the picturesque effects of the past', *Werther* 'attempted the more accurate delineation of a class of feelings, deeply important to the modern mind'.[22] Few novels, especially one so short, had displayed the intensity as well as the hopelessness of human passion.

By the last quarter of the eighteenth century Germany lay under a deep cloud of melancholy; despite the spring orchards and summer flowers, beloved of her poets for they were under the influence of *empfindsamkeit*, sensibility, coined, in Lessing's words, in the German translation of Laurence Sterne's *Sentimental Journey* (1768).[23] This book enjoyed an even more enthusiastic reception among German readers than it had in England, for the cult of feeling had already begun to spread under the influence of Rousseau. Young German men were now encouraged by Goethe to bare their souls. To have a passion, even a hopeless one, was better than to have no passion at all. *The Sorrows of Young Werther* inspired a fashion for smart lovers' clothing, for azure coats, yellow breeches, and jackboots, and suggested that a way out of life's perennial sadness was suicide. Rousseau had championed the cry of *Back to Nature*, which Goethe believed was incarnate in Ossian's Romantic wildness, and even Lotte's virginal reserve was nearly broken by Werther's reading to her his (Goethe's) translation from Ossian.

* * *

The Sorrows of Young Werther preceded Rousseau's own *Confessions* by a decade but it established a taste for confessional writing. How far was Goethe himself plumbing his own experience? He had parted abruptly from his 'blue-eyed Alsatian', Frederike, as soon as marriage appeared to be the logical conclusion of his attentions, but then Goethe did not commit suicide.[24] Though most people thought that the claim that it had only taken him four weeks to write the book hinted at its autobiographical nature. Goethe's own tormented passion for young women may have started with Charlotte Buff whose marriage to Christian Kestner seemed to parallel Lotte's to Albert, and the coincidence of the two Charlottes suggests that it was written in a white heat attempt not only to exorcise her memory, but also to give it a certain objective reality.

Goethe's 'confession' marked a conversion to the Enlightenment ideal of perfected humanism. It was encouraged by his voyage of self-discovery to Italy, when from 1786–8 he basked, not in Ossianic mists and tempests, but in sun and optimism. Surrounded by the docile countryside, classical statuary and calm, reflective Renaissance Madonnas, he re-learned classical symmetry and peace. The *sturm und drang* in his Germanic soul relaxed. If there were to be a national literature, it needed to calm down, become naive again, and drink from the Pierian spring of intuition and naturalism that typified the poetry, not only of the classical world, but of Shakespeare and, now, of Goethe himself.

The Robin Hood fantasy, *Götz of Berlichingen,* had been pure *sturm und drang* in its Shakespearian pace, roll of characters and language (Frederick the Great thought it an 'abominable imitation' of a 'ludicrous Shakespearian farce'[25]) but his voyages to Italy between 1786 and 1790 and his reading of the resident German Graecophile, Johann Winckelmann, persuaded him to trim his exuberance to a Greek economy of cast and unities.[26] His later plays, *Iphigenia in Tauris* (1789) and *Torquato Tasso* (1790), were in Byronic modes and demonstrated an almost classical calm, even optimism.[27] *Iphigenia* demonstrated a classical spirit, which he had always held as the model for Germany, a concern for the public good and for human improvement.

* * *

Goethe had emerged from a swirling soup of theology and law, which had been traditionally the principal professions of university graduates. In the eighteenth century Pietism had given a fillip to the traditional Lutheran pastorate and, as with the Church in England, holy orders remained a common career for educated sons who were not nobles, a class destined, throughout the Holy Roman Empire, for military service. Between 1676 and 1804 it has been calculated that 120 men of letters had a grounding in theology, either as pastors or the sons of pastors.[28] The pastorate provided a comfortable living in which to cultivate intellectual interests, especially letters. It had the time to read and translate Edward Young's *Night Thoughts on Life, Death and Immortality* (1742), its 10,000 lines of blank verse appearing in the next 50 years in over 100 collected editions.[29] In 1748, the year before Goethe was born, three cantos of an unfinished poem were published anonymously in a Leipzig periodical. *The Messiah (Der Messia)* is credited with launching a new literary era in Germany. Its author was Friedrich Gottlieb Klopstock (1724–1803), a Saxon student of theology at Jena University, from which he had 'dropped out'. Klopstock never made holy orders, for his sentimental poetry, which Carlyle compared to 'seraphic music', was too spiritual and successful for him to pursue a career of crabbed orthodoxy.[30] Unrequited love for his cousin 'Fanny', however, nearly unhinged him and he was saved from insanity by the care of the Swiss translator of *Paradise Lost* in Zurich, Jakob Bodmer. But Bodmer was to be no Watts-Dunton, who cared for Swinburne. He was too easily shocked by the young poet's unpoetic lusts, and only a pension from the King of Denmark to live in Copenhagen and finish *The Messiah* allowed Klopstock to escape his spiritual captivity and to settle in Hamburg. But Bodmer, who had translated Milton, had given him the necessary support to embark on an epic poem which was to commemorate, not Winckelmann's Greek or Roman heroes, but the Christian story of Salvation.

Klopstock married, and added 12 cantos to his poem until his wife died and plunged him into a melancholy, which unhinged this time, not his mind, but his poetry. Despite his failing powers, his pension continued and he began to see in North Europe's myths and legends the roots of a German poetic renaissance. He wrote five more cantos of his Messianic life's work, and then entered the service of the Margrave of Baden, who added a pension to that of Denmark's king, so that he was able to return to Hamburg to finish his life work and die in 1803 lamented throughout Germany.

The sprawling *Messiah*, written over 25 years, made Klopstock, 'the Milton of Germany', famous. Despite its uneven, often laboured portrayal of the Christ story, the poem was translated into 17 different languages. It was not, however, the lengthy reaction of divine and angelic bodies to the sacred story, which imparted to the poem an altogether unreal flavour, that made *The Messiah* so influential on German writing. It was the use of free verse, and liberated language, not dominated by reverential Pietistic overtones, which suggested a more lively discourse on important themes. This and Klopstock's intense lyrical odes made it seem as if the well-spring of the German language was bubbling up from a deep, silent past. His readers eagerly embraced what seemed to them the dethronement of French disciplined, if melodic, classicism. When his poetic vein ran dry, he turned to a study of German philology, to find the lime and mortar for his edifice of German speech in which Germans could break loose from the thrall of France. His *Messiah* was, according to Dr Burney, 'the first poem of the Germans as the Iliad is of the Greeks'.[31]

Klopstock had a contemporary, 20 years younger, who was also caught up in the quest for the revival of the German language. Goethe's first patron, Johann Gottfried Herder (1744–1803) was born a Prussian, and had attended Kant's lectures at Königsberg. But he did not become a Kantian. Rather, under the influence of Johann Georg Hamann (1730–88), an eccentric hypochondriac, a hater of French and a dabbler in the arcane mysticism of seventeenth-century German mystagogues, like Eckhart and Paracelsus, the young Herder became a Lutheran minister. Hamann was a Pietist who repudiated Kant's reliance on reason. 'I look upon the best demonstration in philosophy', he told Kant, 'as a well-bred girl looks on a love letter.' Reliance on the existence of God was alone the way out of the vexing problems of existence and doubt. Herder thought he was a genius, a prophet, 'a great awakener, the first champion of the unity of man'.[32] Passionate in his view that Germans must think in and speak German and 'spew out the ugly slime of the Seine', Herder made a special study of Hebrew literature as part of an investigation into comparative philology. After five years teaching in the Hanseatic port of Riga, then part of Prussia, he visited France and, in 1770, Strasbourg where he met the young Goethe, who was instantly fired by his enthusiasm for Shakespeare and his fervent ideas of Germanism. There, some say, was born the movement which swept Germany with *sturm und drang* (storm and stress), which held that true living could not be experienced under the calm predestinarian optimism of Lutheran thought and the false order of French classicism.

In 1771 Herder accepted the position of court preacher, at Bückeburg, then the capital of the tiny Pumpernickel principality of Schaumburg-Lippe in the Saxon heartland, where one of Johann Sebastian Bach's sons was *Konzertmeister*. From Hebrew literature he was lured by the English (and Scottish) exploration of a mythical and remote past contained in the work of James Macpherson (*Ossian and the Songs of Ancient Folk,* 1773), Chatterton and Percy (*Reliques*), to do something similar for medieval German lyrics and songs. Herder was fascinated by the roots of national culture, the stories and sagas of primitive folk deriving from the people not the court, and he lit the fire of nationalism with the idea of the *Volk* and the *Volkslied*. 'The poet is the creator of the nation', he remarked, pre-dating Shelley, and in the simplicity and power of a primitive *Volk,* he found a people whom civilisation and the affectations of civilisation, that is, French culture, had not overwhelmed, and he blew the embers of an ancient literature into the fire of nationalism.

As Goethe shared Herder's philological enthusiasm for the old *Volklied*, or popular balladry, he engineered a post for him at the court in Weimar. Being close to Dresden and its pretensions to be the Florence of Germany, Weimar seemed destined to become a new Urbino under an enlightened prince. When Herder joined Goethe there, Germany seemed to have begun its renaissance. The Duke of Weimar was like a renaissance princeling and these were the 'noble Spiritual Men working under a noble Practical Man, ... a new noble kind of Clergy, under an old but still noble kind of King'.[33] When Herder renounced classical constraints, making Shakespeare his god, the scales had fallen from the eyes of the young Goethe in Stuttgart and he became like 'a blind man upon whom the power of sight had been suddenly conferred'.[34] Shackles of style and content were now struck off; the ghost of Shakespeare haunted the courts of Germany like Hamlet's father the walls of Elsinore. Weimar, under its philosophic prince, illuminated its humbler pretensions by attracting writers living as in a commune, so small was the principality, and had now become a beacon for other literary moths, Christoph Wieland, and Friedrich Schiller.

* * *

Christoph Wieland (1713–1833) was a pastor's son from Württemberg, well-, even over-educated, being precociously well-read in Latin and French before he was 16. He had decided he would be an intellectual and a poet. His early poetry was Pietist in flavour and, inspired by the same religious fervour as Klopstock. He was taken up by the same Swiss patron with whom he lived until his host, as with Klopstock before him, lost confidence in his attachment to 'elevating' poetry when Wieland emerged from a severe moralising phase to take a more relaxed view of humanity. Once introduced to the work of Shakespeare and Samuel Richardson, he abandoned the eternal sphere to wander again among the sons of men. *Clementina von Porretta* (1760) was a German adaptation of *Sir Charles Grandison*. His prose translation of 22 of Shakespeare's plays introduced readers to the greater part of his dramatic works. It was, however, a work of pedagogy, a set of oriental tales adapted for the education of children, which attracted the attention of the Duchess Anna Amelia of Weimar and induced her, in 1772, to appoint him as tutor to her two sons. Wieland was to remain, like Goethe, in Weimar for most of his life, editing for 16 years a literary review influential throughout the German-speaking world.

Wieland's enduring legacy outside that German world was a poetic fairy tale, *Oberon,* taken from a French story, *Huon de Bordeaux.* Set to music as a Romantic opera by Weber, *Oberon* was first performed at Covent Garden in 1826 and still tantalises would-be directors. Is it a Romantic opera or a simple (for simple read, in usual libretto-speak, complicated) Oriental fairy tale in the tradition of *The Magic Flute*? It has been performed with spoken dialogue and recitative; it was modified by Gustav Mahler who tried to make grand opera out of it, and in one form or another, because of Weber's (and sometimes Mahler's) music, it has remained in the repertoire.

Wieland was nothing if not prolific. He wrote novels with rather obstructive, philosophic themes, he translated Horace, Lucian and Cicero, he wrote his own fairy tales on the French model, and the older he grew the more he reacted to his severe Pietist formation and adopted a frivolous, even a mocking, sceptical, almost Voltairean style. As a poet Kant likened him to Homer, but his light fantastical style marked the decline of the 'Piety poetry' with which he had started his poetic career. He was shortly to be joined by one whom enthusiasts claimed to be second only to Shakespeare. It was to be the consummation of the greatness of Weimar.

CHAPTER FIVE

Genius: Germans in Search of Man (2)

Schiller to Grimm

Mit der Dummheit kämpfen Götterselbst verbegens.
(With stupidity God himself struggles in vain.)
(Friedrich Schiller, *Die Jungfrau von Orleans*, act 3, scene 6)

His works are the most famous and the most unreadable in all
Germany. Surely you have heard of his *Treatise on Man*? A treatise
on a subject in which everyone is interested, written in a style
which none can understand.
(Disraeli, *Vivian Grey*, book 7, chapter 3)

THE FOURTH MAN of the tetrad that was to form the glory of Weimar
was Friedrich von Schiller (1759–1805). He was another
Württembourgois, born to a military doctor and christened Frederick after
the King of Prussia with whom his father's employer, the Austrians, were
then at war. Intended also for the Church, the young Schiller used to
dress up in clerical black and deliver childish sermons to the air. When
his father moved to the royal palace, effectively the new Württemberg
capital, Ludwigsburg, he attracted the attention of the Duke Charles
Eugene, who sent the young Friedrich in 1776 to study medicine at the
school he had founded in Stuttgart. There Schiller, being the son of an
officer, was ranked and treated as a noble, as distinct from the sons of
common soldiers who were not. For eight years he struggled with military
discipline 'but the passion for poetry is as vehement and fiery as first love.

What discipline was meant to extinguish it blew into a flame.'[1] He joined the school drama group and at a theatrical event held there he met both Goethe and the Duke Charles-Augustus of Weimar. From that moment he knew what he wanted to do. He shut himself in his room and turning night into day he read the poems of Goethe, Klopstock, Herder and Wieland and all the books of history and philosophy he could get hold of. Above all he read Shakespeare and, finally, in 1776, at the age of 17, he wrote a play.

'I intend to write a piece that will be burned in the main square by the public executioner,' he averred and the reception given by his comrades to this declaration of war on the class structure of the day, meant that he had to present *The Robbers (Die Rauber)* in a theatre in neutral territory. He chose the Palatinate capital at Mannheim where he had the play printed at his own expense from florins raised by his comrades. It was revolutionary stuff, making Beaumarchais's, *The Marriage of Figaro*, which appeared five years later, seem tame. The director of the Mannheim theatre had to insist that all references, however oblique, to recognisable persons, were expunged, that its extreme views were toned down, and that its period was set back from the present to the fifteenth century. Schiller was then 17, and taking French leave from the school, he assisted at the premiere in its modified form in January 1782. Advertised as the story of a great, misguided soul who from 'unchecked ardour and bad companionship' becomes the head of a gang of murderers and is restored to virtue by misfortune, it was a wild success among the young, for whom it paraded the '"interior economy of vice" leading to terror, anguish, remorse and despair which follow close upon the heels of the wicked'.[2] The theatre resembled a madhouse, eyes rolled, hair rose, members of the audience hugged one another and women fainted. A German Shakespeare had arrived.

Not everyone joined in the plaudits. One noble member of the audience wrote to Goethe, that if he were God and had he known that one day someone would write *The Robbers*, he would not have created the world![3] Frederick II felt he had to read it towards the end of his life and dismissed it as 'like a parody of the very worst efforts of Shakespeare'.[4] Duke Charles Eugene was furious and threatened Schiller and his family with imprisonment if he published anything else without his prior approval. Schiller was destined to be a military doctor like his father and knew he was too valuable to sack, but he disliked the profession and decided it was time to go.

During a feast to welcome the future Tsar of Russia, Paul I, on an incognito visit to Württemberg, when all eyes were elsewhere, he left Ludwigsburg and went into hiding, away from the Duke's territories. He emerged from it to see his next play produced at Mannheim in 1784, and after some time in Saxony, the asylum of scribblers, he was persuaded to settle near his great hero, Goethe, in Weimar. Here he found political tranquillity, freedom, 'a select society of interesting persons and thinking heads and respect paid to literary diligence'.[5] After a few years he was appointed Professor of History and Philosophy at Jena University. Ten years later in 1799, he was lured by Goethe back to Weimar, there to establish and write for the theatre and, to spend the rest of his comparatively short life, dying at 45 from tuberculosis. The American Declaration of Independence and the Beethovenian Hymn to Joy echo his young passion for the liberation of the soul from the bondage of Pumpernickel.

* * *

Goethe persuaded Schiller to adapt his historical researches to drama and from his pen flowed *Don Carlos* (1787), the *Wallenstein* trilogy (1799), *Mary Stuart* (1800), *The Maid of Orleans* (1801) and *William Tell* (1804).[6] Performed at the Weimar theatre, they transformed German dramatic writing. Schiller was hailed as heir to Shakespeare, and six of his plays were to be adapted for opera.[7] Hazlitt was fired to enthusiasm and *The Robbers* inspired Coleridge to write a sonnet to him. Indeed, Coleridge determined to translate the second and third plays in the *Wallenstein* trilogy.

As the fashion for so-called realism grew, *sturm und drang,* a storm headed by Johann Herder and Friedrich Schiller, filled the theatres, discarding restraints and unities. It broke like waves on the classic conformity of poets. 'Truth still lives in fiction', Schiller proclaimed, 'Man has lost his dignity, but art has saved it.'[8] Schiller, when he produced *The Robbers,* had denounced the established order to applause from his delighted audiences. The original script, which had caused such a sensation when produced privately in Stuttgart, was a cloudy story of conflict between a 'natural' man, Karl von Moor, upright, strong and generous, who becomes a revolutionary anarchist in the Bohemian forest, and his brother, Franz Moor, who loves money and power and is, thus, 'unnatural' man, selfish, vain and weak. Of Karl von Moor, on the other hand, 'strength, wild impassioned strength' was the distinguishing quality.[9] Schiller had Milton in mind; his Robber is an angel outlaw, like Satan, an 'honourable malefactor, a majestic monster'. The 'natural' man, like Satan, has a team of angel outlaws, other young 'natural' men outlaws in a society that has rejected them.[10]

Karl von Moor, the outlaw chief of a robber band, disinherited by his father through the malice of his younger brother, Franz, has visions of Plutarchan greatness as a benefactor of ordinary humanity. The motley crowd of fugitives who make up the robber band, more like operatic extras, are devoted to their chief and will commit any enormity in his service. But about this Karl is most ambivalent. Any modern bandits would quickly have identified the ambivalence in their chief's dedication to fire and plunder and have cut his throat in a succession struggle. But Karl von Moor parades before them the conflict between his need to be ruthless and his desire to benefit the poor and dispossessed. While applauding his sentiments, they are, however, more interested in booty

Franz meanwhile has shut up his father in a deserted cave to die of starvation, and then raves and rants against the thought that there might be a deity who will exact reparation for his evil deeds. He calls in a pastor to try to convince him that such a God exists, in the expectation that he will fail. The end comes when Karl in disguise finds Franz in command of what should be his inheritance, and releases his bemused father. The robbers attack Franz's stronghold and set it on fire. Franz, seeing the flames, believes that, notwithstanding all his protestations that there is no God, they are the flames of hell and strangles himself.

Karl having recovered his inheritance cannot desert his robber band by whom he has promised to stand. This is inconsistent with his finer aspirations, but he knows that one 'cannot make the world a fairer place through terror and uphold the cause of justice through lawlessness, calling it revenge and right'.[11] His moral conflict deranges him and when his betrothed promises to be his Maid Marian and join the robber band, he cannot bear the thought of so pure a spirit descending to a life of crime, and stabs her to death. Realising that he has nothing left now to live for, he must die for something. He can benefit a poor man who would be able to collect the reward for his capture if he betrayed him. The robbers think he is raving mad.

This youthful account of the struggle between tarnished good and conscience-stricken evil seemed, to its audience, to portray a revolt against authority, and its violent language and almost hysterical treatment of the moral conflict marked it as a prime example of *sturm und drang*. The robbers, despite their lawless behaviour, had right on their side; Franz for all his deceit and wickedness, had, in the limited judgment of a repressive society, right on his. The tortured conflicts in the souls of both brothers were the stuff of Romantic melodrama, and Schiller loved melodrama. As a student actor he once ruined one of Goethe's plays by portraying the villain in a risible parade of facial contortions and grimaces.[12]

If his efforts to be Shakespearian appealed to his fellow students, it constituted subversion in the view of his sovereign, Charles Eugene, who was shocked that the son of his regimental doctor should be so deranged. It spoke to a Carlyle, on the other hand, ever-willing to hear the voice of bold determined action:

> *The Robbers* is a tragedy that will long find readers to astonish ...
> It stands like some ancient rugged pile of a barbarous age: irregular,
> fantastic, useless, but grand in its height and massiveness and black
> frowning strength.[13]

Its effect on contemporary German drama can be compared to Jimmy Porter's vicious, anarchic iconoclasm on the English stage in John Osborne's *Look Back in Anger* (1956).

∗ ∗ ∗

Schiller, meanwhile, was to be tamed under the lambent style and metaphysical influence of the friend with whom, from 1794 to 1805 through the most turbid time of the French Revolutionary Wars, he shared Weimar. Storm and stress gave way to lyrical ballads, a still small voice of calm in the clamour of arms, while Goethe wrote *Wilhelm Meister,* his most German novel, and with Schiller's active encouragement resumed work on *Faust*. If this, on which he worked for nearly 30 years (1775–1808), is acknowledged as his masterpiece, it is the first part that most people know. Faust sells his soul to the devil for happiness according to his desires, and in the ruin of Gretchen shows how treacherous these desires may be. In Part Two (published only in 1832) Faust is redeemed by love and by a realisation of his essential sin. To the English imagination, which was largely baffled by a wordy style that made Shelley seem almost economical with words, Goethe had toyed with the affections of too many susceptible younger women to make him a role model. John Sterling enjoyed and admired him but was in fact afraid of his attraction, being unable to accept that he was 'the most splendid of anachronisms' living a 'thoroughly, nay intensely Pagan Life in an age when it is men's duty to be Christian'.[14] To such as thought like Sterling, Faust's redemption was suspect, and when Thackeray visited Goethe in Weimar he thought he was 'an old rogue'.[15]

John Lockhart at dinner told Sir Walter Scott that when in Weimar he had asked the waiter at the inn whether Goethe was in town. The waiter looked puzzled but when the landlady suggested that the diner might be referring to the *Herr Geheimer-Rath Von Goethe*, the cloud of unknowing vanished. It was unlikely, Scott interjected, that anybody would call at Abbotsford to ask for 'the Sheriff' Scott,[16] but for all the pompous formality, which emanated essentially from the aristocratic goldfish bowls of Pumpernickel, the Germans saw in Goethe's essential genius the spirit of an age that did not fall into categories.

He lived through *sturm and drang*, Napoleonic conquest (Napoleon made a point of giving him a medal in 1803 and receiving him in audience in 1806), and Metternichian repression, with a profound detachment and freedom of expression that gave to the age a label, the *Goethezeit*, the age of Goethe. This was because, although he thought Napoleon the saviour of European civilisation, he felt himself above politics. But there may never have been a *Goethezeit,* for his life covered a remarkable intellectual change from 1790 to 1820 which brought about almost as radical a political and cultural change in Germany as that which had already occurred in France. To all this Goethe had responded in his own detached way, even resisting many of the shibboleths of the age. According to Nietzsche in 1880 he was but 'a conceited fanfare trumpeted from time to time across the

German borders ... an episode without consequences in the history of the Germans'.[17]

Creativity, *his* creativity, was all important to Goethe and when, in 1776, Duke Charles-Augustus ensured that he had time and freedom to write, it was not clear whether this freedom was freedom from oppression or freedom from rules. Certainly Goethe meant to use it to advance humanity's emancipation from religious orthodoxy by the banishment of a potentially interfering God to the Divine Watchmaker's workroom. There He could keep the universe ticking over on its predestined course, in which the sunny land, where the lemon trees bloom, would prosper with its diminished sense of sin and its appetite for pleasure. In the last analysis, Goethe was an apostle of the contented life, not the prophet of change.

∗ ∗ ∗

Goethe's may have been the great name in Pumpernickel when he domiciled himself in Saxe-Weimar, but it was not so in England. *Wilhelm Meister* and *Werther* may have been popular, *Werther* ran to 17 English editions, but they were depressing, and depression, when not bucolic high spirits, was the prevailing image of Germans and of Germany. Dr Burney had found that 'except in the great trading towns or those where sovereign princes reside' the Germans seem very rude and uncultivated.[18] It was not until George Lewes's monumental *Life of Goethe* appeared in 1855, did opinions begin to change. Perhaps the strongest impression the British had of Germany was to be gleaned from what the brothers Jacob Ludwig Carl and Wilhelm Carl Grimm believed would be a contribution to a much greater, encyclopaedic study of German literature: their fairy stories. The Grimms were native to Hanau in the state of Hesse-Kassel, born in 1785 and 1786, sons of a lawyer who prepared them for the law. Their mother dying young, they were brought up successfully, surprising, given the treatment in their tales of second or surrogate parents, by their aunt who was in service with the Margrave.

While they were both at Marburg University, Jacob's imagination was captured by the early texts of the German Minnesingers. His interest was soon anchored in philological studies, which he pursued in Paris whither he had followed his professor. Back in Hesse-Kassel in the war office of the state, exchanging under protest his loose Parisian clothes for a uniform and pigtail, he was appointed in 1808 head of the private library of Jerome Bonaparte who had incorporated Hesse-Kassel into the kingdom of Westphalia. Until the fall of Jerome, Jacob served in small diplomatic duties for the Hessian state, but quickly adjusted himself to Jerome's disappearance and was appointed minister to the Hessian contingent in the army of the nations and then as secretary to the legation at the Congress of Vienna.

During those years from 1812–15 the two brothers collaborated on the work which will always bear their name, their fairy tales, *Kinder und Hausmarchen*. These were reconstructed from oral tradition, old books and manuscripts and were intended as part of an investigation into old German. Some of them had assumed international clothes and Charles Perrault had prettified *Cinderella* by endowing her with a fairy godmother, her coach, her slippers and her tryst with midnight, as well as two ugly rather than beautiful half sisters who would be as stupid as they were malevolent. The brothers wanted the authentic original tales and followed them with a systematic study of the old German sagas of which they were held to be a significant part. From then onwards Jacob applied his energies to German mythology, but his pioneer work is quite eclipsed by the fairy tales.

They were Germany's *Arabian Nights Entertainments*. *Rapunzel* (whose tower can still be seen at Marburg), *Hansel and Gretel, Rumpelstiltskin, Snow White, Cinderella* and *The Dancing Shoes* are as well known as the stories of *Aladdin* and *Ali Baba*, and Germany became a land of romantic fantasy. They also seemed to confirm Carlyle's view that German letters dwelt 'with peculiar complacency among wizards and ruined towers, with mailed Knights, secret tribunals, monks, spectres and banditti', which had certainly influenced Walter Scott when he wrote his Swiss-Burgundian-German romance, *Anne of Geierstein*.[19] Disney's saccharine may have sweetened the savage flavour of many of the stories, but they were not collected for children, but as part of the linguistic reconstruction of German national identity. Malevolent stepmothers, dim-witted fathers, ambivalent dwarfs, talking animals, witches and warlocks were not creatures of fantasy, but lurked in human nature, in castles and among forest-dwellers. Above all, the forest was a sinister, endless labyrinth, in which malevolent spirits lurked to add to the very real danger of becoming lost and where divine protection was almost invariably invoked.[20] This Grimm world was threatening and dangerous and, by understanding that it existed, it was to be exorcised.

As moralities the tales had a didactic purpose. Wilhelm, shocked by their raw violence, bent some of the legends to his own Christian principles, so that their protagonists were given rewards for kindness and generosity, and penalties for meanness and cruelty. In many tales, however, the rewards were unearned except by guile, and, despite Wilhelm's ameliorative influence, some of the penalties were horrendous. One wicked stepmother is danced to death in red-hot shoes, another is rolled down a hill in a barrel lined with sharp knives, and a lazy step-sibling is covered in pitch for life.[21] Cinderella's sisters have their eyes pecked out by pigeons. Their fates may have been deemed appropriate when the tales were first written, when people were haunted by wickedness towards the innocent, and by injustice perpetrated by the guilty, but the brothers Grimm gave Germans a reputation for mindless cruelty.

The class divisions in the tales, too, are almost stereotypes, being a worm's eye view of human nature. Kings and queens are either wicked, or foolish or improvident, landlords and inn-keepers are greedy, crafty or mendacious, artisans and peasants are either astute or doltish. They belong to an ancient past but are timeless. They also reflect the limited social range of the Pumpernickel states. In all but the largest, the sovereign was the centre of most activity, art, letters, entertainment and almost all social life. The kings and queens in Grimm's tales tend to have only daughters. Given that German princesses were fodder for dynastic alliances, it was expected that they would be beautiful and submissive, but in Grimm's tales, the choice of princess's partner is usually subject to a democratic process, just as aleatory as most dynastic matches. Her hand is to be awarded to whomever succeeds in some seemingly impossible task. When the king's daughters are not beautiful and submissive, they are capricious, sensual or improvident, in which case their fates are unhappy. Though as a rule in fairy tales innocence lives happily ever after and love is forever, the Grimm brothers claimed that their fairy stories were 'the pure uncontaminated national products of the *Volk*'. That meant that the spirit of innocence and love did not always triumph. Pumpernickel lived in terror of itself.[22]

Jacob Grimm did not rest after the fairy tales. Having let loose the genie of imagination, he tethered it to a History of German speech, delving into the remote past to establish the vehicle of a nationalism based on language. If Germany did not exist politically, it did linguistically, in the centre of a sea of Germanic related dialects which had evolved into discreet languages, among which were Old High German, Dutch, Scandinavian and English. In Grimm's grammar, as in his fairy tales, the philological concept of Gothic was given a sinister image. Freud may have read into them some of man's perverse and subconscious urges. Its nineteenth-century readers saw in them some of the evil roots of Romanticism.

* * *

What exactly was meant by the term German Romanticism was as much in the mind of the reader as in the pen of an exegete. Frederick Schlegel (1772–1829) filled 125 manuscript pages in an attempt, which he abandoned, to define it, though in the course of attempting to draw analogies with the world of Romance he coined the actual word Romanticism. As an opposite to Classicism it suggested the abandonment of classical order and unities, an emphasis on sentiment and feeling, and a projection of forces outside human control like nature, wild and dangerous, in the form of tempest and disorder. Some would claim that this description suits storm and stress rather than Romance, but if the *sturmers und drangers* were not 'classical' they were admirers of Greek poetry and saw no disjunction between contemporary German and ancient Greek ideas. Werther's favourite reading was Homer. Schiller, therefore, observing that the Greeks were included in every writer's knapsack, defined Classical as naive and Romantic as sentimental, but this definition was not acceptable to those whose artistic aim was to sentimentalise the naive.

Late in his life, Goethe claimed that he and Schiller were the architects of the definition of Romantic as opposed to Classical, and that Schlegel had merely carried their ideas further, so that everyone now (1830) used the definitions Classicism and Romanticism in which to enshrine their ideas. But even Goethe and Schiller did not seem to be in complete agreement. Goethe had originally laid down 'the maxim of objective treatment in poetry and would allow no other, but Schiller, who worked quite in the subjective way, deemed his own fashion the right one'. He had even written a treatise on Naive and Sentimental Poetry to prove that Goethe's play *Iphigénie* was not so much in the classical and antique spirit as some people supposed.[23]

The Enlightenment professed many things but its disciples generally agreed that the world, or nature, was 'a single whole, subject to a single set of laws'. All mankind, as were all other sentient and insentient beings, was governed by these laws, which could be discovered by the exercise of the rational mind and, if interpreted rightly, led to such attainable objects as happiness, justice and liberty.[24] How these were to be achieved, which would flow from the possession of *virtus*, or virtue, prompted lively debate and discussion and by the end of the century animated the minds of the educated, for there was little else for them to do in a country still locked in ancient habits. As a result, freemasonic lodges, which grew up from the 1740s onwards, enlisted nearly all German thinkers.

German freemasonry expanded as fast as it had in England and France, being in effect debating societies for the exchange of new and advanced ideas, but it was soon infected by peculiarities and eccentricities from what had become known as 'Scottish masonry'. It was certainly not Scottish, but it was supposed to be superior to the model order adopted in England and in France, having its own rituals and secrets. It was patronised by the princes and aristocracy, who found the English model of social equality disconcerting, and though they espoused the usual cloudy rhetoric of human improvement and enlightenment, they also pandered to some of the German appetite for the improbable, mysterious and bizarre. This was partly in reaction to the French insistence on order and reason – the language of the first lodges was ritually French – but their leaders, some of whom fostered alchemical researches, quickly fell into some of the byways of German mysticism. Lodges were also infiltrated by ideas that had been particularly held by Rosicrucians – Frederick William II of Prussia was a Rosicrucian adept – but the most bizarre affectation was to adopt one idea of a Scotsman, Andrew Michael Ramsay. Ramsay seems to have started the canard that his newly founded order had an intimate union with the Knights Hospitaller of St John of Jerusalem. The supposed connection with chivalry, the inspiration of Sir Walter Scott, was becoming one of the spirits of the age and a connection with the crusading orders became, with some, an obsession. When the Jews had rebuilt Jerusalem upon their return from the Babylonian Captivity, they were assisted by warriors who protected the builders. These were surely the progenitors in legend of the chivalrous Knights Templar, whose arcane knowledge and fabulous wealth became an *ignis fatuus*.[25]

First, the idea that masonry might be connected with the Templars, whose Grand Master, a title they shared with the Grand Lodges, had been sentenced to death for forbidden practices, seemed to originate in Scotland, not England, a more hard-headed, non-fantastical, even irreligious country. Secondly the belief chimed in with other preoccupations of adepts, kabbalistic lore, 'Egyptian' hermetic thought, and the transmutation of metals, which were among the forbidden practices that had led to their dissolution and which had contributed to their hidden and legendary wealth. Lodges were usually short of money and the hope that alchemical success, if not the wealth of the Templars, might offer tangible gains from membership. Masonry, moreover, was also backward-looking, to an ancient and possibly better past, and conservative in its attachment to the old social order. If they were not wholly impervious to new ideas, they were suspicious of the more radical, and were censorious of Kant whose writing demonstrated 'a rationalistic or enlightened tendency'.[26] German freemasonry became dominated by the Templar obsession, one branch of it, the Strict Observance, wanted to create a Templar rite and raise funds to buy back the Templar treasure, presuming that it was to be found. Claiming that Germans were the proper heirs to the Templar knowledge and fortune the Strict Observers helped to create a pride in their mystical and medieval past.[27]

With the dissolution of the Jesuits in Bavaria in 1773 one of their former students, Adam Weishaupt, decided that the way was clear for a sect, which would display the learning and knowledge of the Society but embrace the more daring theories of egalitarianism and the amelioration of a society that had been intellectually over-controlled. To make his aims less alarming he did not discard an earlier penchant for the Eleusian and Pythagorean mystagogues, and these provided the enticement of mystery, secrecy and nonsense, and camouflaged his more radical ideas, to which adepts would be cautiously introduced. Creating a secret society within a secret society, which he called the Areopagus, Weishaupt inspired by the subversive ideas of Rousseau overstepped the mark. Talk of Rousseauan democracy and republicanism, even in an association of the well heeled, was dangerous. They might call themselves the Illuminated Brethren or Illuminati, but when 'illuminated' adepts began to infiltrate the more sedate, less secretive masonic lodges they were subversives. In 1785 both Illuminism and masonry were banned in Bavaria, and suspicion of the hidden agenda of Illuminati became common with authorities elsewhere.[28] The Lodges had started with secret rites and rules of membership, but their often noble aspirations were tainted, not by nonsense from which all suffered in one measure or another, but by secrecy which hid subversion.

Though this world was a Tom Tiddler's ground for mountebanks and quacks, it was not the farrago of nonsense that attracted men like Kant, Herder, Lessing, Wieland, Goethe and Klopstock. All were enrolled as masons and might be counted as Illuminati, but they sought less the lost key to sacred sciences than a forum for free discussion. This was open and often appeared in writing, thus constituting no perceived threat to princes beyond hope of a fairer society for paupers. In 1765, however, Charles Eugene, the Duke of Württemberg, was sufficiently anxious about free discussion to propose the formation of a (similarly secret) society to combat rationalism and irreligion.[29] To counter the seditious aura of masonry, the foundation of scientific and other academies was encouraged, dedicated to useful activities which could be observed and measured, like the Erfurt Academy of Useful Science, with its library, laboratory and botanical garden pioneering substantial improvements in agriculture. In addition to its universities, reading rooms and discussion societies numbered over 300. Germany seemed to have produced its own encyclopedists. Even so, they were scarcely revolutionary, though free expression and membership of a Lodge carried its risks. Charles Eugene even shut up one outspoken legal academic in prison for five years, and Joseph de Maistre, apostle of reaction, who called the Illuminés 'criminal associations dedicated to killing off Christianity and sovereignty in Europe', had his support among the ruling class. [30]

Not everyone believed that the world was susceptible to control by reason. The cultivation of virtue had led to some of the most violent abuses of the age. Pietists had violently objected to Christian Wolff's view that Christ's ability to turn water into wine, or Joshua's ability to stop the sun were not miraculous acts but the exercise of superior, superhuman knowledge. Other irrationalists believed that virtue was only achieved by the understanding and practice of ancient beliefs like religion, chivalry, altruism, even romantic love, agreed by mankind to save him from his own weakness, and which prevented him from becoming a monster of rational behaviour.[31] The pursuit of virtue by a Robespierre, a Pol Pot or the Taliban, in the pursuit of a programme to purge and perfect society, reveals how irrational behaviour can hijack a rational reform programme.

This was what 'Romantics' feared from a culturally neutral enlightenment. They looked to Britain as a nation which enjoyed a 'natural society', for the British seemed to enjoy a high degree of prosperity with a high level of freedom of expression, achieved it would appear, if its poetry and novels were regarded as representative, by their freedom to behave naturally, even wildly.[32] Poets of temperament, Edward Young and Thomas Gray, dwarfed and humbled man before the inexorability of nature, and novelists of behaviour, like Goldsmith and Richardson, had transformed the picaresque, non-consequential English novel into a coherent narrative within a fixed framework. Romanticists (as opposed to Romantics), like Horace Walpole and Ann Radcliffe, unveiled mystery and passion as a determinant of human behaviour. Rational behaviour could be oppressive; natural behaviour could be both liberating and fantastic. The union of both was to inspire the work of the doyen of British Romanticism, Sir Walter Scott. The legacy of French rationalism, in the English language that was acquiring world status, began to seem unattractive.

As the eighteenth century progressed, overtaken by the excesses of a French model revolution, a retreat from rationalism became almost a stampede. The Illuminati, ragged revolutionaries in philosophic clothing, were threatening the ordered society with disorder, irreligion and chaos. Enlightenment was proving to be a nursery for upset; it had diminished what had been the deep spiritual longings of a people predisposed to mysticism and obscurity. The roots of Romanticism in Germany lay in something less cerebral, more instinctive. It accepted that nature was governed by its own laws against which Man was historically in conflict, but it could be tamed. It could be rendered sublime, not by reason but by imagination.[33] Man's taming of nature was creating a new destiny, which could not always conform to rational behaviour; it inspired the *sturm und drang* movement to excess; and this continued, after it had calmed down, to cling like ivy to a ruined tower, particularly in the person of the Schlegel brothers, August William (1767–1845) and Charles William Frederick (1771–1829). Sons of a Hanoverian pastor, they were intended like many of the sons of clergy for the law but chose instead a career of letters. They grew up in the silence of the French domination of Germany, studied at the Hanoverian University of Göttingen, and between them began a study of literary texts which espoused if not dangerously political at least radical ideas of Romantic freedom, in which the creative arts of man could alone develop. August William developed these in a journal edited in collaboration with Schiller at Jena, but the two men shared no identity of ideas, and they quarrelled. August William then started another journal, *The Athenaum*, with his brother in 1798, and though it was short-lived it was to prove a seminary of literary ideas, which were to influence German writers. In it, Frederick Schlegel used the term Romantic to describe the retreat from rationalism and materialism, which his journal was trying to promote.

Frederick, who nursed a passion for his brother's wife, moved to Paris in 1802, where he married the daughter of Moses Mendelssohn, and concentrated on the philosophy and philology of the Orient, producing in 1808 a book on the language and wisdom of India. On their conversion to Rome, Frederick and his wife became pillars of religious and political conformity and, in this acceptable role, Frederick served as the Austrian councillor to the Frankfurt Diet; but the aura of his early radicalism never entirely deserted him. He had nailed his credo to the supremacy of the individual, who would make his own tryst with destiny, or, if he chose, God, free from dogmas, conventions and institutions.

When Frederick Schlegel went to Paris, his brother, August William, stayed in Berlin, which was becoming now the capital of intellectual Germany. Fluent in both English and French, he was deep into the translation of Shakespeare's plays, which continue to be one of the glories of German letters. His lectures on drama and dramatic art established him as a universal critical master. His attack on French classicism in 1807 caught the ear of a generation of writers still reeling from the humiliation of Prussia after Jena. Enticed by Germaine de Staël to join her travelling caravan, he became one of her authorities for *De l'Allemagne*.[34] His later concentration on Sanskrit and editions of its sacred dramas pioneered the primacy of German scholarship in eastern studies. The depersonalisation of the deity and its identification with and immanence in all created things, harked back to Spinoza and Jakob Böhme, the seventeenth-century Lutheran mystic who had seen all creation in a sunbeam. Sunbeams were available to all poets and thinkers, and their visions in them were now the legitimate province of art.

This may have been the credo, too, of *sturmers und drangers*; 'the criticisms of Lessing, the enthusiasm for Shakespeare – the mania for Ossian and northern mythology, – the revival of ballad literature and imitations of Rousseau – all worked in one rebellious current against established authority'. For George Lewes, 'with the young, Nature seemed to be a compound of volcanoes and moonlight, her force explosion and her beauty sentiment'. The template for recognising genius was to be 'insurgent and sentimental, explosive and lachrymose' even if their visions had been too chaotic in the face of the Enlightenment's faith in the naturalness of natural law and the essential orderliness of the creator.[35] The upheavals of the French Revolutionary and Napoleonic Wars were, however, to politicise and vitalise Germany into an interest in its own history; its own school of mystical thinkers, and in speculation on what was to be its future.[36]

The general public may have been bemused by the fact that the proponents of German Romanticism were elites, professors and intellectuals, many of them sons of Lutheran pastors, who lived in cities like Berlin, where the king and his court still conversed in French, where the theatres put on French plays or Italian operas. They should have been almost the last people to be mesmerised by the ballads of Bürger, whose work presented Coleridge with an idea of the mystery of a supernatural and a mysterious fate on a rational human being, the inspiration for *The Rime of the Ancient Mariner*. Set in a seascape that Coleridge had viewed from his Pomeranian sojourn in Stettin, *The Rime* reeked of north European fantasy in the calms of a deserted sea, replete with loathsome things. They were fantasies projecting a land of enchanted and illimitable forests, of water-nymph-infested lakes, of magic and deformity, of dark spells of a deep, Germanic pre-Christian past. To this, the poets of an earlier age, whom Coleridge was studying in a literary-laden infusion of German thought and romance, added a medieval Catholicism and a chivalry practised by Round Table Knights on a quest, of Minnesingers, of virgins on the brink of sexual awakening, of a Lohengrin towed by enchanted swans and a Tannhäuser in thrall to Venus.

The German dreamers of this vision were in revolt against the rationalist, post-enlightenment parade of Napoleonic power across Europe. The philologists, who collected popular ballads for Bürger and tales for the Grimms, were on a quest for the authentic voice of a Germany, which told of a stronger, more enduring Germanic power, rooted in its glorious past, the age of the Minnesingers and alchemists seeking gold. Some went further back still, to the time of Germanic resistance to the power of Rome at the beginning of the Christian era when the renegade mercenary, Arminius, (Germanised as Hermann) had led his free forest autochthones in a successful battle in the Teutoberg Forest with the Roman legions under Publius Quinctilius Varus (AD 09).[37] Goethe took special pleasure in recording Germanic resistance to the Asiatic hordes which swept across Europe in the thirteenth century. If Italy looked back to her Roman past, Germans should look back to the great saviours of their nation and discover their destiny in the Grimm exploits of the time of the Hohenstaufen Frederick II, and of Duke Henry the Pious who died in the great battle of Liegnitz (Legnica) in 1241, which, though a defeat, stemmed the Mongol advance into Europe, and of Henry the Fowler and Landgrave Hermann.[38] These were the nursery fodder of the future high priest of Gothic Romanticism, the Saxon-born (1813) Richard Wagner.

CHAPTER SIX

Potentates and Patrons (1)

Hanover, Saxony and Brandenburg

> The old Margrave was a perfect specimen of an old-fashioned
> German Prince; he did nothing but hunt and think of the
> quarterings of his immaculate shield, all duly acquired from
> some Vandal ancestor as barbarous as himself.
> (Benjamin Disraeli, *Vivian Grey*, book 6 chapter 3)

> All Valoroso wanted was plenty of money, plenty of
> hunting, plenty of flattery, and as little trouble as
> possible. As long as he had his sport, this monarch
> cared little how his people paid for it.
> (W. M. Thackeray, *The Rose and the Ring*, chapter 2)

*T*HE DUKES AND bishops who had acquired from various Imperial
Diets the privilege of electing the Emperor had on the whole
simple ambitions: to acquire territory, either by marriage, war or bequest,
and to increase and spend their income so that they could be a monarch in
the mould of Louis XIV. The rulers of the larger states had another aim: to
upgrade their Duchies into kingdoms, but only the Elector of Brandenburg
had so far achieved this when he became King in (not of) Prussia in 1701.
The Electors of Bavaria, Saxony and the Duke of Württemberg only
received their kingship when Napoleon dismantled the Holy Roman
Empire in 1806. The Electoral Prince and Duke of Brunswick-Lüneburg
acquired his kingdom by inheriting the throne of Great Britain, through
a daughter of James I who had married the then Elector of Hanover and
was thus the nearest Protestant in the line of Stuarts not barred from

the throne by Act of Parliament. His electorate, Hanover, only became a kingdom at the Congress of Vienna in 1814. As Salic law forbade the monarch to be a queen, on the accession of Victoria to the English throne, the younger brother of William IV became King of Hanover.

At the beginning of the eighteenth century, the future King of Great Britain, the Elector George Louis, was quite at home in Hanover. The court in which he grew up was a very German one. For the courtiers, the whimsical Thackeray's Frau von Kielmannsegge and her dance partner Count Kammerjunker Quirini, sat at tables spread with *schweinskopf*, *specksuppe* and *leberkuche*, which, despite the appetite for all things French, were preferred to French cuisine, and sang French songs with the most awful German accent.[1] Lady Mary Wortley Montagu was impressed to find all the women there had 'rosy cheeks, snowy foreheads and bosoms, jet eye-brows and scarlet lips to which they generally add coal black hair', though she added that the colours lasted them for all their lives as long as they kept their distance from the fire which would otherwise cause it all to run.[2] Not everyone was impressed by the general female pulchritude in north Germany. Dr Burney in 1772, travelling in pursuit of music and musicians found the ladies ugly, less in their face than in their dress and in neglect of their complexions. Coleridge thought them plain ugly.[3]

The Hanoverian Electoral court was richer than most and George Louis, Duke of Brunswick-Lüneburg from 1698, and Prince Elector of Hanover to which he was elevated in 1708, presided over a court of officials and flunkeys, including instructors for his pages, of over 150 persons. Thackeray insisted that food and drink were the province of a *maître d'hotel*, a French cook, a body cook, ten other cooks and six assistants, two masters of the roast, a pastry cook, a pie baker and three scullions, with four pastry cooks in the sugar chamber, seven officers to supervise the cellar, four breadmakers and five men to polish the plate.[4] It was an inference that the new monarch brought with him to England a legendary German appetite.

George Louis had arrived in London aged 50, too late to become an Englishman, so he remained a Pumpernickel German, graced by two newly created peeresses for services to the royal bed since he had put away but never divorced his wife. One was very fat, known to the flunkeys as The Elephant, the other tall and lean and known intimately as The Maypole. They were both ugly and rapacious. The 'Maypole' was created Duchess of Kendal, and the 'Elephant', Countess of Darlington. The boy, Horace Walpole, saw the 'Elephant' once, with her 'vast red face; cheeks running into neck blending indistinguishably with stomach – a mere cataract of fluid tallow.'[5] The politeness of Pumpernickel princes was to be more faithful to their mistresses than to their wives. George Louis, for one, had experienced what had become almost the model for a Pumpernickel marriage. In 1682 he wed Sophia Dorothea of Zell (Celle), his first cousin, a legitimated daughter of his uncle. George Louis's mother, who nursed dreams of royalty for her children, had never approved of the match because Sophia Dorothea's mother was not royal but it ensured that George Louis would enlarge the electorate by union with the Duchy of Zell. It was not in itself a consideration that made for a happy marriage.

Sophia Dorothea grew bored by her phlegmatic and cold husband, and allowed her affections to wander. She was to pay heavily for being the protagonist in one of the most celebrated romances of the century. It was an age of soldiers of fortune who took allegiance where the pay was good and Philipp Christoph, Count von Königsmark, was one such. The Königsmarks were originally Brandenburgers and had properties in what was to become Prussia, most of it then ruled by Sweden. They had made their fortune under Gustavus Adolphus, who used the German plains as his playground and battlefield, and whose militant Lutheranism had made his handsome and indigent countrymen much desired as hired swords. Philipp Christoph had an elder brother who sought his life's adventures as a Knight of Malta, described by Thackeray as 'a favourite of Charles II, a beauty, a dandy, a warrior, a rascal of more than ordinary mark'[6] who escaped being hanged in England for a murder.

Count Philipp had moved after his brother's scrape to the service of George Louis's father, Ernest Augustus of Hanover. There he renewed his acquaintance with the Princess Sophia Dorothea, whom he had earlier met while serving as a page at her father's court at Zell. It was inevitable that he would agree to help her escape from the graceless court of her husband, George Louis. Escape, however, proved to be futile, and in 1694, four years before George Louis became Duke of Brunswick-Lüneberg and Elector of Hanover, Philipp Königsmark disappeared. The mystery deepened when it was rumoured that he had been Sophia Dorothea's lover, and that George

Louis had had him put to death.[7] He was drowned, it was rumoured, in a sack by an Italian adventurer and his confederates, who were handsomely rewarded. The future King of England suppressed all talk of the incident, and confined his wife to a castle. He never divorced or remarried, being content with the undisputed affections of the Elephant and the Maypole. From what he believed to be letters between Königsmark and Sophia Dorothea, uncovered in the University library at Upsala, Thackeray wove a sinister tale of amorous intrigue, jealousy and murder; of a jealous old harridan, former lover of the elector, a sharp tongued wife, a quiet, selfish and silent husband, and a young Lothario 'than whom one cannot imagine a more handsome, wicked, worthless reprobate'.[8]

Count Philipp Königsmark had a sister of remarkable beauty, a star of the Swedish court until 1691, and then the aurora borealis of Hamburg. Maria Aurora, in Voltaire's words, was 'one of the most delightful persons in Europe celebrated throughout the world for her wit and beauty'.[9] She was determined to unravel the truth of her brother's disappearance and her quest elevated him to the world of romantic fiction, to which she was to belong herself. In Dresden in 1694 to see if she could discover any news of him, she fell to the priapic charms of Augustus the Strong, Elector of Saxony and King of Poland, who, one calculation had it, was father of one legitimate and 385 illegitimate children.[10] Augustus was not above using some for personal diplomacy, as he displayed his illegitimate daughter, the Countess of Orzelska, in a diaphanous nightgown to Frederick William of Prussia and his son, Crown Prince Frederick (later 'the Great') as an erotic bonne bouche during their state visit to Saxony. The Prussian Elector recoiled in horror, propelling his son out the room before him.[11] In the event, only one of Augustus of Poland's extensive progeny was to achieve fame: the son of Maria Aurora, a legend in himself, Count Maurice de Saxe.

Compromised in the matrimonial stakes as Augustus's 'stale', Maria Aurora decided to establish herself as Abbess of Quedlingburg, to the west of Leipzig, which position carried the title of princess in the Holy Roman Empire, and from which vantage point she hoped to recover some of the family fortunes. She never achieved her aim, though she became coadjutor abbess and was sent by Augustus on a diplomatic errand to Charles XII of Sweden. Though she lived until 1728, her quest died with her, but the disappearance of her brother and the fruitless search for him by a sister with the beauty of a film star, gave them the aura of romance before Romanticism and Hollywood were conceived.[12]

* * *

Maria Aurora's romance had not been in Hanover but in Saxony, for she was one of the many mistresses of Augustus the Strong, King of Poland and Duke of Saxony. Though her son was among the bastards whom Augustus actually recognised as his own, there was little he was prepared to do for him in either Saxony or Poland. He had sired so many bastards that there were too many to provide for. So his son, the young Maurice, aged 12, with the Königsmark good looks ('circular black eyebrows, eyes glittering bright, six foot in his stockings'[13]) and the Saxon sexual appetite, took service with the Austrians, displaying his capacity for fatherhood and for reckless bravery before his fourteenth year. He fought under two great commanders, Marlborough and Eugene of Savoy who advised him not to confuse bravery with recklessness. Maurice's career now began to glitter. After service with Peter the Great against his mother's people under Charles XII of Sweden, Augustus began to see that he had been careless to neglect his son and by the age of 17 he commanded his own regiment in the Saxon service.

His exploits in the stables and in bed became legendary. Like his father he was inexhaustible in both, breaking horseshoes in his hands, and popping hymens like champagne corks. His father contracted for him a marriage with the richest heiress in the kingdom, but he ran through her fortune in no time. The soi-disant Count of Saxony, everyone admitted, was brave, promiscuous and extravagant, a king's son without a kingdom, and a soldier without a cause. His bid for the Duchy of Courland, which would have meant marrying the plain Archduchess failed as he would not marry her. He could only sustain his position in the face of the Archduchess's fury, by borrowing money from an actress in Paris who had joined his seraglio.

Maurice eventually decided to cast his lot with France and, following the death of his father, he joined another royal bastard, the son of James II, to fight in the century's second war of succession, this time of Poland.

France was supporting Louis XV's father-in-law and an earlier occupant of the throne of Poland, Stanislas Leczynski, but family loyalties were not a factor that determined the loyalties of soldiers of fortune. Maurice distinguished himself at the siege of the Rhenish city of Philippsburg, at which the Duke of Berwick was killed and Frederick II made his military debut, so that when the next succession war, that of Austria, broke out in 1741 Maurice led a French invasion of Austria, and by a brilliant coup de main occupied Prague before even the garrison knew he was there.

Maurice, Count of Saxony, was now a Marshal of France and continued a string of victories that made Louis XV revive a rank that had only been conferred twice on French commanders, Marshal-General of the King's Camps and Armies. He defeated an English army at Fontenoy, titularly commanded by George II, and his victories in the Low Countries brought the end of the war nearer. Despite Saxe's brilliance the peace of Aix la Chapelle (1748) changed very little. The principal gainer in Europe was Frederick II, who had demonstrated that a national army could achieve more than an army of mercenaries commanded by a soldier of fortune, and the battle lines were drawn for another more decisive combat eight years later in America and India. The reputation of French arms remained formidable but the war itself, which had in one way or another involved most of the states on the continent, seemed to the French as stupid as the peace.

Maurice had shown brilliance, bravery and remarkable gifts of generalship which in some way foreshadowed the career of another soldier of fortune, Napoleon Bonaparte. Maurice, however, was fighting, unlike the generals of Frederick II, for a king not his own. He had no expectations beyond personal glory, riches and pleasure. He was to be eclipsed as a military commander by a Corsican, and as a lover by a Venetian. He left a treatise on the art of war, disguised as his dreams, *Mes Réveries*, which Carlyle epitomised as 'a strange military farrago, dictated, as I should think, under opium'.[14] He also left a remote, and surprising, fruit of his loins. At 52 the Saxon's inexhaustible sexual appetite resulted in a daughter by a girl 30 years younger. She was named after Saxe's mother, Maria Aurora Königsmark, and was to be the grandmother of Amandine Aurore Lucile Dupin, born in 1804, in Turgenev's words 'a brave man, and a good woman', calling herself in the androgynous taste of the time,

George Sand. Her links to Poland through her great grandparents were to be revived in her ten-year liaison with Frédéric Chopin.

Maurice de Saxe, however, is better remembered as the tenor role in Francesco Cilea's opera, *Adriana Lecouvreur*. Premiered at La Scala, Milan, in 1902, the part of Maurice was sung by Caruso. Saxe was portrayed as the famous military commander masquerading as a green young ensign, in which improbable guise he had captured the heart of an actress. She was to lend him money to sustain his bid for the Duchy of Courland. The demanding singing roles usually pit a middle-aged tenor with a robust soprano (Saxe was nearly 30, admittedly a general at the time of his Courland bid), but the romantic intensity of the music, eclipsing a plot of great complexity and manifest absurdity, has made it a favourite role for *prime donne* since it was first sung by Angelina Pandolfini (1871–1959, *floreat* 1900). It was the recording of her voice, with that of Caruso, which was rated by that inveterate collector, John Paul Getty, as the Holy Grail among the early recordings of opera. Of Augustus of Saxony's hundreds of children, the most distinguished has ended as a Neapolitan voice on a Bakelite disc.

* * *

Saxony was in many ways the true home of Pumpernickel. Flanked on the north-west by the picturesque peaks and valleys of 'the Saxon Switzerland', she was plentifully watered by the Elbe, rising in Bohemia, flowing into the North Sea and navigable as far as Dresden. She was as a result the principal bread-basket of Germany, producing the rye from which pumpernickel was baked. With tributary streams to drive her mills, her abundant orchards, her dense forests, her urgent stallions, her black cattle, boars and venison, her deeply veined silver mines, her quarries of marble and precious stones and her fine Spanish sheep, whose wool was most highly prized by her weavers, Saxony was pure Snow White country.

There was no historical connection between Saxon England and what came later to be known as Saxony. Any connection with the English Saxons, paradoxically, was closer to the Electorate of Hanover from which England had lately taken its king. In the twelfth century, what were still then identified with the historic Saxons, conquerors of England and enemies of Charlemagne, were incorporated into an Electorate and the Saxon name migrated to the Duchy of Saxe-Wittenberg, where Luther nailed his theses to the church door. The passage of centuries, the bewildering transfers of power and titles, dynastic marriages and alliances was marked by the survival, through many blood-ties, of the electoral Duchy of Saxe-Wittenberg, spawning Saxe-Gothas, Saxe-Weimars, Saxe-Coburgs, Saxe-Meiningens and Saxe-Altenbergs. Under the Electors in the sixteenth century, Maurice (the eponymous ancestor of Maurice de Saxe,) and Augustus, Saxony acquired the virtual intellectual supremacy in Germany. She was the centre of the book trade in Leipzig, which at the beginning of the eighteenth century had emerged as the commercial heart of Germany. She had four universities, at Jena, Leipzig, Erfurt and Wittenberg, and the language of Luther's Bible, with their combined help, had become accepted as the Saxon dialect and the fountain of modern German.

Religious strife, mainly between Lutherans and Calvinists, created instability and weakness and when Saxony became the epicentre of the Thirty Years War she was devastated by the armies both of the Imperialist Wallenstein and of the Swedish Gustavus Adolphus. She never recovered her position as the home of the German soul, and the Polish extravagances of Augustus the Strong (*regnavit* 1697–1704, and 1709–33), which embroiled him with the Swedish meteor, Charles XII, did little to improve it. Augustus became a Roman Catholic in 1696 in order to be King of Poland, and as Prince Elector of Saxony, he established an uneasy pluralism, enduring enough for the Bach family to compose music that appealed to all ears, Lutheran and Roman Catholic, if not to the deeply Calvinist strain that still ruled in some churches.

Augustus the Strong, in addition to siring a regiment of bastards, also aspired to creating the most brilliant court in Germany; pageants, opera and hunting parties were brilliantly stage-managed, Dresden and Warsaw attracted jewellers, painters, architects, dancers and singers who helped to make the eighteenth century and particularly the reign of King Frederick Augustus (third of that name of Poland from 1734 and Electoral Duke of Saxony Augustus II from 1733–63, and the one indisputably legitimate heir to Augustus the Strong) Saxony's great age of art and music. The

King-Elector's wish to convince Europe that Saxony was a European power to be reckoned with may not have done much for the German soul, for the debts incurred by his father's extravagance rendered it vulnerable to the ambitions of the miserly, and therefore richer Hohenzollerns in Prussia,[15] but during his rule Dresden 'was regarded by the rest of Europe as the Athens of modern times'.[16] Though more modestly dubbed by the poet, Johann Gottfried Herder, as 'Florence on the Elbe' (*Elbflorenz*), the city rose from its river banks linked by bridges of peculiar grace, resplendent with spires and cupolas, citadels of poetry and music, towered over by the Renaissance royal palace, the Georgenschloss (1530–5) and the Italianate Hofkirche (1739–51) with its three score human statues. Palaces, churches, libraries, galleries and chapels were built to house their Elector's treasures and adorn the skyline, making Dresden a worthy capital for a monarch. Its luxurious environs of vine-clad hills and waving rye fields were an auditorium for nightingales and skylarks, inspiring poets. From 1747–57, Canaletto's nephew, Bernardo Bellotto, put on canvas the slowly rising glories of the city, in which, in 1787, Schiller wrote most of his *Don Carlos*.

What was to sustain Saxon fortunes was an alchemical discovery. Alchemy was still a feature of German experimentation, buoyed up by credulity and fancy. Casanova was able to convince one impressionable patroness that he could restore her youth and get her pregnant by the moon, and Cagliostro was an adept in pretending to transmute base metal into gold, while as late as 1774 Mesmer was peddling mystic magnetism to the Viennese public, which included the supposedly illuminated masons, the Illuminati. It was not strange that Goethe, in this Saxon heartland, should conceive of Faust's lust for the elixir of perpetual youth.[17]

The China trade had introduced Europe to hard white porcelain, the secret of making of which had hitherto remained with the Chinese. The French had managed to produce a translucent pottery made with glass, that looked Chinese, but it was Augustus the Strong, an avid collector of Chinese porcelain, who was determined to find the secret of its manufacture. He had inherited the laboratories and the alchemists, which were an adjunct of every court that wished to discover the shortcut to riches. Ores, potions, elixirs, gases and crystals were one thing; to discover the secret of making porcelain was another, which promised returns almost as fanciful as those that would follow transmutation of lead into gold.

One of Frederick Augustus's professional alchemists, Johann Friedrich Böttger, was only 24 but he managed to create a hard redstone ware which was fired at such a high temperature that it could be cut and polished like a gemstone. Augustus recognised that Böttger's ceramic, crude though it might be, was at least porcelain and removed him and his workmen to the fortress at nearby Meissen, where they were virtually incarcerated. In 1710, Böttger broke into the Chinese secret, for he managed to produce, from white kaoline clay and powdered feldspathic rock, a crude, off-white porcelain, closely analogous to the Chinese *petun-tse*. When it was modelled, fired, painted and then glazed, and fired again at a very high temperature, it made a hard resistant product. Böttger died in 1719, but the Meissen technique was developed and refined, like the formula for Coca-Cola, in such secrecy that Napoleon had to use his personal authority to have it revealed to his own expert. The secret did not in fact stay confined to Meissen for too long, as workmen managed to break free from their prison-like conditions and to sell the secret to other manufactories, which began to compete with the popularity of Saxonware. By the 1740s, however, Dresden porcelain had so perfected itself that it was often considered superior to Chinese originals and became the most prized in Europe, even finding a market among the Ottomans.

The Meissen factory began to move away from wholly Chinese designs and its chief sculptor to experiment with statuettes of people and animals, which became so popular that they were boldly copied by other manufactories. The Dresden figurines were prized as icons of fashion and their dainty poses and brightly coloured costumes became models for the Pompadour and Petit Trianon fantasies of the daughters of great houses who wished to dress as dairy-maids, or shepherdesses. They continue, to this day, to be the most accurate rendering, in every film studio, of how to make costume dramas of the period. Every bodice that is ripped in romantic fiction can trace its rape to Saxon porcelain.[18]

* * *

One other achievement of Frederick Augustus was to make his accession to the throne of Poland in 1734 the occasion of the first performance of Bach's *Mass in B Minor*. Though some of the Mass, the Sanctus, had been composed as early as 1724, the main body was presented for performance at the accession of the new king, along with a petition by Bach to be appointed court composer, a distinction he obtained three years later. Frederick Augustus ruled Poland as a pretty well absentee monarch from 1734–63, and was uxorious and fat. His father may have been called 'The Strong', a physical rather than a political soubriquet; the son was dubbed 'The Corpulent'. He found Dresden a far more agreeable capital than Warsaw, where he spent only three out of his 29 years as King of Poland. In between fathering 15 legitimate children by his Habsburg archduchess, daughter of the Emperor, Joseph I, he spent his time, hunting, attending operatic and theatrical performances and collecting pictures, particularly the work of Canaletto's nephew, Bernardo Bellotto.

Casanova claimed to know the Elector well, and as his mother lived in Dresden as a member of the theatrical troupe he was a constant visitor, even writing a parody of Racine for performance before the court. 'Never was a monarch such an enemy to economy,' he wrote, surprisingly for him with a note almost of criticism. Augustus laughed at penny-pinchers and spent a lot of money ensuring that he had something to laugh at. Not quite liking to mock the follies of his fellow sovereigns he employed to keep him amused four buffoons, who were the channels for most court patronage. Casanova thought the court of Frederick Augustus, where the arts flourished, was the most brilliant in Europe, but he found it the least 'gallant'. The Elector was uxorious, active only in the matrimonial bed, and the Saxons took their cue from their sovereign. Nevertheless Casanova was clapped at Dresden, and it took him six weeks to recover.

Frederick Augustus's family were in their own way a family portrait of Pumpernickel. Of his 15 children, four died in childhood. His eldest surviving daughter married Charles VII of Naples who exchanged his crown to become Charles III of Spain. Another daughter married the Elector of Bavaria and a third was to be the mother of the ill-fated Louis XVI of France. A third son secured the Duchy of Courland, to which his uncle the Marshal-General of France had unsuccessfully aspired; his youngest son became the Electoral Archbishop of Trier and two younger daughters became Princess-Abbesses of aristocratic nunneries.

When not arranging their complex inheritances, marriages and sinecures the Elector acquired paintings for his gallery. The core of this remarkable collection was transferred by fiat of Augustus the Strong when he became King of Poland, from the Wawel castle in Cracow.[19] Two Rembrandts were its modest beginnings and when in 1745, Frederick Augustus acquired the bulk of the collection of Francesco III, Duke of Modena, for just £60,000 the collection became eclectic and European-wide, numbering six Coreggios and paintings by Annibale Caracci. He then bought the contents of the Prague Gallery in 1748 from the indigent Maria Theresa and, as there was insufficient room to hang all the pictures, those that could not be hung were stacked up against the wainscotting. The collection was crowned by the gift to Frederick Augustus in 1754 of Raphael's *Sistine Madonna*.[20] The royal collection became a nucleus for the study of art and Dresden a centre to rival Vienna, for in 1755 a pamphlet entitled *Reflections Concerning the Imitation of Grecian Artists in Painting and Sculpture* and published in Dresden, was to ignite passions that were to divide artists and art critics for a century, enlisting partisans as fervid as those who rose to the great religious debates of the time on the divinity of God. Johann Winckelmann, who became the archpriest of classicism, was a young protégé of the Elector, Augustus III. He had never been to Rome, or indeed any other art collection than that of Dresden, where the arrival of the Sistine Madonna was to start him off in his bid to become the Führer of German art historians.

If Augustus managed to choose his artists well he chose his allies badly. In the conflicts culminating in the Seven Years War, which left many Saxon towns in ruins, his currency was devalued, his treasury emptied and his population diminished. In 1772 Dr Burney found everything in the utmost indigence, most of the nobility and gentry too impoverished to patronise music or encourage their children to be musical, and what had formerly been 'the seat of the Muses and habitation of pleasure, was now only a dwelling for beggary, theft and wretchedness'.[21]

Frederick Augustus's eldest surviving son was Elector for only three months in 1763 before succumbing to smallpox but he had already set about the revival of his country's fortunes by a campaign of extreme economy which his successor, Frederick Augustus III, continued. In 1806 he assumed the throne as King of Saxony, which he ruled for another 21 years. But the great days of Saxony had passed, and though a precarious alliance with France, largely in despite of Prussia which had done her such harm, allowed him to become the first King of Saxony by fiat of Napoleon Bonaparte, the new kingdom found itself wholly overshadowed by its more powerful neighbour.

* * *

Saxony may have been in its time the most admired of German Electorates but her northern neighbour, Prussia, was to be her nemesis. She was the least admired but the most powerful of the purely German sovereignties, ranking only after the Imperial superpower, Austria. At the end of the seventeenth century there had seemed little promise of this, for the kingdom of Prussia, at its creation in 1701, was an eastern German province (now largely in twenty-first century Poland) much of it outside the recognised boundaries of the Holy Roman Empire. The Prussians were originally a Baltic forest people who had prospered under the Teutonic Knights. They had formed a Grand Duchy under their Hohenzollern leaders who acquired in 1618 the Margravate of Brandenburg, elevated to an Electorate. In 1701, for services rendered to the Imperial cause in the War of the Spanish Succession, the Hohenzollern Elector was given the title of King. The Hohenzollerns also ruled the Duchies of Pommern, Magdeburg and Cleves, the Principality of Minden and Halberstadt, the Counties of Mark and Ravensburg and the Principality of Neuchatel. These territories were scattered across north Europe and some were separated by several hundred miles, so that their ruler had to cross different territories to visit each. So Bavaria and Saxony, with natural frontiers, richer soil and larger populations, seemed more likely to compete for primacy among German states.

The first king, Frederick I, who ruled Brandenburg as King *in* Prussia (the first to be styled King *of* Prussia was his grandson, Frederick II) from 1701–13, was dazzled by French example, and had no intellectual power to rise above it. His third wife might give asylum to an independent mind like Leibniz, but Frederick remained a philistine. Its second king, from 1713–40, was the slightly crazed martinet, Frederick William I, whose passion for recruiting tall grenadiers and black bandsmen was emblematic of his desire to have a reliable army to weld his disparate territories together and to enforce his will. On one occasion his passion for tall grenadiers led his officers to try to press-gang an exceptionally tall Imperial diplomatist, Baron von Bentenrieder, into the regiment of giants.[22] It was Frederick William who established the martial discipline with which the state was run.[23] He also acquired from Sweden in 1721 the port of Stettin (Sczezcin) and the western Pomeranian coast. The influx of many industrious Protestant refugees in the 1730s from Salzburg helped Stettin to attract much of the trade of the virtually closed Baltic Sea.[24] The kingdom had its capital in Brandenburg, first at Potsdam, then at Berlin, which began under Frederick William I to take on the airs of a significant city. Its second largest city was far to the east, at Königsberg in the former Duchy of Prussia.[25]

The philosophy and imagination of a regimental sergeant-major precluded much in the way of cultural patronage; Frederick William I closed his court, disbanded its orchestra and appointed his court dwarf President of the Leibniz inspired Berlin Academy.[26] But he applied his mind to the administration of his scattered possessions and their concentration in an efficient, absolutist realm. He mobilised the sense of honour in his nobles and the capabilities of the upper bourgeoisie in royal service. This was most noticeable in his army, in which frugal management and organisational discipline made Prussia the most powerful state in the old Germany. The army was the core of the state, a national not a mercenary force for the monarch to hire out for gain to France or Austria. Most of the nobility held commissions in it, and one in 25 of the male population served in it. Most of the state revenue was devoted to its upkeep. An 80,000 strong force in a population of 2.5 million was too large for pure defence, but Frederick William had no aggressive use for it. It existed to show that, in his realm, 'I must be served with life and limb, house and wealth, honour and conscience. Eternal salvation belongs to God, but all else is mine.'[27]

* * *

His son, Frederick II, was to see the army's potential. He believed that the first duty of a prince was to survive, the second to expand his dominions.[28] His own courage, daring and military skill used the disciplined tool of his father to command a force which could hold most of Europe at bay, and put Prussia on a par with states of greater size, populations and natural wealth. He used it for his national purposes of survival and expansion, to seize Austrian territory, like Silesia in 1740, to consolidate Brandenburg-Prussia, and to deter invasion, his invasion of Saxony in 1756 being interpreted as a pre-emptive strike. By the time of his death his kingdom was, after Austria, indubitably the most powerful state in central Europe, and supreme in the north, though only the tenth in size, and the thirteenth in population. But it had the third largest army in Europe and was well set upon the process of becoming more *Junkerstadt* than Pumpernickel. Frederick despised most of his fellow monarchs who aped France without understanding where power lay. Though one of the foremost Francophiles among European monarchs, Frederick did not adopt French manners or dress and, if he built palaces, they were not pale reflections of Versailles. The Charlottenberg was not one of Frederick's; it was built in a village like Versailles, on the outskirts of Berlin, for the Electress Sophia Charlotte at the end of the seventeenth century. Though embellished by Frederick II he did not live there, but it remained a residence of Prussian royalty until the death of Queen Victoria's son-in-law and first Emperor of Germany, Frederick III. The main centre of Prussian royalty was at Potsdam, the old capital of Brandenburg, where were clustered the Royal Palace, the principal winter home of the Hohenzollerns until 1918 with, in its grounds, the treasure of Berlin baroque, Sanssouci (more a pleasure dome but favoured – as it was partly designed – by Frederick II as a summer palace), and the New Palace, built to celebrate Prussia's survival, even victory, in the Seven Years War. The cupola over the New Palace was crowned by naked statues of Maria Theresa of Austria, Catherine of Russia and Mme de Pompadour, linked like the Three Graces in a chaste embrace, to show Frederick's contempt for the rulers of the three enemies he had been fighting.

Like his father, Frederick wore military uniform; he made his family serve in the army, and spoke German to his men. Otherwise Berlin was intellectually an outpost of Paris, but Frederick did not allow this to warp his judgment, unlike his younger brother who spent half his life wanting to live in Paris and the other half, after he had lived there, regretting that he was not still there. Frederick II was the walking model for an enlightened despot. He was certainly a despot but was he enlightened? He encouraged Leibniz's Academy of Arts and Sciences (which his father had closed but which he re-opened) to recruit an international body of savants who were free to discuss abstract subjects, he encouraged industrial and agricultural improvements, he imposed religious toleration, and these were enlightened acts. But they in no way diminished the power of the state, only made that power more acceptable. He might toy with the ideas of Voltaire and take pleasure and profit from their association, but any notion that put limits on the power of the monarchy received short shrift. Military discipline remained as brutal as it had under his father.

His preservation of a noble officer caste, to secure support from a class that had imposed regimes on their estates almost as total as that of their monarch on them, encouraged the future dominance of the Prussian Junker families. Under Frederick the number of middle class civilians in the government declined.[29] Tax on land remained static, so as not to disturb the supply of officers and men to the army, while other burdens on the peasants were only relaxed to ensure their availability for military service. Peasant mobility was discouraged to keep the economic viability of estates belonging to a servile aristocracy. Nobles owed a prime duty to the state and the king alone could approve their travel abroad or their marriage. Their privileged status depended on the royal whim; and to preserve it they became like Teutonic janissaries.

Frederick's much-famed religious toleration was more a case of religious indifference, for he was in effect an atheist, and accepted that thought could be more constructively controlled by freedom than by coercion. In Lessing's words toleration was little more than a licence to make fun of religion.[30] Criticism of anything more fundamental to the administration of the state called down immediate suppression. Lessing had little doubt which society was the most slavish in Europe.[31] Yet there were few more slavish than the Duchy of Württemberg.

CHAPTER SEVEN

Potentates and Patrons (2)

Württemberg

You may make merry over little potentates ... But do not cross
their paths. Their dominion may be circumscribed but they have
it ... my power equals that of the Kaiser and the Czar.
(Prince Ernest of Eppenwelzen-Sarkeld, in George Meredith's
The Adventures of Harry Richmond, chapter 32)

*M*ONTESQUIEU BELIEVED THAT Louis XIV had established the power
of France by building Versailles and Marly.[1] Just as President
Reagan beggared the Soviet Union by building his nuclear shield, and
inviting competition, so the German princes spent money they did not
have on palaces which were to show that they were every bit as civilised
as the Sun King. Palaces at Mannheim, Munich, Louisburg, Rastadt, rose
before the weary eyes of the citizenry between 1695 and 1730. The
Electoral Bishop of Cologne moved his episcopal see to Bonn, and the
Elector of Trier moved his to Coblenz, and built accordingly. The motives
were not dissimilar from those that led to the creation, in our days, of
the new capital cities of Ankara, Brasilia, Islamabad and Ajuba, to build a
national centre away from the corrupted traditions and historical baggage
of old metropolises. But in the decisions of German princes deranged
hubris also played its part.

The Swabian duchy of Württemberg had been created by Maximilian,
King of the Romans and grandfather of Charles V, who elevated the Count
to Duke on condition that he always acknowledged his fealty to the House
of Habsburg. Wedged between the Black Forest, the old Palatinate and the
Duchy of Baden, its capital of Stuttgart lay in well-watered land, rich in

cattle, with deposits of marble and copper. During the Thirty Years War, the Duke had cast in his lot with France and Sweden and as a result the Duchy had been devastated in the march of conflicting armies. During peacetime, restoration of the Duke was dependent on Württemberg's remaining firm in its subservience to Vienna, and its Dukes accepted commissions in the Austrian army, which resulted in more devastation in the ensuing War of the Spanish Succession. Visitors found Stuttgart, which had suffered a three-day sack at the hands of the French in 1707, a depressing place, hot and damp in summer, freezing in winter, and when it rained as it did often, there was little to be found in the scanty shops.

The new Duke, Eberhard IV, was only a year old when he succeeded his father in 1677 and as soon as he came of age on his sixteenth birthday he had set off on his travels. He made straight for France, and was graciously received by Louis XIV who hoped to wean him away from subservience to Vienna. If he did not succeed in that, he was nonetheless able to turn the young Duke's head. Louis showed him how a sovereign should live, wrapped in majesty and splendour, at the lifting of whose eyebrow men waited anxiously for their instructions. Württemberg was not a rich state but refugee colonies of Waldenses were gradually restoring its shattered economy. If cleverly milked, Eberhard calculated that it should be able to pay for his Versailles.

He set about recruiting Frenchmen to lend lustre to his court and when his own nobility proved stuffily unappreciative of his efforts to liven up Stuttgart, he imported nobles from neighbouring principalities to join in his palace parties. He took a mistress; she was not up to snuff so he took another. She was a disaster, for she reigned as *maîtresse en titre* for 20 years, and beggared the state. She was the sister of one of Eberhard's fellow officers who had served with Eberhard under Marlborough, but her introduction to the Duke's *ménage* was an elaborate plot on the part of her family to gain lucrative positions at court. She was not attractive, but had penetrating and lustrous grey eyes, of almost sinister power, so that she attracted the sobriquet of The Sorceress. By 1705 she was installed in a hunting lodge, suitably improved in the French manner, and there she held court. Eberhard was totally captivated. He made her a countess and then married her in a morganatic but bigamous marriage, for his wife, the daughter of the Margrave of Baden-Durlach and mother of his heir, still lived. But, as he declared, 'I am the pontiff of this country and therefore everything is in order with the good God.'[2]

The French occupation of the Duchy in 1707 temporarily disturbed this idyll, but at the peace at the Countess Christiana Wilhelmine von Grävenitz was ascendant at court. Naturally the new countess's brother took his place there and her royal bawd, who had engineered her intrusion in the first place became 'her dame of dishonour'. Eberhard ignored general disapproval. He had to advise the Habsburgs of the new arrangements. He expected his legitimate child, a sickly son, to die soon, and his lady could become Duchess of Württemberg, and provide him with a new heir. He even approached the Vatican with an offer to become a Catholic and to establish the Roman Catholic church as the state church if the Pope would annul his marriage to the Margrave's daughter. Vienna refused to accept the new concubine as duchess and ordered Eberhard to dismiss her, and the Pope, though threatened by Eberhard that he would do as Henry VIII of England, refused to do more than appoint an enquiry into what was going on, and gave the legitimate Duchess pecuniary help to fight her cause.

This was a blow to Eberhard, who did not have the power of Henry VIII, so he pretended to comply with the Imperial order and quickly arranged a marriage for his mistress with a 60-year-old Bohemian noble who, once installed in the hunting lodge with his wife, was despatched to Vienna to represent the Duchy of Württemberg as minister, leaving his new wife to resume her position as *horizontale* first lady, with the title of Grand Mistress of the Household. The abandoned duchess left the duke 'to swash about in the pool of amatory iniquity'.[3]

∗   ∗   ∗

At the end of the seventeenth century many of the existing princely dwellings in Germany were little more than fortresses, and often in poor repair, the efforts of the military engineers to modernise and beautify them being often bizarre and maladroit. Foreign architects and designers, Italian and French, laboured to impose their baroque style on existing buildings and gave work to German craftsmen to provide the rococo ornamentation of the interiors, in which workers in metal and stucco created an almost subaqueous world of vegetation, corals and shells, peopled by putti and porpoises gambolling luxuriantly among the fronds. It caught the eye at every turn, creating art in perpetual movement and busyness, exhilarating and breathless and exhausting. This extravagant, opulent and often visually fraudulent style lasted for about 70 years until Germany's influential pundit on classic order, Johann Joachim Winckelmann (*floreat* 1760s), called its creators to order.

Eberhard of Württemberg was determined to have such a palace and because Stuttgart had bad memories of French military occupation, and stuffy disobliging citizens, who had pelted his favourite's carriage with rubbish, he decided to build a new palace in the forest 12 miles from Stuttgart, where he could hunt to his heart's content and where his mistress could preside over a court which had no memories of Eberhard's lawful wife. He had already started to erect a hunting lodge in the grandiose Viennese style adopted by Prince Eugene in the Belvedere, but under the influence of the now irresistible Countess Wilhelmine von Grävenitz he invited, in the usual German tradition, a military architect, Jean-Frédéric Nette, to extend the lodge to house the reigning Prince and his court. When Nette died in 1709, the extensions and decoration of the interior were given to two Italian stuccoists, uncle and nephew, who just built sideways, linking 18 different buildings by corridors and galleries to form a huge quadrilateral square, 140 metres long and 69 metres wide. The Castle of Louisburg (Ludwigsburg, by which it will be known hereafter) was largely finished by 1730 though it was much altered in later years. Its core was a chapel dedicated to St Hubert, the patron saint of hunting, whose conversion had followed his hunting a stag with a cross growing between its antlers. Round his token presence Eberhard established a chivalric order of St Hubert to sanctify the almost daily slaughter that he and La Grävenitz perpetrated in the surrounding woodlands.

The main bulk of the palace was represented by the hunting pavilion and Great Hall, clad in false marble and bedizened by the cross of the Order of St Hubert, membership of which was not based on blood, chaste morals or good works but on prowess in the hunting field, and at the table after the chase. John Jorrocks would have swiftly established his qualifications for membership. Though ministers, functionaries, courtiers and shopkeepers were obliged to move to tied housing erected for them,

Ludwigsburg was never a jolly community, except for those involved in the court hunts or participating in the extravagance of La Grävenitz. Though the chateau was the metropolis, the town remained a sad garrison of periwigged soldiers in uniforms with yellow facings (the Duke's colours), and of functionaries in confections of lace.[4]

At the chateau, however, gaiety ran amok. La Grävenitz moved into her sumptuously furnished and decorated chalet, La Favorita, and for nearly 20 years held court there when Eberhard was busy hunting or drilling his soldiers. In 1711, Eberhard was 35, very fat but still agile on his feet, a superb horseman, and inexhaustible in bed. In German court circles, that of Ludwigsburg was accounted one of the most brilliant, its Grand Mistress of the Household kept her striking looks and penetrating eyes by, it was rumoured, the plentiful use of alchemical compounds manufactured by sorcery. She was quick to see any possible slight or solecism in the strict etiquette that prevailed on her instructions, while the state gradually faced ruin. Her name was added to those prayers seeking a blessing on the principality, where the last sentence of the Lord's Prayer – *Libera nos a malo* (Deliver us from evil) – was held to refer to her. On her husband's death, she revived the idea of marrying the Duke, but the Duchess was still living. Eberhard may have insisted that he was Pope in his own domains, and could do as he liked but he could not actually defy either the Catholic or the Protestant clergy by a bigamous marriage.

However, La Grävenitz was to overreach herself. In 1731, Eberhard fell ill, and his mistress was rumoured to be using strange potions to cure him, mixtures of the blood of a newborn child with the entrails of a fighting cock, herbs gathered at midnight and the beard of a dead man. Then she fell out with her brother over her failure to share her ill-gotten gains with her family. Despite the well-known antipathy of the Prussian King, Frederick William, she had insisted on presiding over his reception at Ludwigsburg on a state visit in 1730. The blunt Prussian monarch asked Eberhard why he allowed himself to be so dominated by an old woman rumoured to be a witch, and the reproach penetrated the Duke's normally thick skin. The favourite's brother did nothing to soften the coming blow. She beat a cautious retreat to one of her chateaux whence the soldiers sent to arrest her had to haul her out of bed by her feet, and carry her off to strict imprisonment.

She only escaped a sentence of death on the somewhat strange reason, given Vienna's aversion to her, which was that as a countess of the Holy Roman Empire she could not be executed like a common felon. In 1732, two years after the Castle of Ludwigsburg was virtually complete, the Duke pardoned her on condition that, in return for a lump sum, she would renounce everything and go into exile. Eberhard died of apoplexy the following year, worn out by feasting and hunting, 'an elderly gentleman [who] had distinguished himself ... not by political obliquities and obstinacies but by matrimonial and amatory'.[5] Nothing was ever proved about La Grävenitz's sorcery or the effects, if any, of her magic potions upon him. He left no heir but a more lurid chapter yet was to open in the history of Württemberg.

* * *

Eberhard's successor was his cousin Charles-Alexander, aged 53. Charles-Alexander, a veteran of Austrian wars in Italy, the Low Countries, Hungary and Serbia, had been right hand adjutant to Prince Eugene, the victor at Belgrade where, wearing the collar of the Golden Fleece and with the rank of Marshal, Charles-Alexander was appointed Governor. A bluff soldier he inherited a state that was pretty well bankrupt, and his first action was to dismiss all the family of Eberhard's mistress, and appoint a chief minister.

The wags said that he only exchanged a sultana for a Grand Vizier, for the new minister was a Jew, born in Heidelberg in 1684. Süss Oppenheimer, known to history and legend as Jew Süss, was a graduate in mathematics and law, and spoke several languages. He had made one fortune supplying the Habsburg armies in their war on the Turks. German states were no different from other Christian countries in placing restrictions on Jews, on where they could live, what they should wear, how they could travel but, despite these inhibitions, Jews could become rich and command extensive credit among their co-religionists. This was particularly true of what were known as 'court Jews', who made themselves available to fund a prodigal prince's insatiable demand for money. They were not subject to the petty restrictions on residence, or on carrying arms. They adopted the prevailing dress of the day and wore wigs, which, however, they were still required not to powder. One of these so emancipated was Joseph Süss Oppenheimer (1698–1738).[6]

He first met Charles-Alexander at the castle of Wilbad, where the Duke's future wife was residing, but when Charles-Alexander was married, Süss, who was nephew to one of the Emperor's bankers in Vienna, insinuated that he could find money for the lifestyle in which the new couple wished to live. This was not one of economy and frugality. Süss bought a house in Ludwigsburg, filled it with servants, good food and fine wines to show off his wealth, and to demonstrate his capacity to add to it. He created a boom in local industry, raised loans, started a lottery and found the cash to meet Charles-Alexander's needs. The duke's militia had new uniforms, the palace once more hummed to parties. Soon Süss was recognised as the all-powerful minister and, if court was paid respectfully to him, the Jewish community sensed the growing dislike.

Whether Süss Oppenheimer was a real financial wizard or just a gifted extortionist, he was able to keep the Elector well supplied and in return received expensive gifts. The large diamond he wore on his finger came from the Duke who seemed to live as a pensioner of the all-powerful Jew. Süss was certainly a gifted *boulevardier*. Small and fastidious, he filled his house with entertainments that added to the lustre of what went on in the palace. His hospitality was spread widely and perhaps indiscriminately. It only required a small dent in his credit for the whole edifice to come tumbling down.

The mysterious death of his daughter, a Jessica trying to shake off the attentions of an admirer, temporarily unhinged him; he saw possible agents of her death everywhere, among court officials, among the public, even among highly placed ministers of the Church. Charles-Alexander, in order to marry the rich heiress to the Prince of Tour and Taxis, had agreed to become a Catholic and Süss's demand, that a prominent Catholic should be arrested and arraigned, troubled the Duke. He agreed nervously and then on the eve of going to Danzig to take medical advice on a troublesome old war wound, he threw a leaving party and was found dead in the Hall of Mirrors, lovingly and lavishly decorated by his former mistress. It was 13 March 1737. The Duke was overweight and had danced nearly all night. He was 57, and though it was pretty clear he had had a heart attack, popular legend broadcast that he had died in the arms of a concubine and his soul had been carried off by the devil.

The three children of the Duke were all minors, so that the Duchess assumed the Regency with the Imperial Arch-Chancellor, the Count von Schönbrun, now Prince-Bishop of Wurzburg. The dead Duke, however, had nominated his uncle, a fierce Protestant, Duke Rudolph of Württemberg-Neuenstadt, who refused to work with a Catholic Bishop. Schönbrun retired and Rudolph was determined to dispose of the Jew. Süss had already decided that flight was the better part of valour, but was recognised by peasants who had no reason to love him and handed him over to those looking for him. His residence was sacked by jubilant crowds, and the Jew was accused of pretty well every crime in the book: treason, lese-majesty, assaults on individual ministers and on other dignitaries, and falsification of money. His end in 1738 was frightful. Confined in an iron cage, a noose around his neck, he was hoisted up a tall gibbet where the noose slowly throttled him to death. He was left in the cage until his cadaver was reduced to a skeleton, only being buried six years later in 1744.

* * *

Württemberg's fortunes improved a little with the Jew's death. The Duchess sent the actors and other agents of licentious pleasure packing and despatched her sons to the austere court of Berlin to learn the arts of ruling. The new Duke, Charles-Eugene, twelfth Duke from age nine in 1737 to 1793, started well by marrying his childhood sweetheart, the daughter of the Margravine of Bayreuth and a niece of Frederick II, in 1748 when he was 20. It was a good marriage because it seemed to reconcile Württemberg to the northern Protestant states, and the young princess seemed well endowed with both beauty and sense. Later Casanova was to dub her one of the most accomplished of German princesses.

Charles-Eugene too was intelligent, had a good memory and some taste for state business. He patronised all the right things, savants, hospitals, libraries, was a keen botanist and an accomplished player of several musical instruments, perhaps even more accomplished than his wife's uncle, Frederick the Great. He was generous and hospitable, but unfortunately nurture had not expelled the demons of nature, and he was already displaying signs of the extravagance that had possessed his predecessors. His marriage entry into Bayreuth was in a coach that cost 24,000 florins and was drawn by six bay horses, followed by an escort of 53 courtiers. In addition Charles-Eugene's appetite for women began to put the marriage under strain. The auspices for marital bliss were poor. In addition Charles-Eugene had become very self-centred, and his mind uncritically dedicated to absolutist rule. He also wanted to be among the first princes of Europe. 'I am the Fatherland,' he declared in the spirit of the times, 'and the image of the deity on earth.'[7]

His half million or so subjects soon found they were supporting a royal household of 1,800 courtiers, including a Grand Marshal, a Grand Chamberlain, 169 chamberlains, an army of valets, cooks, pages and a personal guard of Hungarian *hajduks* as an indoor bodyguard, and a body of Turkish mercenaries to guard him when he ventured outside. In his stables there were 800 horses for his personal use and, whatever else Charles-Eugene had learned in Berlin, he had developed the taste for soldiers. He increased the 6,000 he had in uniform on his accession to 17,000. Men were seduced to enlist by offers of good pay and a smart uniform and those who declined to be enlisted paid a capitation tax. Citizens were obliged to stop and raise their hats to a soldier in uniform and, for neglecting to do so, he ordered one to receive 25 blows with a regulation, disciplinary cane.[8] This swollen army was supported by French subsidies in return for the loan of some of those resplendent soldiers, 6,000 of which were committed to enter the war in French service when required. For this Charles-Eugene received, between 1752–6, 1.5 million livres. He also sold troops to the Dutch to serve in the Cape, and later to the English to fight in their war with the rebels in America. The streets of Stuttgart were full of bravely moustachioed warriors, walking in clockwork order to frighten the citizens, though this was not the effect they had on the Prussian grenadiers when the Duke, true to his alliance with Austria, entered the Seven Years War in 1756, the year that his wife left him.

With his wife's departure, the Duke also showed that, despite the early promise, his rule was proving no improvement on that of Erberhard. He increasingly ignored his advisers and ministers and held Dukely audiences for his subjects, listening to but not remedying their grievances, and running his timetable with a punctilio that required a large number of unnecessary people to be present. He employed one of the largest orchestras in Germany and spent huge sums importing dancers and singers from Italy. To Dr Burney on his musical tour of Germany in 1776, the Duke seemed as passionate about music and shows as the Emperor Nero, but half the population of Württemberg seemed to be 'stage-players, fidlers (sic) and soldiers and the other half beggars'.[9]

In 1760 that sexual butterfly, Giacomo Casanova, was flitting from deflowered matron to deflowered maiden across Germany. In Stuttgart he met some of the Venetian girls he had known at the time of his escape from the Leads. They were part of the corps of Italian dancers who took principal roles in the ballets and operas staged by the companies of French and Italians who mounted both serious and comic operas and French plays. All the ballerinas were pretty, and all boasted that they had at some time or another 'made their amorous sovereign happy'. One of the corps de ballet, the daughter of a gondolier married to one of the regular dancers, became the Duke's mistress, and ran his court like a Sultana, arranging for his nights of dalliance with the rest of the corps and thus enjoying the honours that went with being Grand Mistress of the Household. Casanova got a worm's eye view of His Most Serene Highness, who did what he did,

> only to get himself talked about. He wanted it said that no living prince was more intelligent or more talented than he or more accomplished in the art of inventing pleasures and enjoying them, or better fitted to reign, or possessed of a better constitution for coping with the pleasures of the table, of Bacchus, and of Venus, without ever infringing on the time he needed to rule his state and manage its departments of which he insisted on being head.

His mistake, said Casanova in disgust, was to want to govern like the King of Prussia, who in reality called him his pet monkey.[10]

All this had been the root cause of the estrangement between the Duke and Duchess, who had despaired of being able to remedy her husband's folly. His court may have acquired a reputation for brilliance, but with her departure Charles-Eugene had gone to stud, mixing his bevy of young Italian concubines with a selection of young Württembergeoises whose parents he bullied into complaisance. Soon the shade of La Grävenitz in the person of the gondolier's daughter, La Gardela, was stalking the endless passages, commanding an entourage of pages and valets and demanding carriages. Charles-Eugene felt impelled to add to the palace he was building as his own Versailles in Stuttgart. Boswell may have dubbed his behaviour euphemistically as 'gallantries'.[11] In 1770 the state of the finances dictated bigger power intervention and, while the Duke was on an amorous visit to Venice, homeland of his current mistress, they moved in commissioners and appointed a Finance Council to curb the Duke's extravagance.[12]

Reform came from an unexpected source. A young woman, unhappily married to a boor, caught the Duke's eye. She was 20, he 44, but the encounter was a *coup de foudre*. She was not pretty, or particularly well educated; she spoke German in dialect and did not know French. She was interested in cooking, dressmaking and other forms of domestic economy. But she was socially acceptable, coming from a distressed but noble family. Charles-Eugene was captivated. He had her marriage annulled, he installed her in the palace formerly inhabited by La Grävenitz, and persuaded the Emperor, for a monetary consideration, to make her an Imperial countess. The Countess Francisca de Hohenheim was no Grävenitz. She was pious in a discreet, non-threatening way; she took no part in court intrigues, and was faithful for over 20 years to her middle-aged lover. Under her influence, Charles-Eugene became a reformed character. He adopted economy as formerly he had embraced extravagance:

> No longer did he construct lakes on the top of mountains or force the peasants to fill them with water to give him the pleasure of a deer hunt. No longer were immense forests illuminated, fauns and dryads were no longer assembled to dance nocturnal rounds. No longer did one find gardens filled in winter with spring flowers.[13]

Soon the opera was playing to houses filled by soldiers under orders to attend, and the principals packed their bags.

The Countess urged her besotted Duke to think about his people, their education and welfare. Under her influence he confessed to his entourage that he was a changed man, no longer an unrestrained demon but a man passionately dedicated to science, to creating a botanic garden, to learning, to building up a library and, to satisfy a residual desire for high spending, buying pictures and antiques for his museum in Stuttgart. In 1780 his first wife died and he married, not without difficulty, Francisca, who was a Protestant, but his Cinderella was supported by the state dignitaries who esteemed her so much that they offered the Duke 50,000 florins if he married her and not one of the other possible wives on offer.

∗ ∗ ∗

In one sense, Charles-Eugene had not changed. He still demanded obsequious obedience, tempered as it was by his Countess's influence on what he demanded obedience for. His Military Academy, the Karlschule, founded to provide a free education for 300 sons of officers and men in his army, was to be an Academy of art, music and architecture, of religion, medicine and languages. Eventually its products would replace the imported priests and functionaries staffing Church and State and the artists employed in building and decoration. Dr Burney was surprised to find 18 *castrati* on the pupil strength along with surgeons from Bologna experienced in emasculating boys for Papal choirs. The school was run on military lines. Discipline was severe. The sons of officers were distinguished from the sons of commoners by dress, and separate living. But the penalties for infraction of disciple were common – bastinadoing, solitary confinement and deprivation of food – and the only women allowed in the building were those who presented little temptation to adolescents.

The unreformed temper of Charles-Eugene was shown in his treatment of the poet and musician, Daniel Christian Schubart. Schubart had dropped out of his priesthood studies for love of drink and had become a hedge preacher, who could actually extemporise a sermon in verse, until he landed a job in Ludwigsburg as an organist, praised for his playing by Dr Burney as a truly great master.[14] He had to leave Württemberg purportedly for 'denying that there was a Holy Ghost' and followed a peripatetic career teaching music and inveighing against the clergy, which lost him employment at most places in which he found it. At the recommendation of Frederick the Great, who admired him for his bold anti-clerical utterances and loudly expressed admiration for Voltaire, he became general manager of the Stuttgart theatre, where he was reported as referring to the Stuttgart Karlschule as 'a slave factory'.[15]

'When Dionysius ceases to be a tyrant,' he remarked mordantly to anyone who could hear him, 'he becomes a school-master.' The real cause of his ultimate downfall was a misreport of the health of the Queen Empress of Austria carried in a newspaper he was editing from Ulm, and on a visit to his wife in Stuttgart he was arrested at the request of Vienna. His 'Serene Transparency' shut him for a year in solitary confinement, forbidden to read or to write, and then sentenced him to a further five years with visitor privileges. There both Goethe and Schiller came to see him, Schiller bringing the first draft of his play, *The Robbers*, and Schubart was allowed to write again as long as Charles-Eugene enjoyed any income he might make. Frederick II again intervened and after ten years secured his release. Those ten years had further softened Charles-Eugene's temper, so that he received the poet without rancour, which Schubart, glad to be free, reciprocated. However, incarceration had affected his health and, though he continued writing, meditating an extensive account of the Wandering Jew, it was never written and he was surprised by death in 1791.[16]

Charles-Eugene's other act of intolerance was to have a longer-lasting effect. Friedrich Schiller, studying medicine at the Karlschule, was treated as the son of a noble as his father enjoyed a commission in the army. He nearly suffered a similar fate to Schubart for *The Robbers*, which he wrote and produced there. After the school production he was reprimanded but its production professionally in Mannheim, to attend which Schiller took French leave, could not be overlooked. A doctor in the army was, however, more valuable to the Duke than an organist in the chapel, so he escaped prison. But the play going round in Schiller's head, *Intrigue and Love (Kabale und Liebe)*, was to portray a debauched professor, an insatiable sexual hyena, whipped up by the desire for, and chase of new victims.[17] The target of its polemic was pretty obviously the court of Ludwigsburg, the insatiable hyena was Charles-Eugene, and the Countess Francisca was the model for the young *bourgeoise* whom the insatiable hyena wished to corrupt. The better to get away while he could, Schiller took himself off one night, abandoning both his career and medicine. Carlyle believed that the fate of Schubart encouraged Schiller to flee Ducal service at Ludwigsburg.[18] His self-imposed exile was not to be permanent, for he did return to Ludwigsburg in 1793, when Charles-Eugene was on his death-bed. Francisca, now married to her widowed lover, gave him rooms in the palace where he assiduously wrote the *Wallenstein* trilogy through the nights, with his feet in a bowl of cold water, writing a masterpiece while hastening the tuberculosis to which he succumbed ten years later.

Charles-Eugene may have espoused economy – Dr Burney thought it was more apparent than real for, apart from maintaining an immense theatre, he employed 90 performers and scores of menial extras. 'Indeed the expense so far exceeded the abilities of his subjects to support ... to such excess as to ruin both his country and his people' but he could not suppress his passion for building.[19] In 1768, he had renovated a semi-ruined palace at Hohenheim outside Stuttgart that had once belonged to the family of Theophrastus Paracelsus, which he gave first to a singer who was sharing his bed and then to Francisca. After a visit to England in 1775 he surrounded it with a garden, *à l'anglais*, complete with cottages, a model farm and a mill, and a rustic hut, which Francisca made into her Pavilion of Fantasy. In memory of a visit to Naples and of the Roman pleasure grounds of Baiae, he then added a miniature series of Roman villas, grottoes and temples, surrounded by a landscaped chaos of rocks, trees and statuary, and enclosing a small concert hall. But Europe was growing out of the fantasy of dairies without milk and hermitages without hermits. Goethe, visiting in 1797, was shocked at the evidence of extravagant and useless spending represented by the Ducal palaces in Stuttgart, Hohenheim and Ludwigsburg, each of them monstrosities, as he saw them, of a restless and small-minded fantasist.[20]

The fantasist was stimulated by the foreign travels he made with Francisca. Though she loved domesticity and rural bliss she also had a royal taste in jewellery. London society – being a 'good' Protestant princess, Francisca was given a royal audience – was impressed by her simple and modest demeanour and her shepherdess's *chapeau*. But they were to be astonished, at the banquet given by the Prince of Wales, by her collane estimated to be worth a quarter of a million livres. The Duke also decided to improve his mind by visits to universities, believing that the students of Cambridge, no doubt with memories of Schiller in mind, had far too much freedom, which was dangerous. The Grand Duke of Weimar, Charles-August, told Goethe that he found that this elderly general of hussars ridiculous, assiduously taking notes, with his great round Swabian head adorned by a grotesque moustache.[21]

The couple were in Paris shortly after the fall of the Bastille – Francisca actually attended a dramatic representation of that epochal event at the theatre, and in 1791 Charles-Eugene attended a meeting of the National Assembly. But he recognised that he was no longer safe in Paris, despite having a revolutionary cockade about his person. Back in Württemberg he tried to preserve his Duchy from French anger by refusing the émigré Prince de Condé more than a few weeks visit to his family in a modest inn.

Charles-Eugene died in 1793, and was succeeded by his two younger brothers who were both over 60 when they came to the throne. Their reigns were short and undistinguished. The elder was effectively a Frenchman, having served with the French army, and as a resident in Paris, he had become one of Voltaire's circle and entered into the spirit of his times by a series of liaisons with actresses, once even competing for favours with Casanova. Then he suffered a sea change, resigned his commission and his mistresses and told Voltaire he was tired of pleasure. He retreated to a sylvan chateau with a beautiful Saxon, whom he later married, until he became Duke of Württemberg. Francisca went into self-imposed exile, the new Duke insisted on the use of French for all official business and closed the Karlschule as being a hotbed of Germanism. That did not make him a liberal and he was among the first to volunteer to lead his troops into action against Revolutionary France.

His successor, Frederick Eugene, had also been a soldier but this time in the service of Prussia and had found himself at the time of the Seven Years War ranged on the opposite side to his brother. He had married a niece of Frederick the Great and was much concerned over the education of his sons, even consulting Rousseau, who told him that as he had not had the ill-fortune to be born a prince he could not really help. Württemberg was to be engulfed in the wars with France, and Frederick Eugene died in 1797, after being chased out of his Duchy by the army of Jean Moreau. For the revolutionary wars were changing the dream of Pumpernickel into a nightmare, now to afflict the peaceful and Catholic south.

CHAPTER EIGHT

The Catholic South

Bavaria and Würzburg

At the time of my father's birth, the language spoken in his
family was French, the temper and setting of their lives retarded
eighteenth century, their seat had always been in a warm corner
of Baden, that mild, bland, rural country of meadows and trout
streams, small farms, low mountains and small towns; their
world was Catholic, Western, Continental Europe, and the
centre of their world was France. They ignored, despised and,
later, dreaded Prussia, and they were strangers to the sea.
(Sybille Bedford, *A Legacy*, 1964, Penguin paper edition, p. 28)

O F THE SOUTHERN states that clustered round the Black Forest and
the Rhine, the largest and most important was Bavaria. She had
emerged from the Thirty Years War, though devastated by French and
Swedish armies, not only intact but also larger by the incorporation, at
the peace of Westphalia, of the Upper Palatinate. This made her, after
Austria, the largest single principality in the German world, and her
rulers found that their existence as a marcher state between France
and Austria made for uncomfortable and often tragic choices. Elector
Maximilian II (*regnavit* 1679–1726) espoused the wrong side in the War
of the Spanish Succession and his electorate was marched and fought over
once more by rival armies. He was lucky to retain his Electorate whole at
the peace. Under his successor, Maximilian III (*regnavit* 1745–77), Bavaria
enjoyed a relatively tranquil time. He curbed the financial extravagance
of builders, which after 1720 had become almost drunk with decoration,
founded an Academy of Sciences, did what he could to reduce clerical

power by suppressing the Society of Jesus (1773) and tried to increase prosperity. His death without an heir in 1777 was to plunge Bavaria once more into war.

The new Elector, from a branch of the Wittelsbachs, was a dynast with, himself, no legitimate heir. Charles Theodore (*regnavit* 1777–96) had ruled the Electoral Palatine from 1742 reasonably well, but despite being affectionately known as First Cavalier of the Holy Roman Empire, and reputed to be the father of over 1,000 bastards, he was to enrol himself in the ranks of those Pumpernickel princes who were obsessed by dreams for their bastards and indulgence for themselves.[1] Disputes over his succession to the Electorate erupted into a 'potato war' (War of the Bavarian Succession, 1778–9), a Pumpernickel conflict between rival German states who spent most of it trying to deprive each other of food supplies, at the end of which there was further exchange of territory.

Charles Theodore, having gained an Electorate, would not abandon his intrigues to gain a crown. He proposed that he should be King of Burgundy, exchanging Bavaria for the Austrian Netherlands, a project thwarted, if it was ever seriously proposed, by a league of princes headed by Frederick II. So he used the wealth he had acquired from the suppression of the Jesuits, originally intended to endow more educational establishments, to set up in 1782 a priory of the Knights Hospitaller of St John of Jerusalem, Rhodes and Malta.

The Elector believed that this was what the Bavarian nobility wanted and, to give it more status, he wanted it elevated into one of the national Tongues (*Langues*) of the Order. Elaborate diplomatic manoeuvres secured the cession from England's George III of the Order's defunct title of Tongue of England so that it could become the Anglo-Bavarian Tongue. To this was added the newly created Priory of Poland in the territories recently acquired at its latest partition (1796) by the Czar of Russia. The English Tongue when it had existed had provided the senior chivalric soldier of the Order, the Turcopilier, commander of the light cavalry force, known as Turcopoles which, from their great fortress of Krak, had contested the land with raiding bands of Arabs ('Turks'). That title now passed to the new Tongue. Bavaria had last been involved in a war against the Ottomans in the 1680s, but though Charles Theodore claimed that he had endowed the Priory to fight against the enemies of Christendom, he really intended the Grand Priory for one of his bastards, a dignity the Grand Prior continued to hold when he was married, contrary to the rules of the Order.[2]

The Priory, along with that of Poland, was created to satisfy the appetite of the central European nobility for titles and orders. They had little intention of fighting the Turks; many of them were in the employ of sovereigns who had special relations with the Ottoman Empire and increasingly accepted its legitimate membership of the comity of nations. It was a reflection of the growing popular passion for medievalism feeding on the carcase of ancient chivalries, about to be slain by the oncoming tempest of the French Revolutionary and Napoleonic Wars.

The Bavarians had 'something of the healthy vitality and directness of the peasant', unsophisticated, conservative and traditionalist by nature.[3] By and large they were loyal, if rather oppressed, Roman Catholics, living in a rich environment of gorgeous churches, with comforting and well-organised pilgrimages to numerous shrines, collecting alms and sustenance from well-endowed abbeys. They shared with Austrians the southerner's delight in pageantry and ritual; the drama of both was a constant pleasure so that the delight that their lay and religious superiors took in the baroque theatricalism of their palaces and churches was also that of the common man. The baroque sensuality of rhythm and tone entered their sense through the eye, rather than the ear. If anti-clericalism had manifested itself in the suppression of the Jesuits this was not because the Society had built extravagantly but because it had seemed to stray from its primary purpose. The suppression, moreover, had showed few of the promised benefits, as the educational colleges the government promised did not appear. It had only 'liberated' the population from a Society that had, after all, educated it. With nothing but a fanciful charade of Knights of Malta to replace it, the faithful slipped into intellectual torpor. A largely rural community was more interested in agriculture than culture, in the simple and traditional feasts of a people who did not like change, and in the intellectual ferment that was stirring the rest of Pumpernickel any voice from Bavaria was either inaudible or easily silenced.

* * *

A characteristically Pumpernickel principality of the Catholic south was not an Imperial duchy, but a bishopric, which also beggared itself in wanting to out-Louis Louis XIV. The Duke of Marlborough's victory at Blenheim in 1704, during the War of the Spanish Succession, had brought most of the Rhineland and south German lands under Imperial control. The Elector of Bavaria and the Archbishop Elector of Cologne, being brothers, and imprudent allies of France, prudently took themselves to France, where Bavaria married a Bourbon princess. For ten years they enjoyed the hospitality of Louis XIV during his declining, increasingly solipsistic years, and they became heavily influenced by French taste and dreamed of living, when the war was over, a life surrounded, as was the Sun King's, by magnificence. On their return to their Electorates at the Treaty of Utrecht, the princes revived earlier building plans. They both engaged French or French-trained architects to build and craftsmen, long domiciled in Germany, to decorate the buildings they created. Though the model for a German princely palace might be Versailles, this was more a cultural statement than an architectural. The monarch in his palatial city might imitate the pomp and circumstance of *un petit Roi Soleil*, but the palace itself was likely to be partly designed, partly built and largely decorated in the Italian, late baroque style by Roman or Swiss-Italian architects and craftsman, often trained in Rome and in France, but more often than not in Habsburg Vienna.[4]

The result was a series of elaborate confections, churches, hunting lodges and palaces, each one a paradise of cherubs and angels, in an Eden-like forest of curlicues, and arabesques of carved wood and stucco, of intricate iron gates and grilles, of frescoed ceilings and vaults, in which scenes of gruesome martyrdom were performed in exuberant frames of decorative joy. Art historians argue on the chronological shifts in the rococo and baroque styles,[5] but as the limitations of ecclesiastical power and influence helped to create, in the Protestant Pumpernickel states, a passion for the biblically sacred music of Bach and Handel, in the sunnier Catholic south church lands were still profiting from a lucrative pilgrimage traffic, and as a result enormously rich. The passion of its princes was for building, or for rebuilding and adapting existing spaces as replicas of an opulent, generous, Paradise, in which the senses could enjoy an almost Islamic indulgence. Their palaces were not usually more extensive than the Anglo-Palladian mansions that the Whig aristocracy was ordering in Britain; they were just more sumptuous, florid and gorgeous. Much of the decoration, particularly of their churches, was illusion; scagliola imitated marble, gilded whitewood replaced gold, frescoed ceilings pretending to be domes banished vaults, and windows gave illusions of space, the cunning positioning of light and statuary in altar pieces creating an impression of dramatic activity.[6] Indeed by 1720 few churches had any straight lines or flat surfaces at all. 'Arches swing in all directions. Wall surfaces seem in rhythmical movement. Concave curves interplay with and set off convex ones.'[7] The primary object was to give the eye something of joy to behold, leading heavenward to the realms of paradisal bliss, serving for the eye what Bach in Lutheran churches had intended for the ear.

If the monasteries and religious houses had money to embellish their abbeys and pilgrimage churches, the territorial, electoral Bishops were ready to spend their secular revenues on building palaces. The palaces were a blend of the triumphalist style of Louis XIV and the interior splendours of Papal Rome, to emphasise that they wielded both royal and temporal power. Würzburg was a Princely Bishopric in lower Franconia, on the River Main. It was significant as the burial place of the great Minnesinger and noble aspirant to Wagner's *Mastersingers of Nürnburg*, Walther von der Vogelweide. The Bishop's palace was a fortress, on a hill overlooking the town, until the election of Johann Philipp Franz von Schönborn, who found it lacking in features worthy of a Prince-Bishop. In 1720, a year into his reign, he was successful in a lawsuit that awarded him a princely, non-ecclesiastical fortune, and at once he decided to build something worthier of his rank. Balthasar Neumann was his military architect, 32-years-old and still studying in Paris, which was where artistic taste was to be acquired. A ground plan was ready within months but Neumann's ideas were not grand enough for the Bishop's relatives.[8]

The Schönborns were an extended noble family, whose tentacles had already spread over south Germany and whose accumulated wealth had made them all great builders. One was the Prince-Bishop's uncle, the Elector of Mainz, and Prince-Bishop of Bamberg. He had already constructed his *Schloss* from 1711–18 to house a family picture gallery, with an Italian frescoed ceiling, and with public rooms and a chapel decorated by German stuccoists. The other was his brother, the Arch-Chancellor of the Holy Roman Empire in Vienna, who had already used the leading Viennese architect, Lukas von Hildebrandt, to remodel and decorate his *Schloss* in southern Austria.[9] The Schönborns had their own ideas and their own architects. The building in which the Bishop wished to live was designed to be a masterpiece of individual splendour. It also initiated, in its eclectic and lavish style, what came to be known as Würzburg rococo[10].

The influences are both French and Viennese, and the Prince-Bishop who could not wait to see building start moved to a nearby house, so that he could supervise progress. He did not live to see it completed, dying in 1724, cordially detested by his subjects as an exacting and single-minded autocrat. Despite the election of a modest scholar as Prince-Bishop, the von Schönborn family did not stop employing Neumann to continue work on the palace, until the Viennese Arch-Chancellor was elected Bishop five years later in 1729 and imported his architect from Vienna. Thereafter Neumann had to deal with an opinionated and irascible Lukas von Hildebrandt but, despite this, there was rapid progress with building until the death of the Bishop and the succession of a prelate whose avarice was legendary. He suspended work and dismissed Neumann. After three years he died unlamented and another Prince-Bishop, not a Schönborn this time but a cultivated and ambitious prelate, re-engaged Neumann and pushed on with the gardens and interior decoration.

Würzburg is a showcase for German taste, a daring fusion of the French Regency and Viennese Imperial styles, and Balthasar Neumann engaged craftsmen from all over the empire to create the 'Würzburg rococo', and made it a distinctive residence among palaces. For one thing it did not celebrate a dynasty but a place. The mythical heroes and Roman dynasts, from whom so many princes liked to give the impression that they were descended, were inappropriate for a Prince-Bishop whose ancestors may have been swine-herds. Instead the palace celebrated the ecclesiastical events of the diocese, culminating in the magnificent frescoes by the Tiepolo family (1750–2) depicting *The Marriage of the Emperor Barbarossa to Beatriz of Burgundy* in 1156, *The Granting of the Title Duke of Franconia by Barbarossa* in 1168, and *Apollo Driving the Bride of Barbarossa in the Sun Chariot*.

The munificent Bishop who commissioned what was intended to be the largest fresco in the world, Carl Philipp von Greiffenklau, allowed himself to be commemorated in the fresco over the staircase, as patron of the arts under the protection of the sun god Apollo. Balthasar Neumann died before the Tiepolos finished the great fresco, and the Prince-Bishop died a year after his apotheosis had been completed. Neumann's design for a huge Imperial palace at the end of an immense square, to emphasise the particularity of power, was not untypical of princely palaces, though none quite matched it for size, grandeur and decorative genius. The grandeur of the conception was, however, designed not only to serve the greater glory of God, but also the greater glory of the Church, which had for centuries claimed a primacy over princes. Though that primacy was being eroded by secular powers, the surviving symbolism of the medieval division of the world between Papacy and empire, two co-equal authorities, was played out in the art and architecture of Würzburg.[11] It was almost the last time that the Church was able to compete for magnificence with the secular princes of Pumpernickel. Another domain in which the Church reigned supreme was in the glory of God celebrated not in the visual and plastic arts but in music.

CHAPTER NINE

Magic: Musical Germany

The Well-Tempered Clavier

To anyone walking though the streets … during summer this
place must seem to be inhabited only by a colony of Musicians,
who are constantly exercising their profession: at one house
a fine player on the violin is heard; at another a German
flute; here an excellent oboe; there a bassoon, a clarionet, a
violincello or a concert of several instruments together.
(Dr Charles Burney in Schwetzingen, the summer retreat of the
Elector Palatine, 1771)[1]

*T*HE CIVILISATION OF Pumpernickel may have struck its more
sophisticated visitors as gravely in need of uplift, more washing,
more forks, more refined plates, more conversation, less drinking
and stuffing itself with gamey meat and spiced pies, fewer robust and
energetic dances, and fewer buffoons, but in one respect they did not
need to keep referring to the superiority of France. Its princes, secular
and clerical, absolutist, enlightened or not, even the burghers of its free
cities, preferred cantatas to controversy, symphonies to society, passions
to politics and quartets to quarrels. By the turn of the eighteenth century
music, unconfessional and migratory as it was, was part of the cement
that joined Germans in a common culture, no matter how otherwise
politically or religiously divided.

There was, however, a reflection of the cultural inferiority in the
preoccupation for technical wizardry not innovation. In 1705, two of the
supreme performers of their day went to hear Dietrich Buxtehude play
the organ of the Marienkirche at Lubeck, then part of the kingdom of

Denmark. Johann Sebastian Bach walked 200 miles across the patchwork country from Arnstadt in Thuringia, and Handel travelled from the free city of Hamburg to see if he might succeed the Dane in his post. Musicians were mobile, seeking patrons who either wanted better music, or paid better. Bach himself, in his professional life, changed his residence three times, moving from Weimar to Arnstadt, from there to Cöthen and finally to Leipzig. His son, Carl Philipp Emanuel, served Frederick the Great in Berlin for 27 years before moving to Hamburg and comparative freedom. Telemann migrated from Frankfurt am Main to Hamburg; Gluck, born in Bavaria, worked in Paris and produced his operas to classical themes in libretti by an Italian, ending as virtually court composer to the Emperor in Vienna; Haydn spent most of his time in the service of two Hungarian princes, and both Mozart and Beethoven moved to Vienna from the clerical/Electoral states of Salzburg and Bonn. This cosmopolitan world of music was to provide the seedbed of the German intellectual revival. The human voice required words to sing, and the demand for songs to add to the hymns of Martin Luther which were the staple of church music, for devout texts to sing as cantatas, and for new operas to exalt princely prestige gave the German voice a chance to compete with, even supplant, the *lingua musica*, Italian, and its assertive rival, French. James Boswell, by no means a music lover, was impressed enough by the Duke's chapel at Brunswick in 1764 to write: 'I hear a psalm performed with magnificent music, eunuchs and other singers from the operas, an organ, a French horn, flutes, fiddles, trumpets. It was quite heaven.'[2]

Johann Sebastian Bach, George Frederick Handel, (to give him his English name) and Domenico Scarlatti (born in Naples and choir master at St Peter's in Rome from 1714–19) all shared the same year of birth, so that 1685 marked an *annus mirabilis* in the birth of baroque music. They were, each of them, virtuosi performers on the keyboard. The Bachs were a musical dynasty; Johann Sebastian's father was music director of the town of Eisenach in Thuringia; his uncle, Johann Christoph, was an organist and composer. Throughout the Thirty Years War, the earlier family had survived and proliferated and in neighbouring Erfurt musicians were colloquially referred to as *Bachs*. Church music was the popular, indeed perhaps the only generally accessible, art of the time, and Johann

Sebastian could not study enough of it. His elder brother, who took on his upkeep when their parents died, tried to curb his enthusiasm, either out of envy of his prodigious musical facility or to save him from overwork. It was said that Johann Sebastian's eyesight was ruined by his copying, by moonlight, the music he could snatch from his brother's collection, much of it Italian and French. He was 19 when, as organist at Arnstadt, he walked to Lubeck to hear Buxtehude play, overstayed his leave of absence, and further upset the church elders on his return by his daring and exuberant harmonisation at the organ.

In that world of precocious and experimental musicality, Johann Sebastian was already an acknowledged master in his twenties, and when appointed in 1714 as *hofkonzertmeister* to the Duke of Weimar he could give full reign to the composition of sacred music. From Weimar he went to Cöthen and, after six years, to Leipzig in Saxony where he stayed as paterfamilias to an ever-expanding family of Bachs, finding time to compose a cantata a week, copy or supervise the copying of the parts, and rehearse and perform them with his church choirs. But even in the sophisticated musical world of Saxony, the elders of the Thomasschule, where he was cantor, were critical of his style, finding the 'well-ordered music in the honour of God' too theatrical, too unecclesiastical, which to their ears marred what to our ears are his greatest triumphs, the *Mass in B Minor* and *The St Matthew Passion*.[3]

Yet few of these compositions were published in his lifetime. Rameau still reigned supreme as the model for 'modern' music and Johann Sebastian was prized by his employers as a performer; as a composer he was too overshadowed by his son, Carl Philipp Emanuel (1714–88), who, when appointed court composer by Frederick the Great in 1747, invited his father to visit the Prussian court. For the father this visit seemed the summit of felicity and recognition, but it was short-lived and he was going blind. Three years later he was dead, his musical compositions passed to his five musical sons and, though he was honoured as perhaps the greatest keyboard player of his age, they fell into neglect. Despite Goethe's admiration for his work, Bach was considered a 'learned and arid pedant', half his compositions remained unpublished and unperformed, and it was mainly his instrumental music that was published during his lifetime and that of his children. Samuel Wesley, no mean organist himself, might call him St Sebastian but it was not until Felix Mendelssohn conducted *The St Matthew Passion* in 1829, only once performed in the 100 years since it had been written, that Johann Sebastian was accepted as not merely a musician's musician but one of the glories of German music.[4]

∗   ∗   ∗

There was only one other musician who could share this plinth with Johann Sebastian Bach, as master performer of the age. Despite their peregrinations to hear Buxtehude play and despite invitations to visit Leipzig, Bach and Handel, both born in the same golden year, never met. Handel's father was surgeon-barber to the court of the Duke of Saxe-Weissenfels, some 20 miles from Halle where Handel was born. The Duke, Johann Adolph I, was a music lover and employed the organist of the Liebfrauenkirche at Halle as resident court musician, who endowed his church with an extensive collection of German and Italian music. This proved a gold mine for the young Handel who, despite his father's wish that he should study to become a lawyer, could not resist playing any keyboard instrument he could find. He even smuggled a little clavichord into a disused room at the top of his father's house, so that he could play out of earshot and uninterrupted. He had to be content with this reclusive music making until he accompanied his father to the Duke's court and found a harpsichord to play on.

The child was insatiable; only the removal of his fingers would have prevented his playing any keyboard instrument in sight. His prodigious talent came to the attention of Duke Johann Adolph, who tactfully agreed with his surgeon-barber that, while music, as a profession, was not one in which pre-eminence could be as rewarding as the law, George Frederick was, nonetheless, clearly a musical virtuoso. Princes liked virtuosi, just as the Soviet state was later to do, as giving distinction to an otherwise uninspired court. While Handel could be prepared for the law, he need not be discouraged from becoming also a master in what was an elegant art and a fine help to the digestion of gross meals. The barber-surgeon allowed himself to be persuaded; his son should have a professional music teacher and George Frederick left the court with his pockets full of the Duke's largesse to find one.

This tale epitomised the virtue of a little court and a reasonably enlightened ruler, and Germany through the ensuing century was fortunate that the prevailing climate of relative peace and order (relative, that is, to the period of the Thirty Years War) allowed music to flourish as an essential attribute of princedom. It was so essential that musical court service became a form of caged slavery, while princes presided over a musical establishment that could be both a zoo and a prison, musicians of varying distinction being bound in contracts of service that impeded movement and development. Archbishop Colloredo of Salzburg has his place in history for the short rein on which he tried to keep Mozart while Frederick the Great made it very difficult for Carl Philipp Emanuel Bach to leave his service in Berlin. The young Handel, and his father (for different reasons) were determined to avoid this form of slavery. The father refused an offer from the Hohenzollern King of Prussia to assume responsibility for his son's musical education in Italy in return for a contract of service that would have bound him to Berlin, because he needed his son to look after him in his declining years. The father died in 1697 when Handel was only 12, but the son still never allowed himself to accept a court appointment. Because it would have entailed marrying his plain daughter, he had early decided not to accept, if offered, the post of successor to Buxtehude at Lubeck.

By 1704, already his mind was turning towards opera. Poverty dictated that foreign composers and singers, mainly Italian, were too expensive for smaller courts like Saxe-Weissenfels, which hoped to find its music and performers homegrown. The richer opera houses, founded between 1679 and 1692, were those of Hamburg, the oldest opera house in Europe, Hanover, 'much finer than that of Vienna',[5] and Brunswick. Leipzig's, (modelled on *La Fenice* in Venice) was built as the largest house north of the Alps by Augustus the Strong to mark his election to the throne of Poland in 1733. Dresden's, in an exercise of civic pride and competition, was built in 1741. These civic houses were large and rich enough to compete in the international market, and the *singspiels*, ballets and musical presentations were usually sung by Italians, performed by Germans and danced by French. By the middle of the century an opera house and theatre were accepted as essential requirements of each principality. Frederick II, released from the philistinism of his father, opened one in

Berlin (1742) to make its mark on a musical and literary culture that was otherwise essentially Italian or French. Even so, the works performed may have been by Germans, but they were performed in French or Italian.

Handel's first opera, *Almira*, performed in the Free City of Hamburg in 1705 in German, was adapted from a Venetian libretto and the music reappears in later Handelian works. It was repeated over 20 nights, as much from fear of the cost of a new production as from the quality of the music. Public taste, however, in Germany was shifting towards coarse comedies or spectacles, which were more easily understood in the German language and which in their turn attracted the hostility of the Lutheran Church, which only promoted their success by unsuccessful attempts to ban them. Handel was now 21 and saw little future in this market, so he decided to go, as any writer of vocal music knew he must, to Italy, 'the great school of Musick and Painting'.[6] Italy was even more Pumpernickel-oid than Germany, but it was richer and more confident, parts of it belonged to states of universal importance, like Tuscany, the Papacy and Spain, and it was blessed by nature and, even more attractive as a substitute for power, by art.

Despite his Lutheran upbringing, Handel found an immediate welcome from influential Catholics. He had already met the Medici Prince Ferdinand in Hamburg who, impressed by his musical skills, had offered to take him to Florence. But, ever independent, Handel made his own way there, where, plundering tunes from *Almira*, he wrote his first Italian opera, *Rodrigo*. Thence, no doubt with a Medici recommendation, he went to Rome. His performance on the organ of the church of St John Lateran was enough to find him immediate patrons. The Princes of the Church made no fuss about his religious affiliation, and were more munificent than the princes of Germany.

There was however one big difference. Clement XI, in the pontifical chair from 1700 to 1721, had something in common with the stern Pietists of Hamburg, a fear that opera was demoralising, none more so than for the roles it gave to women. So he had decreed that the great gift which God had given to the Italian voice should be devoted to sacred music, in which there should be no place for a woman. The first night of Handel's sacred oratorio, *La Resurrezione*, in 1708, mounted opulently by the Marchese Ruspoli, featured a woman singing the role of Mary Magdalene, but for subsequent performances, on Papal orders, she had to be replaced by a male castrato. The Papal decree however did not apply to secular courts, only to music performed in churches so Handel, using his Medici contact, picked up commissions from Naples to Venice for operas as well as for cantatas and oratorios, employing both male and female voices.

Handel's reputation as a harpsichordist had preceded him on his travels in Italy. Scarlatti, hearing the instrument played at a masquerade in Venice by a masked player, vowed that he was either the 'Saxon' or the devil, and the diplomatists at the Serenissima, especially the ambassadors of Hanover and of England, began to negotiate for his services.[7] Hanover had a magnificent opera house with famous stage machinery and its Elector, who kept a musical household of organist, two cantors, four French fiddlers, 12 trumpeters and a bugler, was quick with an offer of the post of *kapellmeister*.[8] The Elector's offer of employment included a grant of 12 months leave of absence with pay before Handel should take up the appointment. In Venice, Joseph Smith, banker, connoisseur and patron of Canaletto, spoke seductive words about the wealth and generosity of his countrymen, and Handel decided to take advantage of the Elector's offer to go to England, but not as court composer. In 1710, still free but wanted, he went to London to produce his Tassonian opera, *Rinaldo*, to an English libretto 'Italianised', for the occasion. It was an instant success, playing for 15 nights on its first presentation, and Handel knew where his future lay. In 1714 the Elector, who had offered him a most enticing contract, became the King of England, but Handel steered clear of royal appointment and became instead musical director of the Queen's, now the King's Theatre in the Haymarket. Resident in England, his lifetime's achievement was not to create a German operatic tradition in Germany, but Italian opera in England and a choral repertoire for English singers.

* * *

Italian opera ruled in England, France, Austria and Germany. It was dedicated to showing off the human voice in static arias with endless reprises, the singer rendering all the human emotions as he or she stood on the stage before making a dramatic exit to applause. Through the recitative that moved the story on to its next set piece the audience chatted away, drank coffee and even played cards. Operas were like staged chorales in church; only they were performed in a theatre and portrayed pagan heroes, and heroines, represented by real and very often by unreal women. The *castrati*, the international celebrities of the musical stage, whose doctored voices could range across the emotions, both male and female, competed to display the flexibility and agility of their *coloratura*. The plots were of little interest, mostly adaptations of what seemed to be a template of classical drama, or a rendering of Ovid. Everyone knew the drama; it was the voice they came to hear.

Typical of the musical taste of Pumpernickel was the northern state of Prussia, observed by Dr Burney when he visited Berlin in 1772. Frederick II had opened his specially constructed theatre in 1742 on assuming the throne, and provided entertainments there for free. None, however, was extravagant, since Frederick controlled the content and timing of the programmes, often checking that the performers were playing the music correctly. Frederick himself may have been a competent flautist but he did not play in public for he insisted on being both the undivided ruler of his state and the doyen of its intellectual and musical life, but also its first critic. Dr Burney was never presented to his musical majesty but did hear him perform. His musical taste was, however, circumscribed by the controlling influence of his flute masters and his aged *kapellmeister*. The operatic world was Italian. Though composers might be German they composed what were in effect Italian operas. A Brandenburger, Carl Heinrich Graun, (1704–59) as Frederick's *kapellmeister*, composed 32 operas to Italian libretti, one of which inaugurated the Berlin opera house in 1742. Another was actually set to a libretto by Frederick himself. Johann Adolph Hasse (1699–1783), a Rhinelander married to an Italian singer, was also an immensely popular composer and a friend of Metastasio. He composed operas for the Saxon court at Dresden and Warsaw,[9] and flute works for Frederick, moving later to Vienna, where the immense popularity of his work was to be eclipsed by Gluck. Frederick, moreover, was a musical martinet: 'His Majesty is such a rigid disciplinarian,' wrote Burney, 'that if a mistake is made in a single movement or evolution, he immediately marks and rebukes the offender.'[10] Frederick may have known genius when he heard it, but his own performances never did justice to the music of Carl Philipp Emmanuel, the Bach whose reputation had quite eclipsed that of his father, and he was for nearly 30 years (1740–67) virtually captive in Berlin.

The third son of Johann Sebastian, Carl Philipp Emanuel Bach was born in Weimar in 1714 and, though educated at the Leipzig Heilige Thomasschule where his father was cantor, studied law at the university. But he abandoned jurisprudence for music, taking a post under Crown Prince Frederick Hohenzollen, becoming, on Frederick's accession to the throne of Prussia in 1740, a member of the royal orchestra, rising to accompany the royal flautist on the harpsichord. Carl Philipp Emanuel then slowly built up his reputation, not as an accompanist to the flute, which gave him too subordinate a role but like Handel before him, as the foremost harpsichord player in Europe. He was restive in the service of Frederick, who did not understand his genius. The king preferred his earlier musical director and tutor in the flute, Johann Joachim Quantz, who as a polished courtier 'appreciated' the king's musical skills.[11] As no musician could leave the court without the king's permission it was not until 1767 that Carl Philipp Emanuel was able to accept a position as successor to his godfather, George Philipp Telemann, in Hamburg. There he was able to develop a style 'imitated and adopted by the performers upon keyed instruments in every other part of Germany'. Dr Burney met him here in 1772 – in Bach's words 'fifty years too late'. Though he found some of his music 'long, difficult, fantastic and far-fetched' he believed he was far 'before his father in variety of modulation; his fugues ... always upon new and curious subjects, and treated with great art as well as genius'.[12]

Burney was only reflecting the taste of his time in depreciating Johann Sebastian – this Carl Philipp Emanuel never did – but if Burney found the son's music often difficult or fantastic he was nonetheless one of the most innovative and prolific composers in Germany leaving, in addition to symphonies and operas, at least 200 sonatas for the clavier. As *kapellmeister* at Hamburg he was able to follow in his father's tradition and compose church oratorios, passions and cantatas. More important for Bach himself, however, he could experiment with the form that Stamitz was developing and Haydn perfecting, the symphonic, which he could not do in Frederick's service. Carl Philipp Emanuel spread his fame by judicious publication of his music so that his work became more popularly performed even than his father's. Mozart later acknowledged his musical parentage.[13]

* * *

Tastes, meanwhile, were changing. Audiences sometimes laughed at operatic fustian, and the success in 1752 of an Italian troupe in Paris playing *opera buffa* started an almost Aristophanian war between the classical and the modern. Giovanni Battista Pergolesi (1710–36) was a Neapolitan meteor who in his short life succeeded in changing musical taste. *La Serva Padrona (The Maid becomes the Mistress)* was produced in Paris in 1733, as a diversion midway through a serious Lully opera. The result was a furore and a pamphlet war known as *La Querelles des Bouffes*, which claimed that opera should not always be about serious matters but could be amusing, a cause supported by such Parisian luminaries as Denis Diderot, the Encyclopedist, and Jean Jacques Rousseau who composed his own diversion, *Le Devin du Village*. The quarrel established an acceptable operatic divide, admitting that both *opera seria* and *opera buffa* had their place in the opera house, even if Paris was to consign them to separate houses.

Audiences had been invited to laugh with operas like *La Serva Padrona* not at them, and the lilting melodies and animated ensemble singing captured the changing spirit of the popular age. An appetite for rustic ballades and folk songs, and an enthusiasm for nature and dancing milkmaids, began to wean German taste from both coarse buffoonery and classically grand arias and stately reprises. Comic operas in the German language now vied for performance with heroic dramas in French.

For the plots from which to choose, libretti, largely confined to classical themes or adaptations of Ovid, were so limited that they appeared more than once in operas by different composers, and it was common for a new work to be the re-working of an old subject. The most popular and so often re-worked were the works of Pietro Metastasio, court poet in Vienna since 1729, and author of no less than 27 operatic libretti, some of them set to music by Handel and Mozart as well as by Graun and Hasse. Both new subjects and a new voice were needed if serious opera was not to die with the death in 1759 of Handel in London.

* * *

It was to take a Bavarian composer and an Italian poet to render audiences of German opera straight-laced again. But the Bavarian, Christoph Willibald Gluck (1714–87), was reared, not in German Bavaria, but in Czech Bohemia, the son of the gamekeeper to Prince Lobkowicz's estate. In nearly all schools, in villages as well as in towns, boys and girls were taught to sing and to play a variety of musical instruments, harpsichord, violin, oboe, bassoon and others, primarily so that the village schoolmaster who was also church organist could provide music in church worthy of his Maker. They were also prepared for service, each Bohemian noble family being able to mount a concert 'in-house' from among his servants. The general results of this system, in both Bohemia and Saxony were, according to Burney both 'rude and coarse', perfection not being the aim. Anyone who became an admirable musician would run away to a city where he could enjoy the fruit of his talents. 'If an innate genius (for music) exists, Germany is not the seat of it; though it must be allowed, to be that of perseverance and application.'[14] Gluck spent his adolescent years becoming a proficient fiddler, which helped to pay his way through the Charles University in Prague, and at the Lobkowicz Palace in Vienna he was, like Handel before him, persuaded by the patronage of an Italian prince to have his rustic skills honed and perfected in Italy.

The Italian appetite for opera soon took him over and he was composing lively scores and ballets to standard operatic settings. Invited to London in 1745, the year of the Jacobite invasion that closed the theatres for most of his time there, he found the huge shadow of Handel almost too oppressive. In Handel's view, Gluck 'knew no more counterpoint than his cook'[15] – not perhaps as contemptuous as it sounds as Handel's cook was a fine bass opera singer – but Gluck's work was not as musically sophisticated as Handel's, and Gluck knew it. He returned to Germany and joined an Italian operatic troupe which began to pick up commissions for him.

Gluck was never considered a German composer in the sense that Graun and Hasse, despite composing in Italian, were German. Only his parentage established him as the countryman of Bach and Handel but being born in Bohemia and steeped in the Italian tradition, he did not consider Germany as his homeland. All the time he was perfecting his technique until 1756, when Maria Theresa appointed him her court *kapellmeister*. What made him more than another faithful interpreter of Metastasio, the supreme creator and arbiter of classical drama across Europe – and who considered Gluck's renderings of his work that of an arch-vandal – was his partnership there with an impulsive Italian, Ranieri de Calzabigi. Between them they were to effect a sea change in the traditional rendering of classical drama, epitomised by the plays of Metastasio. They both wished to escape from the rigid Metastasian canon with its characters, who were often both musically and physically castrated, and to create tragic heroes and heroines of passionate flesh and blood. If in their operas, *Orfeo e Euridice* (1762), *Alceste* (1767) and *Paride e Elena* (1770), the dramatic intensity of Gluck's music and Calzabigi's words had too much of the northern *sturm und drang* to be wholly acceptable to the more relaxed and sybaritic Viennese, they inspired one of his former music pupils, the Archduchess Marie-Antoinette, who had just married the heir to the French throne in 1770, to invite him to Paris.

He went without Calzabigi, but with the support of the Dauphine *Iphigénie en Aulide* was performed in 1774. There he saw off a challenge to his ascendancy by the 'Italian' claque, headed by Mme du Barry. Even his grand rival, Niccola Piccinni (1728–1800), had to admit that Gluck's *Iphigénie* was finer than his own version, composed at the same time. But the war between the supporters of Gluck and those of Piccinni, the Viennese as opposed to the Parisian tradition, continued. The 'Piccinnists' refused to accept that Gluck's triumphant *Armide* (1777) and *Iphigénie en Tauride* (1779) made him the heir to Lully and to Rameau. His Italian claque determined that his next Paris opera should not enjoy the success of its predecessors, and though Gluck was now rich, secure and a society cynosure, they succeeded well enough for him to return to Vienna disillusioned in 1781. There, after a triumphant German version of *Iphigénie en Tauride*, he was revered, as Europe's most consummate writer of dramatic music, until the effect of early syphilis and drink brought on the stroke that killed him.

Dr Burney visited Vienna in 1770, before Gluck went to Paris, and the British ambassador was able to arrange a meeting with the composer, who like Handel had become 'a very dragon of whom all are in fear'. Burney impressed Gluck with his musical sensitivity and soon the composer played him the whole music of *Alcestis* and the score of *Iphigénie*, which existed so far only in his head and was soon to take Paris by storm. Two further meetings followed, one spent listening to Gluck's niece playing the harpsichord and to some early quartets by the young Haydn, after which they heard the Abbate Casti give one of his interminable improvisations. Before Burney left Vienna Gluck presented him with some of his manuscript scores. It was a successful visit.[16] Otherwise Burney was not overimpressed by the music he heard in Vienna.

∗   ∗   ∗

Burney remained devoted to the work of Handel, whose life he wrote in 1785, and to Metastasio, writing a memoir to accompany the publication of his letters in 1796. Though he admired Gluck's compositions, he did not remark on his skill in welding a dramatic impact from ensemble singing, or on his melodious ballet music and sharp delineation of character in music, without long autobiographical arias. These had been developed in Paris after Burney had seen him, and were an obvious inspiration for the work of Mozart and Beethoven, whom Burney never met – though he only died in 1814 – and eventually of Wagner.

With Mozart's own final return from Paris and movement to Vienna in 1781, music could be said to have outgrown the constraints of Pumpernickel court patronage. It had failed him in Mannheim, where he had spent a year from 1777–8, hoping to be commissioned to write an opera, and there musical performances were about as good as they could get. Boswell in 1765, though annoyed that the Elector Palatine had refused to ask him to dinner, acknowledged that 'he gives an opera and a French comedy and a concert, or an Academy of Music, as he calls it, all of which entertainments are really magnificent'.[17] Mannheim's orchestra was in Dr Burney's estimate second to none, and this he put down to the efforts of Johann Stamitz, (né Jan Stamic, 1717–57)) who joined the orchestra in 1741 and became a prolific composer of chamber music, symphonies for small ensembles and concerti for a variety of instruments. He was a pioneer of the classical symphonic structure of four movements, with opening theme, minuet, trio and a *prestissimo* last movement. On Stamitz's retirement in 1774 his place was taken by Mannheim's own son, pupil of Jomelli and Stamitz himself, Christian Cannabich, whom Mozart praised as the best musical director he had ever met.[18]

Dr Burney while acknowledging the orchestra's excellence thought its expense was prodigious, for it employed real musicians, many of them composers and soloists on their instruments, not just palace servants who happened to be able to play an instrument, 'an army of generals equally fit to plan a battle, as to fight it'.[19] Though Mozart's reputation had preceded him, the Electoral musical intendant thought he played the clavier only passably well. Mozart for his part had to admit that the orchestra was very strong, but the music it played was either too short – the prevailing taste was for brevity – or commonplace. Mozart told his father that the *kapellmeister*, Abt Vogler, was 'a dreary musical jester, exceedingly conceited and rather incompetent', who even disparaged Johann Christian Bach.[20] When Mozart did play before the Palatine Elector, Charles Theodore, and his children (mostly illegitimate), he suggested he might write a German opera for Mannheim but received a noncommittal reply. His hopes that the Elector might he a more generous and suggestible employer than Archbishop Colloredo came to nothing.

Though Mannheim had become the centre for German singers, money was short, and Mozart was only rewarded with a gold watch for his first concert. Any hope of an appointment at court – despite the fact that the musicians referred to him as *Herr Kapellmeister* – gradually wilted. He stayed as long he did because of the 'superb cantabile singing' of Aloysia Weber, whose sister he was eventually to marry and who sang his arias exactly as he could have wanted. The Elector would listen as often as he could manage to hear her and this influenced Mozart's expectations that he might be invited to compose an opera especially for her.[21] In the event, both the Elector and Aloysia turned him away. Due to his father's querulous anxiety about Wolfgang's morals, easy-going nature, and seeming incapacity to earn significant fees Mozart eventually decided to move. Leopold wanted him back in Salzburg, where there was steady if mediocre employment for the Mozart family team. Wolfgang, however, believed he had reached maturity enough to compose operas, which would earn good money in Paris. 'German Princes are all skinflint.'[22] To Paris he would go.

* * *

Carl Philipp Emanuel Bach's sonatas and his piano manual were the necessary bridge between music as entertainment, the background to card parties and gargantuan meals, and music for musicians. They anticipated the work of Haydn and Beethoven in Vienna where the house of the former Austrian ambassador to Berlin, Baron Gottfried van Swieten, who had commissioned six symphonies from Carl Philipp Emanuel, became a centre of musical creativity. There, Mozart presented his arrangement of Handel's *Messiah* and Haydn married music to the words of *The Creation* and *The Seasons*. Beethoven dedicated his first symphony to van Swieten. This courtly patronage was continued by Prince Paul Anton Esterhazy. He provided the studious and domestic Joseph with an orchestra, which he trained, both instrumentalists, soloists and chorus, for whom he composed music, copied all the parts and directed from the harpsichord, until it was as accomplished as any in the service of sovereign princes of German. This enabled him to develop Stamitz's symphonic form in 98 symphonies (numbers six to 104) of his own, and secure for the symphonic form its place as queen of the orchestral firmament from Königsberg to Naples, even reaching to Pennsylvania in the USA.[23]

Haydn never quite escaped from the need for music that could be played by amateurs, entertaining and light-hearted in the spirit of Pumpernickel and suitable for the out-of-door entertainment of which the Viennese were fond. But it was in the string quartet that Haydn sought the intelligence of music, in conversations between four instruments that could rise from the most exquisite dance to a profound fugue, which harked back to the age of Johann Sebastian Bach and Handel. Goethe in Weimar heard this 'conversation of four sensible people' and expected to learn something from their discourse.[24] The Pumpernickel musical centres of Dresden, Hanover, Berlin, and Mannheim, however, by the end of the eighteenth century, under pressure of war and French invasion, had ceded place to the Vienna of Mozart, Haydn and Beethoven. Haydn was the darling of its new, middle-class audiences, though Prince Esterhazy was not among them. He found Haydn's music too serious for his taste and, anyhow, he had built a new palace with a brand new opera house, and Haydn had to turn his hand to theatrical music again. There followed four operas; *L'Infedelta Delusa* (1773), to celebrate the name day of an Esterhazy princess, a marriage imbroglio pre-echoing Mozart; *L'Incontro Improvviso*

(1775), a harem romp set in Cairo – the original libretto had been written for Gluck; *Il Mondo della Luna* (1777), a satire on astrology and moongazing in a comedy to celebrate an Esterhazy wedding; and finally *L'Isola Disabitata* (1776), a deserted island fantasy looking backwards to *Robinson Crusoe* and forwards to *The Admirable Crichton,* and serious enough to call forth music strongly influenced by Gluck.

These operas all make gentle fun of their characters in the manner of Pergolesi and *opera buffa,* ideal for their setting and the occasions they celebrated. The Esterhazy palace was another princely Versailles, to which the new middle classes did not ordinarily go and their ideal setting was a garden like that of Garsington. Musically delightful, the libretti did not demand that Haydn delved into the raw emotions of his protagonists. They were variously entitled *un dramma giocoso per musica, una burletta* or *un dramma pastorale.*

It was to be Mozart, perhaps more than Haydn or Beethoven, who took the music of Pumpernickel and transformed it into music of the heart. His astonishing skill in hearing first, then reproducing and then improving upon the music of the masters who had gone before, allowed him to outstrip his models, whether they were Stamitz, Handel or Carl Philipp Emanuel Bach. Van Swieten's house was where Johann Sebastian Bach, neglected and almost forgotten, was rediscovered. Tamino and Pamina in *Die Zauberflöte* walk through fire and water to a Lutheran chorale from Johann Sebastian. In his piano concertos Mozart tried to revive and capture the kingdom of the clavier from memories of Johann Sebastian and Carl Philipp Emanuel Bach and of Handel. Mozart called his mature operas, performed ten years later than Haydn's, *giocosa* but they were also in their subtle delineation of the human personality, *seria.* Mozart insisted that *Don Giovanni,* was a drama *giocosa,* but in its penultimate scene, the appearance of the statue and the Don's descent into the underworld, stretched the opera to limits beyond what was expected of an *opera buffa.* The operas he composed to libretti by the spoiled abate, Lorenzo da Ponte, escaped the courtly shades of Pumpernickel and entered the market place of humanity, where laughter mingled with calamity, conclusions were not final and the human comedy was never ending.

∗ ∗ ∗

The dominance of the musical establishment of Vienna, no longer another Pumpernickel court, seemed to have established that if anywhere, it was to be the home of German opera. Yet Mozart's and Beethoven's two *singspiel*, *Die Zauberflöte* and *Fidelio*, had not shaken the belief that opera should be sung in Italian (or French). The protégé of the Bonapartes, Gaspare Spontini (1774–1851), was *kapellmeister* and chief conductor of the opera in Berlin, where he presided over the Italian preference and showed a marked hostility to any German, like Felix Mendelssohn, who wished to challenge it. Despite Spontini, however, the Italian preference was shaken by the production of a German *singspiel*, *Die Freischütz*, in Berlin in 1821.

With its production rocketing skywards, it became a new stellar luminary to rival and even outshine Rossini. The cousin of Costanze Weber, who married Mozart, Karl-Maria von Weber was born in Holstein, a German-speaking province of Denmark, and received his musical formation in Hamburg and Munich, and not Vienna, but he nursed ambition to do what the Viennese, Mozart and Beethoven, had not done: to create a Grand Opera for Germany. *Die Freischütz* was, for Weber, not to be it for, written in the tradition of the German *singspiel,* its characters spoke rather than sang the dialogue. He was on the threshold of writing seamless operas which would match the extravagant splendour of Paris, where Rossini had recently become Director of the Italian opera. Weber lamented that Gluck had gone to Paris rather than stayed in Vienna to effect his revolutionary ideas, and therefore had not written a 'German' opera. What Gluck had done for classical, essentially Mediterranean (Metastasian) themes, Weber intended to do for German.

He was in Dresden when a commission for an opera for the 1822 season came from Vienna. He had no subject and had to find a librettist. Ernst Theodore (Amadeus) Hoffman was in Berlin and as the author of numerous extravagant tales and an opera, *Undine*, loudly acclaimed; he seemed the obvious man to choose. Weber, however, selected instead a local poet and a woman, Wilhelmine von Chezy. Born in Berlin in 1783, granddaughter of a woman who had been dubbed the German Sappho, her life so far had been eventful. She had fled from an arranged marriage to a titled swindler, had almost been a model for Baron Ochs in *Der Rosenkavalier,* and under the protection of Shakespeare's German translator, Frederick Schlegel and his wife, who was Felix Mendelssohn's aunt, she established herself in Paris as a luminary of the German-speaking colony. She made a second, equally unhappy marriage to a French oriental scholar who preferred dusty archives and arcane Sanskrit texts to looking after his wife and children and Wilhelmine, keeping his name, went to settle in Dresden.

Weber had read her work and liked it. It satisfied his nascent Romantic imaginings, and when he met her on the bridge that spanned the Elbe he asked her to write him a libretto. She had no experience of the theatre, much less of the opera house, but the request was too flattering to refuse. Their collaboration was not a success. The libretto was either too Romantic or not Romantic enough, based on a medieval romance that Wilhelmine was to publish as *Euryanthe of Savoy*. Goethe was very decided that Weber had made a bad choice of material of which nothing could be made and should have known better.[25] The plot was obscure and complicated, resolving round a bet on the fidelity of a woman beloved by two men, who agree to a monstrous pact under which, if her infidelity was proved, all lands would pass to the lover who proved it. To unravel the plot would be a tedious venture, but it is embedded in Weber's melodic score: and featured what were becoming standard for a Romantic, German tale: a suicide, a poisoned ring, a tomb, a ghost and a secret. Euryanthe's story, when told by a jealous woman to her lover's rival, leads to her denunciation and the loss of her lover's lands. The ending is happy, owing to the intervention of a dragon (echoes of Mozart's *Die Zauberflöte*) which saves Euryanthe from death at the hands of the man who thinks she has betrayed him, and the revelation, at the prompting of a ghost, that the accusation was false.

Wilhelmine's original tale had included a telltale mole on Euryanthe's breast, the knowledge of which was 'the secret.' Knowledge of this mole, however innocently obtained, prompted a suspicion of carnal knowledge, and thus of betrayal. It was a device used often before, in *Le Roman de la Violette* in the fifteenth century, by Boccacio and by Shakespeare in *Cymbeline,* but Weber thought that the suggestion of intimacy was indelicate and preferred that the secret should require supernatural revelation. In addition to satisfying Weber's scruples, this gave him an opportunity to repeat the success of his sinister supernatural music, which had scored such a success in *Die Freischütz*. Poor Wilhelmine was to 'fire him, give him wings'[26] but her talents did not run to a fantasy that might have amused Fuseli. She tried to meet Weber's demands for a suitable text with such limited success that the composer changed one act 11 times. Despite its imperfections, Weber completed a score which moved from darkness into light, from complication into simplicity, from aria and declamation (in German) into a seamless musical whole which even his illustrious cousin-in-law had not achieved in *Die Zauberflöte*, and which was not to be surpassed until Wagner. Three years after its performance in Vienna, Weber died of tuberculosis before he could perfect the marriage of words, voice and music, which had evaded other German composers since Mozart's da Ponte operas.

Music was now transcending the baroque courts of Pumpernickel. It was no longer wholly aristocratic, performed according to strict ground rules (strictest in Berlin where Frederick refused to allow a minuet to form part of the newly emergent symphonic structure being tried by his clavichordist, Carl Philipp Emanuel Bach, on the grounds that it was frivolous, feminine and too pleasant to listen to). In the easy-going atmosphere of *fin de siècle* Vienna, Weber's was a new note to be heard, a yearning, human, almost personal voice of felicity or longing, even of disappointment, something which smacked of romance, indeed Romantic. Gluck's French and Mozart's Italian operas had prepared the ear for Weber's operas, which were to find apotheosis in the works of Richard Wagner. Under the revolutionary influence of France music was to become *sansculotte*, migrating from the courts to the drawing room, preparing an audience for Schubert, Schumann and Mendelssohn. Opera had become almost too grand, too expensive for the smaller Pumpernickel houses, requiring elaborate stage sets and machinery, and too many extras, though Liszt was able mount *Lohengrin* at Weimar in 1850. Yet it was to be the Pumpernickel sovereign *par excellence*, Ludwig II of Bavaria, who was to make it his lifework to beggar his state to promote singers, words and music that were essentially Romantic and German. Paris was to meet its match at last. German had become, not just a crutch for opera, but a language that touched something: the sublime, God, human greatness, nature, love or passion, what you will, over which her philosophers and poets had been wrestling for a century.

CHAPTER TEN

Pumpernickel Discovered

Boswell to Coleridge

Kant once set about proving the existence of God and a
masterly effort it was. But in ... the *Critique of Pure Reason*,
he saw its fallacy; and said of it – that *if* the existence could
be *proved* at all, it must be on the grounds indicated by him.
(S. T. Coleridge, *Table Talk*, 22 February 1835)

Know'st thou the land where the pale citrons grow,
The golden fruits in darker foliage glow?
Know'st thou it well, that land, beloved Friend?
Thither with thee, O, thither would I wend!
(S. T. Coleridge's translation from Goethe)

*E*NGLISHMEN IN THE eighteenth century seldom went to Germany unless
they were Baltic traders, mercenaries, or diplomatists though many
Germans came to England; apart from Hanoverians, the father of that
model for the *Boy's Own Paper* image of the resourceful Briton, Robinson
Crusoe, originated in Bremen.[1] The land was beautiful but savage, the
inns were more like barns than hostelries, and she was not Italy. But
there were those who were prepared to brave the delays incurred by the
inquisition of toll houses that peppered the bewildering proliferation of
sovereign states, and the misery of the wagon-like conveyances which
carried passengers along roads that were more like tracks through forests
popularly haunted by wolves, witches, goblins, demons and brigands.

In June 1764, Boswell left his law studies in Utrecht in exalted
company for the court of Frederick II in Berlin. The head of the party
was one of those Scottish nobles who had cast their lot in the Stuart cause

but whom the twists and turns of fortune had befriended. George Keith, the tenth Earl Marshal (Marischal) of Scotland, had fought in the German campaigns of Marlborough but chose to follow the Old Pretender in 1714 and abandoned his home country with his chief. In 1719 he led a Spanish filibuster expedition from Spain much of which was wrecked on the west coast of Scotland and Keith had an experience worthy of the pen of Robert Louis Stevenson in returning to Spain, where he was to spend the next 15 years. He found in Bonnie Prince Charlie an uncongenial chief and had no confidence in the 1745 rebellion. Instead he took employment with Frederick II, who sent him as his ambassador to the Bourbon courts in both Paris and Madrid. Frederick later appointed him as Governor of Neuchâtel where he met and befriended Rousseau.

Keith, for services discreetly rendered the Elector of Hanover, also King George II of England, was pardoned and pensioned and was able to buy back some of his estates in Scotland, but not to enjoy his hereditary title of Earl Marischal of Scotland. But he was loyal to his new chief, Frederick, and he was returning to Berlin with the Turkish ward he had adopted when his brother, another soldier of fortune, had found her abandoned at the siege of Ochakov. The lady, Mme de Froment, was married to a French resident in Berlin and was a veritable silent Sybil on all subjects except her hypochondria. Boswell, aged 24, had no difficulty in resisting her charms.[2]

The party called briefly on Hanover and the court of Duke Charles of Brunswick, where Boswell dined in 'the presence', and was later to his distinct gratification introduced to the Duke's family. The wife of the hereditary prince was disarmingly open, warning Boswell that his breakfast would consist of bad butter and brown bread.[3] Once in the Prussian capital there was plenty of cosmopolitan company with whom Boswell could play billiards and drink, though he remained surprisingly chaste. He met princes and princesses without number, with whom he was 'awkward', but not overawed.

In fact Boswell generally enjoyed himself in the little courts of Germany, where he traded heavily on his being the prospective laird of Auchinleck, and was very ready to accept that its equivalent rank in Germany was baron.[4] The princes by and large were affable, their female relatives were glad to talk French with a stranger whose French was less good than their own. He was decidedly put out when he received a less than cordial welcome from Charles Theodore, the Elector Palatine, at whose 'scurvy court' he was not invited to dine, the 'inhospitable dog'![5] At Karlsruhe he had the gall to ask the Margrave of Baden-Durlach, to be admitted to the Prince's Order of Fidelity, on the rather specious grounds that he was related obliquely to the noble Scot, Lord Keith.

✳   ✳   ✳

Boswell had gone to Germany to relieve his boredom at Utrecht. In 1796, 30 years later, two Romantic poets went with more serious intentions. Samuel Taylor Coleridge had conceived the idea of going to Germany before she was, like France, closed to English visitors by war. The fame of her scholars, the teaching of Kant himself and above all the chance to immerse himself in German poetry in its original language, and to translate 'all the works of Schiller' seemed an opportunity not to be missed. He would use the temporary benefits of Wedgwood generosity to complete his education at a university like Jena, which had become a beacon of 'the German enlightenment'.[6] He would return, bringing with him all the works of 'the German Theologians, and of Kant, the great Metaphysician' and would set up 'a school for eight young men at a hundred guineas each' and perfect them in universal knowledge, and wisdom.[7]

Wordsworth and his sister, who travelled with him, were looking for time and inspiration, he to write, she to motivate, but they were soon disenchanted by the Germany they encountered, dirty inns, incivility, overcharging and linguistic incomprehension. Coleridge, who did not share the shrinking solipsism of his fellow passengers, caroused and danced and talked incessantly in rough and ready German, and felt at home. Despite the dirt and dismal appearance of Hamburg, he and Wordsworth stayed two weeks and met Klopstock, where discussion of poetry ranged from Milton in French and the older German poets in Latin. The news at the time was dominated by Nelson's victory of the Nile, and everywhere the English went they were greeted with kindness and generosity. The poets, like Klopstock, Goethe, Wieland and Schiller, who had hailed the dawn of freedom in the 1790s, were now united in seeing Liberty metamorphosed into a Fury and England emerge as the remaining land of the free. Coleridge's ambition to socialise, to learn German, to broaden his conversational skills to entertain and illuminate, and his temporarily rather greater means, meant that he was inevitably to part company with the Wordsworths. William was in compositional gestation and wanted solitude and Dorothy wanted to be his solitary muse. They found the environment they needed deep in the Harz Mountains at Goslar in lower Saxony, while Coleridge went north.

The joint visit was originally planned for three months but Coleridge extended his, as he became the cynosure of society in Ratzeburg in the Duchy of Saxe-Lauenburg in Schleswig Holstein, which was soon to be absorbed into the kingdom of Westphalia and later given, at the peace, to Denmark. There, in a sort of Baltic Paradise, he lodged with the pastor, and was generously absorbed into the family, learning more German than he confessed he would have acquired from polite literature or even from polite society. His letters to Wordsworth at Goslar describing skating on the frozen lake found an echo in Wordsworth's own memories of skating in Cumbria in *The Prelude,* and the verses of *The Rime of the Ancient Mariner* are resonant with memories of the sombre Pomeranian coast and casually violent Baltic storms.[8]

Eventually Coleridge had himself enrolled as a student at the University of Göttingen. Founded in 1737 by George II of England as Elector of Hanover; it was a popular place for the English to study German, and Coleridge had plenty of convivial company before whom to show off. He became friendly with the Blumenbachs, father and son, and Blumenbach *père* being the most eminent ethnologist of the time Coleridge acquired from his teaching some advanced racial theories on the origin of language. By that time he was pretty fluent in German, though his accent was atrocious, and so he threw himself into his studies in the morning, walked in the afternoon and talked and drank the evenings away.

Carlyle recognised that Coleridge was one of the great talkers, perhaps the greatest of his age, but most of it was in the nature of a monologue 'like a lake or sea, terribly deficient in either goal or aim ... so that you felt logically lost, swamped near to drowning in this tide of ingenious vocables spreading out boundless as if to submerge the world'.[9] His fellow students were entranced. With exalted self-discipline, he set about a study of German poetry, intending to write a life of Gottfried Lessing, whom Frederick the Great had excluded from the Berlin Academy but whose *Laoköon* had become an iconic text. He was assiduous in following his work plan, and baffled his confused companions at night as he expounded what he had learned from the early German mystics and Immanuel Kant.

The university had become one of the most visited in Germany. Under Hanoverian electoral rule it enjoyed religious peace and little distraction from deep study and convivial conversation, comparing most favourably with the Cambridge where Coleridge and most of the English students in Göttingen had studied. Apart from his Germanic studies Coleridge also attended lectures on physiology, anatomy and natural history, so that his mind was in a constant ferment of information and speculation. He, too, enjoyed the wild, often savage countryside; he climbed the Brocken – site in the Harz Mountains of Faust's *Walpurgisnacht* – where he hoped to see the spectre. He did not. He accepted the often bleak savagery of peasant life, its superstitions and survivals, many of which appeared in his later poems, and which seemed to explain why Germans could be both religiously sceptical but also devout. He translated the lyric verses of Stolberg, and other Swiss poets, he loosely adapted the poems of Goethe, Lessing, Schiller and German folk songs, and he amassed notes and memories for the works on Lessing and German metaphysics which he proposed to write on his return to England. The books were not written but his notes did provide matter for the lectures on Germany he was later to give in London.

Coleridge suffered from a mixture of homesickness – his wife had had to cope in his absence with the untimely death of their second child – and elation with his German experience. It was the latter that made him postpone his return long after the Wordsworths had packed up and gone. He eventually left Göttingen in June 1799, in a social blaze. Blumenbach gave him a party; his guests were astonished at Coleridge's flow of fluent talk in execrable German and his exposition of the thought of Kant. His confidence that he understood the sage astonished one auditor who had entirely failed to do so.[10] He then walked most of the way home, searching for Lessing papers in libraries, and laughing delightedly at the vagabond appearance and smell of him and his companion. His travel letters were to light a trail of pedestrianising which has enriched the English language from Borrow to Gissing, from Belloc to Leigh-Fermor and beyond.

* * *

Before he went to Germany, Coleridge claimed to have studied in the School of Locke, Berkeley, Leibniz and Hartley without finding in them an abiding place for Reason. What he claimed to be searching for was the truth behind appearances, which to his mind, was poetic. He worked through Plato and Plotinus, and the Renaissance Platonists, until he reached Descartes, and Spinoza, whom he admitted as a true saint but whose thinking he was beginning to hold as inimical to free will and moral responsibility. Many desired the Great, the Whole and the Indivisible, but for Coleridge Spinoza's One Substance had a dimension missing. What Coleridge sought was the truth to be found in the philosophy of the heart, not of the head. Philosophers tended to despise the mystics, whose thinking was confused with anti-reason, but Coleridge was fascinated by their perception of reality. It was as valid in its appeal to the heart as Platonism and Cartesianism to the head, though that validity might be as difficult to prove as to disprove. It could not be corralled in any dogmatic or pantheistic system and, by seeking it, Coleridge was prevented from 'crossing the sandy deserts of utter disbelief'.[11]

It was Kant, the illustrious sage of Königsberg, with his 'novelty and subtlety, yet solidity and importance of the distinctions; the adamantine chain of the logic'[12] who was to bridge for him the gap between head and heart. *The Critique of Pure Reason* took possession of him with a giant's hands. Coleridge's thinking was usually in need of a helping hand, and for him Kant had reconciled religion with pure reason. He established the existence of a deity, not a divine watchmaker, and he had also established that the will was free and choices real. Coleridge explained the obscure meanderings of Kant's thought by asserting that the sage was not prepared to elucidate, even to explain, everything. The climate in which Kant wrote, of 'lawless debauchery and priest-ridden superstition' that characterised the Prussia of his day – and of course the England of Coleridge's – left him too tired to try. That explanation suited Coleridge, who was dazzled by the German capacity to wrap several concepts into portmanteau words, Fichte's *Wissenschaftslehre* (Lore of Ultimate Society) or Schelling's *Transcendentalen Idealismus*. The autonomy of the will being accepted as a given, Kant's *Categorical Imperative* had to be a given too.

Coleridge thought that Kant's disciple and follower, Christian Wolff, had wanted to clarify Kant's obscurity but was prevented from doing so by the governments of Saxony and Prussia who banned him from teaching at Jena. As a consequence, Coleridge thought, Kant was wise not to try to do it himself. In his late seventies he had explained that he was then too old and busy about more important matters to write a commentary on his own work. Coleridge claimed that he understood what Kant had learned from his study of Jakob Böhme and Giordano Bruno, both of whose works were condemned by theologians of the day for their daring and unorthodox opinions.

If German philosophers like Fichte and Schelling believed that Coleridge was borrowing from them, then Coleridge stoutly affirmed that they were wrong. He may have thought much the same as they, but he had arrived at his conclusions independently. He recognised there was a 'scanty audience for abstrusest themes and truth that can neither be communicated nor received without effort of thought, as well as patience of attention'; those that had neither were to be pitied. Few could have stressed the problems of Coleridge's obscurity better.[13] For William Bell Scott, Coleridge's Victorian editor, the poet 'had no clearness nor wholeness in his metaphysical life, we never find that he has led us forwards but rather we have been following detached indications and curves, – eccentric ones having one end only fixed, the other waving about in space.'[14] It was a view that Thomas Carlyle was later to express with far greater bitterness. Coleridge thought he held, 'he alone in England, the key to German and other Transcendentalisms; knew the sublime secret of believing by "the reason" what "the understanding" had been obliged to fling out as incredible'. Sadly, Carlyle concluded, he did not.[15] But he accepted that the philosophy of Kant might, despite its 'ponderous, unmanageable dross, bear in it the everlasting gold of truth'.[16]

∗ ∗ ∗

Coleridge had gone to Germany to study and collect its poetry, not to plumb, as he claimed to have plumbed, the depths of German thought. But at this stage German thought was not going to make him any money, so on his return to England he finished *Christabel* and tried to turn his knowledge of German to financial profit. He wallowed with 'wild ecstasy' in Schiller's *The Robbers,* and its Gothic horrors:

> Schiller! that hour I would have wished to die,
> If through the shuddering midnight I had sent
> From the dark dungeon of the tower time-rent
> That fearful voice, a famished father's cry ...
> .... A triumphant shout
> Black horror screamed, and all her goblin rout
> Diminished shrunk from the more withering scene.[17]

But for all his love of the melodrama, he preferred to translate a more mature play and in 1800 he published his translation of two dramas in Schiller's *Wallenstein* trilogy, on which he had been working for the best part of a year. His critical judgment was suspended during the translation and he embellished and improved on Schiller, in his opinion, when he was not quite certain of his meaning. In Coleridge's hands the two plays became loquacious and lengthy, the brevity and density of Schiller's 'Shakespearean style' lost in the unfolding of a complex history.

Even so Coleridge made it read as an English play, full of puppets dancing to the drama, and he and his publisher, Longman, who had harried and chivvied him for it, had high hopes that it would attract some of the European excitement roused by *The Robbers* when first printed in 1781. Schiller only finished *Wallenstein* in 1799, and Coleridge was working from a manuscript copy. Despite Schiller's name, it was a financial flop, costing Longman money and putting an end to any idea of a proposed *Life of Lessing.* It was not until 1819 that J. G. Lockhart, on the editorial board of *Blackwood's Magazine,* wrote that it was a wonderful translation, even an improvement on the original.[18] Coleridge, though disappointed by his meagre earnings, was buoyed by the thought that the exercise of translation had sharpened his appreciation of Shakespeare's dramatic technique.

Schiller's *Wallenstein* is a leisurely progress through three separate plays, written through the nights while Schiller enjoyed forgiveness for his youthful indiscretions from Charles Eugene of Württemberg, obtained through the good offices of the Countess Francisca. What he was writing was a faction, a novel, in verse drama, a by-product of his researches into the Thirty Years War while professor at Jena. To keep alert and awake as he did so he sat with his feet in a bowl of cold water. There is only one fictional character in the *dramatis personae*, the son of the Italian condottiere, Max Piccolomini. For Schiller the historian, the war was a conflict of Napoleonic proportions, affecting all manner of men in the paths of the conflicting armies. It was a time of fierce tribal loyalties in a war of ideologies where leaders exhibited the sort of charismatic leadership that Walter Scott was to admire in Scottish highland chiefs.

For Schiller the playwright it was a psycho-drama revolving round the character of the Duke of Friedland, Albrecht Wenzel Eusebius von Wallenstein (also Waldstein). Born of Czech parents in Bohemia, Wallenstein was a typical soldier of fortune. He engrossed lands and titles in the service of the Emperor, to whom, for all his rewards, his loyalty was ambivalent, and Coleridge recognised the contradictions in Wallenstein's character, as Schiller portrayed it: his love of power and his weakness of resolve. Twice, Wallenstein was to be dismissed by the Emperor from his post as Imperial commander in chief. On the first occasion it was as a result of caballing by jealous junior commanders, but he had been reinstated to fight off the Swedish advance into German lands under Gustavus Adolphus. Schiller's drama is about his second dismissal, in the final year of Wallenstein's life, when the Emperor suspected that he had designs on power that would unseat him. Schiller leaves Wallenstein's real motives far from clear. Was he aiming at supreme power, or at the settlement of a war that had gone on, already, for 16 years and was to go on for another 14?

The play was performed in Weimar at a time when it seemed that a modern avatar of Wallenstein had just created himself First Consul in Paris, won a decisive victory over the Austrians at Marengo, and seemed to have the fate of Europe in his hands, just as Wallenstein had seemed to have it in his. Wallenstein had been as ambivalent in his intentions as Napoleon. In Schiller's fiction, we are encouraged to believe that he had decided that the only chance of peace in a bitterly divided Europe was for him to negotiate a peace from a position of power, even if this meant virtually renouncing his allegiance to the Emperor, from whom all his huge acquisitions of land had come. Was he intriguing with the virtually invincible Swedes to impose a peace of the undefeated on Europe? Was he ingenuous in his confidence that his officers would back a man who had given them continuous victories; was he blinded by a sort of Herculean hubris, like Napoleon, that he was always right or, as Coleridge highlighted in his translation, did he believe the future had already been determined by the conjunction of the planets?

Schiller plunges us straight into the world of tribal loyalty in the first play, *Wallenstein's Camp*, which Coleridge did not translate. Here Croats, Uhlans, Bohemians, Walloons, Italians and Germans are bound together in a fierce comradeship of great battles and a tide of victories under the munificent Duke of Friedland, and in a vaguer, but strong, loyalty to the Emperor. It is the war that has created them, without which they are nothing, and they resolve to stick together, come what may, even if a peace would remove their reason for living. All are encouraged to assume that their commanders think like their men, and Bedrich Smetana, a fellow Czech, was later to catch the spirit of this polyglot camaraderie in a concert piece called *Wallenstein's Camp*.

Carlyle, who saw a hero in Wallenstein, gave the drama his highest praise. 'Except in *Macbeth* or the conclusion of *Othello*, we know not where to match it. Schiller in his finest mood is overwhelming.'[19] Like Shakespeare, Schiller understood that at the heart of all men there is a conflict, never clear-cut, between self-interest and loyal disinterest. 'The truth of history has been but little violated,' wrote Carlyle, 'yet we are compelled to feel that Wallenstein, whose actions individually are trifling, unsuccessful and unlawful, is a strong, sublime commanding character; we look on him with interest, our concern at his end is tinged with a shade of kindly pity.'[20]

Schiller believed that faith in Wallenstein's 'loyal disinterest' had been misplaced, and this conflict with self-interest becomes clear in the second play in the trilogy, *The Piccolomini*. The Emperor has become convinced that his commander in chief nourishes an ambition to assume all power in the empire. Wallenstein is suspected, not entirely unjustly, of conspiring for a general peace which may benefit the ordinary people, but which will leave the Catholic cause unfinished. Wallenstein's religious affiliation is therefore opportunist and his loyalty to the Emperor doubtful. His principal lieutenant, the Italian *condottiere*, Octavio Piccolomini, also believes that Wallenstein's weakness, his love of power and his hubris, will be fatal to the Emperor. The Piccolomini are the key to what happens next. Octavio's son (Max, a fictional character) loves and is loved by Wallenstein's daughter, but their union is a match neither parent desires, and this presents Max with an intolerable choice between his oath to the Emperor and his care for the father of his beloved.

As Wallenstein tries to secure the signature of all his commanders to a manifesto of defiance of the Emperor, they learn that he has already been dismissed and is to be succeeded by the son of the Emperor. The artful Octavio Piccolomini exploits the conflict of loyalties when he begins to weave his general's doom. Some of the commanders conspire to solve their dilemma by removing themselves and their divisions from Wallenstein's camp; others plot to kill him. His immediate family resolves to bluff it out, relying on the loyalty of what is left of the army. Bit by bit Wallenstein's support falls away and, when his secret negotiations with the Swedes are exposed, he is branded a traitor. A final test of loyalty is now precipitated but, as a fallen giant, like Napoleon at Fontainebleau in 1814, Wallenstein is friendless. The end is inevitable. Ask Schiller why the titan had feet of clay and his answer is ambivalent. As Wallenstein's gloomy fate gathers, his intrinsic nobility manifests itself; but the very expression of this nobility, his disinclination to act ruthlessly, is his undoing. His desire for peace in a world not ready for it and his faith in the loyalty of men he had raised from the dust, above all in Piccolomini, whom he cannot believe is motivated by the baser expectation of advancement in Imperial service, condemn him to a degraded death.

In his last year the historical Wallenstein had appeared 'vindictive, changeable hesitant, a sick superstitious man surrounded by doctors and astrologers'.[21] Schiller accepts that Wallenstein's confidence had depended more on astrological prediction than on observable fact, and Coleridge was excited by 'the diffused drama of history', which was how he thought of Shakespeare's historical plays. In passages where he believed Schiller's drama needed enlargement to include psychological truth – not in fact

Schiller's forte – Coleridge added it. For both Schiller and for Coleridge, Wallenstein was noble if flawed and his end was a despicable murder by men without principle or mercy.

* * *

Despite the meagre rewards he received for *Wallenstein*, Coleridge was convinced that the German playwright would prove a meteor to revive the effete and trivial contemporary English drama, and he resolved to translate Schiller's next drama, *Mary Stuart*, as soon as he could get his hands on the text. The chief protagonist of *Mary Stuart* has had an enduring interest for British historians and Coleridge thought that, in Schiller's rendering, she was a subject that could not fail. The drama was written for the Weimar theatre in 1800, while central Germany was enjoying a period of peace, Weimar's Duke having studiously kept out of the Austrian entanglement. It was Schiller's post-Shakespearian play; the subject itself could not have attracted Shakespeare as it hardly glorified the Tudor dynasty. In it Queen 'Elizabeth is depicted like one of the French Medici [rather] than like … the true-hearted "good Queen Bess"'.[22] Schiller dipped into the well of tortured motives and helpless regret that had tinctured so many of the Master's plays. Set in Elizabethan time, historically manipulated to give the story dramatic action, Schiller manages to leave us in doubt about the motives of his principal players. All but two, Lord Burleigh and Hannah Kennedy, have mixed and uncertain motives, slipping and sliding in the dangerous loyalties of the Elizabethan court. Of those two, William Cecil, Lord Burleigh, has one simple objective: the death of Mary Stuart. Hannah Kennedy, Mary's faithful nurse and maid servant, wants her to live. The others are enigmas. Was Mary Stuart really repentant at the end or just seeking an effect; did Elizabeth really want Mary dead; was Leicester traitorously luring Mary into his fateful coils; was the Earl of Shrewsbury on Mary's side or just a time server; was Mortimer a political schemer or a religious fanatic?

Above all was Mary ill-treated and ill-judged? Could an encounter between the two sovereigns have turned out in reality as it did in the play? Elizabeth's reluctance to grasp the nettle of Mary's life has puzzled historians. Mary's undoubted descent, in Henry VII's legitimate line, did give her a claim to be Queen of England if Henry VIII's marriage to Anne Boleyn was accepted as null and void. Could some diplomatic solution, whereby Mary resigned her claim, have led to her partial release and rehabilitation? To most students of her character, such a démarche was rendered impossible by unalterable defects in her character. She had been a queen since she was a year old and she believed she was queen, to the end, of the three realms of Scotland, England and France. To keep that title she was prepared to countenance murder and assassination, and that qualified her as a villain in an Elizabethan drama. Whether or not she was implicated in the plots against Elizabeth's life, she was ready to accept and profit from them. Schiller portrays her belief in herself as a wronged woman, despite the catalogue of crimes stacked up against her. Are we, like Leicester, to believe her?

Schiller's Weimar plays all suggest that the greater power in any situation will always prevail. Resistance, not backed by equal power, was bound to lose. In that lay the power of tragedy. How much this loss was due to ineluctable forces or to character defect he left for us to decide. He had moved on from the black and white delineation of character that he had shown in his youthful *The Robbers*.

At the start of *Mary Stuart* Elizabeth is contemplating a French match, to the chagrin of Leicester who has staked his ambition on being Elizabeth's chosen partner. Did he for that reason champion the cause of Mary Stuart or was he another victim of her charm? Schiller allows the doubt (unlike the librettist who produced the play for Donizetti's opera). Leicester appears to be playing a double game for survival in whatever is decided in the passionate conflict of princes, but he also appears to be a little in love with Mary. Leicester persuades Mary to meet Elizabeth and by casting herself on Elizabeth's mercy, to beg for her release from confinement. Then he persuades Elizabeth to hear Mary. The encounter is fatal. Mary finds it impossible to be wholly humble, wholly penitent. She is a queen, a more legitimate queen than Elizabeth, who taunts her that she thanked 'God in heaven that it was not His sovereign will that I should kneel to you as you now kneel to me'. Mary tries to excuse her past; she was young, she was in danger, she was ill advised, but 'in the gap between disagreeing monarchs furies fly'. Burleigh has warned Elizabeth not to trust Mary, and Elizabeth pours contempt on Mary's professions of misguided action, traducing her character, her links with the enemies of England, with the Pope, with monkish Catholicism and with suitors, all of whom die before they reach the altar. She has caught Mary on the raw. What right has Elizabeth to insult her, for everyone knew for what crimes her mother had been executed? By what right does a 'vile bastard' have to criticise one who should have been her queen?[23] This is too much for everyone.[24]

As far as Mary is concerned, by her dramatic reference to Elizabeth's bastardy she has triumphed; she has humiliated the English queen as she has been humiliated. She has sealed her fate. The rest of the play is concerned with the historical truth that Elizabeth vacillated over the decision to have Mary beheaded and after a long soliloquy of self-justification, she remembers that accusation of bastardy and determines that this vile accusation will die with Mary. She signs the order of execution. The last act, in which Mary's house steward turns out to be a priest in disguise with powers to hear her confession and give absolution, lends itself to opera rather than stage, and this is where it has ended. As Mary proceeds to her execution she takes her leave of Leicester with a double-edged valediction: 'True to your word, Lord Leicester, as you swore, you lead me out of prison on your arm.' Was Elizabeth's real hatred for Mary inspired by jealousy of her beauty that had turned Leicester's head? For that crime they must both be together at the end, one to suffer, the other to witness the execution.

Coleridge was too discouraged by the reception of *Wallenstein* and *Mary Stuart* to proceed to Schiller's other work. In any case Southey had produced his heroic play, *Joan of Arc,* in 1795, six years before Schiller wrote *Die Jungfrau von Orleans,* (1801), in which Joan dies not at the stake but on the battlefield. Charles Lamb whose admiration for Southey's epic – 'why, the poem is alone sufficient to redeem the age we live in from the imputation of degenerating in Poetry' – would also have been a disincentive to Coleridge's tackling of Schiller's other English history play.[25] Schiller had tried to present the 'darkness and delusions' of Joan's understanding and the 'radiance of her heart' which made her the 'most noble being in Tragedy'.[26] Such a challenge might have tempted Coleridge, but he had lost his enthusiasm.

* * *

When Mathew Lewis, author of *The Monk* (1796), translated Schiller's *Kabale und Liebe* (*Intrigue and Love*) as *The Minister* shortly after its appearance, his reputation for gruesomeness was so pronounced that he caused a jaundiced light to fall on the work of German writers. Though he had already translated a German novella set in Venice, *The Bravo*, it, like its successor *The Monk*, had been set in the territory of a Catholic country, haunted by the terrors imagined by Ann Radcliffe. Lewis's morbid interest in sex and religion gave the Gothic novel a reputation for something lubricious and unhealthy, and when he translated Schiller's 'coarse and overcharged' tragedy, *The Robbers*, he tarred German drama with the same brush by association with his own 'pernicious novel'. Suddenly, 1797, Germanness became a threat that might pervert English taste.[27] Had not Lewis himself claimed that some of his sources for *The Monk* were German? Had he not strayed into 'the world of spirits, and all the fictions of the nursery, and the bugbears of romance become realized – the illuminated oratory, the aerial music – magical every note of it – and the determined silence of the praeter-natural visitant'.[28] The Shudder Novel (*Schauerroman*) became as popular as the Omens and werewolves of late-night TV dramas in the late twentieth century. Byron was not the first to seek the sort of late night excitation that produced Polidori's *The Vampyre* and Mary Shelley's *Frankenstein*. German spectres almost 'drove Shakespeare and Congreve from the stage'.[29]

Gottfried Bürger's ballad, *Leonora* (1773), in which a maiden is carried off on a ghostly ride through an eerie countryside lit by flashes of lightning was translated five separate times in 1797 suitably chilling its readers, and even tempting imitation by Walter Scott. For the rider is not the maiden's dead lover, as she supposed in her terror, but death himself. Charles Lamb recommended its refrain, that the dead could ride apace, to Coleridge with multiple exclamation marks.[30] Burns had given in 1791 his account of an eerie night ride in a land of witches and warlocks, but Tam was drunk and the ride was a *jeu d'esprit*. Bürger's ballad was deathly serious as well as weird, and gothic weirdness had reinforced the appeal of Ann Radcliffe who, after the seemingly supernatural events in *The Mysteries of Udolpho* (1794) were revealed as having purely natural causes, was essentially not a fantasist. Coleridge, who admired Radcliffe – he thought *Udolpho* 'the most interesting novel in the English language' – deplored Lewis's *The*

Monk for its tales of enchantment and witchcraft, which he had contrived to make 'pernicious by blending all that is most awfully true in religion with all that is most ridiculously absurd in superstition'.[31] Ann Radcliffe had never resorted to witches and warlocks. Malevolence and villainy were purely human qualities, but Coleridge's translation of Schiller was to perish in the general suspicion of the demoralising effect of *sturm und drang* drama.[32] By that time however, Pumpernickel was being confronted by a cataclysm that thrust *sturm und drang* into the shadows. Armies were on the move again and their aim was revolution.

CHAPTER ELEVEN

Revolution Across
the Rhine

Napoleonic Germany

*Il y a des grands intérêts attachés à ce que font les souverains, au lieu
qu'aucun intérêt n'est attaché à ce que fait la grande duchesse.*
(Napoleon Bonaparte, 17 December 1811)

You must be master and win or servant and lose,
grieve or triumph, be the anvil or the hammer. ('I have
always commanded ... from the moment I came to
prominence I recognized neither master nor laws'.)
(Goethe, *The Grand Cophta*, 1791 [Napoleon Bonaparte, *Mémoires*,
ed de Bourienne.])

FRANCE HAD SO dominated the manners, the literature and the thought
of Germany throughout the *Aufklärung* that, when the French
Revolutionary Wars began, many continental European thinkers could
see no danger in them. The ageing Kant indeed had long preached the
abolition of all hereditary privileges and equality before the law, so that he
saw the fall of the absolute monarchy as the first step towards a reign of
peace and harmony founded on reason. So it seemed, in its own way, to
Klopstock, Wieland and Herder. Gotthold Lessing had all along held that
existing institutions should be challenged and replaced with better ones
that enthroned reason as their arbiter. Rule by popular sovereignty would
embody the incarnation of common sense and rational thought. Goethe
was less confident that an Age of Reason had dawned; he was enjoying

being Platonic guardian to a small, well-organised state and did not repudiate the aim of the revolution, only its methods. He was prepared to accept that the forces of democracy spelled the end of autocracy and the birth of a society owing more to Rousseau than to St Paul or St Augustine.

Though German intellectuals had fallen on the works of Rousseau, Voltaire, Montesquieu and Diderot with the healthy appetite with which they consumed their Pumpernickel, the yeast of their ideas was believed by Germany's rulers to be unsuitable, indeed too fervent, to 'prove' German bread. Germany remained predominantly a land in which conditions were still medieval but, even before France burst into revolution, change in the time-warped sovereign states had already begun. In 1764, when Boswell set off gaily to visit Prussia, torture in the pursuit of justice was abolished and, before 1779, Baden, Mecklenburg, Saxony and Bavaria had followed suit.[1] It had become almost fashionable to be an enlightened autocrat introducing reforms that often annoyed the privileged aristocracy, while preserving the state's medieval character.

At the beginning of the French Revolution the rulers of Europe may have wished to rescue the beleaguered King of France, reinstate the Church and defend the institution of nobility. However, to enlightened liberals these were the props of autocracy and their disappearance must follow in their own territories. Goethe, however, held that reform, though highly desirable, should come in an ordered way from above, from an enlightened aristocracy, not from below, from a 'trouserless mob.' Goethe's dislike of extreme radicalism led him to approve of the post-Napoleonic Holy Alliance, 'nothing greater or more beneficial for mankind was ever devised'.[2] He was ready, therefore, to welcome Napoleon as bringing that order from above, in fulfilment of the revolution.

In 1792, Frenchmen were not listening to German poets. They heard only the chiefs of the Austrian and Prussian armies vowing to restore order and the king's lawful authority. In reply the French assembly promised Europe that it would enforce revolution in any territory it occupied, offering liberty, fraternity and equality to all those peoples who wished to assert their freedom. The armies of Europe, used to fighting territorial wars that altered maps but not minds, were surprised by the new spirit of French soldiery. Gone were the days when a Marlborough or a Frederick could discomfort and defeat the forces of Louis XIV and XV. The Prussians were routed by a citizen army and Brussels, the capital of the Austrian Netherlands, was occupied or, rather, liberated, by revolutionaries.[3]

The *levée en masse,* introduced in August 1793, seemed to give the French army an irresistible impetus. Though only bachelors and childless widowers were liable for conscription, they gave it a mass strength, which, with good organisation, was to prove too much for the carefully drilled, drawing room grenadiers of the Germanic enemy. French borders had by 1799 been extended to her 'natural' frontiers, of the Rhine and the Alps. What Louis XIV had failed to do had then been achieved by a revolutionary army. To indemnify the princes who lost lands on the west bank of the Rhine, the French resorted to wholesale secularisation in the occupied territories, a popular move, as it freed people from onerous and unproductive feudal impositions. Above all, the sale of church lands created a new class of peasant proprietors; agricultural development was assisted and the long period of peace and relative prosperity that followed disguised the fact that French administrators, tax collectors and recruiting sergeants ruled where once theologians, philosophers, musicians and actors had been 'the unacknowledged legislators'.[4] The occupied Rhenish provinces accepted their change of masters, at first, peaceably enough.

The horrors that followed the death of Louis XVI, and the civil war between parties that made the guillotine an instrument of terror weakened but did not overturn confidence in the benefits of liberalism. The fact that, as Schiller held, the French were not yet worthy of freedom did not discredit the positive first fruits of the revolution. The work of education still had far to go, and the princes on the east bank were not too disconsolate at losing the west bank. They expected to do well out of the indemnification process, and secularising church lands to pay for it appealed to them, especially if the princes were protestant, as a way to increase their wealth. They brushed off the protests of the church leaders who forecast the end of the Holy Roman Empire and the Roman Catholic church.

Needless to say, like beneficiaries of a disputed will, they started to quarrel over the division of the spoils and Napoleon had to intervene to settle the situation, with Russia's support, for the Tsar numbered many of the princes as relations by marriage in one degree or another. The Diet in 1803 eventually approved a new Imperial constitution, under which a few secular states benefited from considerable accretions of territory, population and wealth. The principal beneficiary was Prussia, but Bavaria, Baden, Württemberg and the two Hesse principalities also did well out of the deal. Maximilian II of Bavaria had decided to entrust his fate to Napoleon and, as he had hoped, he was progressively rewarded with former bishoprics, abbeys and free cities which were being suppressed to reward those German princes for their acquiescence in the loss of the west bank of the Rhine. His final reward was to be elevated in 1806 as King Maximilian I of Bavaria, though the price he paid was that his daughter was given in marriage to Josephine's son, the Viceroy of the kingdom of Italy, Eugène de Beauharnais.

The losers were the main supporters of the Austrian Emperor, the ecclesiastical principalities, the Orders of Imperial Knights, most of whom lost their sovereignty, and the free cities, reduced from 50 to six. Napoleon had created a change in the balance of power in Germany, reducing Austrian prestige and power and securing the neutrality if not the active support of those large states that had done so well out of the new arrangements and saw France as their protector.

The Electorate, and then later kingdom, of Saxony enjoyed ten years of peace from 1795, when Prussia withdrew from alliances against France, and was free to develop its mines and forests off which it lived profitably enough for Leipzig to continue as the centre of the book trade and for Dresden to remain a beacon of civilised urban life. The little Duchy of Saxe-Weimar, made itself by its enlightened, unambitious politics a home for poets and philosophers, allowed Goethe and Schiller to cultivate the garden of their minds.

Those minds were not, however, as dangerously critical of authority as had been the French *philosophes.* Voltaire's ridicule was a more potent lever of change in France than the cloudy rhetoric of Goethe or Lessing in Germany. While critical of the lifestyle of the princes and nobles, most German writing towards the end of the eighteenth century, even Schiller's, preserved a due respect for prince and Church. As it extolled the virtues of the English commercial and intellectual bourgeoisie, it brought the class war up a class. German thinkers may have been in tune with the encyclopaedic devotion to liberty, political, religious and social, but it was liberty rather of the mind, not the body. It expressed more a theoretical partisanship of truth and beauty in a more perfect world, than any political plan to bring it about. The liberty of the mind was an idea too idealistic, too ethical, too Pietistic, so that it only slowly dawned on the intelligentsia that liberty of the body could never be achieved without a social upheaval. Of this, after *sturm und drang* and the French 'liberation' wars, some Germans, like Goethe, and most of her rulers, felt they had already had enough.

The benefit of releasing humankind from the social constraints that had otherwise held it back had been belied by the violence of the revolution in France. The Romantic image of Man standing in defiance of Fate, real enough in the visions of Schiller and Byron, suggested that the silver bullets they fired might also be lethal. The Romantic visionaries began to glorify 'the Middle Ages as they saw them, [when] modern doubts and divisions were unknown and the Christian order of a truly organic society was guaranteed by Church and State'.[5] If Goethe viewed this as a vision of phantasmagoria, he did not choose to raise his voice against it, though privately he believed that man was sufficiently saddened by his own passions and destiny 'not to make himself more so by the darkness of a barbaric past'.[6]

* * *

A new social vision and a broad horizon of equality might have been the benefits of French rule; but they did not derive from a spirit of generosity and idealism on the part of either Napoleon or the territorial princes. The people were not sovereign, only the French. Yet the seeds of political nationalism were being sown. Reform had been brought about at the point of foreign guns. The new laws and systems of government were French, supported by an army that was fighting a new form of warfare, one more rapid, more mobile, more flexible and more capable of tactical superiority at short notice, by troops inspired by a feeling of invincibility. It also carried with it, not just liberal ideas, like the emancipation of serfs and the abolition of restrictive craft guilds, but also an oppressive burden of taxation, conscription of labour, and the imposition of laws the people did not understand.

The worst effects of French rule were noticed in the Rhineland. It began by being liberating but soon became oppressive. The relentless demand for money and troops, the perambulation of armies over lands that had not been so afflicted since the beginning of the eighteenth century and the wars of Louis XIV, and the casual imposition of French systems, which confused and baffled the 'liberated' territories, resulted in a general breakdown of society. In the Palatinate and neighbouring, and more intractably, forested parts of the Lower Rhine banditti were to flourish as they did in the Abruzzi and bad lands of southern Italy. One notorious Rhinelander was to enter the robber's pantheon, along with Robin Hood and Fra Diavolo.

Hannes Buckler was born in 1779, son of an Austrian deserter who had fled into the Prussian Rhineland. He was brought up in the severely moralistic Lutheran faith but at 16 succumbed to temptation to use money he had been given for another purpose to buy some smuggled brandy, and then, alarmed at what he had done, he absconded on a stolen horse. He found work as assistant to a public executioner, supplementing his income by rustling livestock for a butcher, until he was arrested and sent to prison. It was not difficult to escape and he joined a band of outlaws in the high region of the Hochwald.

Displaying a debonair ruthlessness and desperate leadership, enhanced by a reputation both for breaking out of prison, which he did three times, and for breaking hymens and hearts, Buckler soon headed the most notorious band of outlaws in the area. He acquired, in the pretty daughter of an itinerant musician, his Maid Marian who put on male attire and accompanied him as a member of his gang. He was not a freedom fighter in outlaw's dress for he plundered indiscriminately. He was said to have acquired a certain immunity from the attention of the local police by robbing Jewish houses, and, it was believed, had once fallen in with the watch who smilingly let his gang pass unhindered, when they learned that they were on their way to 'rob a Jew'. Jews were fair game in a time of distress and when Buckler's gang held up a caravan of Jews who turned out to be not worth holding up, they were subjected to a malevolent game of striptease, the one who found his clothes and dressed last was threatened with death.[7] Eventually the Jewish community asked the French authorities for protection though that did their cause no good, as they were now seen as friends of the enemy.

Buckler's gang moved up and down the Rhine, carrying out their raids on both sides of the river until the peace of Lunéville in 1802 restored a semblance of order to the Rhineland. His gang was soon on the run, and Buckler tried to pass himself off as part of the flotsam of war in order to enlist in the Austrian army, when he was recognised by one of his victims and handed over to the authorities at Mainz. He was subjected to a trial after two years, during which his accomplices and mistress were rounded up, and he was guillotined in 1803 along with 19 of his gang, all in a space of 26 minutes. The French had less trouble dealing with bandits than they had in Italy because Buckler and his gang had inspired popular terror, not grudging loyalty among fellow sufferers from the French.

* * *

Before Napoleon became First Consul, France was engaged in defending her new frontiers. Afterwards she expanded them. Austria was overwhelmed, first at Marengo by Napoleon himself, then by Moreau at Neerwinden. An agreement was struck with the Vatican, so that France no longer appeared as the hammer of Roman Catholicism, and one by one Russia, Naples and Portugal made peace on terms of what one had, one held. The Second Coalition collapsed like its predecessor in 1793 and by 1802 Britain followed its allies into a cessation of war.

Whatever Napoleon was to become – a crowned Jacobin, a monarchical republican, an insatiable autocrat, an inspired legislator, the embodiment of the myth of liberation, or the avatar of conquest – at the time he needed peace to complete his reform and systematisation of France. Just as the French language had been the preferred medium of political change, and of philosophic thought, even of polite interchange, so now Frenchmen considered it natural that French administrative and legislative models should assume the same position in European society. France's immediate neighbours should be the first to enjoy them.

Napoleon had shown in Egypt that he was both a true child of the scientific renaissance and a disciple of English pragmatism. His dedication to this pragmatism over ideology dictated the Vatican concordat, the assumption of royal titles and the creation of a class ennobled for achievement not birth, all to lend the regime respectability in the common mind, still groping in slowly receding darkness. But behind the modernity of his power, he knew as instinctively as Chairman Mao that power flowed from the barrel of a gun. Unless England was overcome, with her capacity to subsidise coalitions that came from her unrivalled economic power and control of the sea, France would not prosper. The 12 years that followed the end of the Peace of Amiens, though accompanied by years of increasing French power and even prosperity, were to match them against increasingly effective forces of resistance, which her very conquests raised against her.

The first recipients of French rational government were the Germanic territories on the west bank of the Rhine, which were absorbed into France as part of her historical entity. There was no popular objection to the imposition of the *Code Napoléon* or to the abolition of the feudal remnants of society. Reform followed the French insistence on the abolition of serfdom, on equality before the law, on universal liability to taxation and on freedom of conscience and of the press from ecclesiastical limitations. The reforms were then extended to those allies of France not absorbed into her empire. The Bavarians accepted them all in the expectation of benefits, but despite a certain latitude in their duties as members of the Napoleonic Confederation of the Rhine, they saw little abatement of French demands for men and money. Napoleon blamed Bavarian troops for failing to suppress insurrection in the Italian territories they had been assigned, and in 1813 Bavaria decided to change sides. Though the chief minister told the French ambassador that his country still needed France, he foresaw an inevitable loss of territory if she was on the losing side in a great pan-European conflagration. In 1806, however, there was no hint of this. Napoleon had carried all before him. Prussia had been humbled at Jena and now it was time to re-order Europe.

At Erfurt, near Weimar, he ceremoniously met Tsar Alexander. Behind him the kings and hereditary princes sat in tamed homage and above them were officers in full dress uniform and princesses in royal finery. The two Emperors were saluted by triple drumbeats, kings by two, except the King of Württemburg who was mistaken for his betters but, before the triple beat could be given, the officer commanding shouted, 'Hold it. He is only a king.'[8]

Goethe, who was not even a king, was presented to the French emperor who graciously launched into a monologue about literature. Later he was summoned to breakfast with the Emperor, who was accompanied by Talleyrand and his generals. Napoleon scrutinised his visitor and announced to his entourage that 'There was a Man!' He thought Goethe very well preserved for 60 years old and invited him to talk about the tragedies he had written. On being told that he had translated Voltaire's *Mahomet*, he criticised a drama that failed to do full justice to the conqueror of the eastern world. He then turned to *Werther*. He had read it, he said, seven times, latterly in Egypt and asked why Goethe had written about a suicide so contrary to nature. Goethe did not think the question was worth answering, but hoped a poet might be pardoned for artifice. Napoleon warmed to his theme; he could not accept any drama that was not true to Nature. Fate had no part to play in man's affairs. That belonged to an obscure period in the past. '*Que veulent-ils dire avec leur fatalité? La politique est la fatalité.*'[9]

There were other encounters with Napoleon, in which Goethe kept his peace listening patiently to the Emperor's views on the drama, on Shakespeare who, he could not suppose, had any attraction for a well-ordered mind. He invited Goethe to write a play about Julius Caesar who could have done so much to benefit mankind had he been allowed to live. Goethe should not write a tragedy in Voltairean mode but dwell on the mighty potentiality for good that died with Caesar and which, he implied, it was Napoleon's destiny to fulfil. He extended an invitation to Goethe to come to Paris, where he would find 'a vaster circle for his observing spirit and immense material for his poetic creation'.[10] If he was attracted, Goethe was too old and settled in Weimar to uproot himself. He accepted instead the cross of the Legion of Honour as an honour due to him, and he was flattered, who would not be, by the attention of the Man who thought he had met another Man.

The foremost German of his time on the whole remained supportive of the French changes, but, then, Goethe was never a political animal. He was no friend, he insisted, to the people who behind the mask of public welfare made their object robbery, murder and destruction, any more than he was a friend of Louis XV. He hated every violent overthrow because as much good was destroyed by it as was gained by it.[11] Beethoven might tear up the dedication of his symphony to Napoleon following his proclamation as Emperor, but then he was a citizen of Austria, which had remained detached from the French Imperial *zeitgeist*. Goethe, on the other hand, snug in the Saxon fastness of Weimar, was a servant of Pumpernickel provided that its Grand Duke ensured real benefits for its people. Heaven preserve him, he had said in 1772, from anything so monstrous as Roman patriotism.[12] Providing he kept his distance, Napoleon embodied the spirit of the new century, 'always enlightened, always clear and endowed at every hour with sufficient energy to carry into effect whatever he considered advantageous and necessary'. Even after the war was over and Napoleon was safely buried in St Helena, Goethe could see his life as the stride of a demi-god, from battle to battle, victory to victory, a man of destiny more brilliant than ever the world had seen before or would, perhaps, see again.[13] That was very much his prevailing sentiment when Germaine de Staël had visited him in 1803. Resistance to France or French ideas was muted.

Despite his gracious recognition of the Goethean genius, Napoleon, in fact, had no feeling for Germany. Such a venal and self-indulgent coterie of princes had to be brought head first into the modern, French world. He spoke no German though he claimed to have had read *Werther* seven times, almost certainly in translation, and he considered Kant one of the 'useless dreamers and impostors of the world'. The Emperor, in the words of Carlyle, found Kant's philosophy 'not only an absurdity, but a wickedness and a horror; the pious and peaceful sage of Königsberg passe[d] for a sort of Necromancer and Black-artist in Metaphysics'.[14] It was expedient, no more, for Napoleon to honour Goethe as an exemplary spirit, just as it was expedient for him to woo his defeated enemies in the interests of preserving a bulwark in east Europe against his other formidable enemy, to flirt with the Queen of Prussia, though giving nothing away, and to marry an Austrian Archduchess to create a dynasty.

After his victory over Austria at Wagram, Napoleon in 1805 had briefly put his mind to the future of Germany. As in Italy, the logic of his policy was to create a surrogate France. It was halfway there in its devotion to the French language, in its palaces and temples, even its admiration – at a distance – of Jacobin principles. Now it was to have the last dressed in monarchical clothes. Austria and Prussia were to be excluded from the settlement, as their role, as defeated enemies and complaisant allies, would be to hold the east against the Russians in case the lure of Ottoman Europe and Asia was not sufficient to divert the Tsar from his preoccupation with western Europe.

First, the Holy Roman Empire was deconstructed. The empty title had acquired in 1803 ten electors as opposed to the former seven, six of whom were Protestant. The Electorates of Bavaria, and Württemberg, in return for faithfully allying themselves with France, now became kingdoms and the constituent principalities, with the exceptions of Austria and Prussia, were grouped into a Confederation of the Rhine, becoming effectively satellites of France. The Confederation's affairs were to be managed by a Diet at Frankfurt, with two Colleges, of Kings and of sovereign Princes. The first included the new kings (Saxony became a kingdom, and joined the Confederation only in 1806) and the Grand Dukes of Baden, Hesse-Darmstadt and Berg, (whose Grand Duke was Joachim Murat, husband of Caroline Bonaparte, and which had been especially recreated as a Duchy for him in 1806). The director of these assemblies was the Elector and Prince Primate of Mainz, Archbishop Otto von Dalberg, who was given a principality at Frankfurt. As an Electoral prelate, he had shown himself to be complaisant to the new order, helping with the abolition of Church principalities and believing implicitly that the greater good of the former Pumpernickel states rested with France.[15] As a result of the abolition of clerical principalities nearly half the population of Germany now lived under Protestant rulers, a situation enshrined in the eventual peace after Waterloo.

At a stroke the Imperial dukes, counts and knights, principal supporters of the Austrian emperor, lost their sovereignty but not necessarily their feudal rights, and they kept their palaces. Certain territorial adjustments were made. The surviving potentates acknowledged Napoleon as their Protector and agreed to recognise and respect each other's territorial boundaries. On the first day of August 1806, they announced that they no longer owed any allegiance to the Holy Roman Emperor who, Napoleon's envoy had informed them, was not recognised by the French Emperor. As the Holy Roman Empire, however, still existed, though in legal tatters, the new Charlemagne impressed upon the Emperor, that it was a meaningless charade. Five days later, this medieval myth was finally consigned to oblivion, when the Holy Roman Emperor Francis II became the Emperor Francis I of Austria.

In the following year Napoleon created, as a throne for his brother, Jerome Bonaparte, a kingdom of Westphalia, from the former Duchy of Brunswick, the Electoral landgravate of Hesse-Kassel, which had earlier benefited from French compensation for loss of territory on the left bank of the Rhine, part of Hanover (whose Elector was his enemy the King of England) and the Saxon lands seized from her by Frederick the Great. The Bonaparte brothers and sisters were to become almost as Pumpernickelish as the sovereigns they replaced; they were rich, courtly and impotent, since their brother recognised no relatives but those who were prepared to serve him, and that service had to be blind. He wished the electorate of Hanover onto Prussia because it belonged to his implacable enemy, thus involving the Prussians in an involuntary conflict with their former ally, who devastated their ports and merchandise in return. Napoleon was as cavalier with the disposal of land as he was of titles and when it was revealed, on the death of Pitt, that without consulting Prussia he had offered Hanover to Charles James Fox in return for a peace, the Prussians decided that subservience to the new Charlemagne was too one-sided, and they mobilised for war. Their ensuing, crushing defeats at Jena and Auerstadt in 1806 resulted in a humiliating peace. Prussia's western border became the Elbe, and she lost half her land and population to the vultures of the Confederation.

How did the superbly drilled armies of Frederick the Great, which were kept up in numbers and drilled by his successors, Frederick William II and III, fare so badly against the French? Partly it was because Napoleon was a general of genius, but so much had been made of Prussia's military strength that it had become a delusion of Frederick himself who, having beaten and drilled his army into drawing room perfection, believed it was better than it was. It had become the model for all German soldiery, commanded by martinets. Frederick himself might have given Napoleon a battle, but under Frederick William III Jena was a rout. His troops had not seen war service for ten years; their muskets were highly polished but were among the worst in Europe.

Moreover the officers, recruited entirely from the Prussian nobility, lacked the youth, dash and conviction of the French. The army, which had beaten the French at Rossbach in 1757, was much the same as that beaten at Jena, but the French had learned all the lessons taught to Europe by Frederick the Great himself and showed the advantages to be gained by delegated command, speed of deployment and a final hammer-blow strike.[16] Napoleon tore down the monument of that French defeat and collected the sword of Frederick from his tomb in Berlin to adorn the *Invalides* in Paris. 'I always admired Frederick II,' he sneered after Prussia's dismal performance on the battlefield, 'but I admire him twice as much since I have seen what kind of men they were who resisted Austrians, French and Russians.'[17] The defeat of their army was not altogether lamented by a citizenry, disenchanted by the boorish behaviour of its officers and men. On the eve of Napoleon's triumphal entry into Berlin, the opera was full of an audience enjoying the trials and tribulations, not of their monarch, but of Iphigenia.

* * *

In 1807, to consolidate this rearrangement, Napoleon elevated his youngest sibling, Jerome, then 46-years-old, to a newly created kingdom of Westphalia. Jerome was good-looking and energetic, but that was where his qualities for kingship ended. He had started his career in the navy and, during a visit to the United States, though he was technically still a minor, he had married an American girl. Napoleon refused to accept the marriage or allow her to enter France, and while Jerome returned to the French navy Elizabeth Bonaparte, née Patterson, settled with her son in Camberwell in England. Jerome was promoted to the rank of *chef d'escadre* (rear admiral) which was also the rank of France's great sailor, the Bailli de Suffren, who had he lived, Napoleon believed, would have been his Nelson. There the comparisons ended, but Napoleon had a use for all his siblings and, after Jerome had distinguished himself in the Jena campaign, he decided to make him a king.

First of all he had to shed his American wife and, when the Pope would not grant a divorce, the Emperor ended the union by Imperial fiat. Jerome went to his new kingdom with a new German wife, Catherine of Württemberg, daughter of the only German monarch for whom Napoleon had any regard. Jerome, buttressed by two French minders, started well enough, dismantling the relics of German feudalism, introducing the *Code Napoléon,* emancipating the Jews, and even employing as librarian one of the Brothers Grimm. But the minders could not control his extravagance, as he set about building the ostentatious palaces of Napoleonshöhe and Catharinental, and providing himself with a profuse number of bemedalled uniforms and bejewelled mistresses. He opened his legislature in a suit of white silk, a purple cloak and diamond-encrusted turban. He was as merry a monarch as his new father-in-law, Friedrich I, the Napoleon-created King of Württemberg, holding a succession of lavish entertainments and theatre parties. Jerome had succumbed to the particular pleasures of Pumpernickel. His uniforms were extravagant and meaningless, his mistresses were greedy and spoiled and his court was obsessed with the pursuit of entertainment. While he spent his time hunting and eating, he was the puppet of an Imperial master, more exacting than the Emperor *fainéant* in Vienna, who had been both Holy and Roman. The entertainments did not disguise the ruin of the kingdom, and by 1809 he could not pay his troops. Napoleon might reproach him explosively for not behaving like a king and the brother of an Emperor, but he did not remove him. He just reneged on his promise to add the rest of Hanover to the kingdom of Westphalia, and this was a bitter blow to Jerome who hoped that this rich province would repair his finances. The contingent he was obliged to send to support Napoleon's Moscow campaign actually bankrupted the state. After the Russian debacle, he and his Württembourgeoise wife and children were forced to flee to Switzerland, and much of their short-lived kingdom reverted at the peace to the Prussia from whom it had been forcibly removed.[18]

* * *

In 1806, having established peace over central Europe, Napoleon doubled his efforts to cut off the dark hand of England which seemed everywhere to be frustrating him, blockading his ports, subsidising his enemies, even engaging in a successful combined operation which denied him total control of the Mediterranean. In his dreams, the fantasy of a French eastern empire, to rival and eclipse the English in India haunted him, and he needed the silence of the lambs in Europe to enable him to bring

England to her knees by reversing the blockade. Austrian, Prussian and Russian armies had been finally fought to a standstill, though Napoleon had learned that Russians could not be defeated; they must be killed. Peace and the diversion of their ambitions towards the south east of Europe and towards south Asia was to be the new drive of French foreign policy. Russia was to help bring England to a peace in which Hanover would be returned to her if she allowed complete freedom of the seas and returned those overseas possessions she had acquired in acts of war.

In all this Germany counted for little. Prussia was saved from almost total obliteration after Jena, and only kept what she had, because of the regard Napoleon claimed that he had for the Tsar. Napoleon regretted that he did not extinguish Prussia as a sovereign entity, especially before he ventured on his invasion of Russia. It would have suited him to make the Vistula the common frontier between the Napoleonic and the Tsarist Empires. Instead, from the Prussian and Austrian annexations in Poland of the last century the French carved out a Grand Duchy of Warsaw which was put under the nominal rule of the King of Saxony, to compensate him for the loss of his former lands, transferred from Prussia to the new kingdom of Westphalia. With the creation of the Grand-Duchy, Alexander now had the French on his borders and wanted Prussia as some sort of buffer state.

Saxony had stayed out of the French Revolutionary Wars, and so great was her rancour against her neighbour that she actively sided with Napoleon in 1806 and sent 22,000 troops to help the French defeat Prussia. She kept her independence by this alliance. But it was an independence dependent on French goodwill, and membership of the Confederation of the Rhine. Prussia, though shorn of territory, remained as a glacis against Russia. Had Napoleon restored Silesia to Saxony, and imposed a constitution after abolishing all feudal dues, rather than giving her titular responsibility again for Poland, he would have created a more contented population.

This was the climax of Napoleon's power. Europe appeared to be in no position to unsettle him, but the decrees he issued from Berlin to deprive England of any European markets turned out to be a policy of desperation. In Germany the elan of revolutionary idealism was beginning to fade. Napoleon had reduced the medieval trappings of empire, chastened the Catholic Church, liberated the Protestant churches, rationalised the legal codes and, despite the almost continuous wars, seen an increase in agriculture and population. But the effervescence of liberal ideas had become flat; the French control of information was obsessive and draconian. The ceaseless demand for 'volunteers' to man the Imperial armies, the taxation and forced levies to meet the demands not of peace but of almost perpetual war were creating a climate of resentment and discontent.

The grand Napoleonic design, large, even magnificent and liberal seemed moreover increasingly unattainable. It had started with Egypt and the revival of France's oriental dreams. These had been dashed by England. The dissolution of the venal Ottoman Empire, its European and Levantine corpses shared with Russia, had been prevented by England's subsidies to the Tsar and her refusal to abandon the Mediterranean to France. The Tsar, 'England's last hope', had yet to be persuaded to relinquish his own dream of a 'barbarian' empire of the north by the promise of gains in the Ottoman Empire.[19] Until England was defeated, the settlement of Germany and Italy as French satraps was incomplete. The new Charlemagne had work still to do. If he failed, Europe would fail.

A new and resplendent Paris had to be created as the centre of civilisation and art, the joint seat of Pope and Emperor, the fount of all liberal ideas, the university of the world, the *pépinière* of princes and academy of enlightened autocrats. His continental system would inspire such a demand for European goods and services that England, no longer the workshop of the world, would shrivel away. But the closer the Europeans looked at this dream, it seemed as if Pumpernickel would be consolidated by secular power and be transformed into a new Holy Roman Empire, a Carolingian super power. The miscegenation of the daughters of an ancient nobility with the meritocrats of a social revolution, from which France would forge a new aristocracy, looked very like the *ancien régime* writ large. Napoleon's vision of a new, vitalised aristocracy was certainly genuine, and much of the new class survived the Restoration.[20] The old Electors had become kings, and the new kings looked little better than the old.[21]

* * *

Prussia after Jena was humiliated; she lost territory and her army was reduced to 42,000 men under arms and, to make sure that she did not recover quickly, Napoleon levied an immense financial forfeit. The king retained his crown but was reduced to parity with the Pumpernickel kings of Bavaria and Saxony, less potent indeed than the Napoleonic kingdom of Westphalia. It was now that the system of Frederick the Great was put to use. It proved easier for an autocratic monarch to introduce a more democratic style of government. The brains and intelligence were provided not by the king but by ministers determined to introduce the sort of changes that, to their mind, had made France so peculiarly powerful, and had enabled Britain to resist her. The imposition of austerity ensured that royal extravagance was not a problem. The improved educational reforms ensured that there were educated and able people, not necessarily nobles, to run the county, to ensure that the indemnity was quickly paid and that Prussia returned to productivity.[22]

The limits Napoleon had put on the size of the army were put to a use Napoleon had not expected. The limits virtually confined it to the enrolment of Prussians not foreign mercenaries who had to be deterred from desertion by horrendous penalties. This meant that by passing men though the ranks and basic training for short periods of service, Prussia planned to put into the field, when the moment was ripe, a larger force than expected. As the fitness of many Prussian officers for command had been their upbringing as landlords and masters of near slave labour who jumped to their master's voice, no matter how stupid it was, Frederick William III was persuaded, despite the protests of his older officers, to relax the mindless discipline that had hitherto prevailed in the ranks and to introduce some of the more democratic forms of the French armies. The ranks of the nobility were no longer the sole source of officers, and Prussia's unexpectedly rapid military recovery, culminating in the timely appearance of Marshal Blücher on the field of Waterloo, was to give her a special place in the reconstruction of Europe.

After Prussia's defeat at Jena the pace of social reform, too, had quickened. Peasants were liberated from feudal obligations. They could acquire land, as well as lose it to enclosures to allow more scientific husbandry. The hold of the nobles on the ownership of land and eligibility for office, both civil and military, was relaxed. By resisting the call of some officials to rise against Napoleon when war with Russia seemed imminent, Frederick William III cautiously ensured that Prussia did not risk another catastrophic defeat. He even supplied 20,000 men for Napoleon's invasion of Russia, but his generals, by deploying them in the Baltic provinces, kept them out of the main army that suffered so much on the retreat from Moscow. With Napoleon in full retreat, the Prussian commander signed an armistice with the Russians without the king's approval, and Prussia was able at last to throw off French thraldom.

The motive for Frederick William's prevarication over responding in 1812 to a national feeling of outrage against the French may have been based on his fear of further defeat and spoliation, and from a prudential hope that, in grateful recognition of his loyalty at a critical moment, Napoleon, if successful against Russia, might allow him to recover lost territories and with them the power that was leeching away to his ministers. He had not given expression to any spirit of national outrage at the end of the previous century when the wars had seemed like the traditional play of dynastic policies and royal ambition. Perhaps he assumed these would be resumed after a stalemate peace. But if it had not awakened Frederick William III, the social upheaval of the revolution and the reformist administrative influence of Bonapartism had awakened a new sense in others that there was a better life waiting for humanity in general. Goethe's vision may have embraced all humanity in the spirit of freedom and equality, but there was a growing sense that, in some mystically purged way, the German people were ordained to lead this humanity towards a higher goal.

∗ ∗ ∗

The German reaction to Napoleon only became articulate after 1806. Before the Germans became aware of France's insatiable demand for men and money, the philosophic ideas of the conflicting schools of local thought had been theoretically concerned with the status of God, of nature, of the individual, of poetry, of religion, but hardly of the nation. A change, however, had been detected in the poetry of one who was to become the arch-poet of German spiritual revival, a young Saxon noble, who took the nom de plume of Novalis. George Frederick von

Hardenberg, (1772–1801), had been brought up on his family estate and educated at the Universities of Jena and Leipzig, where he studied law. When appointed financial auditor of a salt works, he dedicated his time to a study of practical geology, mathematics, chemistry and biology together with a parallel course of historical and philosophical enquiry. His encyclopaedic collection of knowledge was in the Germanic tradition, and he now joined a group of like-minded men and women who were using the end of the century period of German peace to discuss Man's place in the evolving world. He had heard Schiller's lectures on history at Halle, he was a frequent guest at the house of August and Caroline Schlegel, making up a house party that included Friedrich Schlegel, Fichte and Schelling, and he paid his visits of homage to Goethe and Herder at Weimar.

Novalis wanted to prove that the demonstrative certainties of science did not render the spiritual truths of art, religion and poetry of no relevance and though his work was cut short by his death from tuberculosis in 1801 it had already taken him deep into a mystical, imprecise vision of God, Christianity, and faith generally as the key to universal harmony. His poems, especially the six *Hymns to the Night,* written between 1797 and 1800, explored his lyrical view of the relationship between life and death, death being the everlasting night that is one of the great truths of life. Between man's happy life and the fear of unhappy death reconciliation is achieved with the Divine through a mediator, a loved one who has passed on before. Through love one conquers death and arrives at the universal harmony, a sort of spiritual Nirvana.

Germaine de Staël came close to being fair to Novalis's dedication to the reconciliation of nature and spirit. To understand it properly one needed, she wrote, '*une vie poétique et recueillie, une âme sainte et religieuse; toute la force et tout la fleur de l'existence humaine sont nécessaires pour la comprendre*'.[23] Novalis shared a vision that was echoed by William Blake. As Blake could see a world in a grain of sand and heaven in a wild flower, Novalis could see, in a leaf or a twig, an epoch in the life of the soul.[24] To refute the claim of the Enlightenment to have thrust God into the metaphysical boiler room, he dived into German medieval history to seek a pattern for the universal harmony he believed could be achieved, despite all the horrors of the revolution in France. The key to this harmony lay in poetry, which was true religion, not based on dogma or Levitican prohibitions, and harked back to the strong mystical tradition of Jakob Böhme. 'With his stillness, with his deep love of Nature, his mild, lofty, spiritual tone of contemplation, he comes before us in a sort of Asiatic character, almost like our ideal of some antique Gymnosophist.'[25] Without any sort of religion, however, 'of the world will be made a machine, of the Æther a gas, of God a force and of the Second World – a coffin'.[26] His marriage of what were in effect literary fragments about life and death to a poetic religiosity which was not religion, provided the yeast for German Romanticism which was to be 'proved' in the heat of the revolutionary and Napoleonic experience.

Shakespeare, Goethe and Schiller had stirred up an appetite for historical drama. Romeo and Juliet, though medieval Latin lovers, were archetypes of the new, spontaneous and passionate love that was to achieve its apotheosis in Tristan and Isolde. Novalis wanted Germany to cast off her subservience to French language and culture and range herself on the side of the world being created by its poets and philologists. Hesitatingly he saw a new Germany being created out of the old. He did not live to see the revival of German solidarity with which his poetry was to be linked after the humiliation of Prussia. But he had provided a basis for it by reflecting on a past, refulgent with the traditions of knightly excellence, of the Dantean vision of a purified *imperium*, with its rich, free cities full of architectural and artistic splendours, and its Minnesingers and its celestial harpists like Luther, Eckhart, Böhme and Paracelsus. Its language, in which once one used only to address one's horse, was now, in defiance of French linguistic domination, becoming, in the mouths of its poets and dramatists, a German *lingua Toscana*. Germany and German seemed on the brink of a remarkable rebirth.

CHAPTER TWELVE

The Return of 'Pumpernickel'

Germany after Napoleon

The Emperor is everything, Vienna is nothing.
(Clemens Lothar Wenzel, Prince von Metternich, 1848)

*I*T WAS NOT Germany, however, that was to be reborn, but Prussia, and the rebirth was to be personified in the Humboldt brothers, William (1767–1835), and Alexander (1769–1859). They were both privileged young Pomeranians, born in Berlin to a Prussian middle-level army officer; they did not attend school but were privately educated under the supervision of their mother, and were exposed in early life to a more polychromatic world than that of the solely Prussian intelligentsia, which revolved round the Academy of Sciences. William studied at both Frankfurt and Göttingen universities, the second founded in 1734 by George II of England as Elector of Hanover; he had been exposed to Wolfian ideas of religious scepticism, and had lived in Jena where he cultivated the friendship of Schiller as professor there and of Goethe in neighbouring Weimar. At the age of 35 in 1802 he was appointed to be what was considered a sinecure, Prussian minister at the Rome of Pius VII, now restored to sovereign authority on France's withdrawal from Italy.

There he cultivated the city's faltering scientific and literary community until after a brief period as one of the Berlin ministerial team, he transferred to Vienna in 1812. His intellectual and aristocratic credentials helped him to bring Austria and Prussia into an alliance with

Russia against Napoleon. He represented his kingdom at the Paris Peace Treaty and was to attend the Congresses of Vienna and of Aachen (1818) where he participated in the post-war settlement of Germany. But for 15 months, from March 1809 to June 1810, he had held the headship of the Berlin department responsible for the Church and Education. After the disastrous war with France, the call was all for the regeneration of a people through education. Despite his ignorance of schools, never having attended one, William Humboldt had in 1793 written a treatise on education in which his ideas were first elaborated. The whole personality of a man should be developed by the education he received, representative of the society around him and aiming at improvement not only of the individual but of society. It should be governed not by received but by acquired wisdom, responsive to national need and the extension of knowledge. Though only in office for a short time, and though his plans for a reform of the Prussian education system were not published in his lifetime, they were the basis for a system of technical high schools and *gymnasien*, which were to become the model for state education from America to Japan.

Humboldt's treatise also defined the limits of state action, but this did not see the light of day until after his death, so King Frederick William III did not know the limits that Humboldt believed should be placed on state authority in general – he would have disapproved if he had. The section, however, on education had been published in a monthly learned journal – and appeared to make such sense that the king was persuaded to appoint him to overhaul the education system. The theory appealed to Frederick William's notions of discipline: schools should aim, not just at imparting skills and useful knowledge, but at developing trained minds, capable of applying themselves to matters of national importance. This could be achieved by a methodical and intensive study of the Greek and Roman classics and of mathematics, buttressed by an immersion in general culture. Humboldt's interest in education, if not the king's, was cultural rather than administrative. He had published work on Socrates and Plato and their view of the divine, and he was later in his retirement to translate Pindar and Aeschylus, and to out-Goethe Goethe himself in his passion for the Greek world. Perhaps it was this aspect of classical order and conformity that recommended his treatise to Frederick William.

Humboldt's great work was to be completed by those who succeeded him in the ministry and after the war was over. On returning to Vienna and diplomacy he was able to immerse himself in that German speciality – philology. He had a pedagogue's interest in theory, especially the theory of language for his translations from the Greek gave him an interest in the way language developed itself by cultural assimilation and geographical spread. As he had married a rich wife with intellectual interests similar to his own, he decided in 1819 to retire and devote himself to his real passion. He was anyhow disenchanted with the direction of Prussian policy under the increasingly authoritarian Frederick William III and his reaction to independent thought.

To see if he could substantiate his theories on the formation of language as based on a system of rules and not just a collection of words, he set about the study of one of Europe's unexplained mysteries, the morphology of the Basque language. His theory that the original Iberian peoples and the autochthones of the western Mediterranean basin, including the Berbers of north Africa, spoke an adaptation of Basque may not stand up to scrutiny, but his methodology has. He was to die before he had completed a similar study of the ancient language of Java, to prove in a nutshell that thought preceded words, so that speech was an intellectual activity. He gave linguistics and archaeology a template for investigation into prehistory for which his later countrymen became famous.

William is remembered for the university founded in his name and which he caused to be set up in 1810, before he was posted as ambassador to Austria. It was to replace Halle, which was now no longer in Prussia, and while continuing Halle's distinguished academic tradition in the pursuit of knowledge, the new foundation was to develop students who could use their intellectual resources to tackle any task that might be required of them. Universities should no longer just increase and impart knowledge but be an instrument of national regeneration. With modifications, the Humboldt ideal was to inform higher education throughout the world. However, the university he had founded, itself being wholly dependent on an autocratic state, had difficulty in living up to its foundation.

His younger brother, Alexander, was to become more widely famous. His life belongs more firmly to the history of the Americas, where he is commemorated by the current called after him and by the names of many towns, counties, universities and national parks in the United States and in Spanish America. Schiller thought he was better known than his brother because he bragged more, but his brother recognised in him a capacity for absorbing and synthesising knowledge at a rare speed. Alexander published the account of his travels in 'the equinoctial regions' of the new continent, between 1799–1804, in 30 volumes, encompassing anthropological studies of the autochthonous Amerindians, a geographical study of the distribution of plants native to the continent, and historical and political accounts of New Spain. It was followed from 1815–25 by seven volumes containing descriptions of 4,500 plants which he and his colleagues had collected in the Americas.

His work was encyclopaedic, a quarry for botanists, anthropologists, philologists and all collectors of human knowledge, which Humboldt had assembled from personal observation. He was prevented from entering Brazil, and was suspected as being spy for a Spain, which was then an ally of France. Brazil had to wait for the foundation of the new empire and the first scientific expedition, led by two Bavarians, Johann Baptist von Spix and Frederick Philip von Martius. The new world, which hitherto had been an object of exploitation, was rendered by Humboldt an observatory. Napoleon who met him commented with a wry Gallic envy that his wife, too, was studying Botanics. Goethe was more generous; he said that Humboldt was showering the world with treasures. Darwin, who 20 years later was to enter the same new world, counted him the greatest travelling scientist who ever lived. Prussia had left the world of Pumpernickel for that of universal science.

By the end of the Napoleonic wars there was a Germanic consciousness but it was not a national one, and it owed more to literary efflorescence than to Napoleonic inspiration. The two swans of Weimar, Schiller and Goethe, sheltering in the so-far peaceful embrace of Duke Charles Augustus, concluded that the proper stance of the enlightened in the storm that afflicted Europe was to keep their heads down. In 1795 Charles Augustus had delicately withdrawn himself from any commitment to Austria and his Duchy was to enjoy another ten years of peace. In 1796,

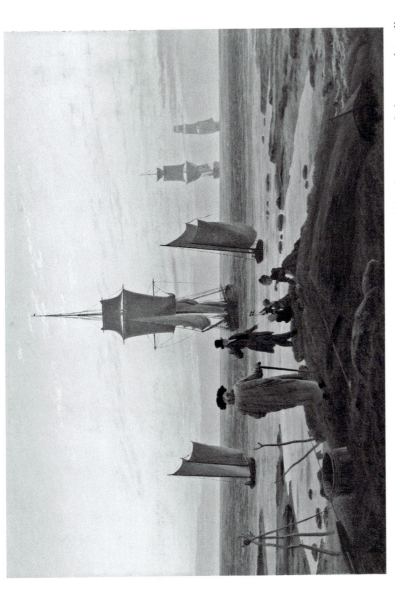

1 Caspar David Friedrich, *The Stages of Life* (1830). The bleak Pomeranian seascape and the three sinisterly looming ships illustrate the sense of melancholy and fatalism that overshadowed Friedrich's view of life.

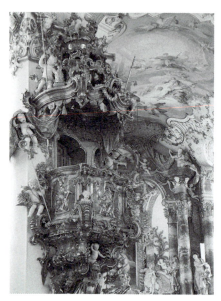

2   Dominikus Zimmermann (1685–1766), Wies Pilgrimage Church, Steingaden (1750s), described by Sacheverell Sitwell (*For Want of the Golden City*, 1973, p. 93) as among 'certainly the most beautiful Rococo interiors in the world.' The 'Würzburg Rococo' pulpit.

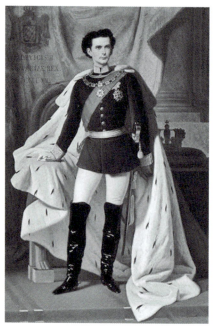

3   King Ludwig II, as a general in the Bavarian army, in coronation robes in 1865, aged 20. A portrait by Ferdinand von Piloty in the *Bayerische Staatsgemaldesammlungen*, Munich.

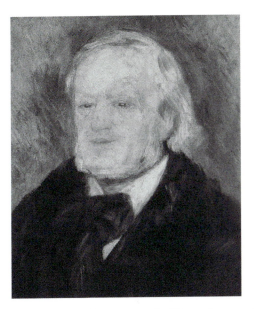

4   Richard Wagner, 1882, a portrait by Pierre-Auguste Renoir, from the Musée d'Orsay, Paris.

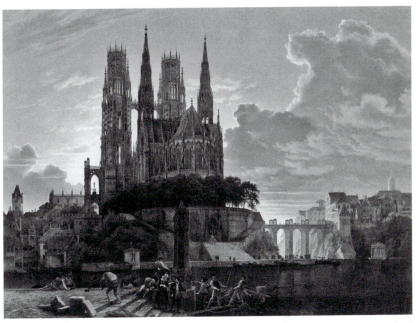

5   Karl Friedrich Schinkel (1781–1841), arch-Romantic and polymath, *A Gothic Temple by Water* (1823). Schinkel was primarily an architect intent on beautifying Berlin in classic style, but in his painting he tried to marry the Romantic Gothic style with the realism of his namesake, Caspar David Friedrich.

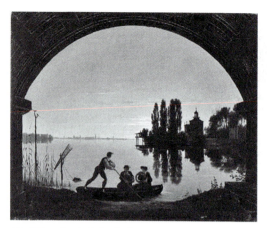

6 Karl Friedrich Schinkel, *A Riverbank in Streslau* (1817).

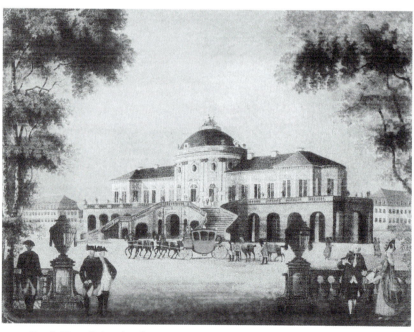

7 Schloss Solitude, the city imitation of Versailles that Duke Charles Eugene of Württemberg built in Stuttgart between 1763 and 1767.

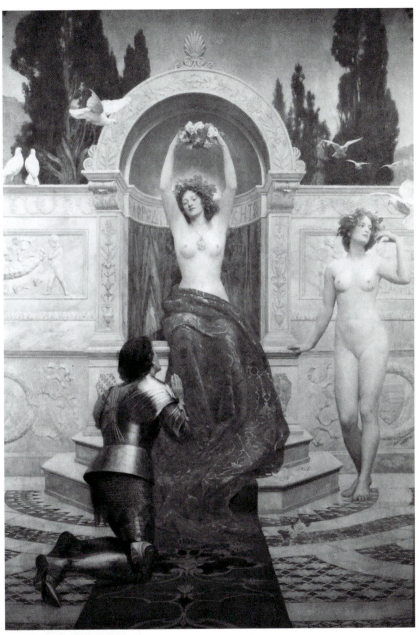

8 *Tannhäuser in the Venusberg*, a painting by John Collier (1901). A rather more explicit illustration of the song that so shocked Elizabeth/ Matilda and the attendant Minnesingers in Wagner's opera.

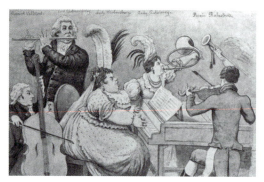

9   A musical party given in a cartoon by Thomas Rowlandson
(1736–1827), which may have given Thackeray his idea
of a typical musical evening in Pumpernickel.

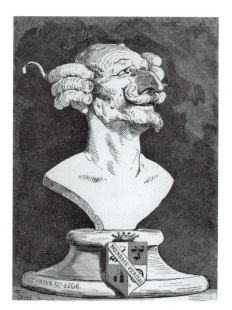

10   The real Baron (Freiherr) Karl Friedrich Münchhausen
according to Gustave Doré. The caricaturist, in the mocking style
of Canova, captures the extravagant mendacity of the man whom
Rudolph Eric Raspe was to make famous throughout Europe.

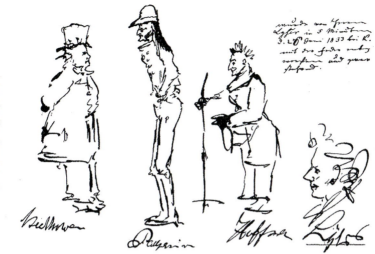

Nr. 30. Lyser. Originalfederzeichnung von Beethoven, Paganini, E. T. A. Hoffmann u. ihm selbst a. d. J. 1833. Originalgröße.

11 A pencil sketch of Hoffmann, third from right, carrying his hat, by Johann Peter Lyser in 1833. The other caricatures are Beethoven, Paganini, Hoffmann and Lyser himself. Hoffmann's dishevelled appearance helps to explain why he never became the 'great lover' of his dreams.

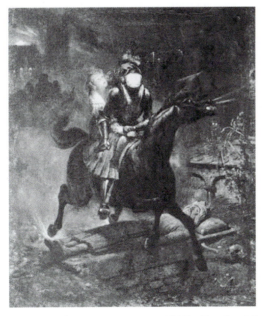

12 *La ballade de Lénore* by Horace Vernet (1849). Gottfried August Berger (1747–94) published the ballade of the ghostly rider posing as Lénore's dead lover in 1773. It was to inspire many of the 'shudder novels' and poems of the late Romantic period particularly Schubert's 'ErlKonig'.

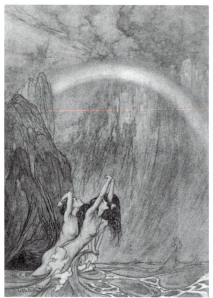

13 The Rhine-maidens in *Das Rheingold*. At its first performance in Munich in 1869 one of them was seasick in what was dubbed 'the aquarium of whores' (the contraption invented for their immersion in the waters of the Rhine), and they had to perform from one of the boxes in the auditorium.

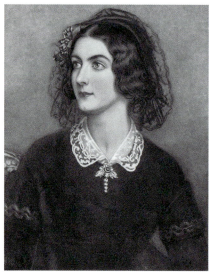

14 Lola Montez in 1847, from a portrait by Joseph Karl Stieler, revealing the expressive eyes, but not the other 28-year-old charms that captivated Ludwig I of Bavaria.

Goethe's *Wilhelm Meister* completed his apprenticeship on a journey through life that started in 1777 and was to end in 1829. Goethe intended his novel to be a morality, seen through the looking glass of Hogarth's *Rake's Progress*. Meister had to learn to disassociate himself both from an arrogant and boorish aristocracy and from a bourgeoisie replete with and obsessed by money. Unlike Hogarth's Tom Rakewell, Meister learned that peace and harmony came from conjugal calm and benevolence, and a usefully productive life.

In 1797, Goethe married Hermann to Dorothea in a long poem in which Dorothea's first husband, a moderate revolutionary, is killed by rabid Jacobins. Herman/Goethe sympathised with their ideals and hopes, but both could be corrupted, and in marrying Dorothea he/ they determined that she should never again be exposed to violence and uncertainty. The two would survive by living a life of moderate behaviour, and simple activities, eschewing hasty and incautious actions. As the storm raged round Europe Goethe, like Hermann, did not strike declamatory, insurrectionary attitude. When asked where the future of Germany lay, he answered: in the German language and culture, not in politics.

Schiller, too, moved on from his youthful sense of rebelliousness. From 1797 his plays explored high political drama in which his principal protagonists were inevitable losers. Wallenstein (1797) was betrayed, Mary Stuart (1800) was beheaded and The Maid of Orleans (1802) was burned (though in his play she was killed in battle). This may have been consistent with Greek drama in which humans fought valiantly but hopelessly with destiny. The revolution in France, which they had all applauded when it started, had consumed its own and spread misery and suffering. Mankind was not yet ready for revolution; reason was not yet enough, for man had not yet learned, through the elevating power of poetry, how to use the knowledge of truth and justice to improve society. Until it had grown out of the frivolity of ordinary pleasures, it could not fully comprehend higher things.

From the ashes of *sturm und drang*, the new Romanticism explored man's relations with God and the world around him, not by abolishing the rules of literary behaviour, like the *sturmers und drangers*, but exercising the same freedom to explore what that relationship might be, in a new pantheism and the spirituality of all things. In his *Hymn to the Night* (1800),

Novalis had expressed the defining spirit of Romanticism in religious lyricism that transcended dogma. The classical Grecian images, which Winckelmann had exposed as the perfect model of harmony and order, and which Lessing and Goethe had accepted, gave place to a search for a soul, which for Germans was to be found more in the German Middle Ages and its mystical tradition than in the groves of Attica.

For Novalis the French Revolution had been a disastrous event for Germany and from that ferment in his mind, he planted the notion of a national identity round which patriots could gather. Germany's Middle Ages provided a new and almost virgin field of examination to German scholars of whom the Brothers Grimm were perhaps the most widely known outside Germany. From linguistic and archival research into the medieval mind, law and culture, an idea of national culture was born, which grew in antithesis to the Frenchified and Italianate predilections of Pumpernickel.

Germany's two most creative writers, Goethe and Schiller, however, had proved too pure for political action. Goethe presided over all the upheavals of Germany with an almost sublime detachment, having grown out of *sturm und drang,* and repudiated Romanticism. Goethe indeed told Eckermann that he considered Romanticism a sickness and the only true health lay in classical law and order. Schiller maintained that the German people still had to be educated, which became his mission, if they were ever to change the political scene in a century dominated by the two competitors for world power, France and England. The sheer prodigality and seeming unattainability of their wealth had made the ideas, that came from both places, exciting and revolutionary, but not dangerous, until the French arrived at the point of the bayonet in 1793. The wars hitherto had been echoes of the Thirty Years War, campaigns of limited duration, fought more for land than ideology. The French revolutionary and Napoleonic armies changed all this, converting war into a matter of cultural survival.

As a result, in 1828 Goethe was not preoccupied about German unity. All Germans needed was to be culturally not politically united. Roads and railways might achieve that in time and in the meantime the nation had done well from Germany's proliferation of sovereigns. For Goethe, a unitary state was where there was homogeneity in weights, measures and currency and where the citizen of one state could move freely in all.

But what would a unitary state do for the culture of the German people? Look at what there was now: 40 universities, 100 public libraries, a great number of collections of art and 'objects belonging to all the kingdoms of nature', over 70 theatres, and orchestras which promoted the higher cultivation of the people. Though many of the universities were little more than status symbols to adorn the principality and were largely used to train administrators and clergy, academics were of all intellectuals among the people the most esteemed.[1] Goethe was worried too about what would happen in a unitary state to the four free cities which had had such a brilliant effect on the prosperity of Germany? 'Would they remain what they are if they lost their own sovereignty and became incorporated with any great German kingdom as a provincial town?' He doubted it.[2]

* * *

Everyone recognised that Prussia was the most successful survivor in Germany, but it was a Prussia, despite Moses Mendelssohn, and the Humboldts, which was to be, after Austria, the most autocratic and conservative member of the Germanic family. Frederick William III wanted no truck with a constitution; the old toothless Estates, easily controlled, were enough, and military conscription remained to remind the people who really ruled. Prussia had to wait for a constitution until the year of revolutions in 1848. In the rest of Germany, eighteenth-century society remained little changed. In nearly all of its states, even in 'reformist' Prussia, the governing class structure had consolidated its power, acknowledging virtually none superior to its own.

Before the wars at the end of the eighteenth century, the predominantly peasant population of central and eastern Europe, with the possible exception of Prussia's, had been kept inefficient and poor by a policy of indolence. Even Prussia protected its peasantry more as a source of well-proportioned grenadiers for its army than as an engine of efficient agriculture. The further east one travelled, the peasantry subsisted in conditions of serfdom. Under the influence of Napoleonic precept and example serfdom was abolished in the western German states, where landlords slowly learned that paid labour was more productive than unpaid, but few expected it to be universally discarded throughout the

German-speaking world.[3] The princes owned most of the available land for farming – the Wittelsbachs at least an eighth part of Bavaria and the Hohenzollerns a third of Brandenburg. Cities seldom had populations larger than 10,000 and though the birth rate rose steeply in the latter part of the eighteenth century, largely because of fewer attacks of bubonic plague and the development of a slightly better diet, there was little migration to the cities, where landless and tradeless poverty was severe.[4] The image of Ruritania (a land of *rus* rather than *urbs*) prevailed, where the *rustics* still ate pumpernickel and the master craftsman enjoyed 'the present with a pure and a perfect joy, expecting tomorrow to be exactly like today'.[5]

The Napoleonic system, however, had been so long imposed that it was not dismantled at the end of the war, for it had provided princes with a model of how to run an autocratic state. The French, when they had the opportunity, had generally reduced the privileges of the nobility and secularised the lands of the Church, and in those southern states that were allies of Napoleon, like Bavaria, Württemberg and Baden, and not therefore occupied, modernising the administration had been pursued on French lines. Christian confessions acquired equal rights, and taxation was levied according to capacity to pay, with no privileged exemptions. If the peasantry, despite the abolition of serfdom, was not entirely free, there was no way of returning to the situation before Napoleon. Such reforms as had been started were not abandoned; they were just appropriated by secular rulers who had either maintained or enlarged their states, and as a result encountered few privileged or spiritual forces to constrain them.

Of all German territories, Prussia changed most of all. The rest of western Germany, brought first into a Confederation of the Rhine and then into Jerome Bonaparte's kingdom of Westphalia, had been used as a recruiting ground for French armies. Napoleon had unilaterally disposed of territories, transferred sovereignties and created kingdoms. He had wound up the decrepit Holy Roman Empire and, with it, Imperial relics like Church princes, imperial knights and free towns. Aggrandisement, by the incorporation of these former statelets, reconciled the larger states to their puppet status. Napoleon had little time or inclination to do more than impose a typically Napoleonic system on conquered territories and then mulct them for men and money. Administrative reform, the

Code Napoléon, and the taming of Church power, did much to release German society from the medieval thrall that stamped it with the image of Pumpernickel, and the shock was to lend strength to the development of a new sense of German nationality, especially among the leisure and reading classes who knew their Klopstock, Herder, Schiller and Goethe. Carlyle described it in his heated prose thus: 'Bonaparte walked through the war-convulsed world like an all-devouring earthquake, heaving, thundering, hurling kingdom over kingdom; Goethe was the mild-shining, inaudible Light, which, notwithstanding, can again make that Chaos into a creation.'[6] It was their common desire to create a new humanity that made it possible for them to accept and develop the social and educational reforms that were being pioneered in Humboldt's Prussia, and to dream that there might be a German nation as well as a German culture.

* * *

Napoleon's banishment to Elba was to reduce him to the size of the pocket-handkerchief principalities that had formerly covered central and southern Europe with a baffling quilt of sovereignties claiming virtually absolute powers. Even before Napoleon set off for his *vita nuova* as sovereign of his island, the victorious powers had decided to simplify that world by reducing the 300 German states to 39. This was not a step in the direction of creating one Germany, which Napoleon's dynastic reshaping of Europe had seemed to foreshadow. There were, in fact, only two German states, Prussia and Austria, which could have laid claim to be the nucleus of such a state. Neither of them had any wish to fulfil what some were already preaching was the historic role of Germans to be an Imperial power.

Prussia was not at this stage a candidate, even though she now ruled over more ethnic Germans than any other state, having been granted at the peace its lost territories and more provinces on the Rhine. Frederick William III, however, did not wish to become a bulwark against France. His ambition was to establish himself as the principal power in north-eastern Europe, nourished on dreams of the Ostmark, the Hansa and Teutonic Knights, and he would have been better satisfied by the cession of more Saxon and Polish territory, than by what he had acquired on the Rhine.

The Austrian Empire itself enjoyed a glittering existence as a multi-ethnic, multilingual, multicultural empire that beat with the heart of a continent. Austria was not a nation but a conglomerate, and as such she saw herself as the natural leader of continental Europe, not just of Germany.[7] She did not want this role to fall to the Romanovs who, since 1613, had transformed the Grand-Duchy of Moscow into a European power. Only a strong Imperial state that stretched to the borders of Poland could thwart Russian designs on the European provinces of the Ottoman Empire and turn her ambitions east, to central Asia.

Neither Austria nor Prussia saw any advantage in unifying Germany, but the Napoleonic confederacy before the creation of the kingdom of Westphalia might be revived as long as it remained a confederacy and not a nation. In 1815, it suited the times to reduce the proliferation of virtually unviable German states, and to preserve a network of viable sovereignties. The winning coalition of sovereigns was rewarded at the expense of those anachronistic anomalies that had survived the Thirty Years War, and the return of monarchies was not opposed. They provided the best guarantee against any return of the dreams to which the French revolutionary and the Napoleonic dreams had given birth.

In crude political terms, in fact, both dreams advanced, not the cause of liberal freedoms, but that of autocratic rule. They had, it was true, ensured the destruction of the old orders of knights, they had contributed to the abasement of clerical power and the disappearance of their temporal lands, and they had assisted in subduing the economic independence of the free cities. The only free cities to survive were Frankfurt, Hamburg, Bremen and Lubeck and these owed more to their distance from both Vienna and Berlin than to their illustrious past. But above all, these dreams had disturbed the fabric of traditional society, with its castes with heritable privileges and autonomies, and made it easier for rulers to rule absolutely. The princes had had enough social revolution. Serfdom had gone, and merit rather than birth were increasingly the qualification for public service, but dealing with the effects of this amount of revolution was enough to occupy the restored dynasties.

* * *

The greater idea of national identity was lost in the challenges of particularism. Napoleon, by the time of his fall was repudiated by both sovereigns and peoples, by the first because he was the embodiment of revolution, by the second because he was the embodiment of tyranny. For sovereigns the defence against revolution was to tighten the screws of absolute rule; for the 'people' free institutions were a defence against tyranny. The two were irreconcilable, and the return of Napoleon from Elba frightened Europe out of any liberal intentions. Some monarchs, like the Grand Duke of Weimar, enjoyed genuine popular support, especially from Goethe who, notwithstanding his conviction that Germany must some day be united, yet hoped that any eventual German unity would not destroy local cultures and loyalties. The other rulers regarded themselves as a benign barrier to revolutionary change.

Kings, Electors, Margraves, Dukes and Prince-Bishops now dominated the 39 survivors of the old German patchwork of sovereignties. The principal states were German Austria, Prussia, Bavaria, Saxony (much reduced in size owing to her mistaken support of Napoleon), Hanover and Württemberg, each with a king; while Baden was ruled by a Grand-Duke. There was an Electoral Hesse and a Grand-Ducal Hesse, for the original Margravate of Hesse-Kassel had been elevated to an Electorate and kept its title after Napoleon's defeat, – even when there was no longer a Holy Roman Emperor to elect – in order to give the elector rank over his cousin the Grand-Duke. The Elector William had been deposed by Napoleon for his alliance with Prussia and Kassel had become Jerome Bonaparte's capital of his kingdom of Westphalia. The Elector William, once restored, was no longer able to sell his Hessians as mercenaries to England, so that he exercised an avarice that eventually led to his deposition in 1830. Schleswig-Holstein was added to Denmark and Luxembourg was united with the Netherlands, but both retained their German identity. Among the other small Pumpernickel states to survive were the Saxon enclaves including Weimar, the two Hohenzollern principalities of Sigmaringen and Hechingen, bordering Bavaria and Württemberg, Hesse-Darmstadt and Hesse-Cassel, the Duchy of Anhalt-Kothen, so small its inhabitants lived off smuggling, and the other tiny principalities round Prussia: Brunswick, Bernburg, Schwarzburg-Rudolstadt, Schaumburg-Lippau, Dessau and Mecklenburg-Schwerin.

Of these, only the Grand-Duke of Saxe-Weimar, in 1816, redeemed the pledge given at the Congress of Vienna that each sovereign would – at some indefinite moment – establish a truly representative institution in his lands. Those German states in succeeding years that accepted or were given constitutions between 1814–20, on the model of the French Charter of 1814, did not interpret their creation as meaning that representative government should rule. They were created to act as a lightning conductor for the ruler, who would appoint ministers with ill-defined responsive powers so long as appointment remained in his hands and ministers did what they were told.

The constitutional story was complicated, spasmodic and mainly futile. The two Napoleonic kingdoms, of Bavaria and Württemberg, who survived relatively unscathed, even liberalised, despite their alliances with France, were the first to adopt a modified form of elected chambers. In 1818 Bavaria became a constitutional monarchy. She had, at the peace, lost most of the territorial gains she had made during the war but she now settled her border disputes and set about becoming the leader of the smaller south German states in their disputes with a prepotent Austria. She also aspired to be a (not wholly) working model democracy, for her parliament was elected on a very limited franchise. For a time, however, she was considered the most liberal, apart from Saxe-Weimar, among the German states. But her liberalism derived less from a conviction of the benefits of representative government than from fear and dislike of the two military monarchies, Austria and Prussia, who had not accepted constitutions.[8] By preserving her detachment from them, and by causing friction between them, Bavaria hoped to enjoy the leadership of the Confederation, but when liberal ambitions became too vocal, the king muzzled them with the threat of Austrian supported sanctions. After which Maximilian then reigned in comparative peace until 1825.

* * *

The spirit of Pumpernickel was to surface in Bavaria with extraordinary vigour with the accession in 1825 of Maximilian's heir, Ludwig (Louis) I. He was 39-years-old, born in 1786 when his father was a French officer, and he had been a godson of the ill-fated Louis XVI, whose name he took.

As heir apparent to the Bavarian throne he had been unwillingly obliged to participate in Napoleon's 1809 war with Austria that ended at Wagram, and Ludwig's was a powerful voice in persuading his father to change sides and join the alliance that followed Napoleon's Russian debacle. Now that he was king, he was able to put the clock back to an ideal world that existed before the great revolution. Even so he was not a complete reactionary. Bavaria needed to generate wealth and Ludwig did not stand in the way of industrialisation, digging a canal between the Danube and the Main rivers to facilitate transport and building a railway as far as Nuremberg. But that was as far as his modernity went.

Ludwig looked back, following the intellectual fashion of the day, to an age of imagined German glory in the Middle Ages. He restored some of the suppressed monasteries and gave himself pompous royal, even Imperial, titles.[9] He revived in himself the Wittelsbach line that had formally expired when Charles Theodore succeeded to the Electorate. Above all he threw himself into building, into collecting art and into writing bad poetry. His passion for all things Hellenic made him an enthusiastic supporter of Greek independence, and in 1832 his son Otto was persuaded to become the first king of an independent Greece. He amassed Greek and Roman sculpture for his classically designed museums, and in addition to altering the largely medieval face of Munich he sent his architects to help his son give his capital at Athens a suitably neo-classical appearance. He even decreed that his country should be called Bayern, using the Hellenic *upsilon* instead of the Latin letter *i*. Above all he had a wholly neo-classical fondness for classical beauties, whom he immortalised in his *Schönheitengalerie* (Gallery of Beauties) and, though he was hard of hearing and married with eight children, he took whom of them he could to bed. For a short time he was lover of the society beauty and heiress, Jane Digby, who left him for another Bavarian nobleman who was father to her son, but he entered into a more enduring relationship, largely for ill, with a notorious Irish *horizontale*, Lola Montez, who was originally christened Eliza Rosanna Gilbert.

Lola Montez was born in Ireland in 1821, child of the 15-year-old wife of Edward Gilbert, ensign in a regiment destined for India, who died of cholera shortly after arriving there. Eliza's mother quickly married another ensign and the young Eliza grew up in that paradise for children, wayward and spoiled. Sent home to England for her education, she grew in wildness and in beauty, mistaken for a child of mixed blood, and acquiring enough learning to wish for no more. To get back to India she eloped at 16 with a Lieutenant James whom she abandoned by mutual consent in Calcutta to become a dancer. Back in London again she assumed a Spanish identity as Lola Montez, dancing wild and faintly lubricious sarabands and seguidillas until rumbled as fraudulently non-Spanish, whereupon she left for the continent to make her name there as a fiery and self-willed but undeniable beauty, performing her Iberian art where she could.

In Paris, Lola managed to captivate Franz Liszt who introduced her to his former lover, the great granddaughter of the Saxon condottiere, Maurice de Saxe. In the salon of Georges Sand, Lola developed some social if raffish literary arts that introduced her to the seraglio of Alexander Dumas *père*. Thence in 1846, on the death of her lover of the day, she went to Munich, where it was not difficult to catch the eye of the sexagenarian king. It was probably malicious gossip that she did this by baring her breasts, to show him that she was really that well endowed, (though it would not have been beyond her) and progression to royal mistress was quick. Soon a reincarnated La Grävenitz stalked the corridors of Munich. The Müncheners were not averse to their monarch's choice of two foreigners as his *maîtresses en titres*, both remarkably lovely in their way, but Jane Digby had the sense not to stay around and interfere. Lola was, by contrast, incautious and greedy. The Müncheners soon realised that she was not good either for Ludwig or for Bavaria, and when they learned that, in addition to all the houses, jewels and works of art that Ludwig lavished on her, she wanted a title and acceptance as a naturalised Bavarian citizen – and as she used to boast that what Lola wants Lola gets – their anger began to show.

Ludwig was tiring of being a constitutional monarch. He had already secured a clerically conservative ministry that was, under the influence of the restored Society of Jesus, inexorably rescinding the liberal laws that had allowed freedom of conscience and the press. It was becoming dangerous to voice any criticism of the royal family or of affairs of State, which seemed to be controlled by Lola. When the chief minister of a subservient but clerical administration sent a memorandum to the king expressing reservations about naturalising Lola, she had him dismissed. She secured her title, as Countess of Landsfeld, and the new ministry accorded her naturalisation papers. But trouble was brewing. The parody of the Lord's Prayer, beseeching God to give Lola her daily perquisites of house and home, to forgive her excesses and lead her not into penury, echoed what had been prayed about La Grävenitz in Württemberg during the last century.

Lola seemed quite insensitive to criticism; and foiled every attempt of the new chief minister to form an administration. When protests convulsed the university, Ludwig dismissed the professors, arrested their students and suspended the constitution. What was put in place of the dissolved assembly was dubbed the Lola Ministry (*Lolaministerium*). But it was March 1848, and the virus of revolution was abroad in Europe. When Ludwig dismissed the Lola ministry but not Lola, the normally complaisant Müncheners exploded in rage. Both Ludwig and his leman had to go. And go they went, Lola to Switzerland, hoping in vain to be joined by Ludwig, who abdicated in favour of his son, another Maximilian.

The fall of the bad angel was sudden and final. Lola retired to London and there contracted another marriage, though bigamously, as her second husband was still at that time living. When that liaison collapsed, Lola took herself to America, where it was downhill all the way. She entered into another failed marriage with a newspaper man and when this ended she took to the stage again with an erotic 'Spider Dance', a tarantella in which she shed imitation tarantula spiders from her capacious bosom. She performed this before gold-diggers on a visit to Australia to recoup her fortunes but her performance was too salacious for their more respectable wives.

Back in America she had a stroke in her 39th year, was partially paralysed, found religion and a priest to look after her — not, she hastened to aver, a Jesuit whose Society had earlier hounded her out of Europe. She died aged 40. Despite the veneer imparted by her short association with Georges Sand and her salon, Lola was not intelligent. She was a naked adventuress with a ferocious temper, to which her trail of husbands was witness, but perhaps she was more genuinely fond of Ludwig than her greed and social ambition indicated. With her passing into self-imposed exile the European story of managing political concubines, one of the vagaries of Pumpernickel, came to a discreet end.

* * *

Württemberg also continued unfortunate in her rulers. Charles Eugene's son, Frederick, was astute enough to please Napoleon, who complimented him on being the most intelligent of German princes, by adopting such Napoleonic reforms as would enable him to retain the absolute rule of his father. He created a new army and established religious equality but he abolished the Estates, which had exercised enough restraint on his prodigal forebears to cause Charles James Fox to say that England's and Württemberg's were the only two true constitutions in Europe. At the end of the war he tried to disarm general disgust at the way he had otherwise ruled the state by promising a constitution, but even Metternich would not support the worthless model he produced. The succession of his son, William, husband of the Russian Emperor's sister, promised better, as the new king wanted to emulate his brother-in-law, then passing through his liberal phase. He revived the ancient Estates, but the dominance there of the nobles and clergy blocked any more liberal proposals, and King William tried to rule, effectively but absolutely, through the bureaucracy his father had created. The reactionaries of Europe accepted, with satisfaction, that even under so liberal-minded a monarch, it seemed impossible to make a constitution work.

* * *

The Grand-Duchy, formerly Margravate, of Baden did little to deserve its tenfold accretion of territory on the east bank of the Rhine, mainly former Imperial Bishoprics and the ill-fated Palatinate. It stretched along the Rhine from Lake Constanz on the south, along the borders of Württemberg to Bavaria on the north. Its heavily forested hills which covered most of its territory provided a perfect climate for the vine and to complement its reputation for wine and song; the Mannheim orchestra was still reputed the finest in Germany. Mannheim as the former home of the Elector Palatine had also staged the first public performance of Schiller's *sturm und drang* play, *The Robbers*. It was incorporated into the Grand-Duchy of Baden by Napoleon, whose stepdaughter, Stéphanie Beauharnais, married the new Grand-Duke in 1811 so that the Grand-Duchy came under France's more direct 'protection'. After the war, Bavaria disputed Baden's ownership of so much of the former Palatinate, and it was the timely concession of a constitution, based on that granted Poland by Tsar Alexander, thus gaining his approbation, that saved the integrity of the Grand-Duchy. Its mineral waters were to give Pumpernickel's Baden-Baden a new lease of life.

* * *

The machinery for inter-state cooperation, which some hoped might jump-start political unity, was the Germanic Confederation. Established at one of the four remaining free cities, Frankfurt-am-Main, the Confederation proved to be a successful barrier to it. Whatever the intentions of its founders, the confederacy was not a Confederation of Peoples but of Monarchs, and of Monarchs who had a highly wrought hands-off policy when it came to issues of governance and sovereignty. It oscillated between membership of 39 and 33 states until 1866 when it was dissolved. Only German-speaking states belonged to it, so that the only part of the Austrian Empire to be admitted as member was the Archduchy of Austria. It had two components: a Diet representative of the sovereigns and an assembly representative of the people. In any confrontation between the two, the people lost. From 1816, the return of Pumpernickel was to retard the cause of German national identity for at least another quarter century. The clock, however, could not be put back entirely. The universities and *gymnasia* became hotbeds of sedition. Formal lectures became manifestos, classes political meetings. The Chancellor of the Austrian Empire at Vienna, Prince Metternich, was convinced that a whole leadership generation was being 'ripened for revolution'.[10]

Austria had always looked not only west, but also south and east. The Habsburgs had been the main obstacle to Ottoman encroachment into southern Europe, and they ruled over a diverse and polyglot peoples, Magyars, Bohemians, Slovaks, Poles, Slovenes, Croats and Italians, as well as Austrians, and the latest Habsburg was unashamedly an autocrat. Francis (the First of Austria and Second of the Holy Roman Empire, *regnavit* as Emperor of Austria from 1804–35), was the son of Leopold who had ruled Tuscany as a benevolent ruler from 1765 until becoming Holy Roman Emperor in 1790. Leopold only lived for two years as Emperor, and Francis, though a humane, even virtuous prince brought to his throne none of his father's loosely liberal attitudes. Rather they were the autocratic preferences of his uncle, Joseph II. For Francis there was only one contract between ruler and people, the duty of the ruler being to rule and the duty of his people to obey. In return for total submission to the prince's will, the prince would try to govern fairly and justly. Unfortunately Francis had very little imagination. Unlike Joseph II whose autocracy was tempered by social adjustments to make it fairer and more efficient, Francis feared change and criticism. What he had inherited he would retain, cocooned as far as he could manage it from reform.

Though the Austrian Empire was run largely by German speakers, it was not German. The administrative languages of Hungary were Latin and Magyar, and the other nationalities were asserting their own brand of linguistic and administrative nationalism. Since Francis had ascended the throne in 1792, he had been engaged until 1815 in a perpetual war with France, punctuated by defeats and truces. After the humiliating treaty of Pressburg (December 1805), when Bavaria, Württemberg and Baden became sovereign states, removed from allegiance to Vienna, and the smaller German states were lumped together in a Confederation under the protection of France, Francis espoused a short period of administrative change. But it did not last for long. Unless the lid was firmly secured on the pot any ebullition of national feeling would in his belief lead to the collapse of the empire.

Francis was supported in his ideas by his Chancellor, Clemens Lothar Wenzel, Prince von Metternich, who was actually born a Rhinelander at Koblenz, where the Moselle meets the Rhine in the former Palatinate (ceded after the French wars to Prussia). Metternich was educated at the universities in Strasburg and Mainz, both cities on river confluences of the Rhine, and so grew up where French ideas and language dominated. The river was a marker of boundaries, and the desirability of natural defences informed and governed his thinking all his life. He was in Austrian service early and in 1801, at the age of 28, was Austrian minister at Dresden, the capital of Pumpernickel Saxony. Thereafter promotion was rapid, to Berlin, then Paris and then Vienna itself as Foreign Minister in 1809. From that moment he was convinced that the only way to keep the multi-ethnic pot over which Francis II reigned from boiling was to draw firm frontiers and preserve the status quo. He believed in the empire's multiethnicity and ensured a steady supply from its many populations to enlist in the service, both civil and military, of the Emperor.

The empire was visible in the person of its Emperor, who was not representative of his people. Metternich shared his suspicion of democratic or representative government. It was argumentative, ill-informed, prejudiced and basically antipathetic to good government – a view of democracy he shared with the younger Disraeli – but Metternich was not ill-disposed to any reform, which in his opinion contributed to his first priority, a general peace. He was sincere in his belief that enlightened rule by an autocratic ruler was the best formula; and he undid none of the often contentious reforms of the Emperor Joseph II. He believed that Napoleon had not broken the Imperial institution. Metternich had, after all, negotiated the French emperor's marriage to Marie-Louise, and had almost to the end believed that the peace of Europe would be better preserved by continued Napoleonic rule in France, suitably tamed. Now the French Emperor was gone, the Bourbons ruled in France and only the Austrian Emperor remained. Metternich was determined to keep that last institution intact, not to add to it by undertaking any pan-German role. The idea of bringing together the fractious and self-important rulers of Germany into a Habsburg-led *reich* was, for him, 'an infamous project'.[11]

By making Prussia, a state he deeply distrusted, the predominant power on the Rhine, he hoped that Prussia and not Austria would become the principal barrier to French ambitions in that area. By keeping all non-German speaking provinces out of the German confederacy at Frankfurt, he hoped to insulate the empire from any attacks of national ebullition. For ebullition there was, and almost straight away. Had this been merely a Romantic revolt against the Encyclopaedia and the Teutonic banalities of administrative, Josephan reform, Metternich could have accepted it as the normal froth of university students – he had been one in his time. But as soon as the infection of liberal thought began to form 'huge cloudy symbols of a high romance', and to inspire noble youth with dreams of German unity, he moved into action.

The University of Jena, in the domain of the liberal Duke of Saxe-Weimar, echoed to cries of liberty and national independence, of which the Diet at Frankfurt was the emasculated symbol. Jena had been the university of Johann Jakob Brucker, born in 1696 and two years younger than Voltaire. He was a deeply religious Lutheran, and had early come under the influence of the Pietists. But they did not stop his exercising a critical mind that was almost French. He quickly assimilated the *Dictionnaire Historique et Critique* of Pierre Bayle (1697) of which he became, despite his piety, a stout proponent. The 'dark Middle Ages' and 'the perversions' of scholasticism needed enlightenment, and this could only be by the exercise of a critique based on true learning. As reason alone had its limitations, there was no single philosophic or religious system that could lay claim to the whole truth. God had, however, endowed man with reason, so he had a duty to see how far he could arrive at it. In 1744 the last volume of his *Historia Critica Philosophiae*, appeared written in both Latin and German, and two years later Diderot was to embark on his *Encyclopédie ou Dictionnaire raisonné des sciences, des arts et des métiers.*[12]

The students at Jena were intoxicated by their local tradition of defiance, which seemed embodied in the person and works of Johann Jakob Brucker, their most distinguished alumnus. Books and pamphlets that preached submission to authority and its symbols, a corporal's cane, a pigtail and a corset, all items of Prussian military dress, were burned in a great bonfire on 17 October 1817. Was this revolution? Copycat demonstrations followed in Breslau and Göttingen, in Saxony and in Swabia. It looked very like it.

Even Tsar Alexander thought it might be. His mystical liberal thought had been buttressed by a belief that liberal institutions figured somehow in God's plan, but when it took on what seemed the very antithesis of religious conformity he began to have other thoughts. A Grand Idea – the revival of Russian nobility through the medium of the Knights of Malta of which Paul I had become Grand Master – had destroyed his father. Was Alexander about to fall victim to another Grand Idea, both dangerous and impractical? The discovery the following year of a conspiracy among free-thinking Russian officers, of the kind that had destroyed his father, made him more circumspect. In March 1819, liberalism seemed to have assumed the mantle of terror. A student from Jena University itself, of 'exemplary conduct and extremely pious sentiments' identified a former student of the same university as an apostate liberal who was the Tsar's evil, anti-liberal genius, and stabbed him while on a visit to report to his master on the current political state of Germany.

The murder of August Friedrich von Kotzebue, playwright, Tsarist minister and critic of Goethe and the intoxication of Romanticism, shocked the entire governing classes.[13] Metternich could claim that this was what he had feared all along. Universities were purged of seditious voices; administrations, even those of Prussia, were cleared of those who had expressed dangerously liberal sentiments, and at Carlsbad in September 1819 were passed the decrees that put paid to any idea of constitutions and liberty for a generation. The sacred rights of sovereigns – when they were suitably repressive – now had the rights of statute.

∗   ∗   ∗

The Tsar retreated into reaction, and Frederick William III dismissed his more liberal ministers, to concentrate on efficiency and discipline under the baton of an arch opponent of representative government. The Prince von Wittgenstein, ironically, bore the same name as the man whose work probably was to do most to destroy German idealist philosophy. Metternich, moreover, had an only too willing confederate in the Emperor Francis I. Neither man entertained any nonsense about the Fatherland; there was just the Imperial Monarchy, as little national as the Indian Empire of which in 1876 Queen Victoria was to become the cynosure and benevolent autocrat. Both men believed that the only protection against the virus of liberalism, which would afflict the empire with the evils of so-called 'representative' – basically unrepresentative – government, was the preservation of the Imperial institution. 'He who serves me,' said the Emperor, 'must teach what I command.'[14]

Prussia had lapsed into a state of constitutional denial, but the time warp that enveloped its monarch did not impede the reforms that appeared to offer no support to liberalism. The revival of provincial government by local Estates which restored the ancient orders of nobles, cities and peasants, provided rubber stamps for monarchy, but they were required to rubber stamp vast improvements in the road and postal system of the kingdom, tariff reform and a huge extension, if not of university, at least of primary education.

Prussian efficiency may have caused resentment because of the inflexibility of its bureaucrats, but Austrian rule seemed just perverse. It saddled her dominions with incompetence as a rule of government. No one could be trusted with full responsibility of his department, reform was not allowed to run its full course; commerce and industry languished before the traditional activities of the noble classes. Prevention was better than cure, and Metternich believed this could be achieved only by repression. To the rest of the world he was like a European chief of police. To himself he was the defender of a Europe that might be approaching its end but which was in every way preferable to one torn by civil war, territorial aggression and supra-nationalism.

Until 1835 and the death of Francis I, the lid on ebullition remained firmly shut. Austria herself and her lands bordering Hungary, Poland and Ottoman territories in the east (Galicia), were largely quiescent, while in Hungary itself, the ancient constitution had so entrenched noble privilege that its Diet was almost as rigorous a defender of the status quo as Metternich himself. Only in Italy was there serious unrest and the Vienna government had little trouble in putting a stop to that. But the Emperor's death, while it did not mark any significant change in Imperial policy, did mark a watershed.

The empire had changed from the primarily agrarian economy that followed the war, when the shortage of manpower had dictated a return to the land. Her population had grown; industrialisation and capital ventures offered an escape from low salaried serfdom (though agriculture itself was afflicted in 1846 and 1847 by such disastrous harvests that the cities were filled with armies of starving beggars). Social unrest did not disturb the central government as much as linguistic nationalism. The Magyars were at odds with the Croats who objected that the replacement of Latin as the administrative language by Magyar would subject them to a tongue known for its arcane and impenetrable nature. In resisting Magyar domination, Croats revived a dream of national identity awakened by Napoleon's creation of the French-ruled Province of Illyria, but as this was a Catholic dream, the Serbs looked south to Orthodox Belgrade. Slovaks looked either west to Bohemian Prague or east to Russia, Romanians and Poles to some ill-defined pan-Slavism. Italians knew that Charles Albert of Piedmont-Savoy was only waiting his opportunity to strike a blow for a new kingdom of Italy.

Only the German speakers of Austria seemed unaffected by the romantic nationalism that was making the other members of the empire drunk with excitement. They, after all, ran the empire, but with that feeling of administrative pride went a spirit of revolt against an unimaginative, often non-German, bureaucracy stoppered in an elixir-bottle of the past. But they were the last to feel any romantic feeling for German nationalism, for many were Jews who invested their identity in the polyglot empire, not in any separate state, and were a nation within a nation, identified by their own Germanic dialect and family networks.[15]

The Paris revolution of 1830 was not a repeat of 1792 for it replaced a monarch rather than beheaded him but it alarmed Metternich enough to allow a lurch towards constitutionalism among the German states. One by one those that had most to complain of about their rulers turned them out. The pathologically violent Duke of Brunswick was forced to abdicate in favour of his brother. The avaricious Elector of Hesse followed. Saxony's nobles themselves turned out the ineffective Estates. William IV, of England and Hanover, was not averse to a constitution over which his brother George IV had prevaricated. Austria was now only the patron and defender of Pumpernickel, and its swollen cosmopolitan capital had no plans for its future. A 36-year-old elected member of the German Diet at Frankfurt had, by 1851, concluded that Austria had no place as the supreme arbiter of the German future, and Count Otto Edward Leopold von Bismarck resolved that this role should be assumed by Prussia.

CHAPTER THIRTEEN

Romance on the Rhine

Byron, Scott and Disraeli

> The mists boil up around the glaciers; clouds
> Rise curling fast beneath me, white and sulphurous
> Like foam from the roused ocean of deep Hell.
> (Byron, *Manfred,* act 1, scene 2, lines 87–9)

> What we heard sounded like a language of the rocks and caves
> … Dumpy children, bulky men, compressed old women with
> baked faces and conical squat dogs, kept the villages partly alive.
> (George Meredith, *The Adventures of Harry Richmond*, chapter XV)

S TURM UND DRANG and the Romance of History, set in a land of swirling clouds, mighty crags and of men reflecting the stormy qualities of both, which could not be dampened by public disapproval, were about to produce in Britain poets to rival those of the school of Weimar. As Byron coasted down the Rhine in 1816 he recollected *Götz von Berlichingen,* musing that,

> Beneath these battlements, within these walls,
> Power dwelt amidst her passions; in proud state
> Each robber chief upheld his armed halls,
> Doing his evil will, nor less elate
> Than mightier heroes of a longer date.[1]

He had set off in his giant travelling coach down the Rhine in April. Though what he saw pretty well matched his own expectations, the sheer beauty of the route surpassed them. The Childe, gazing on 'a work divine', gives in his poem a quick tourist synopsis that would do for today's river trajectories: 'a blending of all beauties, streams and dells, / Fruit, foliage, crag, wood, corn field, mountain, vine'. What spoke to his spirit best were the 'chiefless castles breathing stern farewells'. Tenantless, 'holding dark communion with the cloud', they belonged to history and to Goethe's *Götz*. He could muse on prowess, love, pride and the blood that discoloured the river gliding by. For man, the banks it watered could be an earthly paradise were the memory of the thousand battles, the slaughter and the graves to be washed away.[2]

Byron's lament is not only for the death and destruction the mighty Rhine has had to wash from the memory of the robber barons, for it had seen more recent battles. By Coblenz lay the tombs of Generals Marceau, and Hoche, the first lamented by the tears of rough soldiers, who fell,

> for France, whose rights he battled to resume.
> Brief, brave and glorious'...
> Freedom's champion, one of those,
> The few in number, who had not o'erstept
> The charter to chastise which she bestows
> On such as wield her weapons.

Unlike those robber barons, 'he had kept / the whiteness of his soul'. Byron's salute to the Rhine is brief but heartfelt; none united more 'the brilliant fair and soft, – the glories of old days'.[3] But he declined to enter the French bank of the restored Bourbon monarchy, by Strasbourg. He had no wish to visit the 'cursed crop of rectilignes (sic) and legitimacy', a degraded and oppressed people, who neglected the tombs of its heroes.[4] His indignation is selective; even before *Götz von Berlichingen* had epitomised the Romantic robber, the Rhine had been the scene of bloody contests. Marlborough, Maurice of Saxe, even King and Elector George II of England and Hanover had tramped along its marges, before Napoleon turned 'the peasant girls, with deep blue eyes, / And hands which offer early flowers' first into French maidens and then into Westphalians under his brother Jerome.

One of these girls with red cheeks and white teeth was to enter history when Byron, in a Cologne inn where she was a chambermaid, had ventured on her carnally. The landlord believed the Childe was actually violating his wife and was at the poet's bedroom door swearing like a squadron of cavalry, until the wife emerged from his own bedroom and the chambermaid from Byron's. But Byron was merely applying a salve to his itch to reach the land of vast hills, snowy scalps and icy halls for his Alpine scrambles, to where 'earth may pierce to heaven, yet leave vain man below,' to find 'the apostle of affliction, wild Rousseau.' He left the chamber-maiden, whose most precious possession he may or may not have filched, to the mercy of her employer.

Goethe, though he had handled maidens with similar carelessness in his time, may not have averred that 'a character of such eminence [as Byron] had never existed before and probably would never come again', had he had this memoir to hand.[5] But Byron's interest in Rhine-maidens was kinder than Mary Shelley's, who was not looking for concupiscence, but rather an idealised view of beauty that might be platonic and consistent with that expressed by her husband. In those regards, German women failed badly. She found them 'so ugly, not one pretty or handsome German male or female have I seen – so destitute of grace – so ill-dressed – so dirty and as far as I can make out with few qualities to render their society agreeable'. They might be simple-hearted, good-humoured and willing, but that was not enough to brighten her imagination.[6] As the century progressed the image of German women became one of a severe, subservient, house-proud drudge, when not facing the complexities of life with questions worthy of a female Kant. 'How is it,' Ambrose Harvey-Browne asked Elizabeth von Arnim in Rügen, 'that German women are so infinitely more intellectual than English women?' Elizabeth dodged the question with one of her own. 'Have you not observed that the German *fräulein* is as independent as she is intellectual?' No, he had not. That was where they were far behind the English. 'Their women have nothing like the freedom ours have.'[7] Switzerland, however, seemed to breed a very different woman, more to the English taste.

* * *

One French and one Swiss soldier, anonymous robber barons of long ago, blue-eyed peasant girls and an absentee, anonymous lover, people the vision of Childe Harold. The Rhineland was only half German, being Frenchified marcher territory, and the restoration of the Bourbons to the throne of France in 1815 had offended Byron more than the return of the Pumpernickel despots to their petty kingdoms. Now he was leaving them behind for the pure air of freedom-loving Switzerland, for life between the Villa Diodati on Lake Geneva and for the haunts of the mountain chamois.

French-speaking Switzerland was the abode of Voltaire at Ferney, of Madame de Staël at Coppet and the homeland of Rousseau, a land of civic and religious liberty and of tyrannophobes since the days of William Tell. The mountains, however, were Germanic, where the spirit of man soared naturally free, regardless of political or religious affiliation, where the sure-footedness of the chamois, the keen eye of the eagle, and a bravery bred of battle against natural forces was the stuff of poetry. Grand Tourists were familiar with the landscape of mountain and ravine, waterfalls, trees blasted by wind, but only true Alpinists, and dedicated naturalists, chose to get near to them. The Swiss painter, Caspar Wolf (1735–83), was determined to show visitors to the mountains in a series of engravings what it was truly like to venture upwards into the clouds.

There was nothing prettified about Wolf's vaults and caverns, sculpted in portentous shapes by the elements, in which man was a very small object indeed; but they were not the Romantic pinnacles and precipices from which Manfred would interrogate the spirits of the universe, or summon the Witch of the Alps. His vision, however, made it seem as if the 'landscape were obeying its own independent laws of perspective'. Wolf, who had actually been there, nevertheless evoked a sense 'that the soul ascends, the vision of the spirit tends to expand, and in the midst of the majestic silence one seems to hear the voice of nature and to become certain of its most secret operations'.[8] In the beauty of Nature could be perceived not only the natural resources that gave us life, but also a sense of the sublime, which could be achieved by man-made action enhanced by aesthetic pretensions. There was the voice of the *naturphilosophie* of the German Romantics.[9]

* * *

Like Coleridge, Walter Scott ventured to immerse himself in German, but without going to Germany. In 1792, then 21-years-old, he had started to learn the language with a small group of friends in Edinburgh. They wanted to sample the new German literature in a language thought not to be too far removed from lowland Scots. Most readers in Britain wept over (some even laughed at) *The Sorrows of Young Werther*, but only in translation, while the melodramatic poems of Friedrich Klopstock, whom Wordsworth and Coleridge met in Hamburg, seemed as vigorous and lively as new wine, while Gottfried Bürger (1747–94) had rendered old German ballads in a style with which the young Scott could identify. Students in Edinburgh, moreover, wished to enter the labyrinthine mind of Immanuel Kant, whose ancestors had originated in Scotland itself. All these voices found an eager audience in Scotland. In 1788 Scott attended a lecture on the German theatre at the Royal Society in Edinburgh, and saw a way to escape from pedantic classicism into a world of colour, adventure and romance.

Like all enthusiasts whose teacher wanted them to start on something simpler, the group wanted to read the 'greats', particularly Goethe, and laughed at the puerile sentimentality of the texts recommended by their German tutor. Having studied both low Scots and Anglo-Saxon, Scott grappled ambitiously with the low German language. He never mastered it, but his reading skills expanded and, for a time, he was seized with enthusiasm for his newly discovered wonderland. By 1796 he was confident enough to believe he could translate some of the works he had read. His former teacher at the university had just translated Schiller's *The Robbers,* and Scott was to translate several plays, over the following years, among which were Bürger's *Leonore* and Schiller's *Conspiracy of Fiesco.* He would declaim his translation of *Fiesco* 'to sobbing and weeping audiences'; though he knew his version was poor, he thought the original sublime.[10]

The work which Scott enjoyed translating most was Goethe's *Götz von Berlichingen* (1799). It was, to start with, greatly superior to what he had translated so far. Echoes of Shakespeare were to be heard in the exploits of 'the baronial robbers of the Rhine, stern, bloody and rapacious, but frank, generous, and, after their fashion, courteous in their forays upon each other's domain. Their annals rang with stories of besieged castles, plundered herds, captive knights, brow-beaten bishops and baffled liege-lords' who vainly strove to quell all their turbulence. Scott recognised something familiar to him from the Scottish and English ballads: Götz was a Border chieftain, intrepidly wrapped in a Romantic cloak of equal integrity and crime.[11]

Scott's translation was neither accurate nor particularly exciting, and his clumsy style invited ridicule from a readership, which found too much to ridicule in the flowery excesses and rodomontade of the German dramatists. He professed in a letter to Goethe himself that he set some value on his bold and clumsy youthful excess as it showed 'that I knew how to choose a subject which was worthy of admiration'.[12] Thomas Carlyle believed that *Götz* had provided the inspiration for *Marmion* and *The Lady of the Lake* and it is surprising that it was never adapted to opera.[13] Maybe that was because Schiller's youthful play, *The Robbers*, adopted by Verdi as *I Masnadieri* (1847), pre-empted it, but *The Lady of the Lake* provided Rossini with *La Donna del Lago*.[14] Scott's novels lent themselves to opera. *Götz*, however, had certainly inspired a real life bandit, Hannes Bucker, who in his final trial, attempted with operatic and Romantic nobility to protect the lives of his wife, father and companions, at the expense of his own.

In the exercise of translation, Scott began to understand that the true interest of narrative history lay, not in the events, but in the personalities of the principal actors in them. His translations were made in-between working on his legal cases, and he was helped by his junior who had returned from Germany with an extensive collection of works in German. His other collaborator was the wife of his kinsman, Harriet Scott of Harden, who had lived in Saxony. All this time, he was polishing his craft. Meanwhile, in Europe, what seemed from his birth and history to be a real-life robber baron, two years Scott's elder, had driven the Austrians out of Italy, and was the following year to turn on the British approaches to India by invading Egypt.[15]

* * *

In 1827 Scott published his *Life of Napoleon Buonaparte*. A copy was sent to Goethe, and in his letter Scott wondered whether he was indebted to the man, who for so many years exercised so terrible an influence on the world, for making him, despite his lameness, carry arms in the militia becoming as a result a good horseman, huntsman and shot.[16] Scott must have known that Goethe, at Napoleon's express request, had met the man himself; he may not have known that Goethe, having little sense of national pride, had always admired Napoleon. Goethe acknowledged the gift cautiously, asking

> what could be more delightful to me than leisurely and calmly to sit down and listen to the discourse of such a man (Sir Walter) while clearly, truly and with all the skill of a great artist he recalls to me the incidents on which through life I have meditated and the influence of which it is still daily in operation.[17]

It was a tribute more polite than real, from one old man (78) to another fast ageing (56), and the work, had it been published in the same format as Scott's novels, would have filled many volumes, probably too long for Goethe to have read at all. Anyhow, Scott was still too close to the Napoleonic era for his lofty and impartial treatment of the man's character to be received by all its readers with acclamation.

Goethe admired Scott and recognised in him a master spirit of the age. 'There is finish! There is a hand!' he told Eckermann on 3 October 1828. 'What a firm foundation for the whole, and in particulars not a touch which does not lead to the catastrophe! Then, what details of dialogue and description!' As far as German histories went, by comparison they were 'sheer poverty'.[18] As Scott had never learned to read the Gothic hand, he had to find someone to read Goethe's letter to him. Normally he did not bother about what seemed to be fan mail, but Goethe was 'a wonderful fellow, the Ariosto at once and almost the Voltaire of Germany', and Scott could scarcely believe he would be corresponding on equal terms with the 'Author of *The Robbers*', 'the first-born of the Romantic school'.[19] (He had forgotten that *Götz of Berlichingen* was the work he had translated, not Schiller's *Robbers*.[20]) He hoped to return from his last trip to Italy by way of Weimar and the Rhine, in order to visit Goethe, but the great man died in March 1832, and Scott decided to push on home to Scotland as fast as he could. 'Alas for Goethe,' Scott wrote fearing his own dissolution before he got there, 'but he at least died at home.'[21]

Both men died literary heroes at their deaths, but Scott's imprint on Romanticism was the more indelible. Faust is less real than Mephistopheles who is not real at all, and Napoleon was not the only reader who found Werther's suicide unnatural. Moreover, Scott himself thought that only a German like Goethe would ever have provoked comparison, as he did in his prologue, 'with the Book of Job, the grandest poem that ever was written'. Notwithstanding the free brigand barons of the Rhine, none competes for their revelation of the diversity of humankind – a fact that Goethe had recognised – with Caleb Balderstone, Dominie Sampson, Edie Ochiltree or Dugald Dalgetty.

* * *

In 1829 Scott's German novel appeared. *Anne of Geierstein* owes something to *Götz von Berlichingen*, which he had laboriously translated but its only real connection with Germany is that some of it takes place on German soil, the lower Rhine down which Byron had sailed. It is otherwise a companion novel to *Quentin Durward*, set in the same century and the time of Louis XI of France and Duke Charles the Bold of Burgundy. Scott was lapped in the Gothic history of the early northern Renaissance, and wrote *Anne* largely from memory, deprived at the time of access to a well-stocked library. His main source was Philippe de Commines, whose *Memoires* of the time were the authoritative voice of the apogee and fall of an exotic northern Renaissance court. While there is no golden gallery of Scottish originals, Scott makes a creditable fist of the character of Duke Charles himself, and of the stern and formidable Swiss patriarch, the Landammer Arnold.

The novel opens in a mountain canton of Switzerland, where two English travellers are benighted by a landfall which blocks their road forward and would have cost the life of one of them, but for the mysterious appearance of a girl, the Maiden of the Mist. Intrepid of resolve and firm of foot as befitted a Highland lass, she rescues them from almost certain death. The opening scenes in Switzerland are drawn from the highlands of Scotland inhabited by mountaineers of formidable size and primitive chivalry and tinctured by Scott's familiarity with Salvator Rosa's renderings of wild mountain scenery.[22] He does not reveal the mission of the two English travellers, father and son, until much later in the book, but they forge an identity of sympathy for the Swiss who are to embark on a peace mission to Burgundy, led by the father of their remarkable rescuer. The English are also bound for the Duke's court and they agree to travel together.

The younger Englishman is intrigued, and then besotted by the mountain girl who rescued him, and about whom there is a mystery. Stories of her being the daughter of an oriental magus, who mysteriously appeared and as mysteriously vanished from her father's castle, suggested that she was endowed with the powers of a *doppelgänger,* able to be in two places at once. At that point Scott starts to write a Gothic novel, at once a pursuit and escape story in the genre of William Godwin's *Caleb Williams* (1794), using the Scottish/Swiss terrain with his old flair, as demonstrated in *Rob Roy* (1817). It is also a spine-chiller of strange and sinister mystery. As soon as the joint party emerges into the lowlands of the lower Rhine, Goethe and his *Götz von Berlichingen mit der eisernen hand (with the Iron Hand)* becomes the main inspiration. The Westphalian lands are unruly and treacherous, the rulers are avaricious and corrupt, the landlords boorish and unwelcoming, dangers seem to lurk round every corner. The brigand Barons of the Rhine, however, are not all-powerful. A form of civil control is exercised by a society as secret as the Neapolitan *Camorra* or Calabria's *'Ndrangheta*, which dispenses justice *ad terrorem* of the local population.

Into the hands of this society the older English merchant is winched down in his bed as he sleeps in an otherwise typically unwelcoming German inn. This intricate machinery is reserved for those travellers whom the elders of the secret society wish to examine, to try summarily and to execute either by ritual strangulation or by dagger. Their network extends to any domain where the society has members and its efficient and remorseless spy system is as coldly terrifying as anything that Mathew 'Monk' Lewis had invented in his Gothic tales.[23] Their prisoner on this occasion is released, being innocent as charged, on the word of the tribunal's president, a hooded ecclesiastical figure, a 'mark two' Abbé Schedoni in Lewis's *The Italian*. It is clear that there is something as mysterious about the tribunal's president as there is about the merchant.

Once in Burgundian territory the merchant's son, Arthur, is arrested for behaving suspiciously – which was part of his mission – only to be rescued by what appears to be the *doppelgänger* of the girl who originally rescued him from the landfall, accompanied by the equally if not more mysterious priestly president of the tribunal that had recently tried his father. Scott loved weaving mysteries, in the style of Ann Radcliffe, but as soon as the Burgundian court is reached, the mysteries begin to be explained and rational explanations, also loved by Scott, emerge. The novel, from being one of Gothic pursuit and escape changes, almost in the tradition of Hollywood, into one about the high politics of history.

The riches of Scott's mind are unrolled in his description of the Burgundian camp and in the gallery of historic portraits. There is a certain bathos in the unravelling of the mysteries and Scott loses interest in the love story of Arthur, the merchant's son, and the Maiden of the Mist and her *doppelgänger*, to which he returns in a perfunctory last chapter. From now on he is more interested in how the Lancastrian claims to the English throne, sustained by Margaret of Anjou, have come to roost in the sybaritic, poetry-sodden court of the last King of Provence, and in the nemesis of Burgundian power at the hands of the stalwart Swiss. Anne of Geierstein turns out to be the daughter of the mysterious priest-president of the Vehmic Tribunal, who is responsible, it is implied, for the death of Charles of Burgundy, sentenced by the dreaded court to death, not by the cord but by the dagger. Arthur, being really of noble, not merchant, blood, is finally free to marry Anne. All, save Charles the Rash, Duke of Burgundy, and Anne's father, live happily ever after.

Anne of Geierstein is one of Scott's Gothic tapestried history tales and ends on a theme that Scott might possibly have contemplated for a future novel: the continued fortunes of the house of Lancaster culminating in Bosworth Field. But instead he went north to Scotland with *Castle Dangerous* and south to Byzantium with *Count Robert of Paris,* before exhausting his pen and his imagination with *The Siege of Malta. Anne of Geierstein* is full of Scott's absorption with the influence, often fatal, of chivalry and honour on human behaviour. There are villains, regrettably Templars or Italians (Campo Basso in *Anne of Geierstein*), but Scott's principals are all flawed by caste-driven opinions of themselves, from De Bois-Gilbert in *Ivanhoe,* to Henry Ashton of *The Bride of Lammermoor,* to Charles of Burgundy. Heroes of rectitude in *Anne of Geierstein* are the *landamman* of Unterwalden, Arnold Biederman, and John Philipson, the alias of the exiled Earl of

Oxford. Germanic nobility was, however, tainted by the exploits of *Götz von Berlichingen of the Iron Hand*. Indeed Charles of Burgundy regretted that 'such words as fame, honour, *los*, knightly glory, ladies' love and so forth, were good mottoes for our snow-white shields' but gold now demanded some other impulse, either public good or private advantage.[24] Anne's father, Count Albert, has been so tainted by necromancy, alchemy (shades of *Wallenstein*) and magical influences that he can only support a role of ambivalence, as father of the heroine, the pure Maiden of the Mist, and as the unhallowed terrorist of the Vehmic tribunal.

Scott professed that he hated *Anne of Geierstein*. The source materials were excellent but, on his own admission, his powers of using them were failing. Others, including his publisher, concurred.[25] It had proved difficult to finish; it was clear that the Gothic passages, which make it interesting now, were not really to Scott's taste and he was not impressed by his own heroine. In his words he had to 'muzz' on with it.[26] To everyone's surprise it was well received, and remains a yarn that holds us still. There are few longueurs, if few memorable characters. But if it had been written in his prime, and had he thought more deeply and sympathetically about what he was describing, it might, in the words of one critic, have been 'something not far short of a Tolstoyan epic of a world convulsed by international conflict … Scott's War and Peace'.[27]

* * *

One reviewer in the *London and Westminster Review*, as remembered by Carlyle in 1838, believed that Goethe's *Götz von Berlichingen* and *The Sorrows of Young Werther* had had a profound influence on the subsequent literature of Europe. *Werther* had

> appeared to seize the breast of men in all quarters of the world, and to utter for them the word which they had long been waiting to hear … Sceptical sentimentality, view-hunting, love, friendship, suicide and desperation became the staple of literary ware … *Götz* became the parent of an innumerable progeny of chivalry plays, feudal delineations and poetic antiquarian performances.[28]

Goethe's two novels were, in his view, the prime inspiration for *Marmion* and *The Lady of the Lake*. The grain of sand had lighted on the right soil. Carlyle was not sure he agreed, but he did agree that Götzism in Scott's 'chivalry literature', and Wertherism in the poems of Byron had been carried 'to the ends of the world'. Byron's Wertherism, so potent and poignant, had produced a mighty effect on the languid appetite of men. Scott's Chivalry Romances held sovereignty over Europe and were acquiring a new lease of life with the enthronement of an 18-year-old virgin queen, after two monarchs who had represented the worst of a Pumpernickel principality, imported to England.

* * *

Coleridge, the true apostle of Germanism, and England's most fervent exponent of Kantism, had touched hands and minds with the German colony in Rome in 1805 when he was returning to England from Malta. Most of it revolved round the house of the Prussian minister there, Wilhelm von Humboldt. Humboldt had known Schiller at Jena and was spending what was an undemanding diplomatic assignment, developing his linguistic and philological theories, some of which appealed to Coleridge's vague metaphysical fancies. With Johann Wilhelm Tieck, later August Schlegel's collaborator in the Shakespeare translations, Coleridge struck up a mutually animated friendship, delving into modern German philosophic ideas and the metaphysics of Jakob Böhme. Tieck's sister was astonished to meet an Englishman with such a knowledge of German letters. And the two men maintained a friendship until well after the end of the war.

Coleridge plundered his wide acquaintance with German writing, without acknowledgement, throughout his life but it was surprising that a few years later he allowed himself to be publicly exposed to the charge of plagiarising, in his London Lectures of 1809, August William Schlegel's views on Shakespeare. He had discussed these with Tieck in Rome and they had been published in 1809, so that Coleridge knew that Schlegel had started on his translations and commentaries as early as 1789. He never quite cleared himself of the accusation that he had incorporated in his lecture some of Schlegel's comments without acknowledgement.

The difficulty may have been that Coleridge convinced himself that he had already formed his ideas at much the same time as, and independently, of Schlegel. He may even have been slightly miffed that the German had been able to publish and so secure all the credit for them. Coleridge's ideas were not essentially the same as Schlegel's and, to his mind they were even superior as he spoke the same language as Shakespeare. That he was not aware, as he claimed, of Schlegel's book in its original German seemed most improbable. Coleridge read German avidly, and did not hesitate in his lectures to quote untranslated works, soaring to heights of philosophic rhetoric in which he gave his version of the thought of Kant and the poetry of Herder, Lessing and Schiller.

It was after his eighth lecture in December 1808 that he was visited by a polite German gentleman who presented Schlegel's book to Coleridge remarking that the lecture he had given the night before seemed so remarkably like the lecture Schlegel had given in Vienna, that it seemed he must have either heard or read it, a fair and probably accurate assumption. Coleridge subsequently made much of the new German literary criticism, developed, like his own, as he put it, at a time when the national mind was forced inwards by political repression and received opinion, just as his had been.[29]

In the summer of 1828, Coleridge in a last attempt to resume the former close friendship of equals travelled to Germany with Wordsworth and his daughter, Dora. The companionship of earlier years could not be replicated but the two men rubbed along well enough, complaining bitterly of each other's idiosyncrasies. Wordsworth was silent, mean and an early riser, Coleridge his usual anarchic, expansive and disorganised self. One purpose of the visit was to see August Wilhelm Schlegel at Bonn where Schlegel enjoyed a university post, but most of the conversation was about Scott and Byron, and Coleridge was exasperated. Byron may have been a meteor, but Wordsworth was a fixed star. He was not fixed, however, in the firmament of German Romanticism, while Byron was.[30] German poets had already established their Romantic views of nature, which Coleridge would claim, were Wordsworth's inspiration.

Among them was Frederick Schelling (1775–1854) whose original but convoluted and chaotic mind had embarked on the philosophy of Nature. Schelling was a native of Charles Eugene's Württemberg, and had been prepared at a Lutheran seminary for the Church, but like so many of his day, his theological studies of the patristic Fathers and the ancient Greek thinkers whetted an appetite for speculative thought. The Church was now no longer his aim and by throwing himself into a study of Kant and Fichte he established himself as a philosopher didactic enough to be appointed at the age of 23 to a professorship at Jena. Time spent in Saxony had enabled him to attend lectures in the natural sciences, and he now aspired to the same universal range of knowledge as Leibniz. The period was now 1798 to 1803 and German universities were hothouses of individual enquiry across disciplines, as Coleridge was to find at Göttingen, and the patronal influence of Goethe and Schiller gave Jena a special place in the formation of German idealism. Schelling, with the help of his old roommate Hegel, began to expound his philosophy of Nature. The Absolute, which was the essential study of philosophers, could only be understood through the operations of the spirit and nature, which were essentially the same. This was an approach to truth, which Coleridge took up with enthusiasm, and he saw his friend Wordsworth as the foremost expositor of it. From his experience of and sympathy for the natural world, a truth would emerge, essentially free from religious dogma and pre-conditions.

* * *

That truth, however, seemed remarkably reluctant to be born. German idealism proved too opaque even for a Coleridgean synthesis so that Baron Julius von Konigstein, minister to the Diet of Frankfurt 'from a first-rate German power' mischievously asked Vivian Grey who 'was the favourite master? Kant or Fichte?' and did not expect a reply.[31] But then Vivian Grey's creator, Disraeli, who was then only 21, an auto-didact who was writing his first novel (1826–7) from immersion in a library and listening to the guests round his father's and John Murray's dinner tables, was not concerned to give an opinion as it was too weighty a matter for his brilliantly precocious prose.[32] Germany was a very suitable place in which to complete a first novel which sailed rather close to libellous satire in its early chapters but which had nevertheless sent the author 'to sleep a nameless youth of twenty one who woke to find himself famous'.[33]

So he moved the venue for the second part. Most people only knew Germany from her watering places. Once, observes one of Vivian Grey's interlocutors, you went there to see and be seen in the Courts of Princes. 'You all travel now … to look at mountains and catch cold in spouting trash on lakes by moonlight.'[34] Gladstone thought the second part of the novel trash too, for in it Disraeli relaxed the flippant, political banter of the first part, which had made its appearance a *succès-fou*.[35] It opens with a mock-heroic account of gambling at a German spa, and the eccentricities of German life, and ends as a political *jeu d'esprit*, set at a safe distance from London and from the English counterparts to German palaces, the country houses where Disraeli inferred all political decisions were made.

Disraeli outdid his hero Byron in his romantic view of the Rhineland with its

> vine-enamoured mountains, … spreading waters, … traditionary crags, … shining cities and sparkling villages, … antique convents, … grey and silent castles, the purple glories of thy radiant grape, … the vivid tints of the teeming flowers, the fragrance of the sky, the melody of thy birds, whose carols tell the pleasures of their sunny woods. [36]

But it was a land of make-believe, a mixture of faery, fancy and fiction, with its Grimm forests, pantomime princes and Don Quixote. Vivian's Sancho Panza is a pedlar, part *saltimbanque*, juggler and Papageno. Cast together as master and servant on the run from the spa town where a cards scandal and the mysterious death of a young woman has suggested it might be wise to resume their travels, they are lost in the forest of the Wild Hunter who hunted not game but the child of anyone tempted to join him in the wild chase. They find themselves unwilling participants in a weird banquet given by a drinking fraternity of St Hubert dedicated to inebriation. But Disraeli was not wholly at home in a bizarre eccentricity more suited to Thomas Love Peacock. He wanted to imagine the politics of a post-Napoleonic prince like His Serene Highness the Prince of Little Lilliput, whose life Vivian Grey saves from a wild boar and thus becomes his adviser and friend.

The prince was a 'mediated prince', that is one whose sovereignty, but not whose titles, honours and palaces, had been stripped from him after the Napoleonic wars in order to reduce the legion of sovereignties into which Germany had been divided. Into this principality Vivian Grey strays, to find himself caught up in an intrigue aimed at obtaining a democratic charter from a despotic Grand-Duke, installed to rule over the former lands of mediated sovereigns. Then, having reached the Grand-Duchy to watch the result of the intrigue, Grey finds that the mediated prince has been turned into being a loyal officer of the court that had deprived him of his sovereign status. Its prime minister, a quirky Metternichian character, had successfully diverted his energies from obtaining a democratic charter to swimming in the uncharted waters of courtly life and intrigue. Disraeli in the person of Vivian Grey, being English and supremely neutral, enjoys what his characters were to enjoy throughout his novels, an Olympian view of the uncertainty of politics, the influence of beautiful and witty women and the uncertain interplay of loyalty and temptation.

The aphoristic gibes that pepper a text verging on the absurd (or what Gladstone called trash) were what Disraeli would fling at the politics he had observed from the law chambers in which he was apprenticed. 'In politics there is no feeling of honour'; whatever public benefits may be achieved by a party, everyone is dependent on another, and it is a question of whether in time one is a deserter or the deserted; no one was 'petted so much as a political apostate'.[37] Little Lilliput had committed political apostasy and was petted by all, even the morganatic wife of the Grand-Duke, a Frenchified blue stocking, more sedate but as beautiful as Lola Montes (then still a child in India). In a land of political dependency and no political honour Disraeli essayed his first blueprint of pluto-democracy. He could not resist romanticising as, basically, Vivian Grey was a self-portrait who, in the setting of a Pumpernickel court, meets and falls in love with a proud beauty. He does so too late in the novel to make a love story of it, so the proud beauty is off bounds, being an Austrian Archduchess, destined for the usual loveless dynastic marriage.

For Vivian Grey, his destiny is to love without consummation. His first love dies mysteriously, causing him to seek his fortunes abroad; his second is marked out for other things. Grey rides off with his Sancho Panza for other kingdoms, is overtaken by a dreadful storm and flood, at which Disraeli, aware that this novel could go on for ever, terminates it suddenly, leaving his hero helpless in the middle of a natural disaster, and suggesting that his readers should complete the story themselves. In its wild location, its glittering panorama of a petty court, with its weird proceedings and personal eccentricity, *Vivian Grey* was a madcap fiction which found some of its inspiration in the work of the Brandenburg Hoffmen. The reciprocated love of commoners for royalty has been the stuff of fairy tales and romantic fiction. It surfaced later in novels of George Meredith and Anthony Hope, even recurring as late as contemporary time (1953), when common journalist Gregory Peck and Princess Audrey Hepburn pursue their attachment on the back of a motor bicycle in William Wyler's *Roman Holiday*, 'the fourth best love story of all time'.[38] But who were the 'Hoffmen'?

CHAPTER FOURTEEN

The Tales of the Hoffmen

Kleist, Hoffmann, Fouqué and The Berlin Renaissance

> A lady of unblemished reputation and mother of several well-bought up children [announced] that without knowledge of the cause[she had] come to find herself in a certain situation; that she would like the father of the child she was expecting to disclose his identity and she was resolved to marry him.
>
> (Heinrich von Kleist, *The Marquise of O*—)

> One night he suddenly awakened me, begging me to get up to leave him, to stay no longer in the room 'I feared lest I should harm you,' he groaned. For he felt he was gradually losing all control over his own actions, that something outside himself was continually urging him to violence against those he loved best in the world ... Thus he was ever imagining he heard sounds, sometimes just one note of music perpetually repeated; and then again the tones would be modulated, and vary and combine and weave themselves into melody.
>
> (Clara Schumann, letter of 1854)[1]

*I*N 1810 APPEARED the strange story of an Italian Marquise who had discovered herself pregnant and advertised to know who had put her into this condition. *The Marquise of O* appeared at the same time as Prussia was licking her wounds after the crushing defeats of Jena and Auerstadt. The author was a Brandenburger who, coming from a family that numbered 18 generals, had enrolled in the army at the age of 15, had served in the army on the Rhine and who had secured his discharge aged 22 to go to university to read philosophy and law. Heinrich Wilhelm von Kleist was a restless body, who found his civilian job in the Finance Ministry as tiresome as the army. During the period of Napoleonic peace in central Europe, Kleist secured a prolonged leave of absence and went travelling. He started in Paris, moved to Switzerland where he wrote a gloomy tragedy full of angst and despair, and met Goethe, Schiller and Wieland (whose son had befriended him in Switzerland), before returning to Berlin.

Though he resented the air of incense that surrounded Goethe, and railed at the respect given to the Great Man and at the lack of it given to him, he caught the literary virus in Weimar. He became bitterly anti-French when he was arrested as a spy in Dresden after the Jena debacle, and was imprisoned for six months in France before being released. He now resolved to follow his *lebensplan* (life-plan) as an antidote to what seemed his endemic dissatisfaction with life, and to seek the happiness and confidence that seemed to have eluded him so far by writing. He would build on the life work of Schiller and give German drama a relentless drive for both simplicity and seriousness. He chose as a subject Robert Guiscard, an eleventh-century Norman freebooter who attempted to conquer Constantinople, but writing a Schiller play in a new style eluded him throughout his life. He was more successful with the issues of common humanity faced by crisis. His Wallensteins and Mary Stuarts would be more commonplace people, more like those whom Ibsen would later portray, who had to work out their responses to human crises not by societal rules but by their own personal choices. These could be in conflict, thus thwarting the outcome. It was as if the happiness Kleist had expected from his life-plan was always to elude him by his own contrariness, and the shadow of a self-induced death kept appearing to him as an inevitable outcome.

Goethe did not prove the enlightened theatrical director Kleist had expected, when he turned down his Attic play as being not sufficiently Attic. It smacked too much of the *sturm und drang* out of which Goethe had grown, for its principal characters, the Amazon queen Pentheselia and the Greek hero Achilles, die in a frenzied orgy of savagery. Kleist tried his hand then at a comedy about cuckolds, which owing to feeble direction, was a flop. The flop may have been more the fault of Goethe than of the author, but it cast a pall of failure over his excitable and unstable temperament. In 1809 he produced his 'Hermann play', which paraded the virtues of the forest-loving German patriot in battle with the vicious men of the plain, the Romans (French).[2] Again the implied savagery was 'Penthesilian'.

But it was love and, through love, sentimental bliss, that was to be his undoing. He became obsessed by the accomplishments of another man's wife, Henriette Vogel, who was dying of cancer. Her wish for death to escape more suffering matched the omnipresent disposition of Kleist towards self-destruction, and their joint Wertherism was to end in a double tragedy. Catching Kleist at a moment when he was suffering from what today might be diagnosed as clinical depression, Henriette entered into a death pact with him. They chose the lakeside of the Kleiner Wannsee at Potsdam where, after enacting an elaborate charade of conviviality at an inn by the shore, he consummated the pact by shooting her in the heart and himself in the brain.

The year was 1811. Mme de Staël stuffily dismissed Kleist's motives as posthumously seeking the fame that had eluded him in life. But he had shown, particularly in his last drama *Prince Friedrich von Homburg* written that year, that he believed death, while making a noble gesture, was a suitable end to life. 'I have no other wish but to die,' he wrote to his sister in 1802, 'if I might achieve three things, a child, a beautiful piece of writing and a great deed. For life holds nothing nobler than this: to be able to throw it away with a noble gesture.' Prince Friedrich has been condemned to death for dereliction of duty; he accepts as his conviction that military discipline is so important that he must overcome his fear of death. Only by a national will to put the public good over self-preservation, Kleist was implying, would Prussia become great. In his view she could only survive by harnessing the unconditional dedication of the individual who would put country above all other devotions.[3] Kleist's dramas seemed to die with him, at the height of his hostility to France brought on by her humiliation of Prussia. He did not live to see the revival of either Prussia or his work, which only resurfaced when he was long dead, in the malign worship of the German state.[4]

Kleist's short stories, written towards the end of his life when his powers were at their highest and his sense of *cafard* at its most pronounced, reflected a macabre streak of romantic drama that was to mark the age with a sense of strangeness. They were not just vehicles for his dislike of France; they were international in their locale, they were unadorned by much speech or description, and they were free of moralising, proceeding to their often surprising denouement by bare narrative. Their conclusions were stark and uncompromising, accompanied by very little commentary. Kleist's moral, if there was one, was that human actions had unexpected consequences over which the actors really had no control. Despite his bare narrative, leaving all visual imagery to the imagination, he was still able to achieve one of his life's ambitions: 'a beautiful piece of writing.'

The heroine of *The Marquise of O*, which is set in Italy, is violated while unconscious following an assault and sack by a Russian army, by the very man who had rescued her from violation by common soldiery. Rape while unconscious – before the invention of spiked drinks – was unusual enough to cause family rift, but the Marquise, in boldly inviting public opprobrium by advertising her condition and seeking the identity of the rapist, is surprisingly satisfied by the result of her search. In another tale, *The Earthquake in Chile*, two lovers condemned to death for fornication, leading to an illegitimate birth, are released by a chance earthquake which destroys their place of imprisonment just before their execution, yet they meet their death at the hands of a mob driven half-mad by fear and by their desire to seek a victim whose crime must have brought about the earthquake. The fate of the child who is the fruit of their illicit intercourse is adopted by the man whose own baby had been presumed to be the bastard, and beaten to death.

Kleist's *Michael Kohlhaas*, set in the time of Luther, was written like Browning's *Ring and the Book* from an ancient manuscript found on a stall. It is the story of a complicated lawsuit delayed, unlike Jarndyce vs Jarndyce by the law's delays, but by corruption in high places. It ends with the delivery of judgment in favour of the plaintiff who is then executed for his protest at the delays in its delivery. In *The Betrothal in Santo Domingo*, a Swiss officer, escaping from rebellious slaves in Haiti, in a manhunt for their white oppressors, is befriended by a young *mulata*, whom he shoots dead on the brink of rescuing him, convinced that she has betrayed him. He then kills himself, rendering vain the whole saga of the rescue.

The climax of each tale reveals an irony of which Thomas Hardy was to be the master. There may be a deity but He is inactive. Though in Kleist's imagination the Church, especially the Roman Catholic, is at best hypocritical, and always malign, it is not the social or religious environment but the actions of man that determine his fate. These actions are not governed by design but by the capricious rule of chance. Only suicide, such as that which Kleist committed with Henriette Vogel, could cut the web of fate decisively; but was it ironic fate, or his own ineluctable destiny that caused him to fall in love in the first place with a woman dying of inoperable cancer?

Kleist was certainly unstable. He suffered two breakdowns; he twice tried in vain to seek military death, first by enrolling in Napoleon's army for the invasion of England then, towards the end of his life as Prussia was gearing up for war, by trying to resume his military career. He several times talked about taking his own life or having it taken, as he had early on decided that the dice were loaded against things working out as one wanted. Even the overthrow of the hated French was problematic. After the victories of Napoleon had showed the vanity of *sturm und drang*, of Goethean Atticism and of Schillerian heroicism, this streak of almost Quietist fatalism was to pervade the fiction of the north German story writers who followed Kleist. This was until musical drama rediscovered the fiction that love conquers all, particularly the villainy of humans, the vanity of human wishes, and the prohibitions of the gods. But it was not the love of Klopstock's divine Messiah, or Werther's human love for Charlotte or Max Piccolomini's for the Princess Thekla von Wallenstein, but the sacrificial love of Wagner's women, of a Senta, of an Elizabeth and of an Isolde, for an ideal.

$$* \quad * \quad *$$

Ernst Theodor Hoffmann was born in the same city as Immanuel Kant in 1776, of a race of lawyers and destined for the law. His father was an amateur musician who played the *viola da gamba* in the current enthusiasm for stringed instruments, which was to convert Germany into a nest of orchestras. He did not intend his son to be a musician, but while Hoffman never became an instrumentalist, he grew up to be among other things, a composer, a conductor of operas and a music critic. Two years after his birth his parents separated and Hoffmann stayed in Königsberg with his mother and her unmarried siblings, two aunts and an uncle, who took on the rearing of the boy. The uncle was severe and Pietistic, and gloomily paternal, but the aunts were more indulgent, even if between them they infected Ernst Theodor with their stark notions of Hell and Heaven. He would hear the voice of the Devil on the bleak Pomeranian coast, and learned that life was a serious and thorny path between normality and the abyss. But he did well at school and showed early talent with his fingers, as pianist, artist and scribbler.

Hoffmann's early years were to follow a pattern which the fantasist he became might have written for himself: university friendships with fellow artists and scribblers with outrageous ideas, attendance at the lectures of Kant himself, which were like a draught of strong liquor, and finally passionate love for one of the pupils to whom he was teaching the piano, a married woman ten years his senior and mother of five. His passion became so intense that her family sought the ardent lover's removal from Königsberg.

Another uncle took him in as a clerk in his legal practice in Silesia, pretty well as far away in the same country as he could be sent from Königsberg. In 1798 his uncle was promoted to a law court in Berlin and Hoffmann went with him to taste the delights of a capital city and to flutter his artistic wings. He wrote an operetta, which he was rash enough to send to Queen Louise and, having passed his law exams, he secured employment in Prussian service in the Polish provinces acquired during the partitions of the late eighteenth century. Poland was a happy exile for Hoffmann where, being largely without artistic training, he could amuse himself by composing, drawing and writing to standards that were not overshadowed by censorious and critical peers. He married a young Polish girl and secured a post in Warsaw, which was then a Prussian province. There he was to enter a literary and artistic circle that still radiated some of the intellectual interests of its Saxon past under the King-Electors Augustus, and which tapped into the salons of Berlin. Carlyle, who vaguely disapproved of Hoffmann's dark frivolity, described his time in Poland in suitably Hoffmannesque terms, surrounding him with

> gay silken Polesses, talking and promenading over broad stately squares; the ancient venerable Polish noble, with moustaches, caftan sash and

red or yellow boots, the new race equipped as Parisian *incroyables* with foreigners of every nation, not excluding long-bearded Jews, puppet-show men, monks and dancing bears.[5]

Hoffmann did not intend to practise law as a career if he could avoid it and in Warsaw he was able to develop his musical gifts. He conducted the orchestra of the Music Academy and wrote, among a lot of serious music, two comic operas. He was also able to cover the foyer of the national theatre with frescoes he painted by himself. This happy provincialism ended in November 1806 when the French drove the Prussians out of a Warsaw for which Napoleon had other plans. Hoffmann, refusing to serve the French, found himself back in Berlin. Even there he could not escape them for they had occupied the city after Jena, and Hoffmann survived how he could, on friends, on meagre rations, and on occasional publications. By this time he had decided from which, among all his skills, he proposed to make a living. He was able to secure an ill-paid post as musical director of a small princely theatre at Bamberg, in Bavaria, and, when he lost that through intrigue, he became music critic for a Leipzig newspaper.

Ernst Theodor William replaced his third forename with Amadeus in homage to Mozart, but his musical career was to be dogged by the persistence of war in eastern Europe. No sooner had he accepted direction of an opera company in Dresden than the retreat of the French from Napoleon's disastrous invasion of Russia converted Saxony to a battlefield. With great difficulty, Hoffmann made his way back to Berlin to find a post in the only profession for which he was formally qualified, the law. It was now 1814 and in the renascent society of Berlin, Hoffmann began to flower. Employed by day as a legal arbitrator, he retreated by night into fictional fantasy, and musical creativity. Stories flowed from his pen, and at last an opera, based on a story by la Motte Fouqué, was performed to general applause. *Undine,* ran for 25 performances until fire broke out in the theatre and brought it to a close.

Hoffmann was among the first to recognise the titanic genius of Beethoven, when he reviewed the score of his Fifth Symphony in 1810. In it he gave a definition of Romanticism in music. Haydn and Mozart had established the symphony as 'the most Romantic of the arts, one might say the only purely romantic one'. Haydn's symphonies led their listener into 'an infinite green grove and a cheerful gaily coloured throng of merry people'. Mozart entered the depths of the spiritual world, a foreboding of the eternal, but Beethoven opened up a world of the 'immense and the infinite', making everyone conscious of 'gigantic shadows which annihilated everything within us except the torment of endless longing'. His review was loaded with images: 'the wondrous spirit world of the infinite', the symphony 'stormed past people like an ingenious rhapsody', inspiring 'an inexpressible prophetic longing', and embracing 'the realm of the spirit with torment and joy'.[6]

Hoffmann's Gothic imagination, of the spirit world wrapped in music, was an entirely new appreciation of Beethoven's music, which many in the Viennese musical world found either frantic or noisy. Of Hoffmann's own music, however, five operas, a symphony, much chamber and instrumental compositions, little is performed today. His own critique of Beethoven is a kind of criticism of himself. *Undine* does not take us into 'green groves' or into the spiritual world, does not cast 'gigantic shadows' or induce 'endless longing'. It is, however, as Romantic as Hoffmann could make it, with all the baggage of the time. It takes us into the spirit if not the spiritual world, for Undine is a water nymph, mysteriously found as a child and reared as a human. It is set among lakes, and forests, in the age of questing knights and betrayed love, which is death to the spirit, presided over by a sinister water nymph who presides balefully over Undine's human emotion.

The first eligible bachelor to see Undine falls instantly in love with her in the usual convention of the brothers Grimm. Hoffmann wanted to compose a Romantic German opera, an ambition said also to have been occasionally nursed by Goethe. He and la Motte Fouqué together worked on the libretto, and had Fouqué been collaborating with a more talented composer, like Weber, he could have become another Da Ponte or Hofmannsthal.[7] With its resonances of Gluck and Mozart, and often with some of the fiery energy of Beethoven, *Undine* gave Weber his theme for *Die Freischütz*: the influence of natural spirits of darkness and destiny on human affairs. In his opera, Hoffmann succeeded in writing a Romantic *singspiel,* to a story that appealed to his strangely complex literary taste. His florid and stylised personal behaviour, adopted to expunge the memory of his convoluted and baffled past, attracted Weber who, while he admired

Undine, accepted the open challenge to give Germany its own operatic tradition, overshadowed for so long by the Italians and the French.

But Hoffmann had only a few more years to live, too few to challenge the Italo-French hold exercised by the director of the Berlin court opera, Gasparo Spontini, imported from Paris in 1820. Those hardy Romantic afflictions, drink and syphilis, were attacking a system already much weakened by his rackety life. Hoffman's irreverent and often publicly satirical pen involved him in trouble with the Prussian government of the day, steadily enforcing its own McCarthyite purge of liberals and intellectuals, under the baleful influence of Metternich. But Hoffmann was now too ill to prosecute, and though a reprimand from King Frederick William III was contemplated it was never delivered. Hoffmann died in June 1822, his limbs convulsed by *locomotor ataxia*.

Hoffmann's spirit of satirical fantasy not only got him into trouble but also secured his immortality. From his dark yet light-hearted tales, Wagner found *Tannhäuser*, Tchaikovsky was to weave *The Nutcracker* ballet, Delibes composed *Coppelia* and Offenbach invented his parables of unrequited love. Was Hoffmann a wordsmith or a tune-smith? *Undine* is conventional Romantic opera, but the tales work on several levels. Their setting is often sinister, set in unreal but compelling situations, often gruesome, often in historical fancy dress, like *Mademoiselle de Scudery (Das Fräulein von Scuderi)*, a tale of murder and obsession in pre-revolutionary Paris, and *Doge und Dogaressa*, story of a passion across rank in the Venice of Doge Marino Falieri.

The tales, set bizarrely in a society hovering on the brink of madness, were beloved of Hoffmann's most direct spiritual children, Edgar Allan Poe and Baroness von Blixen (Isak Dinesen). Human behaviour varies from the frantic to the irrational. Love for an unsuitable object is inspired with dramatic suddenness, its genuine nature due not to a natural but a supernatural cause, so often represented in fairy tales. Hoffmann's own history of passions, not only for his long-suffering Polish wife and amanuensis, but for his matronly piano student and a teenage singing student in Bamberg, was marked by delusion, and unconsummated desire.

The mechanical doll that sings Nathaniel to suicidal distraction in *The Sandman (Der Sandmann, 1815–16)* and the daughter of the maker of violins who must die if she sings again (*Councillor Kresler*) were snapshots of the conflict between illusional love and reality in Hoffmann's literary imagination. Illusion gradually took over, like the devil's voice he had heard in Pomerania. Misplaced love, irrational behaviour, unexplained *doppelgängers* and Gothic fantasy appeared increasingly in his fiction in a sinister gallery of actors: inventors of mechanical dolls, necromancers with powers of levitation and murderers with strange delusions. They introduced his readers to a society on the brink of madness, almost of dissolution. Thus may it have seemed in the furnace of the wars of 1806 to 1815.

Hoffmann's obsession with doubles reflected his own almost split personality, the lawyer who wanted to be a great composer, the corpulent, shock-haired piano teacher who wanted to be a great lover, the caricaturist who wanted to be a Great Master. His first published story was of his meeting a composer in a busy Berlin coffee house who was rewriting, and improving, Gluck's operas long after he was dead. Was he mad or actually Gluck?[8] Later, in 1813, when 'he' (Hoffmann) was attending a performance of Mozart's *Don Giovanni*, in a theatre attached to his hotel, he is visited in his private box in the interval by the singer who plays Donna Anna. She tells him that the opera was really all about unfulfilled desire and of regret, a clash between titanic spirits. The Don was the mate Donna Anna desired deep in her vagina, but he failed to rape her. He had to die for his failure, for his preference for other women and for killing her father. That was his destiny, but the agent of it, the bloodless Don Ottavio, would never enjoy Donna Anna, even after the Don has been carried off to hell, even after the year's gap to which Donna Anna binds him in the last scene. The Don as Superman, Donna Anna as Superwoman intrigued Bernard Shaw, whose rendering of *Don Juan in Hell* transformed the conception of the opera from a *drama giocosa* by a drawing room Mozart to what Hoffmann was to describe as a 'foreboding of the eternal'.[9]

The story of the star- or rather father-crossed loves of Robert Schumann and Clara Wieck might have come from the pen of 'Amadeus' Hoffmann, down to the tragic madness of Robert and his incarceration in an asylum, haunted by the single note of music weaving itself in a melody hinting at a tale defying elucidation. There was a daemonic hint in his later work that the orderly symphony of music teetered on the edge of disorder, the signs of mental illness sounding a macabre dance of Romantic frenzy. Like Keats, whose imagination reflected his illness but whose work showed no signs of dementia, Schumann was probably affected by mercury poisoning while treating himself for syphilis contracted as a student. Experimentation rather than dementia may have produced those strains of Romantic excess that Brahms, after his death, is said to have expunged, but the angelic followed by daemonic visions that affected the last two years of his life, may have entered his subconscious from his reading of Hoffmann.

* * *

The author of the original story of *Undine*, which had appeared in 1811, was another Prussian but not another Hoffmann. What he shared with Hoffmann was his experience of double identity, for Friedrich de la Motte Fouqué was born with the poetic imagination of a writer but who became a soldier, what Edmund Gosse called 'a rubicund officer of dragoons'.[10] His grandfather had been a French-born mercenary general in the army of Frederick the Great, and ennobled with the rank of baron. As only nobles could be officers in the Prussian army, Fouqué's father was also a soldier. Hoffmann had been born under the stormy skies and grey seas of Pomerania, where the voice of the devil might be heard on the beach and where wolves and hobgoblins inhabited the forests, but Fouqué was born a year after Hoffmann, in the city of Brandenburg, eponymous centre of the Margravate until the Hohenzollerns moved their court to Potsdam and Brandenburg sank into being a satellite of Berlin. Fouqué's father had retired from the army to be provost of the minster of Brandenburg and the family lived in an old church dwelling of rambling corridors, which the young Fouqué peopled with benign ghosts and spectres. These Ruddigore-like wraiths he identified with the military mementoes that bedecked the walls, and his earliest memory was of a family friend riding off in full military fig to fight a Prussian war. As a boy he had little physique for a soldier, much less a Frederickan grenadier, and his mother before sending him off in his early teens to study at the university in Halle made him promise that he would never become a soldier.

Halle was a garrison town and Fouqué's romantic imagination was fired by the images of cigar-chomping, moustache-twirling officers, latter day heroes of the mighty knights of the Teutonic Order who had fought paynims, Poles and Swedes, and whose armour hung in the Halle museum. These were the beaux who strode the streets, occupied the coffee bars and won the Patiences, and Ladies Jane, Angela and Sophie of Halle. Fouqué refused to tread his flowery way alone and resolved to join them. At 17, breaking the promise to his recently deceased mother, he enlisted as a cornet of cuirassiers in the Regiment of the Duke of Weimar.

It was 1794 and the Duke of Brunswick had been commanded to roll back the armies of revolutionary France, which threatened Prussian territory on the Rhine, and Fouqué went off to fight the enemies of Prussia against whom he had fought spectral battles in his imagination. During peacetime he was garrisoned in Saxony where he made an unhappy marriage, and then in 1800 found himself quartered in Weimar. The choice of the Duke of Weimar's regiment may not have been random, for Weimar was the home of poets, and to poets all things are poetry. Fouqué by now was determined to be the poet of the glory and excitement of war. He met Goethe who invited him to tea with Schiller, but neither was particularly impressed by the poems of the smart young cornet. It was in Berlin that Fouqué found his mentors in August Schlegel and Fichte, for he had been introduced by Goethe to the salon of one of the great poet's admiring acolytes, Amalie von Imhoff. Amalie, on moving to Berlin, had cast herself as both muse and poet, and had become a society queen.

Now 27, Fouqué determined to write drama in the tradition of Schiller, inspired by the poetic effusions of a new Berlin acquaintance, the French émigré Louis de Chamissot, who was also an army officer but who had decided to make a literary future for himself as Adelbert von Chamisso. Chamisso had founded a magazine to publish his verses, and Fouqué was carried along by the rising poetic reputation of a man who in 1805 published a long poem full of Romantic, knightly exploits which bore a strong resemblance to Walter Scott's *The Lay of the Last Minstrel*. Chamisso is perhaps best remembered by the song cycle *Frauenliebe und Leben*, composed by Schumann for his marriage in 1840 to Clara. Chamisso himself had married a girl of 18 when he was 40.

* * *

In 1806 Chamisso's magazine foundered for lack of direction. He had been with his regiment when Napoleon routed the Prussian state at Jena, after which he had been repatriated to his homeland. There being nothing to keep him there he drifted into the company of Mme de Staël at Coppet and spent two years under her dominating control, taking up the study of Swiss flora and laying claim to another, more enduring reputation as a botanist. Joining a Russian voyage of scientific discovery in 1815, Chamisso's journal of the voyage in Pacific waters as far north as the Bering Straits became almost as widely read in the continental world as the more famous *Beagle* journal in England of 15 years later. If Chamisso had not entirely given up his literary ambitions, he had left the field open for Fouqué who took up the editorship of a quarterly literary magazine and it was in the pages of this that in 1811 he published *Undine*.

Fouqué's story appealed to Coleridge as her character, before she acquired a human soul, was marvellously beautiful,[11] and to Hoffmann because it appeared to be about two Undines. The water nymph substituted for a human child, who was believed drowned, was reared by the lost child's parents, an old fishing couple who live on the edge of a lake, cut off from the rest of the world by a wood full of fearful enchantments. Having no human soul, Undine is wilful and capricious but of outstanding beauty, so naturally she attracts the immediate affections of a wandering knight, Huldibrand, who has braved the dangers of the wood and lighted on the fisherman's cottage. She undergoes an almost instant transformation after her marriage to the knight and their return to his castle. She becomes almost saintly, beloved by all who know her, and desperately faithful to her lord.

But she is dogged by the curse of her uncle, a powerful and malicious water sprite, Kühleborn, who cannot forgive her assumption of human qualities. The child for whom she was substituted, however, was not dead; she was found and brought up by a neighbouring noble and inevitably finds herself staying with Undine and her husband. Just as inevitably, being beautiful and wholly human, she captures the heart of Huldibrand, who finds Undine's devotion, accompanied by excessive lachrymosity, tiresome. He cannot accept her clinging love and her queer, unearthly powers, and repudiates her, whereupon her uncle reclaims her. When Huldibrand thinks he is free to marry his new love, he calls down on himself the curse that he had dismissed as impossible when he married Undine: that a mortal who has married a water nymph and then loves a mortal must die. The tale, with its Grimm-like premonition, its phantoms, and implacable curse, its tulgey wood and errant knight, its excesses of sudden love and undying affection, its brooding of the supernatural over the natural, its reverent hermit, dropping not from heaven but from a cenobitic monastic community, has all the standard apparatus of Romantic fiction.

Fouqué claimed that the inspiration for Undine came from Paracelsus, but a closer source would have been the master who had coolly received his early poems, Goethe. For Undine was the name Goethe had given the element of water, and water is the element of Fouqué's story. This time Goethe was enthusiastic: Fouqué had at last struck pure gold and it was a pity that for most of his time he had mined only copper. Heine thought that in the tale 'the genius of poesy kissed the sleeping spring and he opened his eyelids with a smile and all the roses breathed out perfume and all the nightingales sang'.[12] This Romantic effusion is the more remarkable in that Undine was written at a time when Prussia was picking herself up from war and defeat. Fouqué took up arms in 1812 to join the volunteers who were gathering at Beslau (now Wroclaw) to expel the army of Jerome of Westphalia and to prepare to join the coalition that was to defeat Napoleon at Leipzig. He never saw action in that battle as, after a soaking when hurled from his horse into a freezing river, he was advised to leave soldiering. Apart from patriotic and stirring military songs to celebrate the battle of Leipzig, Fouqué's best writing was already done. He died suddenly of no identifiable ailment in 1843.

Fouqué's military career and his quirky sense of German identity made him the special bard of Prussian chivalry. It was a bond between his austere Lutheranism and the starchy discipline of the Prussian cavalry, and the Romantic yearning for honour, glory and love, virtually in that order. He lacked Walter Scott's sense of knightly chivalry as noble but ultimately rather absurd. There was nothing absurd in Fouqué's mind about knights loving wraiths, or walking across the desert in search of an enchantress, or fighting duels to the death on the slightest pretext, or for that matter marrying a water sprite.[13] Why should Amadis de Gaul, Roland, Tancred and Bayard have the monopoly of chivalric legend and glory? Germans had it too and moreover that spirit of chivalry and honour, which would revive the German nation, was to be found in Prussia.

* * *

Both Fouqué and Hoffmann found an unexpected immortality in music. Hoffmann's *Undine* gave Fouqué a more enduring reputation outside his own country than he could have expected. *Undine* is as close as Hoffmann could get to the original, and sired more water spirit works, from Dvorak's *Rusalka* to Sullivan's *Iolanthe*. Hoffmann too could not have expected, given his antipathy to France that his unexpected immortality was to come from the music of a Parisian German Jew, born Jakob Offenbach in Cologne. His father Isaac Eberst took his name from Offenbach in Main where he was born in 1819, and being himself a music teacher, he recognised in Jakob a special talent, and decided to take him to Paris and enter him in the Conservatoire as a student of the cello. Jakob became Jacques and eventually so accomplished a cellist that he accompanied both Liszt and Mendelssohn. Then, after a time with the Theâtre Français, he established his own company to perform the comic operettas that poured from his pen. As a German immigrant he was vilified after the Franco-Prussian war as an agent of Bismarck having mocked militarism generally in *La Grande Duchesse de Holstein* (1867). The Grand Duchess is pure Pumpernickel and General Boum, with his '*pif-paf-pouf, tara-papa-poum*' could be seen as a mindless German militarist, and actually made Bismarck laugh, as he acknowledged 'That's it. That's just how it is.'[14] Offenbach was attacked by royalists for having brought the army, and thus the reign of Louis Napoleon, into disrepute. A discreet absence from France and triumphs in the United States soon restored him to popularity and in the late 1870s he embarked on the composition of his one serious opera.

Les Contes d'Hoffmann was unfinished at his death in 1880 and performed only a year later. His librettists took many liberties with the three stories that they extracted from Hoffmann's work.[15] They are true to Hoffmann in that they exploit what might be called his Baroque Romanticism, within the conventions of elaborate splendour. In palaces in Venice and Paris, the dark stories of Hoffmann's impossible loves are acted out against the malice of sinister people. First there is Councillor Lindorf, an elderly

Parisian debauchee, who fancies Hoffmann's latest love, the diva Stella; then Dr Coppelius, the inventor of Olympia, the mechanical doll, who supplies Hoffmann with magic spectacles though which Olympia appears as a living beauty. The gallery is completed by Captain Dappertutto, the controlling pimp of the beautiful courtesan, Giulietta, and Dr Miracle, who is bent on the destruction of the singer, Antonia. All either exploit or frustrate Hoffmann's Romantic amours, Romantic in that they are sudden, passionate and futile. Hoffmann is the principal in each story, and each episode ends in death or desolation. Finally Hoffmann is persuaded to love, not women who cannot reciprocate his love, like, Olympia, Giulietta and Antonia, and ultimately the diva, Stella, but his Muse who will safeguard his immortality.

Though Offenbach's Hoffmann dreams that in each woman there is an apotheosis of all of them in Stella, the diva singing Donna Anna to the applause of his student friends, he is eventually too drunk to welcome her from her triumph in the opera house, and cedes place to Councillor Lindorf, who has presided over all Hoffmann's thwarted love affairs. Offenbach had no message to his time. The music reflects the sybaritic opulence of Napoleon III's Paris, which post-bellum France was attempting to recapture. The opera is not, however, a light-hearted Sybaritic romp. It carries some of the melancholy melodies of Bizet and Gounod, and echoes of Weber hover over the action. Offenbach, nearing his end, wished to write a more serious, Germanic work; more reflective of Hoffman's world of Berlin's *unter den linden* than the champagne popping airs of the Champs-Élysées. The story is set in a Nuremberg of Hoffmann's era, but though the atmosphere is French it reflects some of the doom-laden melancholy of the other Parisian German, Meyerbeer. It is as if the composer wished to acknowledge his German origins, which otherwise he had ignored or ridiculed as if they had never existed.

∗ ∗ ∗

That was something Wagner never did. Hoffmann was one of his sources – particularly the knightly singing contest at the Wartburg that takes up much of the second act of *Tannhäuser*. *The Singing Contest (Spielerglück)* was one of Hoffmann's *Serapion Brethren (Die Serapionsbruder)*, in which the narrator, while reading an old chronicle, dreams that he witnesses, in a delicious woodland grove, a great concourse of knightly hunters, their pages and servants led by a man of special quality in old German costume, and accompanied by a lady of striking beauty. It is the preface to the appearance in the same dream of the chronicler, who tells him that what the narrator has witnessed was a meeting of six of the most famous Minnesingers of thirteenth-century Germany.

The story unfolds, of the baffled love of a bourgeois Minnesinger, Heinrich von Ofterdingen, for the widow of the Landgrave, Matilda, the beautiful lady the narrator had seen in his dream. She has been wooed and won by the purity of his singing by a knightly Minnesinger, Wolfram von Eschenbach. Heinrich, however, also loves her, and on one of his knightly quests he is accosted by a sinister stranger who promises to teach him the art of his master, Klingsor, widely suspected of trafficking in magic, so that his song might win the next contest and the affections of Matilda. When Heinrich competes at the next contest before Matilda, he wins the crown, but his singing has a strange, uncanny note about it and though the other Minnesingers agreed that he had deserved to win they could not exactly explain why. On being challenged by Wolfram, Heinrich breaks down before the implication that he has sought the aid of supernatural powers.

The other Minnesingers accept this as a confession of guilt, but Matilda stands by him and under the malign influence of Klingsor's musical style, the characters of both change. Matilda becomes obsessed with Heinrich; she composes lays of her own in his style, and abandons all the charms that made her the queen of beauty. Above all, she discards the love of her knightly Minnesinger, and moves to an isolated castle to sing her own songs to her own weird music. Heinrich would have joined her had he not been expressly forbidden to do by the Landgrave.

Being a Minnesinger he is summoned to compete in the next contest, a summons he has to accept and he is out-sung by his rivals. In frustrated rage he bursts out in an angry tirade at the Landgrave and all the ladies of his court, except Matilda. When threatened with his life by the other outraged competitors he begs the Landgrave to protect him and to order another contest where Klingsor may be the arbiter. The Landgrave weakly agrees but rules that, if Heinrich loses, he shall be instantly executed. The end is predictable. Heinrich does not win, Klingsor having declined to be the judge and, as the executioners move onto Heinrich, he disappears in a puff of black smoke. Matilda is reconciled to Wolfram von Eschenbach, whose pure style of singing has virtually exorcised Matilda's enchantment, discomforted Klingsor and rescued Heinrich from his tainted thrall. All live happily ever after except Klingsor, condemned by Wagner to return in *Parsifal*.[16]

Wagner adapted Hoffmann's song contest for *Tannhäuser* but there is no Tannhäuser in Hoffmann's story. For him Wagner was indebted to the brothers Grimm and to a medieval poem, the *Tannhäuserlied* – Wagner being in his full medieval Romanticism phase – but the sinister setting of the dream, the caparisoned knightly concourse and the change of nature in both Heinrich and Matilda, which were Hoffmann's trademarks, were irresistible to Wagner. But he was resolved to make his own tale out of it. Tannhäuser is not Heinrich, but this is the name by which he is known by his fellow Minnesingers and by Elizabeth, who is not Matilda. There is no Klingsor or sinister traveller but Heinrich/Tannhäuser, after earning Elizabeth's love by his singing at an earlier contest, has been carnally polluted by a fairly sustained sojourn with Venus in an enchanted grotto, the Venusberg.

Sated by sexual indulgence, Tannhäuser yearns for the fresh woods and skies and the contests of his singing days. Venus lets him go with dark hints that he will never throw off her thrall. Tannhäuser meets his old companion, Wolfram von Eschenbach, and agrees to attend the next contest when Elizabeth, the Landgrave's niece, will present the crown to the winner. Wolfram loves Elizabeth (as he did Matilda) but realises from the passionately chaste encounter between Elizabeth and Tannhäuser, that however purely he may sing of love, which is the subject of this contest, he does not and will not enjoy the affections of the girl. Elizabeth is a teenage beauty on the threshold of carnal love but sanctified by the halo of her purity. Even so she is surprised by what happens next.[17]

Wolfram sings of love that is like a pure fountain of joy that may not be sullied by impurity, but only enjoyed by spiritual contemplation. This sentimental effusion, being Wolfram's tribute to the maiden innocence of Elizabeth, incites Tannhäuser to contempt. If love is a fountain it is to be drunk from to the full, and enjoyed. The Minnesingers are shocked;

this is not their idea of the courtly, impotent love of troubadourism. Tannhäuser is now possessed by the memory of the Venusberg, for there love was a carnal pleasure, to be enjoyed and enjoyed and enjoyed. This is too much for the assembled company. It is an admission that Tannhäuser had dwelt in Venusberg, and for boasting of that in his song to the maidenly Elizabeth he deserves death. But for her intervention he would have died then and there, but though he has broken her heart by seeming to glory in his sexual pleasure with the Goddess of Love, he must be given the opportunity to repent. Tannhäuser, realising the enormity of his behaviour, agrees to join a band of pilgrims on their way to be shriven of their worldly sins in Rome.

At that point Wagner breaks with Hoffmann. No happy ending can soften the impact of gross sin, penance and pride. Elizabeth is mortified by Tannhäuser's behaviour. Tannhäuser is not shriven in Rome and returns to seek the pleasures of Venusberg, but learning on his way that Elizabeth is praying for his redemption in heaven, and encouraged by a returning pilgrim carrying the symbol of his pardon, he repudiates carnal love and drops down dead at her tomb. Wolfram is left to sing of his pure and bloodless love to an empty world.

* * *

Romanticism was not a definition coined from its interest in love, for the mysteries of the conflict between cerebral passion and carnal fulfilment had preoccupied poets since the time of Homer. The fatal attraction of Venus had then sparked a ten-year war, so that she became the divine temptress, perpetually at conflict with the divine redemptrix. She was the personification of a cult that sanctified an alternative to maidenhood, virginity, continence and fidelity. Venus in her Venusberg, her mountain of delight, was the permanent temptation to gloomy celibacy and frustrated monogamy. Even in Fouqué's cold haunt of northern chivalry, she is desired and feared.[18] But though the Romantics were not bound by the precepts of Christianity, they would not repudiate marital fidelity and idealistic affection. They would, however, exempt it from ecclesiastical censure. Holy men were usually roving thaumaturges or brethren from a community that lived cut off from established morality, like the priest who married Huldibrand and Undine, or Schiller's consecrated priest masquerading as a servant in *Mary Stuart*.

That so many of Germany's writers should have been the sons of Lutheran pastors, destined for the Church, may explain their interest in the interplay of the human inevitabilities of birth, love and death, at a time when an increasing interest in human behaviour around them provoked doubts as to the existence of divinity and divine sanctions. Their interest in the metaphysics of love had been aroused by *The Sorrows of Young Werther*, consumed as he was by love for a forbidden object. Charlotte, too, was pure, like Elizabeth, wrestling with desire, but she was a refreshing change from the carefully married wanton, who was almost an essential feature of eighteenth-century life, like La Grävenitz, Eberhard of Württemberg's mistress. It explored the urban, middle-class, Lutheran domestic scene where an unfulfilled illicit passion was not an uncommon experience. For Goethe, such passions might almost have been autobiographical but, by the time of Hoffmann and Fouqué, passionate love, free from benefit of clergy, was a Romantic theme. The German exploration of its linguistic and literary past, of mystical saints, virgins and knightly troubadours showed that love had been metaphysical and pure at a time when the discipline of marriage, usually arranged and dynastic, had been most rigid and severe. It was poetic, musical, a foretaste of heaven, and being pure could be enjoyed without social sanction.

Wagner made the musical metaphysic of such love his life's exploration. The Minnesingers, usually portrayed in art without musical instruments, were now supported by harp and guitar, plangent instruments that could be plucked like emotions. But he could never quite believe, nor could Hoffmann, that perfect, undying and sacrificial love was wholly natural. It did not exist in their own lives. It could only be induced by supernatural (essentially Romantic) means. Hoffmann's Matilda (Wagner's Elizabeth) was captivated by the magic enhancement of Heinrich's music, his Donna Anna by the uncanny magnetism of Don Giovanni. Wagner's Elizabeth (Hoffmann's Matilda), was torn by conflict between her hormones that were roused by Tannhäuser's singing, and her saintly purity. She might recoil from his suggestion of carnal pleasure, but she desired him enough to prevent him from instant death at the swords of his fellow Minnesingers, provided he repented.[19] Once launched on passion Wagner let it rise like incense to the sky. It could only be consummated in death, for the delights of pure love were not those of the Venusberg but of Heaven, closed to mortals.

Tannhäuser was partly taken from Hoffmann, just as Offenbach had taken *The Tales*. As musical stage-pieces they are poles apart, but each explores the illusion of romantic love, erotic and passionate but false and deceitful, from which the human spirit has either to escape in death or to be violently rescued. Hoffmann did not invent Venusberg, but many of his tales were about other Venusbergs, abodes of false love, which haunted the Romantic stage. Passion rather than love was the aim, and music was to be its elixir.

CHAPTER FIFTEEN

Harmony and Dissonance

Mendelssohn and Wagner

Wagner's music awakens the swine rather than the
Angel. It is the music of a demented eunuch.
(The Paris *Figaro*, 1876)

Die Meistersinger ... is the incarnation of our national culture ...
It brilliantly combines German sobriety, German romanticism,
German pride, German industry and German humour.
(Joseph Goebbels, 1933)

*A*T THE END of the Napoleonic wars Frederick William III might not
be an inspiring monarch but his commander in chief, Blücher,
had settled the victory over the French at Waterloo. Prussia had done well
out of the peace conferences and acquired what were to become the principal
sources of future German power and wealth: northern Saxony, the Saar
and the Ruhr, and the Rhenish (North Westphalian) lands from Cologne to
Aachen. She was now second only to Austria in size and population. Goethe
might still be living in Weimar, revered by all, but Berlin had become the
intellectual centre of Germany. The roll of poets, musicians and writers, the
salons they attended and their fruits now elevated Berlin to a popular parity
with Paris, London and Vienna. The beacon of its cosmopolitanism, its
human appeal and its universalism had been personified, in the immediate
years after the humiliation of Jena, by the Humboldt brothers and was now
to be trumpeted abroad by its own musical genius, Felix Mendelssohn.

* * *

With the end of the wars that marked the age of that arch-Romantic Napoleon, Romanticism fled from the attic studio to the concert hall, to be recaptured in compositions on new, more versatile musical instruments, where musical presentations of nature no longer relied on full symphonic ensembles but could be reproduced in pianistic or solo form. A golden age of Germanic Romanticism in music, embracing the *sturm und drang* of Beethoven, the lyricism of Schubert, the mystical passion of Byron, the pastoral melody of Goethe inaugurated a new age of artistic expression with the Schumanns, Mendelssohns and Wagner. Hoffmann's comment that 'music is the most romantic of the arts, perhaps the only one genuinely romantic' seemed to have been true.[1] Pumpernickel emerged from its forests into the sunlit plains of pastoralism, only to retreat with the braying brass of Germanic pride and Prussian militarism.

Felix Mendelssohn's grandfather was the former Jewish waif who had walked to Berlin in search of enlightenment in his faith and had defied poverty and illness to become one of the major thinkers of his time, a German Socrates, honoured as a 'Protected Jew'. Abraham, the father of Felix, was Moses's second son, and whereas his father was a gifted philosopher, and his son a gifted musician, his gift was for making money. He married into it and continued to make it as he ran a banking house in Hamburg, where Felix was born, financing a highly profitable smuggling business under French occupation until 1811. When the French decided to clamp down on breaches in the Continental System, Abraham left with his family for Berlin.

After the end of the war Prussia wanted stability, peace and prosperity and, with them, Abraham continued to prosper. He was able to give his children a pampered childhood, indulging the precocious musical talents of his daughter Fanny and his son Felix. He and his wife, whose family had abandoned the Jewish surname of Salomon for the gentile Bartholdy, decided to convert to Lutheranism, having the children baptised first in 1816 and then accepting baptism themselves in 1822. Despite the emancipation of the Jews in 1812, Jewish believers who had not converted were still classed as second-class citizens and anti-Semitism was still rife. This was not good enough for the Mendelssohns, anxious that their gifted children should have all the benefits of an emancipated society. Though never abandoning his family name, Felix was ready to add Bartholdy to it.

It was clear from an early age that Felix was a musical prodigy, inviting comparison with the child Mozart, but whereas the Mozart brother and sister were paraded like a musical circus act round Europe, Abraham and Lea Mendelssohn wished to protect their children from undue adulation and publicity. They had the money to indulge Felix's passion for home concerts and ventures among friends, like the first performance of *The Matthew Passion* for 100 years. Felix would offer his services free, if asked to perform publicly, but his real passion was for composition. At 16 his octet for strings followed a year later by the overture to *A Midsummer Night's Dream,* showed a compositional skill that Mozart, it can be argued, could not show at the same age. His versatility as both a performer on the piano and as a composer impressed Goethe in Weimar in 1821, though Goethe could not be said to have a musical taste to match his reputation as The Sun of Weimar. He disliked the music of Beethoven as an assault on his ears and he found Schubert's too difficult to understand. But he liked Felix's renderings of Bach and was heard to hope that the world had been blessed with a second Mozart, bestowing on him a paternal kiss which, from the author of *The Sorrows of Young Werther* and of *Faust,* seemed to its recipient more precious than Mozart's from the Empress of Austria.

The mature Mendelssohn never rivalled Mozart in revealing a deep, instinctive understanding of human desires or follies; he never developed an operatic style, after his few adolescent party pieces, but his ear for natural atmosphere was unrivalled. The youthful overture to Shakespeare's *A Midsummer Night's Dream* was to become one of the most commonly performed pieces in the repertoire Mendelssohn took to London, with its fogs, its bustle, its wealth and its women. In return Londoners took to him.

His first visit was in 1829 aged 20. He had already conducted the Bach *Matthew Passion* before the court and the musical society of Berlin. Goethe had graciously, when he read of its triumph, said that he had heard the roaring of the sea from afar, and Berlioz was soon to add that there was no God but Bach and Mendelssohn was his prophet.[2] London was not the musical epicentre of Europe but it was preferred to Vienna as the city where Felix should appear before a wider audience, because it was rich and a triumph there would be more widely trumpeted abroad. The opera was strongly Italian; serious music, mainly symphonic, following Haydn's successful visit 30 years earlier, was in the hands of Germans.

Haydn's 18 months from 1790–1 had been wonderfully prolific, his 12 London symphonies being presented to full houses and huge applause. He heard enough of Handel's oratorios in London to inspire him to try his hand too at composing choral pieces when back in Vienna. *The Creation* and *The Season* (and the *Kaiserhymne* which ironically finished as the German, not Austrian, national anthem) were among the fruits of his London visits. Having lived so long on the borders of the servants' quarters in the Esterházy palace Haydn was a musical innovator but not a revolutionary. It was easy on the ear, difficult to play, full of cranks and quiddities that appealed to professional musicians who were still viewed as only one step above servants. Within Haydn's music of delight was hidden a respectful satire on aristocratic employers and patrons who were not musical enough to see it. But Mendelssohn was different. He was clearly not a servant, rather a master. He was handsome, he was rich, he had influential contacts and he performed prodigiously without a fee. His public concerts were a sell-out, even though properly the 'season' had ended, his triumphs were a symphony composed when he was 15 and the *A Midsummer Night's Dream* overture composed two years later.

Scotland had become through the influence of Ossian (James Macpherson) almost the prescribed home to Romantic wildness. Klopstock and Schiller had sung its praises and Goethe's *Werther* was steeped in its Romantic gloom. Then Walter Scott had made the country almost as mandatory a centre of pilgrimage as Goethe had made Weimar. Mendelssohn was entranced by the combination of open spaces, wild mountains and the culture of plaids and bagpipes. His Hebridean overture, known as *Fingal's Cave*, captured the Romantic flavour of a land made Romantic by its primitive passions, its freedom from the enervating and soporific torpor of civilisation, yet carrying within itself the sublimity of true sentiment. The portrait in sound of one of the strangest and wildest places in the British Isles, a continuation of the strange columnar basaltic rocks which started with the Giant's Causeway in Northern Ireland, lashed by the incoherent Atlantic waves against which they had stood for many millions of years, was pure Ossianic territory which Mendelssohn bathed both in sunshine and in gloom. Since the age of Handel, Britain had not had a musical experience like it. Mendelssohn seemed, though a German, as was Handel, to belong to Britain.

Mendelssohn was back in London in 1832, received with acclamation by the orchestra as soon as he entered the rehearsal hall; when he played the organ in St Paul's Cathedral the congregation would not leave until he had finished, having to be beaten and chased out by the vergers. On a later visit his playing on this organ was only ended by the sudden departure of the organ-blowers. He was in Birmingham in 1837 conducting a four-day festival in the newly-built Town Hall, a new symphony, his oratorio *St Paul* and a brilliant exposition of Johann Sebastian Bach on the organ. Mendelssohn was now the cynosure of musical life in both Germany and England, director of two national orchestras at Düsseldorf (now capital of the Prussian Rhenish provinces) and Leipzig. His enthusiasm for Bach made him the champion of music that was little played or known; he performed Schubert's great C Major Symphony recently discovered by Schumann in Vienna gathering dust as too difficult to perform. He was surrounded by prodigally skilful performers but seemed able to overtop them all.

Even Chopin and Liszt, both of whom would engage Mendelssohn in friendly rivalry on the pianoforte, admitted that he was their master. His memory was prodigious. After hearing Liszt play a new Hungarian dance with improvised variations, and with a lighted cigar between his fingers for effect, he was able to play it all again immediately afterwards, improvisations and all. He could recall and play new music after having heard it only once, and his mind was a perfect library of his own and other composers' music. When asked whether he knew the music of Handel, he replied: 'Every note.'

His devotion to the choral music of Bach and Handel led to the composition of choral works that became the staple of choral societies across the world. Birmingham was captured by a cantata symphony, *Lobgesang*, or *Hymn of Praise*, so stirring that audiences stood when the choir sang *Now Thank We All Our God*, as they had learned to do for Handel's Hallelujah chorus. His every performance was sold out. Kings walked to his conductor's rostrum to compliment him, orchestras applauded him when he was spotted in the audience. He was to captivate a queen and fill drawing rooms with melodies played by every young lady learning the piano. He was as Romantic as he looked, and his sound, bathing its listeners in liquid angel songs of joy, conquered Europe. His music was not Jewish, despite his *Elijah;* it was not Christian despite his *Paulus.* It was not Lutheran despite his *Hymn of Praise.* Was it properly German despite its debt to Bach? In its radiant harmonies, intensely singable, supremely energetic, it was Mendelssohnian. An English organist was to discover that *Hark the Herald Angels Sing,* Charles Wesley's most popular Christmas hymn, could be sung to Mendelssohn's music.

Mendelssohn had captured the Elizabethan land of fairy in his scherzo for *A Midsummer Night's Dream.* Fairies were becoming a popular subject for imaginative art, and Shakespeare was the main source. Joshua Reynolds had set the trend with his *Puck,* then in the possession of the *breakfasteur,* Samuel Rogers, and Fuseli and Maclise had almost created a vogue for sinister incubi and goblins. Richard Dadd's *Titania Sleeping* and *Puck* had appeared at the Royal Academy exhibition in 1841, and established him as master of the fairy genre. In the first, a Giorgionesque group of semi-naked women surround a semi-naked Venerian Titania, and are themselves surrounded by an aureole of winged goblins forming a snail shell cavern from with which corybants emerge in a twilight erotic dance. A similar circlet surrounds the Puck, an infant cherub, shining like an incandescent light bulb against a grotto of trumpet flowers, merging into pale blue moonlight.[3] Mendelssohn's little people were neither erotic nor sinister. Fairies may have been perverse people, mischievous if not malevolent, and consumed by mortal passions for power and possession, but Mendelssohn's rendering evoked the spirit of Robin Goodfellow, not of Dadd's later pictures from the Bethlem Hospital. Titania and Oberon, the sinister middle-aged denizens of a Biblical fairy tyrant's court in Dadd's *The Fairy Feller's Master-Stroke,* painted in the late 1850s and 1860s, are closer to the malevolent sprites of Christina Rossetti's *Goblin Market* (1862). Earnest evangelism and rampant rationalism had begun to view askance a dangerous psychopathic irrationalism and were busy confining fairies to the nursery or to the end of the garden when not, more sinisterly, to the subconscious.

For now the innocence of the nursery was joyously present in the happy music elder sisters would play to younger and reflected the family life of Mendelssohn's two royal patrons. He dazzled them in Buckingham Palace as he played 'Rule Britannia' with one hand and the Austrian national anthem with the other. Albert invited him to hear him play his organ and to give an opinion on the instrument, while Victoria refused to let the maestro pick up the music which had blown to the floor, doing it herself. This cosy Pumpernickel scene was played out in its *biedermeier* format of musical monarch and more gifted subject, Albert managing the organ stops and singing the chorus of *Paulus*. Queen Victoria would enthusiastically if inaccurately claim Mendelssohn as her singing teacher, and she liked to sing his German songs to her German husband as he accompanied her. Mendelssohn found the Palace the only comfortable house he had met with in England.

Mendelssohn capped his English triumphs with *Elijah* (1846) at Birmingham. He had hoped that the Swedish superstar, Jenny Lind, would sing the soprano role, but she was having contractual problems. Even so and despite the actual singer being 'so out of tune, so soulless and so brainless' it was a triumph, attracting prolonged applause before the last chord had died away. English choirs accepted it instantly as the younger brother of *The Messiah* and *Judas Maccabaeus*.[4] Within a year Mendelssohn was dead. Victoria, when playing the music of so wonderful a genius and great mind, felt that his death was both perverse and incomprehensible.

* * *

Not everyone bowed down before the Mendelssohn sound. He had rejected a symphony for performance at the Gewandhaus in Leipzig, a rejection for which he was never forgiven by its composer.[5] Though in 1855 Richard Wagner, at his first Philharmonic concert in London, conducted the whole overture to 'the isles of Fingal' – never in the recollection of the critic of *The Morning Post* so well played in this country – he seldom allowed his distaste for the music to go unnoticed. He objected in principle to the English custom of expecting conductors to wear kid gloves, which he would ostentatiously take off when he was on the rostrum. For conducting Mendelssohn at one of the Philharmonic concerts he just as ostentatiously put them on again, giving what he thought was an unmistakable message of distaste to the audience. On that occasion *The Times* critic thought his conduct of the baton must have been especially puzzling to the orchestra, and his conducting without a score said, in his view, more for his memory than for his judgment.[6]

Wagner was a Saxon, born in Leipzig in 1813, only four years after Mendelssohn. It was in the same year that Hoffmann accepted the post there as director of an opera troupe. He was to know the Wagner family, both Richard's father and uncle, and his *Tales*, if not his music, were to be favourites of the young man as he grew up in Dresden. Richard Wagner proved a studious if self-willed, and often eccentric student, his literary training spent in translating the first twelve books of the *Odyssey* for his own amusement. His musical training, under the cantor at the Thomasschule in Leipzig, was more professionally thorough and he landed the job of chorus master at Würzburg in 1833 at the age of 20. There he set about composing his first major opera, *Die Feen*, adapted from a play by the Venetian Carlo Gozzi, which he called *The Fairies*.[7] It was only performed in 1888, for these are not Shakespearean fairies, more Hoffmanesque, jealous creatures of a fairyland in which one has renounced fairyhood for a mortal. Wagner wrote the libretto himself and this music was strongly influenced by Hoffmann's *Undine* and Weber's *Oberon* and *Euryanthe*. The story, in the nature of these interactions of the human and fairy world, is intricate, involving fairies determined to keep their half-human fairy from the human lover who, in his turn, is required to save his principality (he is of course a prince) from disaster. Sorceresses and sorcerers compete, not for their souls – it is not clear that either have any – but for reasons of their own. The fairies win in the end; both the mortal and semi-mortal hero and heroine end up as fairies in fairyland and the human protagonists in humanland.

A Gilbertian ending would have been more fun and Wagner was later to disclaim his juvenile work as rather a bore. He only saw *Die Feen* performed in the last years of his lifetime, and in his own Valhalla he may have celebrated or deplored the fact that the original score was destroyed in the Berlin bunker along with Adolf Hitler, to whom it had been given as if from the spirit of Wagner himself.[8] Supernatural motifs were, however, to mark all his subsequent work (with the exceptions of *Rienzi* and *Die Meistersinger*): mysterious strangers, magic potions, talking birds, giants, gods and goddesses, enchanted swans and the Holy Grail play out their role in his world, where reality coexisted with fancy in both human and divine destiny.

From Würzburg he went to Magdeburg in 1833 as conductor of the opera. It was not a wholly successful appointment. He received only a single performance of his opera based on Shakespeare's *Measure for Measure, (Die Liebesverbot)*, and for nine years, during which he married an actress from the theatre at Königsburg, he moved from post to post composing all the time. In 1839 he went to Paris with a suitably stirring unfinished work that he hoped to have performed at the Opéra. It was a musical but not magical extravaganza based on Bulwer Lytton's *Rienzi* (1835), which had recently appeared in translation. Paris was escaping from the thrall of Rossini whose last opera, after Schiller's *William Tell*, had been performed in 1829, launching an appetite for grand stories of a more recent historical past than classical or Biblical times. The heir to Gioacchino was Giacomo, no more Italian than Rossini had been German, for Giacomo Meyerbeer had been born Jakob Liebmann Meyer Beer, in Berlin in 1791 and was in fact connected to Felix Mendelssohn, whose sister had married Meyerbeer's uncle.

Meyerbeer had carefully studied Rossini and in 1831 had been hailed as the new master with *Robert le Diable*, which caused Goethe to believe that he might, if properly asked, have composed music for *Faust*. This was, followed five years later by the even more widely acclaimed *Les Huguenots*.[9] Wagner had already written a rather fawning letter to Meyerbeer, calling him 'almost a God on earth' and outlining his ambitions. He received no reply. When 'God' and his acolyte did meet in Paris, where Wagner and his new wife were living in some hardship while he tried to finish *Rienzi*, Meyerbeer did help the younger man, getting his opera based on *Measure for Measure* accepted at a smaller theatre and his *Columbus* overture by the Paris Conservatoire.[10] Meyerbeer, who was now Wagner's 'esteemed Lord and Master' and 'Protector', took an interest in the struggling fellow composer, recommending *Rienzi* to the new Dresden Royal Opera, where it was performed in 1842.

Meyerbeer had given it a generous recommendation, 'full of inspiration and dramatically most effective' but *Rienzi*, despite being modelled on all its great predecessors, Beethoven's *Fidelio*, Rossini's *Tell* and even the work of the new Paris sensation Vincenzo Bellini, was rejected for the French opera. Despite its sprawling length – the first performance at Dresden lasted till nearly midnight – the performers would not allow significant cuts and the opera was performed on subsequent evening over two nights. Wagner felt vindicated and launched. *Rienzi,* especially its overture, outshines anything Meyerbeer wrote, (except probably the duet in the fourth act of *Les Huguenots* about which Wagner actually raved), but Wagner insisted on being his own librettist, an insistence which seemed perverse at the time and diminishing to local talent. He had in 1839 written vainly to Eugène Scribe, the prolific dramatist, novelist and provider of libretti for 60 operas, among them Meyerbeer's, but he never replied. In future, Wagner would write his own 'Poems'. He would not find himself in the somewhat ignominious position of seeking a plot from a hack librettist; everything would be written by the composer, words and music would come together in physical and psychological consistency. In what he called his 'stage festival plays', music and words would merge in truth.

Paris was not ready for total opera and the opening of *Rienzi*, moreover, was to sound to French ears more like the music of a German bandmaster than the Romantic surge of wild and abandoned horsemen who had emerged from the twilight forest calm that had prefaced *William Tell*. Even so, Wagner had decided that the moment was propitious. The 1830s were turbid times following the overthrow of the Bourbon dynasty in 1830, and Wagner was all on the side of the bourgeoisie. Paris was a big house and needed a big opera, and as he had seen Spontini's sprawling grand opera, *Ferdinand Cortez,* in Berlin, he thought he knew how to produce one, carried away as he was by Lord Lytton's picture of a major political and historical event. '*Rienzi* with great ideas in his brain and strong feelings in his heart, set all my nerves thrilling with sympathy and affection.'[11] But production was too difficult and expensive for a huge opera by an unknown, and furthermore Wagner had not actually finished it when he offered it to the house.

* * *

Wagner's reaction to the ascendancy of Mendelssohn and Meyerbeer was not long in coming. In 1850 an article appeared on Judaism in Music in a musical journal, signed with a pseudonym. The careers of both Mendelssohn and Meyerbeer came under attack, for the article held that it was impossible for a Jew, no matter how civilised or capable, to move both heart and soul. The author was Richard Wagner, whose teeth were growing ever longer to bite the hand of anyone who fed him.

Gone was any sense of gratitude to Meyerbeer for recommending him to Dresden. Pulling strings on the backstairs was dishonest, not a proper case for gratitude, but foremost was the implied insult of rejection of *Rienzi* in Paris. As a result Wagner was filled with immense loathing for his so-called 'Protector'.[12] Wagner's was hardly a musical comment, but Bernard Shaw, an early admirer of Wagner who similarly displayed an irrational anti-Semitic judgment, was to find Mendelssohn's Judeo-Christian oratorio *Paulus* so insufferably tedious that he would rather have engaged in Sunday school talk with a brainless woman for two and a half hours, while the Sunday school sentimentalities of *Elijah* made him pine for Handel.[13] Wagner seemed a heaven-sent antidote.

∗ ∗ ∗

Wagner also had his meetings with the Pumpernickel monarchs in London in 1855. The short, plain, plump sovereign with her trivial musical taste – she loved Mendelssohn – was affable, even enthusiastic. She and her husband attended his concert to hear the *Tannhäuser* overture, and applauded prettily from the royal box for all to see. Wagner, who thought he was hounded in Germany like a highway robber and in France by passport problems, was impressed to find 'the Queen of England is not embarrassed to receive me before the most aristocratic gathering in the world with the utmost friendliness'. Which was more than *The Sunday Times* critic showed; he thought him either 'a desperate charlatan' or else a 'self deceived enthusiast who thoroughly believes his own apostolic mission and is too utterly destitute of any perception of musical beauty to recognise the worthlessness of his credentials'.[14] The critic was not alone. Schumann writing to Mendelssohn from Dresden in 1845 thought that Wagner 'could not write four consecutive bars of decent, let alone beautiful music'.[15]

From 1849 to 1860 Wagner *was* in flight like the highway robber to which he had likened himself. He had incautiously allowed himself to be caught up in the riots of the year of revolutions and was only able to escape arrest by being hurried out of Dresden to Weimar where Franz Liszt was preparing to produce *Tannhäuser*. Liszt then secured him a forged passport as a Berlin professor, Werder, to go to Switzerland while things calmed down. The ban on his residence in Germany – he could still not enter Saxony – was only lifted in 1860. By this time Wagner had had his royal reception and less royal reviews in London, his *Lohengrin* had been performed in his absence at Weimar again under the baton of Liszt, he had completed the 'poems' for *The Ring of the Nibelungs*, finished *Die Walküre* and *Tristan und Isolde*, composed the *Wesendonck Liede,* started on *Parsifal* and enjoyed a platonically devout triangular idyll with his wife Minna, his muse Mathilde Wesendonck, and Franz Liszt's 20-year-old daughter, Cosima, wife of his student, Hans von Bulow.

Wagner at 47 was now the uncrowned king of Germany's musical castle. Whereas Mendelssohn's had flowed like an enchanted Tokay over conjugal love, Wagner's music was the melody of the potion, an envenomed mixture which tested the power of redemptive, though usually thwarted, love. Above the often-turgid prose of his own 'poems', which had to untangle the complications of the story he had chosen to adopt as his starting point, he spun compacted skeins that developed into music of an ethereal and sometimes magical beauty. Unlike the 'Jewish' music of Mendelssohn which Shaw thought had descended into Sunday school piety, Wagner tackled the psychological drama he found in his sources, the sagas of the German Minnesingers, the German folk legends, the Nibelungs of Nebelheim, the German courts, the guild of Mastersingers, and the Germanic amorality of passionate love. 'Your typical Englishman is your typical sheep'[16] and as a groundling his love, presumably, and that of any non-German, must be sheep-like. Wagner for his part had discovered the true virtue of love. If the will was frustrated by human efforts, love despite all obstacles could soar above them, and even when betrayed could achieve redemption for the lover, no matter how compromised. It was no wonder that the grandson of Ludwig I of Bavaria, the lover of the wild Irish beauty Lola Montes, carrying out his grandfather's mission to make Munich the intellectual and artistic capital of Europe, as soon as he had read Wagner's Nibelung poem, saw the intense Germanness of it.[17] In 1864 he invited him to complete the mighty work in his kingdom of mountains, rivers and forests, a suitable home for the modern Nibelung. There true love, German love, could thrive.

The Nibelungs who, after all, were Norwegian dwarves, could scarcely be the personification of the German personality, but the thirteenth-century tale was German enough, with its familiar thread of greed and treachery, sexual attraction and chicanery.[18] The Wagner oeuvre had so far explored this mixture in a purely human forum where, despite the virtue of kings like Henry the Fowler and of knights like Lohengrin, human affairs were subject to corruption and failure, the purest Elizabeths and Elsas crossed by human weakness. Now the role of the extra-human, of fairies, of flying Dutchmen, of gods and goddesses and supernaturally conceived heroes, not subject to the laws of pessimism, or failure of the will — which Wagner had learned from his obsessive reading of Schopenhauer — was to reveal that it, too, was subject to the laws of life and death. In 'symphonic poems on a grand scale',[19] he would demonstrate the vanity of all human wishes. They could also be proof of the redemptive role of music.

Humans, like Tristan and Isolde, might be indissolubly joined in a passionate drug-induced love but, if they might consummate it, they could not enjoy it. Wagner was to show that even love between heroes, like Siegfried and Brünnhilde, could not immortalise it. Love was only a temporary palliative to life's inevitable misery, which is why it could only end in disappointment or in an orgasm of catastrophe. Music alone could extend and support climax, a tonal Viagra, to be 'the fulfiller of our Will to live and consequently our reconciler to night and death'.[20] In the last analysis it was only the Rhine-maidens who were truly and pointlessly immortal, for theirs was a sterile love for essentially useless gold.

* * *

In March 1864 Ludwig II had become the new king in Bavaria. He was still only 18, tall, athletic and incredibly handsome. Moreover, he had the receptive brain of an actor and, as kingcraft was largely an act, Ludwig II filled his role at the outset to perfection. He had already committed most of Wagner's 'poems' to his amazingly extensive memory, and hearing that Wagner was in deep financial trouble he determined to be both his saviour and his patron. Wagner was only too ready to be saved and patronised. He was still struggling with *Tristan und Isolde* and was in despair of ever finding singers let alone a theatre and the money to perform it. Ludwig offered to cancel all his debts, give him an annual pension and a house, and promised that if he completed *The Ring* he would pay him the colossal sum of 30,000 gulden, and build both a theatre in which to perform it and a music school in which to form the singers.

It was like the opening of heaven to Wagner; a God-given dream to find a beautiful, gifted and munificent prince who understood him so well and was determined to make his genius 'free to spread its mighty pinions in the aetherial regions of your heavenly art'.[21] The king ordered productions of *The Flying Dutchman* and *Tristan* in the Munich opera house. Wagner was to be Ludwig's Lohengrin, Ludwig Wagner's Siegfried. They met daily, Wagner flying to him like a lover. They were soulmates. For Wagner it was not a homosexual love affair. He had found a worshipping acolyte who had the means to fulfil his fondest dreams, to have *The Nibelungenlied* performed exactly as he wanted. He was to be his own master, not a *kapellmeister*; Ludwig 'knows everything about me and understands me like my own soul.'[22] That was more than he expected of Mathilde, Minna or even Cosima. For Ludwig the infatuation may have been almost female, and it was not long before memories of the expensive and domineering Lola Montez began to occupy the mind of courtiers, some of whom referred to the king's new crony as 'Lolus' or 'Lotte'.

Despite the exchange of 'love' letters, Wagner's full of thanks, Ludwig's of promises of future support, the hothouse relationship of artist and patron was too heated to last. Journalists unearthed Wagner's revolutionary antecedents in Dresden and began to accuse him of being a danger to both public order and morality, and causing extravagant expenditure that threatened ruin to the Bavarian economy. Ludwig in words which promised an eternal friendship and support advised his withdrawal for a time and Wagner removed himself once more to Switzerland, ostensibly for his health. He would never return to live in Munich unless he was given Bavarian citizenship. That request sealed his exile; it was too close to the unhappy example of Lola Montez. It was now also clear that despite Ludwig's passionate protests, he could only resume the relationship if he abdicated like his grandfather.

This, Wagner could not allow. A penniless king in exile was not his idea of a patron, now that the production of his *Ring* was likely only to be possible in Munich. He advised him to act with circumspection, do nothing rash, and continue to subsidise his work. Public opinion in the city was exacerbated by rumours of Wagner's liaison with Cosima in Switzerland, (hotly denied by Wagner) while Bülow had had to stay in Munich to prepare for the performance of Wagner's operas. But if Wagner had found a new emotional toy, then Ludwig had too, and his courtiers, almost sighing for the days of Lola Montez, tried to encourage affairs with visiting actresses, while his mother schemed with the mother of the Empress Elizabeth – wife of Franz Joseph of Austria – for the hand of her younger sister, Sophie, as a wife for Ludwig. Sophie was a Wagner enthusiast and the young couple referred to each other by Wagnerian names. Soon 'Elsa' and 'Heinrich' were engaged. Both Wagner and Cosima were delighted; Wagner glad to know that the relationship of patron and artist would not be disturbed, Cosima hoping for the distraction of an uncomfortably adoring rival.

Ludwig had partially restored his standing with the Bavarians. He had turned out in uniform to encourage his troops on the eve of war with Prussia, looking quite the young hero on his white horse, his long hair flowing free – he would not wear a helmet as he hated disturbing his coiffure. And though the Bavarian army, which had entered the war allied with Austria, was decisively worsted in battle, Bismarck knew that he might have need of Bavarian support in any future battle with France, and the kingdom was only lightly mulcted at the peace. Though Ludwig had done precisely nothing for his country either at war or at the peace, he took much of the credit and so great was the relief at his proposal to get married that a lavish state wedding was planned. Sophie seemed to have driven a stake into the heart of that enduring vampire, Lola Montez.

The fire that burned for Wagner in the heart of Ludwig, however, was not dimmed by 'Elsa's' apparent passion for him too. Ludwig began to doubt how deep that was, and as the marriage grew ever closer he began to be obsessed by fear of having to maintain the pretence of affection for a woman. Wagner was his beloved, his friend, his God, and Cosima was his *freundin*. That left little space for Sophie. The wedding was postponed and postponed, and when Sophie's father wrote to expostulate, Ludwig took instant offence. The engagement was off. He could not marry someone he did not love and, as he was to tell Cosima, it was a performance of *Lohengrin* that gave him the resolution to 'break his burdensome fetters'.[23]

The relationship with Wagner, despite the metamorphosis of Cosima as mistress, mother and now wife, remained the core of Ludwig's emotional life, but it was to be darkened by the shadows of incipient lunacy. He had attempted to show himself ready to be a public monarch, to marry and perhaps beget an heir, but now he began to withdraw from the world into the solitary quiet of his many chateaux. The knowledge that Wagner owned *The Ring* and that Ludwig had promised to present it in its entirety remained uppermost in his mind. For a time he thought Wagner had no business working on *Die Meistersinger von Nürnberg*, until he heard it performed in Munich, when he became a convert to this hymn to German art and culture, this apotheosis of Walther von der Vogelweide, this dawn of a new age. But the composer was finding difficulties in getting either the singers or the productions that he wanted and had become disenchanted with the Munich opera, despite its tumultuous welcome to *Die Meistersinger* in 1868. Meanwhile Cosima's real status in the Wagner seraglio was becoming known; Ludwig gradually realised that his *freundin* was in fact an adulteress and, moreover, with someone who was his lord and his God. Like Fricka with the errant Wotan, Ludwig felt betrayed by all the lies and tergiversations that had surrounded what he had been convinced was shared worship of a common deity.

The Ring, however, had to be performed as promised. Wagner was prevented by Cosima from breaking altogether with Ludwig and trying his fortune in Prussia, but the 1869 first production in Munich of *Das Rheingold* was beset by problems. Von Bülow had had enough of pretending that nothing was happening to his marriage and been sent off on sick leave to nurse his sense of betrayal. Though replaced by Wagner's other pupil, Hans Richter, rehearsals were dogged by mechanical failures; — one of the Rhine-maidens got seasick in what was later to be dubbed 'the aquarium of whores', — and Richter fell foul of the management claiming that he took orders only from Wagner. He was instantly suspended, and despite Wagner's peremptory order that he be restored, Ludwig showed that he was a king and would not be ordered about even by Wagner. Richter was not just suspended; he was sacked for insubordination and contempt of royal authority. *Das Rheingold* was finally performed in Munich in 1869 – the Rhine-maidens happily earth-bound in the wings – despite Wagner's plea to wait until he had completed the rest of *The Ring* before performing it. The performance was not one that either Ludwig or Wagner had desired. Everything seemed to go off half-cock and Ludwig tried to make the peace by reiterating that his mission in life was to serve the maestro. He wrote a grovelling letter of submission vowing that a rupture could only end in Ludwig's suicide. What was the value of a crown compared to a friendly letter from Wagner? Wagner's reply ended abruptly. Either the king wanted Wagner's works performed as he, Wagner, wanted or he did not.

Ludwig could not wait. In 1870 when he ordered *Die Walküre* to be performed, as was his right, since he owned the score, Wagner then insisted on controlling the performance or he would have nothing to do with it. He had nothing to do with it. It was premiered in Munich by local talent. Brahms, Saint-Saens and Liszt were in the audience but neither Wagner nor, as it happened, Ludwig. It was a resounding success and lavish, with real horses from the royal stables carrying grooms disguised as warrior maidens. But it constituted a final break with Wagner, who now planned to perform *The Ring* elsewhere.[24]

*   *   *

Ludwig was to find a solace for his bleeding heart in that other great occupation of Pumpernickel princes, building. Not for entertainment or for glory but that he might enjoy his dreams in solitude. His mind was still filled with the echoes of Wagner's music, the background to his dream of kingly and knightly splendour and of an eroticism that he did not feel in the presence of real women – and probably not even with men – but only in imagination with Tannhäuser in the Venusburg. In 1881 he commissioned a mural for his study in the fairy-tale castle he had erected of Neuschwanstein. Depicting, in its profusion of sexless nude beauties, the judgment of Paris, it centred on a knight in Gothic garb, his head resting on one arm, a harp in the other, reposing but not actually touching a Venus clad only in her crown. Classic *putti* and doves circled the group which led onto a blue grotto, which Ludwig had also constructed as a three dimensional *Venusgrotte,* complete with cascade, and a moon lit by electric light of different colours to represent its various phases.

Ludwig had visited the Wartburg, in which Wagner had set the singing contest in Tannhäuser, and in 1869 he started to build Neuschwanstein as a shrine to his Friend and God. In a castle perched on a mountain spur, he constructed a fairyland castle that would, unbeknown to him, be the model for Disneylands, Camelots, and dentifrice advertisements extolling white teeth. Its site, 'one of the loveliest that can be found, inviolable and inaccessible, a worthy temple for the Godlike Friend',[25] was stupendous, its gleaming pinnacle providing a view of the surrounding lakes and mountains which was to inspire Hitler's eagle eyrie of Berchtesgarten. Every spare wall was to be bedizened by murals or paintings dedicated to the sagas which formed Wagner's operas, Tannhäuser, Lohengrin and finally Parsifal, which covered the minstrel's hall, in which no minstrels ever sang. Alone the throne room, more like a chapel with a throne for an altar, was not decorated with Wagnerian motifs.

The castle was never finished in Ludwig's lifetime. He was distracted by other building projects, by his growing interest in the splendour of the Sun King and a desire to build his Versailles too, though he never intended to live in it. His love of solitariness, of midnight journeys in the snow or moonlight, for dropping in unexpected on simple peasants from whom he could expect a rude naturalness not the obsequious and often ill-concealed mockery of his royal relations and courtiers, rendered him odd. His younger brother had already showed signs of dementia, from which more and more signs indicated that Ludwig too might be suffering. It took many indicative forms: compulsive present giving, imagining that he was dining with Louis XIV in Versailles, watching theatrical performances alone in an empty theatre. He ordered private performances of Wagner's works, and if these could not be provided he preferred to sit through the dress rehearsal for the public with no other audience present. His interest in public affairs waned; as his appetite for designing the decoration and furnishing of his palaces and houses grew. He could not bear to have anyone but his most intimate servants with him and found public events daunting, even frightening. He ate, slept and walked virtually alone under discreet surveillance.

In his later years he became obsessed by the life and time of the last Bourbon monarchs of France, the epitome of absolute monarchy that Ludwig wished he could emulate, and later by the plays of Victor Hugo.

He formed a close friendship with an actor whose voice he loved to hear proclaiming Schiller's *William Tell* and Victor Hugo's *Marion de Lorme* from high mountain places, and who for a time replaced Wagner as his friend. He never quite abandoned Wagner; in 1874 he came to the rescue of the building fund for Wagner's Bayreuth opera house with a generous line of credit and in 1876 he heard the whole of *The Ring* there, though on rehearsal nights only. When at last *Parsifal* was staged at Bayreuth Ludwig did not go, abandoning the Grail, Wagner remarked, in a huff because Wagner had refused to conduct the *Parsifal* prelude twice in a row and that of *Lohengrin* in Munich the year before. But Ludwig was now increasingly unreliable. He did hear the whole of *Parsifal* in Munich, but that was after Wagner's death and shortly before his own.

Ludwig's death was to prove as strange as his life. In 1866 he was found drowned with his doctor, who had earlier conspired with the Bavarian ministers to get Ludwig committed as irretrievably insane. Had Ludwig in a last moment of madness first drowned him and then himself? Was he wholly mad? Was he driven to a cruel self-destruction by remorseless and selfish people that feared for their own positions? Everyone knew that the king had fits of mad rage in which he would order frightful instructions to be carried out, which were ignored and he then forgot. Humoured, the king was generous and kind, and immensely popular with his people, who tried to rally to his support at his final arrest and incarceration at his Wagnerian lair at Neuschwanstein. Was he fit to rule? Probably not. Monarchs were no longer expected to rule with his notions of unchallenged sovereignty; there could be no return to *L'état, c'est moi*. Ludwig was aware of this and retreated instead into a world where unfettered sovereignty was still accepted in the autonomy of the artist and of the artist's patron. This had been fed by Wagner's own egomania; his was the stronger will of the two, and they were fated not to live for ever in perfect harmony but, where the music of Wagner was concerned, Ludwig was as despotic as he. It alone calmed his obsessive paranoia and nerved him to brave appearing before a public.

The Wittelsbachs had always been obsessive builders. Ludwig I may have squandered wealth on Lola Montez, but never to the detriment of his beautification of Munich in the classical style. His son, Maximilian II (1848–64), had absorbed the medievalism that was to make his son so ardent a disciple of the age of Lohengrin, who was believed to have lived in the castle that Maximilian bought and renovated in the land of the Swan. The walls of Hohenshwangau were decorated with legends of the Grail, of Tannhäuser and of the Swan Knight, for Maximilian had come unexpectedly to the throne in the year (1848) that Wagner completed *Lohengrin*. He was, as the second monarch in ranking in Germany, a conscientious prince, concerned about the state of Europe and the growth of popular feeling. The obsessive mania skipped him to enter his son, who coming to the throne at the age of 18 was ready to be the cynosure of artistic Germany, in contrast to his Hohenzollern cousins who seemed to be philistines. He was in 1871 ready to nominate his uncle Wilhelm to be paramount Emperor of Germany; though he did not like him, for he knew that his capacity to pay for his operas and his palaces depended on the goodwill of Prussia.

Wagner and Ludwig marked the end of Pumpernickel Romanticism. The shadow of Bismarck now stretched its wings over Germany, the domination of Austria and France had been broken. The little courts that had thrived on art and music, had succumbed to the logic of Fichte and Hegel out of whose cloudy and mystical idealism grew, like Aphrodite from the head of Jove or, perhaps more aptly, sin from the head of Satan, the more pragmatic theories of State power and the economic gospel according to Marx. Wagner had never lost his foothold in the practical world, for Titans needed to draw their strength from somewhere and in his case it was from money; he was a prodigal spendthrift, living on credit when out of funds but never curtailing the magnificence of his imagination and the demands it made on human resources. Providentially he found that patron just as his mature work was coming to fruition and a patron who was prepared to be dictated to and bullied, so different from Haydn's Prince Esterházy. Wagner's cloak and hat became symbols of the ruthless exploiter, his craggy jaw the mark of determination while Ludwig, with his flowing hair, trim beard and growing corpulence, became the figure of the exploited.

Wagner died before Ludwig, and was buried in his garden in Bayreuth whither Ludwig paid a secret visit of homage. The town had been part of Bavaria since 1801 situated between Munich and Nuremberg, and had been transformed by Wagner not Ludwig into a shrine for Wagnerism.

Wagner had turned his back on the charming rococo opera house of the former Margraves, needing more space for technical effects and extras of Hollywood numbers. Ludwig did not turn his back on the glories of Bavarian Baroque. His desire was for splendour and craftsmanship, and for his buildings, both his Swan sanctuary and his 'Versailles', he chose an eclectic style, mirroring his enthusiasm of the moment, sometimes medievalism, then the epochs of Louis Quatorze and Quinze, and finally Oriental, inspired by the new Paris sensation, Massenet's *Le Roi de Lahore* (1877). The environment he constructed, using modern steel and concrete and electric light, was one of illusions, of dreams: Hunding's Hut surrounded a huge tree bedecked with mementoes of the Volsungs, the Knight's Hall was dedicated to Lohengrin and the Holy Grail, Neuschwanstein had its grotto to Venus, Herrenchiemsee (his Versailles) was a show-house of Meissen porcelain and Bavarian stucco, Linderhoff a monument to the style of Louis XIV and XV. His standards were exacting and as a result the crafts of Bavaria were given a new lease of life. Though Ludwig had built for himself as part of a private programme of solitary enjoyment, it was a legacy that made him probably the foremost Maecenas of German art, a final organ blast for the glories of Pumpernickel.

As for Wagner, he believed he had laid to rest for ever the *biedemeyer* charms of Mendelssohn and his idea of a comfortable passion, of sunny dispositions, conjugal fidelity and contentment. These were not properly German. Love was raw and all consuming, teetering as had Tannhäuser on the brink of lust, or hopeless and involuntary as with the Celtic lovers, Tristan and Isolde, expiatory and inconsummate as with Senta and Kundry, pure and impossible for Elizabeth and Elsa. Happiness only triumphs in *Die Meistersinger,* for on the whole Wagner did not believe in happiness, though he claimed to have found it with Cosima. Ludwig, who did believe in happiness, failed to find it, but followed its elusive will-o'-the wisp through the medium of art. But when Hans Sachs warned Germans never to betray German art and its Masters in the final tableau of *Die Meistersinger:* 'So heed my words; honour your German Masters if you'd forfend disasters! Let us take them to our heart, though should depart the might of holy Rome, no harm will come to holy German art', Ludwig and his Pumpernickel forebears were not among the audience.[26]

Wagner was looking forward to a nation that would in the end bitterly betray them.

Wagnerians would say that what was betrayed was not the Germany of high art but the Germany of Alberich, the Nibelung, who brought by love of money and power a curse upon the guardians of the realm, the Rhine-maidens, Wotan, Siegfried and the gods. Alberich, the supreme 'scientist', personifies the essential barrenness of 'reasonable' knowledge without Religion or Art.[27] Yet the heroic myth of *The Ring* is about as German as the Arthurian legend is English. It was born in the sagas of Scandinavia and Iceland, just as the Round Table was fashioned in south European chivalry; both myths are about the betrayal of noble aims and the triumph of perfidy, and the Nibelungs are about as weird as the Hobbits of twentieth-century fame ('feverishly, uninterestingly they burrow through the bowels of the earth like worms in a dead body; they anneal and smelt and smith hard metals'[28]).

Alberich by superior intelligence has fashioned a ring, which has given him and the Nibelungs mastery over all. He reduces his fellows to slavery as they amass the Nibelung hoard of noble Rhine-gold. Alberich, master smith, metallurgist, alchemist and potential ruler of the world – the malign soul of Germany – then fades out of the picture as Wagner's tetralogy charts the fate of giants, dragons, gods, Valkyries and mankind in dealing with the extra-terrestrial forces created by the Nibelungs. But their fates have been woven in the tapestry of fate by the Norns, a Wagnerian personification of the classical Parcae. The hero who is to save the world, a Galahad figure who knows no fear, is slain by treachery, and Valhalla, the impregnable fortress of the gods, is consumed in the conflagration of his funeral pyre lit by the daughter of the god-king, Wotan.

It is not entirely clear what Wagner's message was. Do the old Germanic gods, personified by Wotan, perish before the earthly spirit of man, a Germanic hero whom Wagner is wise enough to allow to perish despite the supernatural, alchemical aids to his survival, but through whom the race is saved and its mission to purify the world sustained? That mission was German, or so the meagre mind of an Adolf Hitler was persuaded by music that suspended reality. For the dramatis personae of *The Ring* both human, subhuman and superhuman, are more worldly than

Parsifal and Lohengrin, earth-bound than Tristan and the Dutchman, and more sexually aroused than Tannhäuser and Isolde. The entire *Ring* had its first Bayreuth performance in 1876, after the Kaiser Frederick I had presided over the creation of the new Valhalla, created by Wagnerian man not Wagnerian gods, making *The Ring*, a farrago of dubious politics and morality, into the national saga.

CHAPTER SIXTEEN

Butterflies or Maggots

Caspar David Friedrich, Samuel Prout, Schinkel and the Nazarenes

> Nothing could be more sad and eerie than this position in
> the world, the only spark of life in the wide realm of death,
> a lonely centre in a lonely circle ... and because of the
> monotony and boundlessness, with nothing but the frame for
> a background, one feels as if one's eyelids had been cut off.
> (Heinrich von Kleist on Friedrich's *The Monk by the Sea* in the
> Berliner Abendblätter, October 1810)

> I spin a cocoon around myself, let others do the
> same. I shall leave it to time to show what will
> come of it: a brilliant butterfly or a maggot.
> (Caspar David Friedrich on his life's work)

NO ONE CAPTURED the visual Romantic image of Germany more vividly than the painter Caspar David Friedrich. Born in 1774 in the bleak Pomeranian Baltic coast town of Greifswald, he spent most of his working life in that Florence of the north, the brilliant Saxon capital of Dresden. In 1835, towards the end of his life, he returned in his imagination to that melancholy seascape with a painting of the stages of life, in which three figures, one young playing with his sister and nursemaid, one in the prime of life, the father, and a third staidly standing with protective cape and hat and stick, the grandfather, watch three ships, all of a size to match their ages, sail into a sunset across a placid green sea. There is none of the turbid explosive energy or even the misty deliquescence of his British contemporary, Turner.

For Friedrich the Baltic always seemed calm, as he hoped would be his passage through and from life, fading gently into the mists that enshroud much of his work. With few exceptions, even among mountainous crags and forests tormented by wind, his was the calm after the storm. His snow-covered monastery ruins serenely preside over a quiet procession of hooded monks. His tombstones, covered with snow in abandoned graveyards, or open in moonlight, are silent, his funeral wreaths, gravedigger's tool and watchful owls conjure up ghosts perhaps, but not spectres.[1]

Anna Jameson, visiting Dresden in 1833 was impressed by Friedrich's poetical qualities but thought he was an exponent of gloom, in contrast to Turner, one year younger than he, whose genius revelled in light.[2] That characteristic was evoked by German Romanticism in the sinister and darker music of Weber, the stories of Kleist and Hoffmann, in the tales collected by the Brothers Grimm, and in the *cauchemars* of the Swiss Henry Fuseli (Heinrich Füssli, 1741–1826). But Friedrich's work is bereft of fairies, goblins or sprites, though his melancholic landscapes of blasted trees, tulgey forest and soaring, ruined fanes were their natural abodes. Like Turner, Friedrich filled notebooks with sketches from the natural world about him, but his finished paintings were carefully constructed, often as an amalgam of what he had sketched in different places. He did not imagine, like Turner, that man lived among forces over which he had no control but over which he hoped to triumph. He believed, like Novalis whom he had known at Dresden, and William Blake, that 'the divine was everywhere, even in a grain of sand'.[3] Yet the sense of defeat was also always there, replaying the memory of his brother's death by drowning after rescuing Friedrich from falling through the ice in a skating accident. Men and women hardly existed in Friedrich's landscapes except as minor participants, for he was exploring landscape that was pure but never simple.

Germany had plenty of landscape of a dramatic kind. It was not difficult for man to feel diminished by the size and wildness of it. The British nature poets, especially the Scottish James Macpherson with his Ossianic sagas set among flinty crags, beetling precipices and stormy seas, awoke the nascent German sensibility to the drama of their own wild landscapes. Through them, man arrived at a divine reality, a revelation of pure beauty and freedom, 'a symbolical representation of the infinite'.[4] Friedrich, when he arrived in Dresden in 1798 after four years at the

Copenhagen Academy, found himself in the midst of an esoteric society debating the virtues of classicism, where nature provided a backdrop to an ancient harmony, with a school of naturalists who deplored the intrusion of rustic innocence among forces of potential elemental fury. Among the most potent of these were the armies of revolutionary France.

Friedrich was essentially a man of peace. In his landscapes wreathed in fog, an undisturbed nature peeped out. In his painting 'mountains and mist, forest and cross, sea and boat, tomb and sky are so many poles between which Friedrich drew the threads linking the objective to the imagined and vice-versa'. Friedrich's love of mists was expressed in his belief that 'a landscape swathed in mist appears vaster and more sublime; it stimulates the imagination and increases expectancy, like a girl wearing a veil.'[5] His stark fir trees, jabbing like needles into a dusk half lit by fallen snow, are balanced against the outline of a church tower promising asylum to the man whose exhausted body is supported by a rock. Nature was not always elemental and furious and, being a simple Pomeranian Lutheran, Friedrich knew that the still small voice of God followed the storm and the earthquake. There was nothing to suggest that God might be shaken by the very elements of chaos, and there was plenty of that among the young artists of Dresden. There, naturalists, medievalists and classical landscape painters competed for attention.

Friedrich tried to find the voice he wanted from the nature everyone else was searching for. Remove the often jocular and inappropriate figures that people Poussin's landscapes and they became almost contemporary. Nature must be allowed to speak for itself in a voice people could hear, and if that voice was to accept the transience of life and inevitability of death that was no more than humanity was being required to hear amid the tumult of war. The consolations of religion were represented in country shrines, and ecclesiastical ruins rather than in the erotic apotheoses that accompanied heroes in classical art.

North German Protestantism was tinged with the intense devotion of Pietism, reflected in Friedrich's childhood upbringing in the Marcher lands of the Teutonic Knights. The English nature poets, enthusiastically translated by a Pomeranian pastor, Ludwig Theobul Kosegarten, had suggested that in nature one would find 'Christ's bible', an often solitary study producing melancholy thoughts about one's inevitable end. On the

Pomeranian island of Rugen, the Pomeranian pastor and poet, Ludwig Kosegarten (1758–1818) found a semi-Scottish landscape, complete with dolmens and symbolic oaks which he accepted as necessary for an historic 'Ossianic' past. Friedrich never elaborated the Ossian theme, but painted the dolmens among the oaks as a purely natural setting for something that had a religious significance. As religion meant preparation for one's latter end, dolmens, ruins, shrines, with funeral and other processions in their midst were subjects that came naturally to him.

Friedrich never paid the statutory visit to Italy, but his close student and associate did, and under his influence he began to brighten his canvases and paint large landscapes recollected in tranquillity. The 1820s saw him marvellously productive but, ill, uncertain of the fidelity of his wife, and sensing that he was unable to compete with the exuberant naturalists, painters of the Roman *campagna* and medievalists. He was too quiet for the prevailing taste. He concentrated more and more on the end of life, rather than its turmoil. Cemeteries, ruins, winter landscapes with naked and uncomfortable trees and rocks, sepia sunsets and solitariness pervaded his work. His earlier admirers now found him morbid, but in the early 1830s he was to produce his most atmospheric work, tinged with intimations of mortality. By the time of his death in 1840, the Romantic age was spinning to its climax and Friedrich was lost in the vortex that it had created. When Anna Jameson reissued her *Visits and Sketches at Home and Abroad* in 1842, Friedrich's name was not there. He had not been ready to go against his convictions to conform to prevailing taste. 'I spin a cocoon around myself, let others do the same. I shall leave it to time to show what will come of it: a brilliant butterfly or a maggot.'[6]

Friedrich's brilliant butterfly is like one of those night moths trembling before the dim light of day, alive but still, every sense quivering, in rest but not in repose, in contemplation rather than in action. *The Wanderer above the Mists,* hatless, armed only with a walking stick with which he stands on a rough and perilous crag, and *Woman in Morning Light*, standing more securely on a winding path, bonneted, arms extended in wonder at the golden orange glow over the hills, were both painted about 1818. The figures are isolated and anonymous before what seems an endless vision. The pose of each is appropriate to their sex, but if wonder and delight fill the woman, a sense of challenge and possible helplessness is the reaction of the man. But they are neither of them dwarfed by the mighty infiniteness of nature, as was often the fate of the human figure in Friedrich's sketches. The man is not Manfred expecting spirits to rise from the mist; the woman is not Astarte, alone in her solitude. In Friedrich's palette man/ woman is nearly equal to nature. They will not dominate it but they will not be dominated. The artist has 'naturalised the divine', perhaps become the divine.[7] If God had been displaced in the Romantic imagination, His place had been taken not by man but by nature. The emancipation of man from clerical subservience in the past 50 years put him on almost equal terms with it. He would not rant against his destiny. That of nature was to die and be reborn. That of man was to die. Friedrich's art implied that this he should do in quiet dignity, going down into the vast and sublime.[8]

* * *

The vast and sublime certainly dominated the work of Karl Friedrich Schinkel. Born in 1781 in the Margravate of Brandenburg, Schinkel aspired to be a painter and after the statutory visit to Italy from 1803–5 he returned to Berlin to paint for the stage, creating a sensational setting for Mozart's Queen of the Night against a tenebrous, star-studded sky, fostering the illusion that the queen was a lady of the spheres of night, seeking to illuminate the darkness before the dawn. Schinkel's talent was prodigious and his energy Promethean. He was to be painter, glass worker, furniture designer, stage decorator and architect, all in turn; his early design was to be a landscape artist, absorbing the Poussinesque models of Italy, setting tiny humans against majestic trees and mountains, very much studio pieces. Open to all Romantic *zeitgeists* he went through his Romantic, Gothic, and medieval periods, silhouetting spindly-turreted cathedrals against water and rocks. The influence of Friedrich lay strong upon him but he could not match the atmospheric, haunting quality of Friedrich's work, and he turned his energies instead to designing buildings. With the final defeat of Napoleon, he became a consultant on the Prussian Building Commission.

Berlin was growing, if in a higgledy-piggledy, not-planned way, and was still, despite Frederick II's development of Potsdam, a pokey, unspectacular city, hardly worthy to be the capital of the second power in Germany. Schinkel was to preside over its transformation, not, as in Pumpernickel, with replicas of French Baroque but of Greek classicism. Soon, Berlin and the new territories on the Rhine were to feel his strong classicising hand. He actually designed few buildings himself but he aspired to find a suitably German aesthetic, part reflecting the marvels of the German Gothic, part Wagnerian-Romantic, but wholly Imperial. When Ludwig I of Bavaria's son became King of the Hellenes he designed for him a royal palace incorporating the Acropolis of Athens, mercifully never built. In 1826 he visited England and saw at first hand the rapid industrialisation that was creating new building materials in steel and brick and allowed monumental edifices to be built on the horizontal and vertical lines of Attic building. These only existed in his paintings and designs, for he died before Prussia embarked on her own major industrialisation.

Friedrich's legacy could be detected in many of Schinkel's landscape paintings, in his elegiac settings of boats on water, cathedrals brooding on water, and of distant water, lakes and rivers winding into the far distance. The passion, to make Berlin an artistic and cultural capital, was to lead to his premature death, for he had to fight against the underlying antipathy to change on the part of the king and the still strong belief on the part of his people that France was still the cultural capital of Europe. Berlin, however, was becoming under his influence visually the first city of Germany. Napoleonic Paris may have aspired to be a new Rome but Schinkel's Berlin was to be a new Athens.

It was not only in the cities that Germany was aspiring to rival the cultural icons of Europe. The rivers and forests of Germany had long been one of the impenetrable and invincible fastnesses of Europe, but now they were to be tamed, domesticated, improved. The pioneer was to be a 25-year-old Saxon who in 1811 inherited a vast estate on the banks of the River Neisse, now part of the Oder-Neisse border between Poland and Germany but at the Congress of Vienna annexed to Prussia. Count, later Prince, Hermann Ludwig Heinrich von Pückler-Muskau (1785–1871) was a Promethean figure with some of the characteristics of the hero in a story by Hoffmann.[9] Goethe had designed a park for Weimar and designed others in his head, and with the appearance of a five volume *Theory of Garden Art* which appeared from 1779–84, German landowners were encouraged to create a controlled land-space, not in the regimented manner of Bourbon and Napoleonic France but in the contrived naturalness of Georgian England.[10] Pückler-Muskau was to spend almost a whole lifetime, and two fortunes, creating a natural park that would 'bear the stamp of German ingenuity' while, at the same time, preserve nature's 'own loveliness, and reveal in a German way that a properly designed landscape garden could equal if not surpass nature's power as a force for good'.[11]

For a cultural hero, Pückler-Muskau made a Hoffmannesque start; at 15 he was a student, erotically licentious and emotionally quarrelsome enough to fight duels. At 18 he abandoned academe for the army and by the age of 21 he was a general in the army of Saxony. Unwilling to fight Prussia which he would have been obliged to do when Saxony sided with Napoleon, he resigned his commission and returned to his family estates, emerging later to serve against Napoleon at the Battle of the Nations. His road to Damascus was when in 1815 he went with the entourage of the Russian and Prussian monarchs to England, and saw the tailor-made landscapes of the great aristocratic houses. He knew then what he should do back home.

Home was a large estate of rather dull country on either side of the Neisse River, of sandy alluvial soil with few striking features. On it were 40 villages, housing with the town of Muskau itself 8,000 inhabitants. The estate was heavily in debt. Undeterred, Pückler was to add to it, and on marriage threw in the fortune of his bride, to transform this terrain as if nature had made it differently. He altered the course of rivers and streams, drained marshes, raised hills, physically uprooted and replanted trees, some of immense size, and removed ruins to build them again more romantically. Unlike other ruthless landscape adapters Pückler intended his park to transform the lives of its denizens, by improving their surroundings. The man-made lakes and forests provided fish, game and honey in plenty, and even mines were opened, and their liberal landlord and ruler established schools, and cottage industries. Schinkel was brought from Berlin to advise on rebuilding Muskau town, for the embellishment of which Pückler spent well over its economic value to acquire more land. His vision of a model garden city happily engaged the enthusiasm, and fortune, of Lucie von Pappenheim, daughter of Prussia's chancellor, whom Pückler married in 1817 and who, when they ran out of money, sent her husband off to find another rich heiress to whom she would resign her position while she stayed to manage the estate and, it was thought, to occupy his bed.

Eventually in 1846 the venture had to be abandoned as even the vast fortunes of the young couple could not meet the debts they had both incurred, but Pückler's travels on his unsuccessful search for a second rich wife gave him almost a literary reputation as a Romantic adventurer in the style of Childe Harold. In his *Letters of a Deceased Man* (*Brief eines Verstorbenen*, 1826–9), he described his visit to nearly every English landscaped garden and estate, which were later collected in his *Hints on Landscape Gardening* (1834).[12] These earned him various sobriquets, of Green Prince, and Parkomaniac, and gave Dickens his model for Count Schmorltork in *The Pickwick Papers*. Pückler lived on to age 86, still a visionary, still writing, while some of his plans were completed by the new owners of Muskau. Though the man-made park spans both the modern German and Polish borders, Pückler nearly achieved his aim to improve on nature by making it beautiful *and* useful *and* German.[13]

∗   ∗   ∗

Pückler also became known as the Goethe of Landscape Gardening, and in 1832, the uncrowned ruler of German culture was the ageing Goethe, virtual Archduke of Weimar, cynosure of all the visitors to Germany who had any predilections for politics, art or letters. Mme de Staël had made straight for him when expelled from Napoleonic France; Thackeray visited him often when he was learning German for the diplomatic service. Scott would have come home from Malta via Weimar had he been less ill. The 11-year-old Mendelssohn played to him for hours on end, dedicated music to him and teased the old gentleman with the licence of a child. The polymath panjandram was open and hospitable to all, enjoying their homage and scattering his store of wisdom on all; but he was an icon, not a symbol. Once he might have been an apostle of change and renovation, but his chameleon changes of colour had allowed him to rise above the shibboleths of his day, above *durm und strang*, *naturphilosophie*, classicism and romanticism, liberalism and reaction. He had contributed to all of them in his own way, blazing paths but not following them, finding in the gentle Saxon kindness of Weimar the Leibnizian garden he wished to cultivate. Perfection, he had said in 1812, was so rare. He dabbled in science, he philosophised, scattering aphorisms which Coleridge tried to imitate in his *Table Talk*, most of which were gnomic in meaning. Everything transitory was but a symbol, a maxim he appeared to apply to his own art, when he drew his own illustrations for *Faust*, forsaking his classical bent for the witches and hobgoblinry of Goya.[14] In protest against Newton's optical findings, he wrote a cerebral treatise on colour, attributing to it positive and negative virtues; happiness induced by light, distress by the dark. With it he became a psychological master for German painters who attempted to match painterly practice to his theory. This work, translated in 1840 by the future director of the Royal Academy in London, was a clue to Ruskin's surprising championship of Turner. It helped the bright pageant of German historical painters to turn their backs on the melancholic Friedrich, depressed by the Romantic master's obsession with the symbols of transience and death.[15] Something more cheerful was needed to sum up the German spirit of the time.

∗ ∗ ∗

If Anna Jameson had introduced Friedrich to Britain in 1833, that was the year too in which Germany was to be exposed to Britain's gaze from the windows of print and lithograph sellers in the work of Samuel Prout. He was a west country man, born within sight of Plymouth Hoe. With Benjamin Robert Haydon, another Plymouth boy two years his junior, he had drawn marine subjects, making the most of a sensational shipwreck in Plymouth Sound to explore the marriage of sea and land, rather as Friedrich had done. The two young men roamed round the lush countryside of Devon, so different from the bleak dunes and rugged glades of Pomerania, making sketches of the rural landscape with its symbols of man's peaceful contest with nature, farmhouses and bridges, and tamed agricultural pastures. At the age of 20, Prout knew what he needed to learn and moved to London to develop and perfect his skills in sketches and watercolours.

His moment of truth came in 1818 when he set off in the period of European peace and recovery to capture the evocative and sometimes quaint monuments of cities on the continent, their massive Gothic cathedrals, cobbled streets and over-hanging buildings. He proved to have a Ruskinian eye for architectural detail, and against these monuments of men's past he portrayed the citizens engaged in their contemporary avocations. Though he was no great figure draughtsman, 'Prout's streets,' wrote Ruskin, 'are the only streets that are accidentally crowded, his markets are the only markets where one feels inclined to get out of the way.'[16] It was as if Prout had sensed the threat of railroads and steam engines, factories and slums and wished to preserve in almost pernickety detail a way of life that was to vanish. He almost created the picture postcard that would capture the timeless past and an uncertain future, and his sketches reflected some of Friedrich's obsession with the passage of time and decay.

Ruskin in fact started his collection of watercolours with a vigorous little Prout engraving of a wayside Devonshire cottage, and a few years later he purchased his *Sketches in Flanders and Germany*. By that time, Ruskin had filled his first sketch book with increasingly competent depictions of ancient buildings in south east England and, fired by Prout's rendering of a turreted window over the Moselle at Coblenz, on which his father had commented that they ought to go and see the originals, he decided to travel abroad, sketch-pad in hand. Some of Ruskin's early sketches of domestic architecture in the lower Rhine, so unspoiled and Romantic, were copied from Prout. Prout, however, was too good a master of topographical detail to improve upon and Ruskin was soon concentrating on minute and detailed sketches of what he saw, rather than of the noble sweep of cities and buildings that characterised the work of Samuel Prout.[17]

Ruskin generously gave Prout a special accolade for representing

the influence among the noble line of architecture, of the rent and the rust, the fissure, the lichen and the weed, and from the writing upon the pages of ancient walls of the confused hieroglyphic of human history.[18]

This was not merely from love of the picturesque; there was no stone painting, no vitality of architecture like Prout's. Ruskin, when he came to write *Modern Painters*, had less enthusiasm for Prout's drawings of Italy, of buildings and scenes of which he had become himself an expert miniaturist. It was Prout's sketches of buildings in Flanders and Germany, his love of pictorial truth and atmosphere that made Ruskin include him among the masters. The public buyers of his work were attracted to the crumbling, time-worn and lichen-encrusted exemplars of a medieval world which architects were beginning to tidy up and restore in France but which still preserved across the Rhine the patina of their antiquity. These were the stalking ground of characters from Grimm, Hoffmann and la Motte Fouqué, the background for the ballades of Burger and the robber barons of Goethe's *Götz von Berlichingen*.

Goethe was, however to have a more profound influence on an artist who never went to Germany. The translator, in 1840, of Goethe's *Theory of Colours (Zur Farbenlehre)*, praised by Schopenhauer as so good a translation that it read better and more intelligibly than the original, was one of Prout's fellow citizens of Plymouth. Benjamin Robert Haydon's first Royal Academy student, Charles Eastlake, had already established his reputation as a history painter with the encouragement of the 'Plymouth School', effectively Prout and Haydon, with his portrait of Napoleon proceeding into permanent exile on *HMS Bellerophon*, which he had witnessed as he passed Plymouth. The war was now over, and in 1815 Eastlake started a 15-year residence in France and Italy. There he improved his pictorial narrative skills, latterly in the mountains near Rome to portray bandit life. In his absence in Rome he was elected a member of the Royal Academy and in 1830 returned to England to make his reputation by painting detailed historical and biblical subjects. So impressive was his translation of Goethe and of a handbook on the history of painting by another German, Franz Kugler, that he added a reputation for art appreciation to that of art creator, and was nominated secretary to the Fine Arts Commission in 1841, and two years later as first Keeper of the National Gallery.

Eastlake was now effectively Britain's commissar for the arts and with a German prince as consort of his pliant but basically philistine monarch, he was in a position to influence decisions on public art in a particularly Germanic fashion. The most important commission of the Victorian reign was to be the decoration of the newly-restored Houses of Parliament, after the disastrous fire, with frescoes of the important and striking episodes of English history. The predilection of Eastlake was for the Italian style, that of Prince Albert for the German 'Gothic', meeting somewhere in what was the Italo-Gothic style of Siena, fresh, stylised, narrative and epochal, before the imprint of the High Renaissance humanism of Florence assumed the mantle of the Italian style.

* * *

The impulse for and awareness of Albert's preference came from a group of German-speaking artists who had congregated in 1810 in an abandoned monastery in Rome, under the general patronage of the Prussian consul-general, Jakob Bartholdy, Mendlessohn's uncle on his mother's side. They had dubbed themselves, before moving to Rome, the Brotherhood of St Luke and, joined by other young artists (and one more mature landscape artist who became their leader and tutor), they adopted the habits and lifestyle of what they imagined were Biblical times. In this guise they aspired to rediscover the spiritual inspiration of what they held to be the high water mark of Christian art. Their untrimmed hair and flowing robes attracted the nickname of Nazarene after the early sect of Jewish Christian adepts, who held to the Hebraic torah and the law, but accepted the Virgin birth and called their redeemer Yeshua. The fastidious Felix Mendelssohn disliked their tobacco-censed gatherings in the Caffè Greco near the Spanish Steps, where they shared their vermin with the mastiffs that accompanied them and discussed and abused Titian and Pordenone as if they were present as members of the Brotherhood. Their work, buoyed up on Biblical optimism and historical enthusiasm, was the antithesis of the pessimism of Caspar David Friedrich, and the realism of Samuel Prout. They achieved their apotheosis in Assisi where one of the founder members (Johann Friedrich Overbeck) painted a Vision of St Francis in the church of Santa Maria degli Angeli, built to enclose Francis's own *porziuncula,* close to the masterworks of Giotto and Cimabue further up the hill.[19]

The Nazarenes attracted the interest of Ludwig I of Bavaria who, when still crown prince, had visited them in Rome, whither they had repaired in 1818 as the centre of Christianity, and who shared their ambition to revitalise German art. In 1819, newly ascended to the throne and intoxicated by the prospect of establishing a school of Teutonic painting in Munich and reviving fresco panting as 'practised from the great Giotto to the divine Raphael',[20] Ludwig invited Peter von Cornelius to fresco his

Gyptothek (sculpture gallery) and Pinakothek. Soon Cornelius's students covered many of the public buildings in the city in frescoes, the first fruits of the Teutonic school. Eastlake had known the Nazarenes in Rome and admired their dedication to recapturing historical and Biblical accuracy as they interpreted it, though they were not in truth as good as the painters who preceded Raphael and whom they were trying to imitate. Few were accomplished colourists or first rate draughtsmen – indeed Mendelssohn thought they painted 'such sickly Madonnas, such feeble saints and such milksop heroes' that he longed to have a go at them[21] – but for a short but significant time they had a following among those who were looking for a new style in pictorial art. By 1830 most of them had returned to Germany and to the art schools where their reputation as art teachers was to be higher than as artists, but they had made Ludwig's Munich the centre of excellence in art, especially the art of fresco painting, stealing the reputation hitherto enjoyed by Dresden.

It was not surprising that the fellow German princeling, Albert (Saxe-Coburg-Gotha), should be attracted by Ludwig's example. The success of the Bavarian king in creating a school of fresco painting tempted him to think that this might also be achieved in Britain with such a virgin space as the newly rebuilt Houses of Parliament. That a comparatively minor kingdom as Bavaria should have created its own national school suggested that a similar school ought to be established in Britain, to mark the emergence of a national culture to emphasise her new position in Europe and dominance overseas. The suggestion that the English might use the newly built Houses of Parliament as the easel by commissioning frescoes for its walls seemed to the arts establishment fantastic and far-fetched. Frescoes in Britain were, scoffers said, like shipbuilding in Bohemia.[22] Between them, however, Prince Albert and Eastlake invited the Munich school to submit cartoons in the competition for the decoration of the rebuilt Houses of Parliament.

Their submission caused immediate controversy. Disraeli might be at work on *Coningsby* (1844), elaborating his belief that there were two Britains that needed to be brought together but, if fresco painting was considered to be the highest manifestation of Christian art, that was when western Christendom had been united. That the mother of Parliaments should deny her roots in the protestant Reformation by admitting works so Popish, based on the work of professedly Popish artists in the Popish capital, and working for a Popish king, seemed inappropriate. The Bishop of London not long before had rejected a suggestion from George III that Benjamin West might decorate the dome of St Paul's Cathedral, vowing that he would 'never suffer the doors of the metropolitan church to be opened for the introduction of popery into it'.[23] Suspicion of the personality of Albert, too enthusiastic by far, and news of the lurid political and love life of Ludwig himself, seemed to prove that the German taste was too alien, even advanced, for British stomachs, never particularly receptive of State patronage. Nevertheless, a committee was appointed in April 1841 to consider promoting the fine arts in Britain by patronising the decoration of the Houses of Parliament. On it sat people who had been to Munich and seen what was being done there, and others who knew the work of the Nazarenes, led by Charles Eastlake.

Benjamin Robert Haydon in 1829 maintained that historical painting had been blighted by the reformation and Anna Jameson, who in 1834, had watched a Nazarene painting scenes from *The Nibelungenlied* in one of Ludwig's new palaces, regretted that English painters had not found a space to create glorious scenes from the works of Chaucer, Spenser, Shakespeare and Milton.[24] Now the opportunity seemed to have arrived. Eastlake and the prince were not alone in wanting a new movement. The Reform bill of 1832 had brought to a head the demand for public amenities of the kind that Ludwig had given his country. Art was perceived as a means to educate the people who now had the vote or might get it in the next enlargement of the suffrage. The committee was impressed by the immediacy of fresco painting in enforcing simplicity on the artist, thus making the medium ideal for didactic public painting.[25] In the ensuing argument whether to employ British or foreign artists – Cornelius, though he believed Britain had neither the skill nor tradition of fresco art, was diplomatically aloof – Prince Albert suggested that a competition would decide the issue. It did. English painters frescoed away and finished their work before the new Parliament building was inaugurated in 1847. When Albert decided that the English *Nibelungenlied* would be the Arthurian legend, the Queen's robing room in Buckingham Palace had to be chosen as the venue.

∗ ∗ ∗

The new queen, whom everyone had hoped was about to usher in a new age, had now been on the throne for six years and was in her late 20s. Yet, despite the example of Bavaria, English formal painting was still in the doldrums. Moreover, the enthusiasm for German art soon began to wane. Were English artists, hoping for a commission for the new Parliament building, obliged to follow the wooden style of the Middle Ages, grow their hair long and dress accordingly? This, said *Punch,* was nonsense and un-English, and in Ford Madox Brown's view, it was 'papistical and German and, most abhorrent of all, it was Christian art'.[26] An anti-German aesthetic was forming, religious alarum bells were ringing, the Royal Commission for the Paintings was perceived to be the source of a dangerous mania for all things German, personified by the Prince-Consort, and in 1848 its activities were censured in the Commons for extravagance.

Among artists, blame for the mediocrity of the Royal Academy summer exhibitions, regularly dull and uninspiring, was popularly put at the door of the German school. In 1843 the 24-year-old Ruskin had produced the first volume of *Modern Painters* and had come out as a champion of Prout and David Roberts whose *Departure of the Israelites from Egypt* (1829) and sketches from the east had already established him as an inspired topographer. Above all, there was Turner, already 68, three years from his end, but still energetically flinging his paint pots into the face of tradition. More significantly, in September 1848 at 83 Gower Street, the family house of the Millais family, a coterie of arts students met to issue their manifesto. They were all in their early 20s, Holman Hunt 21, Dante Gabriel Rossetti 20, and John Everett Millais 19. They were to find their particular brand of medievalism not in dry academic rendering of historic subjects but in the far from dry bones of Keats's poetry, republished in 1848 to accompany his *Life* by Monckton Milnes.

Like all youthful manifestos, theirs was full of noble aims; they would espouse only genuine ideas, whatever they were; they would study nature 'attentively'; they would sympathise with what was 'serious and heartfelt in previous art and not what was conventional, and self-parading and learned by rote'; above all they would produce good art.[27] For their movement they adopted the name Pre-Raphaelite Brotherhood. They had rejected 'Early Christian' as smacking of Roman Catholicism and of the work of the Nazarenes, of which they had no high opinion. Even so, Holman Hunt had to admit that without the Nazarenes and the Royal Commission, there would have been no Brotherhood, though he defended it from the charge of Overbeckism, or creating Christian art in the German manner. Holman Hunt too is credited with adopting the Nazarene predilection for the name Pre-Raphaelite, and Dante Gabriel Rossetti, coming from a family of Italian liberals, opted for the *carbonaro* echoes of 'Brotherhood'. Holman Hunt epitomised it all in dismissing Revivalism, whether classic or medieval, as 'seeking after dry bones'. What they were after was 'simply fuller Nature'.[28]

Their connection otherwise with the Nazarenes was minimal. They admired their idealism but rejected their Romano-Germanism. They thought that the Nazarenes had not properly fulfilled their aims, for they had copied their models too closely and were untrue to nature. This was where the Pre-Raphaelite Brotherhood would be different. They would fulfil their aims. Above all, they would be their own masters. The frescoes that were being commissioned for the Houses of Parliament were a dreadful warning of the perils of nationalism in art. Despite their disclaimers, however, Ruskin initially believed they were mere heirs to the Nazarene Roman Catholicism he detested, and when Millais produced his *Christ in the House of His Parents* he was attacked for imitating the most uncouth productions of the German school. Dickens described Jesus as 'a hideous, wry-necked, blubbering boy in a nightgown',[29] not a wholly aesthetic judgment, for the tone of the day was bitterly anti-Catholic.

The Brotherhood survived because Ruskin unexpectedly championed them as they turned from religious painting to the portrayal of nature. As the threat from Rome to the queen's supremacy from 'out of the Flaminian Gate' receded, so the furore over the Westminster frescoes died down. Emerging from it was no great school of fresco painting, no school of English painting which owed its existence to public patronage, but a lively debate about art and its place in religion which elevated the Pre-Raphaelites to the status of a national institution. Britain was acquiring, as people preferred, a national culture without national sponsorship. If the Pre-Raphaelites were agreed on one thing it was that art had never been quite as pure, true or natural since Raphael, who had in Holman Hunt's opinion done great evil. The Brotherhood attracted interest because it appeared to capture the spirit of the age with its love of the past and of nature, linking itself not only with the poetry of the poets, Scott, Keats, Shelley and Byron who were in the vanguard of the Romantic movement, but also with the spiritual proponents of the Gothic and religious revivals, with those reacting against industrialisation, and with the excitement of revolt in 1848 that was sweeping across Europe.[30] In this last they shared something with the Nazarenes, but if the Brotherhood had any homogeneity it was in their staying pretty well united until the 1850s. If its 'Nazarene' religious subjects had attracted hostile criticism – Hunt's *Christ in the House of His Parents* (1850) was accused of being impious if not blasphemous – the movement, by turning to historical and social subjects, made art in the annual exhibitions a draw again.

∗ ∗ ∗

Mendelssohn's death seemed to mark the end of Romanticism in England. Keats, Shelley and Byron had died Romantically before Victoria had come to the throne. Wordsworth was to die three years later than Mendelssohn, laden with honours that had in the view of many reduced his voice from that which, Byron said, had once been of the deep, to that of an 'old half-witted sheep'. Leigh Hunt was summarising a life spent at the heart of it in his *Autobiography*, surprisingly friendly with the Carlyles who had become near neighbours – we shall never know whether Jane (Jenny) really did get up from her chair to kiss him – while her husband strove manfully to get him a civil pension. The Pre-Raphaelites continued in their medievalism but had taken on much of the Sunday school sentimentality that Bernard Shaw had detected in Mendelssohn's music. Their attention to nature now delighted not in its grandeur or ferocity but in exquisite detail worthy of Burgundian miniaturists.

However, Romantic and medieval art were feeling the tedium, shortly to be rocked out of their torpor by Manet's Post-Raphaelitism (termed more for chronological reasons Post-Impressionism) in *Le Déjeuner sur l'Herbe* (1863) and *Olympia* (1865). Once again Paris had seized the cultural initiative. Infinite detail and truth to an ideal of nature to which the Pre-Raphaelite Brotherhood aspired now welcomed (or regretted according to its critics) an impressionistic delineation of form and colour. Trees in landscapes, which Gainsborough had carefully re-worked from models provided by heads of broccoli, were once again worked not from vegetable models but from memory or from sketches, in the studio, not in the field, (where a naked model, contemplating her own figure in Courbet's *Studio of the Painter an Allegory of Realism*, would have been covered in goose-pimples). Romanticism fled from the attic studio to the concert hall, to be recaptured in compositions on new, more versatile musical instruments, where musical presentations of nature no longer relied on full symphonic ensembles but could be reproduced in pianistic or solo form. A golden age of Germanic Romanticism in music, embracing the *sturm und drang* of Beethoven, the lyricism of Schubert, the mystical passion of Byron, the pastoral melody of Goethe inaugurated a new age of artistic expression with the Schumanns, Mendelssohns and Wagner. Pumpernickel had emerged from its forests into the sunlit plains of pastoralism, only to retreat before the braying brass of Germanic pride and Prussian militarism.

'Pumpernickel' by Binoculars

Germaine de Staël, Julius Hare and Thomas Carlyle

> She is a phenomenon of vitality, egotism and
> activity. Her appearance is transfigured by her
> soul and indeed stands in great need of it.
> (Caroline Schelling on Germaine de Staël, 1808)

> The end of man is an action and not a
> thought, though it were the noblest.
> (Thomas Carlyle, *Sartor Resartus*, book 2, chapter 6)

BEFORE GRIMM AND his *Fairy Tales* appeared (between 1812 and 1857, when the seventh edition containing over 200 tales was published), the work of an obscure copper smelter and chemist, employed by a Cornish mining company, had been top of the reading lists of works from Germany. Since Queen Elizabeth's time, German smelters had been employed in the extraction industry in Cornwall because their general training was more advanced than anything obtainable in England. Rudolf Erich Raspe was born in Hanover in 1737; as a graduate of King George II's recently founded University of Göttingen he had found service with the Landgrave of Hesse-Kassel as not only Professor of Archaeology but as Librarian and Keeper of the Medal Cabinet. The Landgrave made him a state councillor but Raspe, who seemed always to have difficulties with money, was detected pawning some princely valuables, and was arrested and imprisoned. His captivity was not particularly strict for he broke out of prison one night and, in 1775, successfully made his way as a subject of King George III to England.

Raspe had reputation as a vulcanologist, having published in Latin a treatise on the formation of volcanic islands. Had the story of his misdemeanours not become known, Raspe would have been elected a fellow of the Royal Society. In 1769, for a paper on elephantine and other animal remains (mainly teeth) found in Latin America, he had been made a corresponding member. This was not the work, pre-Alexander Humboldt, of a genuine naturalist, but he was curiously learned in an eighteenth century way. Deprived of his fellowship for his misdemeanours, he survived by translating German works of practical science, and added to his reputation by another work on extinct volcanoes, and on the amalgamation of metallic ores, especially gold and silver. This was largely based on the work of a former Jesuit, the Hungarian Baron Edler von Ignaz Born, metallurgist in the service of the Empress Maria Theresa, whose travels to the Banat of Tamesvar, Transylvania and Hungary, Raspe translated.

He may also have essayed a translation of the baron's attempts at satire, for Born was a good hater and among his hates were his former Jesuit superior, whom he depicted as Father Hell, and the Royal Astronomer in Vienna. He then directed his anti-clerical venom at the monastic orders in *Monachologia,* a mock serious investigative work describing the inhabitants of monasteries as if they were animals under observation in a zoo. Somewhere in the imagination of the impecunious Hanoverian expert on minerals was born the inspiration that became the adventures of Baron Munchausen.

They appeared first in England in 1785, and by that time Raspe had found a job at the Dolcoath copper mine in Cornwall, first as store-keeper then, as his technical competence was recognised, as chief smelter. The hero of these adventures was a known teller of tall tales, Karl Friedrich Hieronymous, Freiherr von Münchhausen, to give him his full name and title, born in 1720 at Bodenwerder, by the Weser in Lower Saxony, into which the Pied Piper piped all the rats from Hamelin nearby. As an officer in the Russian army, he took part in two campaigns against the Ottoman Turks, and returned in the 1750s to his hometown, to tell marvellous stories experienced during his campaigns. They included travelling to the moon, riding cannonballs and extracting himself from a swamp by pulling on his own hair. Some of these ludicrous anecdotes had appeared anonymously in a Berlin review, *Vade Mecum für lustige Leute (A Handbook for*

Jolly Folk) between 1781–3, and in 1785 Raspe produced them in English as *Baron Munchausen's Narratives of his Marvellous Travels and Campaigns in Russia.*

The eponymous hero of these stories was not well pleased, for though he was a fantasist and born *blagueur,* he now found himself a subject of mockery for the sheer number of improbable stories he was reputed to have told. Some certainly were of his telling but many were fantasies from folk tales that had been in circulation for years. The wretched baron suffered the indignity of a translation of Raspe's work back into German in 1786 by Gottfried August Bürger, who added some tales of his own, and this is the version now current in the German-speaking world. Thereafter the real life baron's life fell apart, and he died with no heir to follow him in 1797.

Raspe in the meantime continued on his impecunious and slightly fraudulent way. Hired to prospect for mineral deposits on the land of a rich landowner in Scotland, he tried to pass off Cornish iron pyrites as copper ore, but he was forgiven by his employer as he had amused the family so much when a guest in his house. But for Baron Munchausen, Raspe would have disappeared as he did, possibly to death from typhoid in Ireland, as a common adventurer in a century that was rather full of them.[1] But the baron was ever with him. Sir Walter Scott took him as the model for Dousterswivel, the German miner in *The Antiquary.*

Raspe was a fraud but not, like Dousterswivel, a quack. Scott knew all about Raspe's deceit over the mineral deposits so Dousterswivel was a so-called mineralogist, deceiving the credulous Sir Arthur Wardour with the promise that he could retrieve his fortunes through the quack's magic arts by finding buried treasure. After much alchemical mumbo-jumbo, accompanied by sepulchral moans and groans from some unintended watchers, a small box of worthless coins, planted by Dousterswivel in the crypt of a ruined and abandoned church, are discovered. The deceit is uncovered when the magus's pretended magic is put to the test in a second dig in which genuine buried, probably Armada, treasure is found without magical assistance. Dousterswivel then falls victim to a practical joke played on him by the Scottish beggar, Edie Ochiltree, who promises him that more treasure is buried where they were digging earlier. Dousterswivel starts digging until he is terrified by the sound of ghostly chanting among the ruins.

Why performed in such solitude and by what class of chorister, were questions which terrified the imagination of the adept, stirred with all the German superstitions of nixies, oak-kings, wer(sic)-wolves, hobgoblins, black spirits and white, blue spirits and grey, durst not even attempt to solve.[2]

Raspe belongs to a tradition of allegorical and fantastical liars made respectable by Cervantes, Rabelais, Swift, Saint-German, and Voltaire. Some had a satirical and didactic purpose, others merely a desire to amuse. Munchausen has given his name to a syndrome by which a patient will lie about an illness to gain attention, but Raspe/Munchausen is a harmless liar. He does not, like Dousterswivel, allow himself to be frightened by his own imagination. He does not invent bogeys; he does not dream alchemical dreams. He is just absurd and a nobody, behind the man off whose reputation as a mad storyteller he lived. The real storyteller is commemorated in his birthplace at Bodenwerder, in the statue of himself riding on the half of the horse which had not been severed by a falling portcullis in one of Raspe's stories.

* * *

Germany had the fortune as well as the misfortune to be visited by someone who dared to challenge one of her most celebrated philosophers by contrasting his metaphysical loquacity with the matter of fact, uncommon sense of the baron. Germaine de Stäel confounded Fichte in Berlin when she asked him to explain what he meant by Absolute Ego. After quarter of an hour's painful exposition, she suddenly explained that she understood him completely, because she realised that Baron Munchausen had already expounded his theory when he crossed a river by taking hold of his left hand sleeve in his right hand and swinging himself across.[3]

In 1803 Germaine de Staël had received her final excommunication from Napoleon who was determined not to be countered or contradicted by a woman, no matter how eminent. She must go from Paris, the further away the better. She had been invited to meet Wieland in Zurich, but Germaine was not ready to go all that way to meet someone who was, in her eyes, a minor poet. She had read The Sorrows of Young Werther and Goethe had sent her a copy of *Wilhelm Meister* but the nearest she got to reading it was to admire the binding. She had mixed freely with the German colony in Paris; one of her correspondents was the foremost French authority on Kant, Charles de Villers, who was to become Germaine's main informant on the country whose language she could read but not speak. Her expulsion from France made her more determined to find a cause that could bring Napoleon down a peg or two. She went to find such a one in Germany, then enjoying, uncomfortably, a period of peace and, as the most celebrated woman in Europe, she traversed the land like a meteor.

The beginning was not good. As her caravan moved further into Germany she found the brutality of German life a sad contrast to the perfections of France, the grave and monotonous formality tedious; and the interest and appetite for bad food deplorable. The Rhinelanders were cautious about the reception of anyone who had upset Napoleon, and the absence of many people of French 'sensibility' put them, for Germaine, almost beyond the human race. She did not disguise what she felt. Poor Frau Goethe in Frankfurt, oppressed by Germaine's torrent of questions, warned her son that she found her as oppressive as a millstone and that she avoided meeting her where possible.

As the de Staël circus moved east towards Weimar, coming under the influence of the scenery, and of the tiny medieval towns and their communal music she began to sense a poetic feeling among the inhabitants, their thoughts contrasting with and elevating their common vulgarity. Even so she thought the endless contrapuntal sonatas that even humble cottagers would play on their spinets intolerably tedious.[4] By the time she reached the home of Goethe and Schiller she had learned to play German folk tunes on a harmonica and become almost tolerant. But the tiny court of Weimar, which had digested Goethe and Schiller, was uncertain of this female phenomenon, a noted Jacobin, best-selling author and sturdy critic of the mightiest man in Europe, one who, Circe-like, enchanted intellectual men when she did not devour them, and travelled with them in her baggage. Above all she was a ferocious and amusing talker, and in no time she had charmed the court from the Duchess down.

In the felicitous phrase of Christopher Herold 'the surprise (of her conversation) could not have been greater if the Queen of Sheba had suddenly evinced an interest in baby care'.[5] Her encounter with the two lions of Weimar was less felicitous; they did not expect the Queen of Sheba to talk baby talk, but they expected her to understand that poetry was the ineffable vehicle of human identification with the Ideal. This was very un-French. Schiller found her torrent of talk in a French of which he was not wholly master, intimidating. 'She insists on explaining everything, understanding everything, measuring everything. She admits no darkness; nothing Incommensurable and where her torch throws no light, there nothing can exist.' Ideal Philosophy, to her intensely French and logical mind, led to mysticism and superstition.[6] The Weimarians were irritated by her passion for treating all great philosophic ideas as suitable subjects for social conversation, especially those matters that, Goethe believed, belonged only to a conversation between man and his maker. But Goethe, who had refused to return to Weimar from a visit to Jena to meet her, even at the request of the dowager Duchess, when he did meet her in Weimar, enjoyed the encounters. He found her stance amusing rather than provocative and he liked taking a contradictory position to Germaine's barely concealed belief that the Germans tended to retreat from theory into the abstract and quickly disappeared into the clouds.[7] He was amused, not offended, by Germaine's lack of sympathy for, even understanding of, complexity, prolixity or cloudy generalisation and by her feeling that German poetry, not being passionate, rhetorical or universal, made no sense.

Germaine, for her part by her provocative notions and plenty of champagne persuaded Goethe to talk brilliantly but never seriously and then, to the relief of the two poets, and perhaps of Germaine herself, she set off in February 1805 for Prussia. She approached Berlin like a ruling monarch. She crossed Saxony virtually unmoved by the romantic beauty of the country, but in Prussia Queen Louise, who later enchanted Napoleon, flattered Germaine by graciously acknowledging her pleasure in meeting someone she had admired for so long. Germaine was pleased and willingly did the round of notables, the royal family, the statesmen, the writers and the thinkers. Of the latter she showed her characteristic impatience of what she considered nonsense, when she cut Fichte short as he was expounding his theory of the Absolute Ego. Fichte dismissed her as a fool but she had perceived that, if she could not understand what he was on about, then no one would. Fichte had the misfortune to be the best that Berlin could parade, coming between Novalis, who had died aged 29 in 1801 – whom Germaine might have enjoyed meeting – and Hoffman, whom she might not. Germaine was becoming bored with Berlin: 'the thinkers soar into the empyrean; on earth you find only grenadiers'.[8] She admitted that the vagueness of their conclusions did constitute, none too transparently, a revolution in thought as radical as had taken place in France, but as long as thinkers were obsequious to authority no one bothered to take them seriously. It might be easier, Goethe gently reminded her, if one realised that a German thinker, '*avance toujours, mais en ligne spirale*'. '*Sur les questions théologiques, sur l'idealisme ou l'empirism, (sans qu') il n'en resulte jamais rien que des livres,*' ('is always going forward, but in a roundabout way'. 'On questions of theology, idealism or empiricism there has been no other result but books.')[9]

She numbered one trophy in a comprehensible German thinker, before she hastened home on the news of her father's death. Goethe had given her a letter of introduction to August William Schlegel, who at 36 seemed to have read everything and had already translated 16 of Shakespeare's plays. Germaine to her amazement found she could understand his directions through the maze of German metaphysics, and determined to give him a richer career in Paris than Berlin, despite his literary fame, was able to give him. Schlegel could not resist the attraction of this brilliant lighthouse of French intellectualism, fell in love with her and accompanied her back to France.

Germaine visited Germany again in 1807–8, accompanied by Schlegel. She was growing a little old to impress people by her youthful passions, and the Bavarians in Munich found her dress bizarre, her manner flamboyant, and her egoism risible. In Vienna, her association with a revolution that had decapitated the Emperor's aunt, and Austria's persistent hostility to French aggrandisement, meant that her reception was lukewarm. The Viennese, like the Bavarians, but for different reasons, refused to take her at her own estimation, even suspecting her of being a spy. Germaine returned the compliment; she found the Viennese morals loose and their opinions frivolous, a not entirely unfair judgment when one considers their reaction to Beethoven. She spent a few days again in Weimar. Goethe was away but she had spied with considerable thoroughness, and unexpected sympathy. She had found the cause she wanted.

In 1810 she produced *De l'Allemagne*. By 1813 it had been translated into English. Her principal object was to mark what she considered the stultification of French creativity by the Napoleonic intellectual dictatorship, by introducing her countrymen to the originality and vitality of a nation whom they despised and thought they had conquered both intellectually and militarily.[10] Germans might be savages but they were noble savages. Gone were the shortcomings she had described so graphically to her father and other correspondents on her first visit. They were the proof, if any was needed, that there was no nation incapable of feeling and of thought, both, she implied, having been denied to France under Napoleon.[11] *De l'Allemagne* was a paeon in praise of a culture that was as creative and dynamic as Napoleon's France was not. There was also the smaller consideration that Napoleon was about to marry an Austrian Archduchess, another good reason for presenting *Germanness* in an attractive light.

In the third volume of her lengthy account, monitored by Schlegel, she tried to rehabilitate metaphysics, which being essentially speculative, she wrote, appealed to the Greek and German mind, whereas the Latin and English mind preferred an 'experimental philosophy'. Leibniz had defended moral liberty from fatalism (*fatalité sensuelle*), ensuring the independence and rights of the moral being (*l'être morale*). Kant had created of the soul the place where all faculties are in accord with one another (*un seul foyer où toutes les facultés sont d'accord entre elles*).[12] The long disquisition on German thinking, letters, even morals, ended with a reproach to her homeland, land of glory and love, where '*une intelligence active, une impetuosité savante vous rendroient les maîtres du monde; mais vous n'y laisseriez que le trace des torrens de sable terrible comme les flots, arides comme le désert*'.[13] The French censorship accepted this as a reason for impounding all copies it could seize. Mme de Staël was able to salvage a copy to have translated into English.

Most important, she divided Europe between the classical, essentially rational, gay and creative south (the Latins) and the north's gloomy, solipsistic and introspective metaphysic that, she claimed, were the essential ingredients of Romanticism, thus inventing the word.[14] She may have said all that she really thought about German metaphysics when she cut Fichte short with Baron Munchausen, but she gave it (and

English and French philosophy) much intellectual space, even conceding that ineffable German thought might yet dominate the new century. With *De l'Allemagne* the notion that there was a Romantic movement was presented to both French and English readers, and the label stuck. With her book, Germaine suggested that Germany was about to challenge the intellectual supremacy of France. Young German intellectuals not only had banished the French language but had made a point of being in every way unlike the French. Shakespeare had liberated Goethe from French classicism, while Lessing 'with iconoclastic wit [was] scattering the pretensions of French poetry'.[15]

✳ ✳ ✳

In England, Coleridge had done his best to present German thought, especially Kant's, as worthy of intellectual study, but his own elusive and opaque style, attended by his erratic mode of lecturing, had left it in a cloud of unknowing. He was more successful with his translations of Schiller, while hovering over his spirit was the reputation of Goethe whom he never met. But the writers of the Berlin school were to establish a following in England when la Motte Fouqué's *Sintram* was translated in 1820, by a Cambridge classical scholar, followed by Carlyle's version of his *Aslauga's Knight* in 1827.

Sintram's translator, Julius Hare, had met Goethe and Schiller in Weimar at the age of nine, and become bored while studying at a law firm in London. Hare had been born in Bologna, the third son of Francis Hare-Naylor and Georgiana Shipley. Georgiana's father was Bishop of St Asaph, and had married 'the beautiful Miss Mordaunt', maid of honour to Queen Caroline. Her sister was Anna Maria Jones who married Sir William Jones, the first Chief Justice in India, and her cousin was the exotic Georgiana, Duchess of Devonshire. Hare Naylor was the improvident son of a clergyman; father and son did not get on, and the son had already been arrested for debt. But Georgiana Shipley fell deeply in love with him and, on condition that they lived abroad, the Bishop agreed to their marriage, made possible by an annuity from the Duchess.

Their second son, Augustus, was given to the childless widow of Sir William Jones to be brought up as her son. Georgiana Hare-Naylor threw herself into the education of her remaining three sons, into painting and into learning languages, one of which was German, to improve which she took her third son, Julius, with her to spend the winter of 1804–5 in Weimar. Being a painter, a linguist and an accomplished conversationalist, Georgiana found herself at home in the hothouse intellectual society of the Duchy. Julius learned to revere the sacred names of Goethe, Wieland, Herder and Schiller, and so was born his lifelong devotion to the literature of Germany. The Duchess became a friend to his mother and, as Georgiana began to lose her sight, a comforting sickbed visitor. Julius listened to the literary giants conversing round her bed, and when Schiller died in Weimar while he was there he witnessed an outpouring of grief that marked a major national calamity. He visited the Wartburg, scene of the great Minnesinger contest between Wolfram von Eschenbach and Walter von der Vogelweide, where Luther had begun to translate the Bible under the protection of the Margrave Frederick the Wise. Here, Julius claimed, 'he too first learned to throw inkstands at the devil'.[16]

Julius entered Trinity College, Cambridge with a formidable reputation both as classical scholar and mathematician. He also brought with him a knowledge of German literature almost as profound as his knowledge of English and greater than any undergraduate before him. Though elected to a fellowship at Trinity in 1818, he was persuaded to study law and took chambers at the Temple. But his heart was not in it. He took more pleasure from his translation, into his strange clipped pseudo-medieval English, of *Sintram and his Companions*. When his aunt, Lady Jones, worried about the distraction of German, suggested facetiously that it might be better if his German books were burned, Julius was outraged. To them he owed 'the best of his knowledge', his 'ability to believe in Christianity with a much more implicit and intelligent faith' than he otherwise should have done.[17]

In 1822 Julius Hare left the law for a classical tutorship at Trinity College, Cambridge, finally taking orders in 1826. The Hares had become heirs to Herstmonceux Castle in Sussex and to an income, so he began collecting books 'to build up his mind'. He collaborated with the Bishop of St David's in translating the early volumes of the Danish Barthold Georg Niebuhr's *History of Rome* (1826–7, in an authoritative edition in 1828–32), with extensive notes of his own. He read the History more as another inkstand thrown at God, since its sceptical examination of prevailing secular history was seen as the precursor of an examination of more sacred texts. Hare vindicated both Niebuhr and himself from the charge of scepticism, but became sensitive to the gibe that he might be too learned for his own good. Sometimes his enthusiasm for the classical world led him to absurdity when, as Archdeacon of Lewes, he lectured the clergy of Sussex on the lyric poetry of the poet of sixth century (BC) Alcaeus of Mitylene, much to their surprise at hearing poems of war, revelry, gambling and love paraded as a model for living.

Hare was fascinated by the German penchant for philology and became in his own words a philologer himself, adopting his own idiosyncratic spelling that had had its first airing in the translation of *Sintram* and later was used on funerary monuments and in the hymn books of his parish church at Herstmonceux. Followers of his style among his Cambridge colleagues dropped the affectation when they finally became known for their publications, but Hare persevered in using it to the end, even as preferment followed. His sermons, often of inordinate length, argued that men were born in light and ventured through sin into darkness, a consistent Lutheran theme. Selfishness was the great sin, 'the disturbing, destructive force, the enemy of the order of the world'.[18] Theology, as the German secular theologians defined it, saw that all true and righteous deeds were the work of the Holy Spirit. Its job was to remind a self-centred humanity of that.

When Hare succeeded to the family living at Herstmonceux in 1832, with its extensive glebe lands, its rich pastures looking down on the Channel and its generous stipend, his library grew to tens of thousands of volumes, many in German, lining every room in the house. He would spend some of his vacations in Denbighshire with Anna Maria Dashwood, a wealthy widow who dabbled in poetry, art, Italian and German literature, and whose attempts to become a literary Maecenas attracted Leigh Hunt in search of an annuity that might lift him from poverty. In her house, 'which breathed of bowers / Of ladies who lead lives of flowers' whose 'walls were books' and 'the rooms / made rich / With knights and dames', they enjoyed a bloodlessly Platonic converse, Leigh Hunt trying not to give Marianne Hunt cause for anxiety and Hare trying to avoid Aunt Jones's anxiety that he might be tempted to marry her.[19]

Hare did marry a dour and religiously Calvinistic lady, one of two grim sisters and, towards Francis Hare's son, Augustus, consigned to his care, Hare became a Murdstone and his wife a Jane Murdstone. For the slightest infraction of what were considered right behaviour or manners he would whip the five-year old in the belief that he was heaving an inkstand at the Devil. Julius Hare did not understand boys, or even parishioners for that matter. He preached them long sermons full of carefully crafted medieval sentiments that flew above their heads. He had a poor opinion of women generally, though had been brought up by a highly intelligent mother. In his mind they saw nothing but religion in religion and knew and cared nothing for science, philosophy or statecraft.[20] To his lasting regret, the English were not Germans. When Julius received the news of Goethe's death he mourned the departing of a spirit mightier than anyone since Shakespeare. He wished he could own the armchair in which Goethe had died, hoping to follow his example when the time came to follow the Master, full of years, learning and contentment.[21] He wept for the death too of Coleridge whom he had known at Cambridge. His had been a great thinking mind, which had embraced German metaphysics, and metaphysics were what he endlessly discussed with his curate, John Sterling.

* * *

John Sterling, the son of a soldier turned farmer, turned journalist, turned newspaper proprietor, was the extravagantly gifted product of Christ's Hospital, joining in time a distinguished roll call of alumni that included Coleridge, Leigh Hunt and Charles Lamb. At Cambridge he was an Apostle and his tutor was Julius Hare, who with Coleridge turned his studies towards Germany. He was to visit Hare later in Bonn while studying with Germaine de Staël's protégé, August Wilhelm Schlegel, the translator of Shakespeare. Sterling vacillated between a career in the law, in politics, in the Church and in letters, choosing at first the last, founding with E. D. Maurice *The Metropolitan Quarterly* and then acquiring ownership and control of a new periodical, *The Athenaum*. John Stuart Mill saw him as a radical anti-Benthamite, but it was to be Coleridge who became his mentor and his hero. Sterling's disillusion with politics came from an abortive campaign of Spanish exiles to stir up revolt under the disaffected General Torrijos, against the established tyranny, supported in its time by Tennyson and his friend Arthur Hallam, but which led to the death by execution of its leader and his English lieutenant, Sterling's own cousin.

When Hare met him in Bonn, Sterling had returned in poor health from a family plantation in St Vincent, frustrated in his plans to ameliorate the condition of its slaves. The offer Hare made of the curacy of his parish at Herstmonceux determined what he thought would be his career. He was ordained deacon and took up residence in Sussex administering to a large rural parish. But his health proved too precarious to continue, and after six months as a curate he retired to a world of poetry and letters. In 1835, his friend Mill introduced him to a fellow enthusiast for German literature, Thomas Carlyle.

Sterling's father met the Carlyles in Chelsea and Sterling now chose him as a subject to champion, despite Carlyle's ill-concealed views of Coleridge who, in his view had 'magicked' John into holy orders by 'moonshine' which had convinced him that the dead English Church must be brought to life again. Coleridge believed that he understood how to harness man's reason to his understanding, by following the German prescription, and in the pure mind of reasonable philosophy one could create a Christianity not influenced by the 'clerisy' and 'hebetude' that crippled the established Church. This was 'moonshine' to Carlyle but Sterling hoped to convert Carlyle to the Coleridgean view of religion and art, and the reconciliation between historical Christianity and modern experimentation.[22] But despite their common interest in German thought – Sterling translated Goethe's autobiography in *Blackwood's Magazine* – he failed. Carlyle disapproved of Coleridge and the 'clerisy' too much to change his views of religion, but he respected Sterling so much that he developed a deep attachment to him that resulted in the deeply moving life that followed his early death in 1844. He claimed that he wrote it to rescue Sterling from his friends who did not appreciate his critical views on God and religion.

* * *

Thomas Carlyle was to translate another of la Motte Fouqué's short stories, *Aslauga's Knight*. It was the tale of a bold Danish knight's passion for a dead woman, who repaid his devotion by appearing as a golden glimmer as bright as was her hair in life, and of his dedicated friendship for a young German knight. It appealed to the Scottish seer's Calvinist belief in single love, male bonding and his Germanic taste for wandering knights in search of moral challenges and battle triumphs. The story is slight. Hildegardis, a beautiful, but living princess, is promised in the capricious way women in folk tales were promised, to the winner of a jousting tournament. The two companions reach the final and the younger who actually loves Hildegardis, loses. The victor, however, cedes his claim to the promised bride because he serves another. Hildegardis is annoyed because she has been rejected for someone else and is not appeased to learn that her rival is no longer alive. She swears that she can only marry the winner, as was the original arrangement.

Hildegardis is then snatched by a gang with supernatural powers (Bohemians, not good Germans) but she is freed by the two friends after fierce battles with the powers of darkness. The Dane then accepts a return match, so that if he loses then Hildegardis can accept her lover. To save his honour – for he cannot lose the contest on purpose – his ethereal lover dazzles him with her beauty at the critical moment, so that he is momentarily blinded and the younger man wins. Hildegardis accepts the verdict of fate and marries the younger man. Their marriage is attended by the Dane, whose lady makes a brief appearance from the dead and carries her lover off to the land beyond death. The whole tale is permeated by pre-Christian echoes of the heroic past of battles and triumphs, conflicts with spirits, and an almost risible sense of honour. Just off centre is the figure of the Holy Roman Emperor, a near sanctified figure, and the Teutonic Knights of the Black Cross who are pledged to fight the pagans, to remind us that this spirit of honour, battle skills and male devotion existed in la Motte Fouqué's Prussia. It is an echo of the old days, for which Fouqué had an unconquerable interest, in his morbid Germanic passion for the throes of death, a pale version of a Wagnerian saga.

* * *

Carlyle was born in 1795 at Dumfries in the Scottish lowlands, on very nearly the same latitude as Pomerania. Brought up as a strict Calvinist, though he abandoned that version of Christianity later, he never emerged from its stern moralistic influence. He experienced his first religious doubts at Edinburgh University, where he turned to the German theologians to help him. He entered fully into their examination of the true nature of divinity, trying to break free from the constraints of so-called revealed religion, and like Coleridge he concentrated on Kant. His principal mentor was to be 'Mme de Staël's Munchausen', Johann Gottlieb Fichte, whose first book, published anonymously, was believed to have been written by Kant himself. The opaque and lofty style of Kant became in Fichte's hands even more abstruse and difficult. His distinctions between *noumena* (things as they are) and *phenomena* (things as they seem) existed in a cloudy land of abstraction, but appeared to suggest that self was only aware of itself in contact with other rational objects. How it dealt with these objects was the basis of individual freedom of action. Thus was displaced the idea of an inherent basis of morality, the trailing clouds of glory that appealed to poets like Wordsworth.

Fichte had decided that there was a Divine Idea that pervaded the visible universe, and that Literary Men were the only appointed interpreters of it. They were, as it were, a perpetual priesthood.[23] The idea appealed to Carlyle who elaborated it in an essay on Schiller, whose life showed 'a priest-like stillness, a priest-like purity' which he likened to a monastic character, where for Faith 'we substitute the Ideal of Art, and for Convent Rules, Moral or Aesthetic Law'. Immured in the cloisters of the mind 'he meditated only on what we may call Divine Things'.[24] Carlyle did not give a capital letter to the word *mind* but its use would have been wholly appropriate. *Mind* was what was said to characterise German letters, a ceaseless quest for rules that were within the understanding of the human mind, like art, aesthetics and nature, rules which had their own validity and did not depend on Divine edict, interpreted by a man-made institution like the Church.

Carlyle, freed from the aura of Divine imperatives, could now examine historical events and their influence on human behaviour. At times of crisis, only heroic decisiveness could create decisive action. Human affairs were directed by the self-conscious action of someone with that heroic character within him, or one who recognised that he must acquire it. In expounding this conviction in his historical works, Carlyle's style affected a breathless incoherence, as he stumbled into a kind of fiction, using the present tense to describe how human beings reacted to the often contradictory challenges of the immediate situation – a technique he developed inimitably in *The French Revolution*.

Carlyle first met Coleridge in 1824 and dubbed him 'a man of great and useless genius', despite the dim view he took of his personality – 'a steam engine of a hundred horses power, with the boiler burst', 'the hulk of a huge ship; his mast and rudder rotted quite away'.[25] Coleridge was then 52, and though under the protective care of Dr Gilman, showed his addiction to opium. Carlyle was familiar with his writing, rather mystical, sometimes absurd, but he read it in hopes that it would not be a fruitless exercise. He had to admit in the end that, despite trying to get 'something about Kant & Co from him about "reason" versus "understanding"', it was all 'in vain'. But the puffy, anxious, obstructed-looking, fattish old man,[26] had made him redouble his efforts to become the British interpreter of German culture.

In 1827 he met the other determinant influence in his German studies, Thomas De Quincey. Already an opium addict he contributed regularly, like Carlyle, to the *London Magazine*, and was then translating chunks of Lessing's *Laoköon* for *Blackwood's*. Carlyle had already read some of his earlier writing on German writers, particularly Jean Paul Richter, who provided the subject for an essay that De Quincey reviewed.[27] The two men nearly fell out over the hostile reference De Quincey gave to Carlyle's translation of *Wilhelm Meister*, but though Carlyle thought that De Quincey was inspired by 'the laudanum bottle in his pocket and the venom of a wasp in his heart', he was later to admit that the criticisms had been just.[28] The two men became friends and Carlyle even invited him to his first marital home, Craigenputtock, a farmhouse surrounded by a peat bog, there to establish a Bog School, which would rival the Lake School of Wordsworth and Coleridge. But De Quincey declined. His drug addiction and poverty would have made him a companion as uncomfortable as Coleridge had proved to those who befriended him, but, though the two men drifted apart, Carlyle read and often reviewed what his friend wrote until his death in 1859.

In 1821, Carlyle met the 20-year-old Jane Welsh, the precociously witty, spoiled daughter of a Tyneside doctor. She had just lost her father and was deep into Rousseau and Byron, and the 26-year-old Thomas took over her mind and her reading. He had applied himself only two years earlier to learn German and by immersing himself in German letters, and his own special study of Richter, he became sufficiently competent in reading German (never speaking it) to take on a pupil. He introduced Jane to Mme de Staël's *De l'Allemagne,* and to the works of Schiller, whose life he was writing, and to Goethe, whose *Wilhelm Meister* he was translating. He was commissioned to review *Faust* for the *Edinburgh Encyclopedia*, and with his *Life of Schiller* which appeared in serial form from 1821–3 and from his translation of *Wilhelm Meisters Lehrjahre (Wilhelm Meister's Apprenticeship*) in 1824, he began to acquire a modest reputation and with it an income. Despite her mother's anxiety that Carlyle, though clearly a brilliant talker and prolific reader, was not really suitable as a husband for Jane, she permitted him to teach her German and inevitably the two drifted into a marriage. They lived together so acrimoniously that Samuel Butler thought that God had been very good to allow them to marry so that only two people not four were rendered unhappy.

In 1825, in his 30th year, Carlyle's *Life of Schiller* appeared in book form; in this he interpreted the respect Germans had for poets, like Goethe and Schiller, as homage to those who must express the ideal in fiction and truth, 'imprinting it in all sensible and spiritual forms and casting it silently into everlasting time'.[29] From Schiller he imbibed the view of history that was to inspire him, as Schiller claimed it had inspired him. 'The business of history is not simply to record but to interpret', he wrote in his *Life*,

> It involves not only a clear conception and a lively exposition of events and characters but a sound, enlightened theory of individual and national morality, a general philosophy of human life whereby to judge of them and measure their effects.[30]

That he was later to attempt in his *History of the French Revolution* (1837).

With his life of Schiller he was now established as an authority on German letters, about which he wrote largely in a mystical contemplation of the German cultural landscape from Jane's inherited farmhouse of Craigenputtock in Dumfriesshire. *Sartor Resartus* (*The Tailor Re-patched*) purporting to be the life and opinions of Herr Teufelsdröckh appeared between 1833–4, an autobiography dressed up as speculation on the symbolism of clothes, written with highly charged mishmash of Richterian metaphysics, Carlylean neologisms, German interpolations and apocalyptic ramblings. It was hard to tell where philosophising degenerated into satire, but it established Carlyle as a writer with a distinctive style.

In 1834 the Carlyles moved to Chelsea where, as he laboured over three years on his *French Revolution*, he became the cynosure of literary London, known from his eccentric behaviour and fiery stance as the Sage, producing in 1840 the book that outlined his concept of the hero. This was a more promising venture than pure metaphysics, and he looked to Schiller for his model. Karl Moor in *The Robbers* had shown heroic qualities in surrendering the price on his head to a poor peasant. Wallenstein had shown heroic qualities, so had Joan of Arc, both in spite of their belief in the supernatural, which was in some ways an abnegation of will. Heroes were not the chivalric nonpareils of Arthurian legend or of German Romance; they had human failings and weaknesses and they were not always men of action. They could be prophets, poets, men of letters, kings or priests. Heroes are those men (none of Carlyle's heroes is a woman) everyone knows about because they stand out as pioneers or leaders or creative geniuses. As heroic priests he chose Luther and John Knox, for they brought down 'a light from heaven into the daily life of their people'. They were battling priests in valorous conflict, and Carlyle viewed Protestantism as the 'prophet-work of the sixteenth century'.[31] It was not that Luther was always right, (indeed Carlyle's view of organised religion was that it was seldom right) but he was engaged on honest demolition of an 'ancient thing grown false, preparatory to a new thing, ... true and authentically divine'. In his search for moral purpose he revolted against historical sovereignties, but without a moral sovereignty life was anarchy. The true sovereign was the Hero who established a union of good men in the sincere search for truth.

Luther was such a hero, a Christian Odin with his thunder-hammer, and the revolution that Luther spearheaded was, for Carlyle, the 'greatest moment in the Modern History of Men'. It embraced English

Puritanism, the independence of America and the French Revolution against 'Semblance and Sham'. Protestantism had also produced Goethe and German literature. As Carlyle purred, it was alive. Though he had abandoned its theology, he supported the dynamic of a Protestant society. That dynamic he attributed to 'kings', who took command of both spiritual and secular destinies. Kings were *Könning*, 'Can-do Leaders', whose status was not necessarily marked by thrones or crowns. These could be the antitheses of real *könning*-ship. Napoleon belied his heroic capacity to create a new society from revolutionary *sansculottisme* when, from being king by nature, he became an Emperor by licence of Pope and aristocracy, enveloping himself 'in a turbid atmosphere of French fanfaronade', and Pumpernickel.[32]

Carlyle was more poet and prophet than philosopher but his elaborate prose constructed a theory of sovereignty that rejected the model of the Enlightenment. Freedom was not personal, it was societal, the freedom of a society to work out its collective destiny. That required a hero to command both belief and action in such a way that both expressed, if it did not actually create, the deepest, even sub-conscious, desires of his people. Eighteen years later, in 1858, he was to begin work on the avatar of a hero, Frederick the Great, who in his excited prose, created a state, not taking its life from the liberal enfranchisement of the French (vaporous and quarrelsome) and English Enlightenments but from the depths of German Romance. His was 'Real Kingship eternally indispensable ... The destruction of Sham Kingship (a frightful process) is occasionally so.'[33] If Napoleon did not bring about the death of Pumpernickel, Frederick dealt it a blow from which it was to expire. Carlyle forgave him for his admiration of the arts and of Voltaire, the first of which he believed to be a sign of dilettantism, the second because he thought Voltaire's thought was ultimately destructive of a system of moral authority. France after the Seven Years War had become doomed to the dry rot that brought about the revolution. Frederick had heroically smashed a system that threatened his country externally and internally. That deep Carlylean concept of a chthonic German romance, attributing moral authority to duty to the leader, was to have a baleful influence on German notions of authority and respect, for it was to culminate in the National-Socialist dedication to a racially pure master-race, by nature predestined to determine human destiny.

Carlyle believed that German thinkers, particularly Schiller, had produced a template by which measurement could be made of cultural movements and achievements, by aesthetic rules that had a universal interpretation. He took his cue from Kant of whom he believed that he, Carlyle, not Coleridge, was to find the gold amid the dross, and be the interpreter to an English readership. Kant had established that 'ever since mankind has existed, and any Reason among mankind, (certain) first Principles have been admitted and on the whole acted upon'. Among these principles, art had 'its basis on the most important interests of man and of itself involves the harmonious adjustment of these'. The application of pure reason wanted, for the poetic nature, 'no Moral Law, no Rights of Man, no Political Metaphysics', no deity even.[34] As Prophets were not without honour save in their own country. Carlyle did not want any honours, not even a pension, from a British government led by Disraeli. He did accept, however, the Prussian Order of Merit from Bismarck, though privately remarking that he would rather have received a quarter of a pound of good tobacco. He hoped that, like Schiller, 'his mind ... will remain one of the most enviable which can fall to the share of mankind.'[35]

To Goethe, Carlyle built an altar before which he offered not uncritical worship. The two men kept up a correspondence, Carlyle's adulatory, Goethe's warm, acknowledging gifts and eulogies. Goethe used him as his interlocutor with English letters, asking him to send medals to Walter Scott and to five other literary luminaries of his own choosing. Carlyle readily acknowledged that Goethe had rescued him from atheism and shown him a way of accepting a secular Christianity shorn of miracles and theology, emphasising that life, perhaps this life only, could be lived creatively in a discipline of duty and renunciation. He greeted *Faust* as a revelation that its author knew what it was like to be an unbeliever driven almost to despair and that Faust's curse had seemed 'the only fitting greeting for human life'.[36] While never disclaiming his role as an acolyte of the German master, Carlyle wilfully misquoted him in vital particulars, underlining the moral and diminishing the aesthetic elements in his theories of life and living. While accepting Goethe's ethic he found his aesthetic almost as unappealing as Christian theology, inducing a quietism that betrayed life's true mission. Carlyle saw in the insensate fury of the French Revolution the birth of a new order, whereas Goethe believed it had brought an era that had nourished genius for a sordid end. Goethe's detachment was, to Carlyle, a turning away from the efficacy of action, to which Carlyle converted the 'hero' of *Sartor Resartus*, Diogenes Teufelsdröckh. 'Only the inspired man of action could save the planet from destruction and chaos.'[37]

Carlyle never finished the history of German literature that he had designed for four volumes. He became increasingly attached to proclaiming the achievements of men of action like Oliver Cromwell and Frederick the Great, the apotheoses of saviours from destruction and chaos. But in that history he had reached Luther and the German reformation which reflected the deep feeling, deep-thinking, devout temper of the German mind, the beginning of a new revelation of the God-like. His enthusiasm for the merits of the German people led him to believe that 'Deutschland will reclaim her great colony, we shall become more Deutsch, that is to say more English.' The German race, he went on 'is more clearly in the ascendant; seems as if it were destined to take the main part of the earthly globe, and rule it for a time'.[38]

Carlyle was no democrat. He believed that there were natural aristocrats, not created by birth but by their capacity to lead, by whom ordinary people were ready to be led. The model for such heroic virtue was the subject of his final work, a giant Pumpernickel loaf, a six volume life of Frederick the Great, written over 14 years and produced between 1858 and 1865. It was yeasty and inspired in parts, but it nearly sank in the prolixity of its materials, given rarely in the original but presented at length, paraphrased in the impressionist Carlyle style, obtrusive, self-opinionated and often obscure. By the end of it, if they had persisted to the end, readers must have felt that they knew all, nay more than all that was to be known about Frederick and his times. In their quest, they had plodded through sloughs of style, like Carlyle's description of the death of George I:

> after sixty seven years ... he has flung his big burdens – English crowns, Hanoverian crownlets, sulkinesses, indignations, lean women and fat, and earthly contradictions – fairly off him ... Wilder puddle of muddy infatuations from without and within, if we consider it well – of irreconcilable incoherence, bottomless universal hypocrisies, solecisms bred with him and imposed on him – few sons of Adam had hitherto lived in.[39]

Precisely!

If English readers found the whole indigestible, Germans were impressed by its coincidence with their feeling that modern notions of democracy and reason were not blueprints for a glorious future, not heroic enough. They felt that Carlyle's belief that Jews were not patriots except in the interests of their homeland, Palestine, and that their espousal of a liberal ethos was to promote these and not those of the nation, was true. What Germany needed was a führer, not an assembly of potential führers. If there is no conclusive evidence that Hitler had even tried to read Carlyle, the life of Frederick the Great proved to be the most quoted work in the diaries of Joseph Goebbels, who read extracts to the führer during the last days of the war to encourage him in the belief that he might still find salvation from the German people and the House of Brandenburg. Though it is hard to see in Carlyle's colourful and dramatic prose any suggestion that Germany might, from the example of the most distinguished member of that house, produce an ideological monster, Carlyle seemed to have produced a blueprint for Germany radically different from that envisaged by, say, Goethe.[40]

For Carlyle, Frederick was 'the last of the Kings', who ushered in the French Revolution and closed an epoch in world history. He did not find the eighteenth century a lovely one; 'opulent in accumulated falsities … it had nothing grand in it except that grand universal Suicide which terminated its otherwise most worthless existence.'[41] Frederick was unlike the other Pumpernickel monarchs. He believed in discipline not dissipation; austerity not ostentation and to the end of his life he would appear in public in a shabby old military uniform and unpolished boots – he would encourage the street boys to polish them while he was on horseback, which, not a carriage, was his preferred form of locomotion. Carlyle held that he was equal to the greatest commanders in history when, by strategic art, human ingenuity and intrepidity he won the battle against the French at Rossbach (1757) with the loss of 157 men. Napoleon in contrast caused Prussian losses of 10,000 men killed and wounded and 15,000 captured at Jena (1806).[42] With Frederick died the deplorable eighteenth century.

* * *

In 1835 Carlyle, who admired admiration, met an admirer through his neighbour James Leigh Hunt. George Henry Lewes was then 18 and studying German. Carlyle furnished him with letters that he took off with him three years later to Berlin and Vienna. There, Lewes applied himself to his studies, reading Hegel and collecting Goethiana, returning to sit admiringly at Carlyle's feet as he worked his studies into an essay on Goethe's character and works for the *British and Foreign Review* (1843). Carlyle was sensitive to any suggestion that he himself was not the authority on Goethe and thought Lewes had missed his mark, so that when Lewes returned to Weimar to continue his research into Goethe with Marian Evans – a liaison of which Carlyle did not approve – he was ready to be hostile to the result.

The *Life of Goethe* appeared in November 1855 and proved an instant success, selling 1,000 copies in three months and being quickly translated into other languages. Not everyone was pleased. Some Germans were annoyed that an Englishman should have become Goethe's most successful biographer. A German biography had been rushed out as soon as it was known that Lewes's was to appear, as it would be to the dishonour of the German people to be forestalled by a foreigner. While individual critics claimed that Lewes had misread and misreported what he had learned at Weimar, most readers had to accept that, short of transforming Goethe into a saint, who had achieved literary perfection, the portrait that Lewes had drawn, warts and all, was a just one. Even the Sage of Chelsea had to admit that Lewes had done what Carlyle's overblown prose had not and thrown a great light on the life and work of the Sage of Weimar. That visit to Weimar with Marian Evans had, however, cost Lewes his intimacy with the Carlyles and Marian was never invited into the Carlyle home.[43] But Lewes willingly acknowledged him as the first who 'taught England to appreciate Goethe'.[44]

Not everyone did. The way he loved and left young women and even girls, his marriage after a succession of lovers worthy of his rank and genius with Christiane Vulpius, effectively uneducated and a servant, his time-serving obeisance to Napoleon, all helped to form Thackeray's impression on first meeting him that he was an old rogue.[45] Lewes did not overlook these, but while sympathetic to a man whose carnal desires were similar to his own, he did not defend his behaviour, but drew from each liaison something good. When some had seen cold dalliance with a married woman, Frau von Stein, Lewes discerned affection, even passion. As for Christiane Vulpius, he was scrupulously fair. She had enough education to be a companion to Goethe and enough charm as his wife to inspire some of the master's finest love lyrics.

One critic, on hearing that Lewes was writing a life of Goethe, thought that he was entirely unsuitable for 'a task for which he must have been as unfit as irreligion and sparkling shallowness can make him'.[46] He judged Goethe's behaviour and Goethe's attitudes to human relationships, holding that 'Goethe was an Artist not an Advocate', and this exposed him to charges of sympathising with immorality.[47] There was a raw honesty about Lewes's approach. Like Goethe he was largely self-educated, his own relations with women were unbounded by conventional morality, and like Goethe he had made science a special study. Some of that honesty rubbed off on his subject, so that Lewes did not feel he had to conceal awkward facts to preserve his subject's blameless reputation. Napoleon had called Goethe 'a Man' and Lewes treated him as such.

Lewes while in Weimar wrote two articles on Heinrich Heine, whose teasing autobiography had appeared in Paris in French and hinted at the poet's abandonment of scepticism, Hegelianism and atheism back into the beliefs of his childhood Jewishness, which to Lewes was 'a ghastly subject'. Marian Evans had already pitched herself into the German cauldron, translating David Friedrich Strauss's *Life of Jesus* in 1846 and in 1853 embarking on a translation of Feuerbach's *Essence of Christianity*. The moral universe was not so much the result of Divine ordinance from God to man, but a reversion from man to God. In anthropological terms, man was God and human benevolence and morals were born of their own experience and development as in the Ten Commandments, which were a man-made blueprint for social cohesion. Their joint interest in German culture and thought ensured both Lewes and Marian social and intellectual acceptance in Weimar and, if Carlyle spluttered, they were received quite naturally. Goethe's non-judgmental Wertherism and his large tolerance of 'living, generous humanity – mixed and erring' was about to be reflected in Marian's own portrayals of Hetty Poyser, Maggie Tulliver and Dorothea Brooke. There was to be no authorial judge and jury determining blame and determining reward and punishment. Marian Evans had become George Eliot.

CHAPTER EIGHTEEN

Power over Genius and Magic

'Pumpernickel' to Potsdam

Soup made of the inner mysteries of geese, eels stewed in
beer, roast pig with red cabbage, venison basted with sour
cream and served with beans in vinegar and cranberry
jam, the pumpernickel and cheese, apples and pears on
top of that and cakes on the top of the apples and pears.
(Elizabeth von Arnim, *The Solitary Summer*, August 1899)

ESPITE THEIR GROSS appetite – it was their language which
sounded like 'glutton's feasting'[1] – it was the grim and fearsome
Hohenzollerns with their Pomeranians, who did for Pumpernickel. Their
highly disciplined armies were for conquest and their trim, be-medalled
aristocratic officer corps, compulsorily billeted on civilians during
manoeuvres, were there for victories. Even Elizabeth, (née Mary Annette
Beauchamp) who had in 1891 married Count Henning August von Arnim-
Schlagenthin, found it all faintly risible, but she loved her Pomeranian
German garden which she was converting from the wilderness, into an
oasis of English amateurism, a wilderness of delightful ease among the
northern skies of the Baltic coast beloved of Caspar Friedrich. Count von
Arnim, otherwise complaisant and good-humoured, was nonetheless her
Man of Wrath. For wrath was what Pumpernickel deserved. Its rulers had
shown an insouciant display of wealth among ignorance and poverty, and
though the competition for buildings, orchestras, festivals and gargantuan
meals may have been shared among most of Europe's aristocratic

caste, who lived like Indian rajahs under growing and greedy empires, Pumpernickel's had shown too great a concern for their dynasties and historic survival. One by one they lost their principalities and powers, even if they kept their titles and their palaces. As the German Empire grew so the national aristocracy declined to provide spouses for dynastic marriages and satraps for their Emperor.

Neither Napoleon nor Bismarck gave Pumpernickel the deathblow. Both believed in the illusion of aristocratic rank and power as long as it remained an illusion. Jerome Bonaparte was permitted to pirouette like a prince as long as he remembered he was a lackey. Ludwig II of Bavaria was ready to nominate Friedrich of Prussia as Emperor of Germany because he realised that it was the only way he could keep his kingdom and finish building and decorating his palaces. France may have remained the lodestar of the south German aristocracy, as so brilliantly described by Sybille Bedford in *A Legacy*, but it was a France that no longer influenced their political or social development. Paris might still be the capital of arts and pleasure, but Wagner wrested away its musical primacy by creating not only German operas but a German stage on which to perform them. Pumpernickel, in fact, destroyed itself.

For all Thackeray's ironic mockery, good-natured in *The Fitzboodle Papers*, savage in *Barry Lyndon*, Carlyle's thundering and Coleridge's philosophic musings, the English decided that it was Pumpernickel rather than Prussia they wanted to visit, the world of Grimm and Hoffman. After all, their own queen had married into it and now the most resplendent Pumpernickel court was at Windsor, Winterhalter was its court painter and Mendelssohn its court musician. Bath and Tunbridge Wells, both of which had prospered during the Napoleonic wars, declined before the lure of the German spas, both cheaper and more fun, where the local royalty extended invitations to rich English visitors to come to their gardens, musical parties and casinos. These visitors, who increasingly consisted of parties of female relatives, ladies' maids and English valets, found Germany cleaner, more polyglot and almost as culturally rich as the Italy to which they had gone (without their families) on the Grand Tour.

Perambulating, as Coleridge did across Germany, was easier, less fraught by fear of bandits, and of social parasites, and attracted the readers of the great perambulators, Wordsworth, De Quincey and

George Borrow, as they found an extended Lake District and a grander Wales in the hills and forests of the Black Forest and the Hochwald. The admiration for the English evinced by Goethe may not have been entirely welcome to everyone. Towards the end of his life he had completely succumbed to Anglomania. What fine handsome people the English were, full of confidence, as if they were lords everywhere and the whole world belonged to them. 'If we could only alter the Germans after the model of the English, if we could only have less philosophy and more practice we might obtain a good share of redemption.' He trembled for the women of his country every time he met a young Englishman, dangerous people whose very merit was their danger. There was nothing vitiated or soiled about them, they were thoroughly complete men. Even though there were complete fools among them that still had some weight in the scale of nature.[2] That was exactly what the English thought of themselves.

* * *

Yet rivalry seemed almost inevitable between Germany and England which though united under common dynastic heads, were developing so many points of conflict. To the orderly Prussian mind, it was a lamentable irony that the essentially frivolous and amateur British had managed to acquire so many places in the sun, which sustained their increasingly obsolescent industries, and gave their badly educated ruling class so many outlets for their incompetence. Admiration for the pragmatism, agnosticism and originality of English Newton and Scottish Hume had given way to contempt for the inability of the English to understand Kant and Hegel and for turning their back on Goethe. Even ineffable, unworthy Cambridge had replaced Göttingen as the lodestar of English philosophic studies. In 1903 the English found their own Kant, who had proved largely impenetrable to the pragmatic English mind, despite the efforts of Coleridge and Carlyle, when the brotherhood of bright Cambridge intellectuals, the Apostles, were overwhelmed by the work of their president, George Edward Moore. His *Principia Ethica* (1903) proved, in the words of Maynard Keynes, 'so exciting, exhilarating, the beginning of a new renaissance, the opening of a new heaven and earth, we were the forerunners of a new dispensation, we were not afraid of anything'.[3]

German thinkers had been saying that of Kant and his successors for nearly a century.

The English, for their part, hankered after an older Germany, the Romantic world of Mozart and Haydn, of Weber and Hoffmann, of an ancient chivalry and a court life of music and love. It found its expression in one of the most famous stories of romantic adventure, set in a land of lakes and forests in a mythical part of Germany, where Undine might have lived. *The Prisoner of Zenda* and its sequel, *Rupert of Hentzau*, appeared in 1894 and 1898 respectively. They were the work of someone who had never been to Germany, the son of a clergyman, with a first class Classics degree from Cambridge, who had been recently called to the London bar, which interested him about as much as law studies had Hoffmann. Anthony Hope Hawkins always wanted to write. His cousin was already contributing to the Yellow Book and was to be the author of *The Wind in the Willows* (1908) and Hawkins himself had already, in 1890, written a novel set in an imaginary country, Aureataland.[4] In 1893, while, he said, pedestrianising in the streets of London, he had the idea for Ruritania. He wrote its first draft in a month and it was an instant success. It might have been the Last Tale of Hoffmann.

Its Germanic links are obvious. The hero, Rudolf Rassendyll, by some genetic freak – they are cousins – bears a twin-likeness (even down to the name) to Rudolf V of Ruritania, a Pumpernickel monarch of uncertain morals and mental stability. Ruritania proved to be an inspired name, giving parentage to ideas of an imaginary European state, and was set somewhere south of Prussia in the hinterland between Saxony and Austria.[5] Hope knew he could not set it in the Bavaria of Ludwig II, so recently dead in suspicious circumstances, and he carefully omitted mentioning the newly-proclaimed empire of the queen's grandson. King Rudolf is a shadowy figure; he is due to marry his kinswoman, the Princess Flavia. He also has a rival, suitably known as Black Michael who wants the throne and the bride, and is prepared to play dirty to get them both. The politics of Ruritania are obscure, but Hope's predilection being for mild autocracy not liberalism we can only assume Michael may have had some unsettling reformist agenda. This does not detract from the evilness of his character, for he has the king kidnapped and held prisoner in his castle HQ at Zenda, while he schemes to secure the throne and the girl.

In this he is frustrated by the king's namesake, Rudolf Rassendyll. He is the antithesis of a Prussian: an English gentleman, well-dressed, affluent, unemployed, with a hearty laugh and an English sense of humour, with lots of soldierly qualities of honour, enterprise, initiative and dexterity, in short what Hope thought might be a portrait of himself. On a fishing holiday he meets two Ruritanians, also fishing, who are struck by the similarity he bears to their sovereign. So that when Rudolf V disappears, a Bismarckian quartermaster figure, Colonel Sapt, and his well-drilled adjutant, Fritz von Tarlenheim, rope him into a wild plot to replace the missing king by Rudolf Rassendyll, while they search for him through what George Meredith had depicted (1871): the forests of Germany, with 'their awful castles, barons, knights, ladies, long-bearded dwarfs, gnomes and thin people'.[6]

Rassendyll behaves throughout in the manner of a well-drilled public schoolboy who finds himself in a *Boy's Own Paper* yarn of skulduggery in a foreign court. He comports himself impeccably as monarch and as the affianced groom of a beautiful woman; he proves to have all the equestrian, gymnastic and fencing skills of an Olympic gold medallist, rescues the king and outwits his alter ego, the brave, resourceful but not, ultimately, gentlemanly Rupert of Hentzau. It was a story made for the cinema, Rassendyll played in 1937 by Ronald Colman and Rupert by the more raffish Douglas Fairbanks Jr. It was peopled by stereotypes like a James Bond movie, the gentleman amateur coolly triumphant through wit and daring, but in this story only the villain, Black Michael, has sex – he has a mistress. Rudolf Rassendyll is too much of a gentleman to take any advantage of the Princess Flavia either in *The Prisoner of Zenda* or in *Rupert of Hentzau*, the inevitable sequel.

Despite his German blood, Rassendyll behaves as the legendary Englishman Hope wanted him to. Sapt and Tarlenheim are honourable but rather thick-witted Germans, fed on beer, tobacco and Pumpernickel. The wronged woman is a Frenchwoman, conforming to stereotype, but her lover, the evil intriguer, Black Michael, pales beside the true, but unintended hero of the novels, Rupert of Hentzau. He steals the show from the hero, who actually kills him but is in turn killed by his henchmen. Rassendyll is thus spared having to carry on the charade of being the last of the Elphbergs and presumed husband of Queen Flavia, who has, naturally, fallen in love with a husband so remarkably transformed into a model man. The rivalry in the two novels between two identikit swordsmen, equestrians and romantic athletes proved a shadowy prelude to the inevitable confrontation between two nations, so alike as to constitute virtual civil war.

∗　∗　∗

George Meredith did not choose a mythical county in which to set his 1880 novel, *The Tragic Comedians*. He had found a living case with which to compare his own fiction of the tempestuous passions of women, and the loyalty of men. His own marriage to Peacock's widowed daughter had been a searing experience, for she had effectively widowed him by absconding with the painter who had used him as a model for the death of Chatterton. But it had given him his life's work, to develop his own metaphysics of love, which was in many ways similar in ingredients to Wagner's. The potions and elixirs, however, were not created in the laboratory but in the chemistry of the mind. They had their own romantic inevitability and in *The Tragic Comedians* were to unfold in the intellectual hothouse of a Germany, where a tragic comedy had been enacted in real life.

Ferdinand Lassalle was a Prussian Jew in the mould of Moses Mendelssohn. He had risen from a lower class commercial background to become an intellectual, a follower of Hegel with whom he was to associate in a learned work on the Greek philosopher, Heraclitus. The work never saw the light of day as Lassalle was distracted by a law case between a husband and his separated wife over property and custody. To take up the case of the wife, he made a special study of the law and pursued her case, with forensic brilliance, through tribunal after tribunal, before forcing her husband to compromise. The case made his reputation as a lawyer, which survived the scandalous attempt on the part of the wife's friends to steal a casket from the husband that contained proof of a financial settlement on his mistress. Though Lassalle was acquitted of complicity, popular suspicion and rumour stuck to his name, not erased by his part in the 1848 rising in Dusseldorf that led to imprisonment and banishment from Berlin. He was reconciled to the Prussian authorities through the good offices of Alexander Humboldt, and while ingratiating himself with the authorities by arguing for Prussian dominance in Germany, he also became a champion of the working class. Though a member of the Communist League he was no friend of Marx, but nevertheless became the father of organised socialist thought, and unacknowledged inspiration of Bismarck's social policies.[7]

This, then, was the character of Meredith's Alvan, Jewish intellectual, protector of wronged womanhood, political firebrand and renowned and perfervid orator. Lassalle/Alvan falls in love with Helene von Dönniges/ Clotilde von Rüdiger. It is a tempestuous wooing and, in Meredith's words, evokes a torrent of infatuation for her brilliance and boldness of spirit and the liveliness of her wit. She is to be the soul mate of the eagle who is the lover, despite their difference in age, class, political proclivities and, above all, despite his Jewishness. The opposition of her aristocratic parents to such a misalliance is absolute. In the conviction that he must win them over by his eloquence Alvan allows his beloved, who has fled to him from her family home, to return to her parents, who then work on her by a mixture of cajolery and force to renounce him. Helene/Clotilde finds the pressure from her parents and from the man they wish her to marry, a decent but dyed-in-the-wool aristocrat, almost unbearable, but they manage to convince her that Alvan has in fact renounced her. She agrees to give him up whereupon Alvan, though a socialist and a man of peace who has no time for the customs of German aristocrats, invites the father to a duel. The challenge is met in proxy by the man Clotilde has consented to marry and, though a crack shot, Alvan is mortally wounded. So, in August 1864 in a duel fought over a similar offence, was Lassalle.

Meredith called his Alvan and Clotilde tragic comedians, playing a tragedy, for the ending is tragic, but also a comedy because, despite all protestations to the contrary, he believed that this happened only too often in real, not only in romantically tragic life. Clotilde marries her lover's killer. 'He was good, her misery had shrunk her into nothingness and she rose out of nothingness cold and bloodless, bearing a thought that she might make a good man happy.'[8] Meredith aspired to be the clinician of the human heart in relations between the genders, travelling so far along the path charted by George Eliot as to show that love and passion are not only emotional, but intellectual states, subject to all the doubts and betrayals of the human intellect. Alvan and Clotilde were (in their incarnation as Lassalle and Helene von Dönniges) fine laboratory specimens for Meredith's theory, that passionate love seldom survives all the pressures of human life. Real women are not Elsas, Sentas and Isoldes. Goethe and Schiller and Wagner may have created a metaphysic of love, but Meredith's was closer to *The Tales of Hoffmann*. His message was that such a metaphysic was a deception.

In the years up to 1871, Meredith had developed this theme in *The Adventures of Harry Richmond*. Through the intervention of his father, a plausible, ambitious adventurer and spendthrift, Richmond has fallen in love with a German princess, Ottilia of Eppenwelzen-Sarkeld, and she with him. Opposition to the liaison comes from both sides, from Prince Ernest who cannot bear the prospect of adulterating his blue native blood with that of an ordinary Englishman, the son of one of his retainers, and from Richmond's grandfather, who is the source of Harry's wealth and who cannot believe that a foreign princess could possibly be a suitable match for him. Meredith used Germany only as a setting for his analysis of relations between unequals – he had already essayed this ten years earlier in *Evan Harrington* – and Ottilia is at best a shadowy creature. The tale ends with both oppositions squared, and both parties married to the partners of their families' (if not Harry's father's) choice. Did they find love and not just contentment?

Harry's was not the alchemical fusion of a stallion of good bourgeois blood with a rich aristocratic filly, but in true comedic form it is a sane ending. Meredith had made Ottilia a princess to place her higher in the social scale, even more difficult to attain than Evan Harrington's upper-class beloved. The action could as easily have been set in any of Henry James's country houses, but that would not have given a role for Harry's father, who wished to overturn his reputation as an adventurer by storming the society to which he aspired with his son's royal marriage. The hero/villain of the book is Richmond père; he dominates the action, trying to rule everyone like puppets to achieve his grand desire, but Meredith, despite his florid language does not pretend that there is a mystical bond between Germany and England. Harry is more excited by gipsy girls, and Meredith's own predilection was for marrying within one's own race if not necessarily in one's own social class. Though Meredith's metaphysic of love was similar to that of Wagner's, he sought its consummation between tepid and comfortable lovers, not in a great symphony of passionate sound. Love in life was usually betrayed and something essentially more pragmatic, more English, than passion consummated in death, was his recipe for endurance.

∗ ∗ ∗

On a less heated level, English readers had been entertained with frissons of horror by tales of mystery since the end of the eighteenth century. Isabella Thorpe had their titles in her notebook when she met Catherine Morland in the pump room at Bath: *The Castle of Wolfenbach, a German Story* (1793) and *The Mysterious Warning, a German Tale* (1796) by Eliza Parsons;[9] *Necromancer, or a Tale of the Black Forest* (1794) translated from the German of Lawrence Flammenberg by Peter Teuthhold;[10] *The Midnight Bell, a German Story* (1798) by Francis Lathom;[11] *Orphan of the Rhine* (1798) by Eleanor Sleath;[12] *Horrid Mysteries, a Story from the German of the Marquis of Grosse* (1796) by Peter Will;[13] and *Clermont* (1798) by Regina Maria Roche.[14] Two of these were translations from the German and three claimed connection with Germany if only through their titles. But the Germans had been only too ready to see their land as fit to cause a shudder, lending itself, with the help of Gottfried Bürger's *Lenore,* to a general disposition to see it as a natural home for ghosts and other supernatural spectres.

Jane Austen, when she began *Northanger Abbey,* was gently mocking the popular taste for stories of horror, which are enjoying a revival in the horrid age of the twentieth and twenty-first centuries, in which the protagonists are rather malevolent extraterrestrial aliens than the walking or riding dead. In not being, like most of Ann Radcliffe's agents of horror, susceptible of a rational, even scientific explanation, the supernatural in these novels revived the English imagination that Germans were obsessed with the spirits of the forest, with witches, necromancers, water sprites and goblins, hostile and unfriendly to man, who was violating their immemorial fastnesses. They were the staple of the Gothic 'shudder' novel, fascinated as it was by the encounter of Romantic purity (the child of nature) with supernatural malevolence (the child of urban society). They pitted the Romantic fantasies of poets against the realities of corruption, deceit and violence. They also explored the shadowy and inexplicable world of spirits after death.

Mary Shelley in prefacing a revised edition of *Frankenstein* remembered the collection of German tales translated into French that had served to entertain the little gathering on the shores of Lake Geneva. In one, an inconstant lover returns to his deserted bride to find that he is embracing a pale ghost; in another the cursed founder of a dynasty is fated, as a ghost, to cause the death of all younger sons of his house to eternity.[15] The collection had appeared between 1811 and 1815. The French translation called *Fantasmagoriana* appeared in Paris in 1812, an English translation in London the following year. By 1831, when Mary Shelley wrote her preface to *Frankenstein*, interest in the ghostly supernatural was waning with a public sated by the fantasies of Mathew 'Monk' Lewis, by the violent wanderings of Charles Maturin's Melmoth, by the cynicism induced by prestidigitators and mediums, and above all by the evidence of a real 'super' in nature. It is most likely that Byron and his guests in the Villa Diodati spent more time discussing the extraordinary power of electricity, demonstrated by the student of Galvani, who had tried to galvanise a dead body, than migrations of the dead and vampires.[16] Nature had things more awesome and marvellous to show.

From this evening of ghostly *rapporteurs* emerged, eventually, Mary Shelley's *Frankenstein,* and the story of *The Vampyre*, abandoned by Byron, but adapted by his attendant doctor, John Polidori. Byron used the phantasm motif in his long poem on *The Siege of Corinth* where the ghost of the Turkish commander's *inamorata* appears to foretell his coming death, while Mary Shelley gave Frankenstein an awful nightmare when, thinking he was embracing his wife, he found it was the corpse of his dead mother. On a wet Sunday in August 1816, Mary had talked long with Byron and 'Monk' Lewis about ghosts, in which neither man believed – how could anyone who did not believe in God believe in ghosts? Mary thought such disbelief in the broad light of day might wane before the onset of night, and Lewis had told a number of ghost stories, which suggested that he collected them. They included one about a lady of the court of the Princess of Wales, Caroline of Mecklenburg, surely a believer in ghosts, witchcraft and magic, who had received a ghostly visitation from her husband when he was already dead of wounds on a battlefield.[17]

∗   ∗   ∗

In the eighteenth century, fear of the inhabitants of the night, of ghosts, werewolves and goblins receded before improvements in transport, in security and in street-lighting. Walking was becoming the most agreeable way of getting from one place to another, and this in it turn encouraged observations on the beauties of nature, even poetic rhapsodies upon it. This awareness was slow to grow. Even by 1749, if he noticed nature at all, Henry Fielding, author of the picaresquely pedestrianising novel, *Tom Jones*, was likely to phrase his description of it in the words of an anonymous classical author. He was more interested in the perversities and eccentricities of human behaviour. So was Dr Johnson; though he christened the periodical he almost entirely wrote from 1750 *The Rambler*, he rambled only in imagination as far as Ethiopia in *Rasselas* (in 1759). He did not actually take to rambling proper until Boswell took him off to Scotland 14 years later in 1773. Though sharing Fielding's poor impression of man's work, he was fired enough by what he saw of God's to record an account of his journey. He followed it by trips to Wales and Paris, his solitary incursion onto the continent.

Around him nature was buzzing. Thomas Pennant (1726–98) had written an account of his tour to Scotland in 1771, which had spurred Johnson to follow him, and was already in correspondence with the father of English naturalists in Selborne, Gilbert White (1720–93). White was not a rambler, for he lived in and wrote about one place only, his beloved birthplace, whence appeared in 1788 *The Natural History and Antiquities of Selborne*. It was written with the encouragement of letters from more travelled naturalists and advanced the growing passion for the picturesque, which between 1742 and 1745 had received a romantic drive from the *Night Thoughts on Life Death and Immortality* of Edward Young. The *Thoughts* had inspired Klopstock to meditate on nature and Klopstock had inspired Goethe, and it was not long before nature began to acquire a personality, even morality of its own, with lessons for humanity, inspiring goodness, peace and love, as well as providing occasions of awe, admiration and envy. Above all, it inspired the pathetic fallacy that it had sympathies and emotions similar to those of humans, seized by poets both as a device to humble man and as an example to exalt him. The discovery of nature in an ancient land during his travels to Italy helped to mature Goethe's belief that beauty and truth did not lie either in human storm and stress or in classical order and dignity, but in the natural word, which incorporated all God's creation, including man.

Coleridge and Wordsworth, who had both stomped along the wooded and mountain paths of Saxony to share Goethe's enthusiasm, rediscovered their charms in Cumbria. Linnaeus was classifying and labelling the contents of the Garden of Eden, inviting men with time on their hands to collect and classify in their turn, and the hitherto forbidding wildernesses of wood, wold and wildacre became the haunt of botanists and lepidopterists as enthusiastic as Johann Friedrich Blumenbach, Professor of Medicine at Coleridge's alma mater at Göttingen, in his search for variant skulls to fix the basis for racial classification. The passion for classification, which was to send Alexander Humboldt (who had also sat at the feet of Blumenbach[18]) and Aimé Bonpland round Spanish America, Spix and Martius into wild Brazil, and then Darwin round the South American cone in *The Beagle,* was not an impulse peculiarly German. It was, in its way, theological in its attempt to discover a non-Biblical rationale for Creation, hitherto just accepted as the work of the 'Immortal, Invisible, God only Wise' and 'hid from our eyes'. Even Joseph Haydn, after his English visit to the astronomer Herschel, saw *The Creation* in swirling, turbid technicolour, in which day followed night, and life followed chaos, and the rules of musical harmony reflected the rules of the Ineffable.

Coleridge, worried that German rationalism would subvert man's understanding of the numinous, tried to see in nature proof that reason was not inimical to an understanding of the goodness of God, to the existence of virtue, and to the triumph of Christian revelation. But he came perilously close to the lessons of nature 'red in tooth and claw', as he sailed in imagination with the Ancient Mariner. No witches or hobgoblins there but the ineluctable consequences of an action, naturally reprehensible. So also were actions to subvert the laws of nature, like creating a man from the galvanised portions of cadavers. Even Mary Shelley held that a man not created by God was irredeemable. Though the unnamed horror that Frankenstein had brought to life was educated by hearing a cottager read Volney's *Ruines ou Méditations sur les Révolutions des Empires* to his children, nature was too strong for nurture. Not being ruled by reason (Kant's *Vernunft*) the electrically animated monster could not understand (*Verstand*) the motives of human beings. Innocent of any deep understanding herself, Mary Shelley had nevertheless embarked on a theological dispute on the role of nature and nurture. No one today wants to animate the inanimate except at the protoplasmic origins of human life, (and the possibility of doing this was what really interested Mary and the Diodati denizens) but this battle still rumbles on.

* * *

The luminary to whom all moths flew to pay their homage had been, for over half a century, Wolfgang von Goethe. In him men saw the beacon for the German Renaissance. Religious innovators, philosophic system-makers, poetic romantics and dramatic tragedians abounded and, though Goethe would not have claimed to be supreme in any of these, he seemed to sit atop the mountain in judgment, dispensing or withholding Divine approval. His reading had been extensive, his learning encyclopaedic and though much of his thought was expressed in a mysterious code of language, he had something to say on everything. Abstemious in tastes, careful of his health, methodical in his lifestyle he was what Coleridge, but for laudanum, might well have been, a supreme interpreter of European culture. His *Table Talk*, in the record of his opinions made in *Conversations with Eckermann*, the authorship of which is sometimes ascribed to Goethe himself, ranges as wide as Coleridge's, delivering judgments on language, literature, theology, philosophy, drama, the novel, poetry, aesthetics, biology and cosmology. At one point he confesses, which Coleridge never did, that German philosophic speculation only made their style 'vague, difficult and obscure. The stronger their attachment to certain philosophic schools, the worse they write'. Even Schiller's noble style was noble only when he left off philosophising.[19] He acknowledged that German writers should 'seek now a stronghold in the literature of so able a nation of [sic, as?] the English'. Germany could not boast three literary heroes to be placed on a level with Byron, Thomas Moore or Walter Scott.[20] They had shown that English history was excellent for poetry 'because it is something genuine, healthy and therefore universal'.[21] His opinion of his countrymen would certainly at that time have appealed to the lighter-hearted English (though light-hearted could not be said of their English admirers like Carlyle), in thinking that 'by their deep thoughts and ideas … they make life more burdensome than is necessary'. Enthusiasm was not a component of his spirit for, in his view, a few centuries would have to elapse before Germans would appreciate beauty like the Greeks, before they would be inspired by beautiful song and before 'it will be said of them "it is long since they were barbarians"'.[22]

His memories of listening to the child Mozart may have faded, but beauty was always, once he had got *Götz* out of his system, Attic, sunlit and simple. Though Franz Schubert, who quarried among his work, died before Goethe himself, his music seems not to have penetrated to Weimar, where Eckermann, who knew that Goethe was not shy of self-praise, makes no mention of it. More poems by Goethe were set to music by German composers than ever English set their own poets, both as a recognition of his lyrical genius and as a reproach that the Master should have thought they would not appreciate songs unless they were Attic.

* * *

On the eve of the declaration of a German Empire under the Hohenzollerns, Goethe had been dead nearly 40 years. It had not taken centuries for Germany to move its heart from Pumpernickel to Potsdam. The Holy Roman Empire of minnesingers, knightly chivalry and mysticism had been reborn, but this empire was neither holy nor Roman, nor would Thackeray have recognised it. It may have had its minnesinger in Richard Wagner, and acknowledged Kant, and Moses Mendelssohn, Kleist, Hoffman and la Motte Fouqué as Prussians but they belonged to that romantic, kindlier, eccentric kingdom of Pumpernickel. Though an embedded and irrational Romanticism defied the Potsdam *Kulturkampf*, as it tried ideologically to Protestantise the empire, religion, of whatever flavour, was eventually to find itself in an embittered battle with Godless socialism for the soul of the people. The chivalry of the new empire was now to be loyalty to caste, neither Catholic nor Protestant, and to nation. It was to prove its credentials in war, and chivalry was only to survive in battles in the air, in which contesting pilots sought to unseat their opponents, not with sword, flail or axe, but with machine guns synchronised with aircraft propellers, and requiring a skill as exacting as remaining seated in a joust.[23]

Its mysticism was expressed in a cult of nationhood which exalted Frederick II as the progenitor of an enlightened Germany, based, as had been Frederick's Prussia, on vigorous discipline. The Hohenzollerns were Protestant enough to believe that a religion which had emerged from Lutheranism and Pietism should restate an image of God purged of superstitious reverence and assert an authority which had, in its time, given the Holy Roman Empire its raison d'être. But in the struggle in which conflicting national myths approached their end, the ideals of Romanticism and the poetry of *Goethezeit* eclogues, in all nations, died, vainly and uselessly, in the mud of Flanders.

Chronological Data

As the text roams freely across the period between its beginning and end, this list of dates, all given in the text, aims to give a timeframe.

1648	Treaty of Westphalia ends Thirty Years War.
1677	Eberhard Louis becomes tenth Duke of Württemberg, when one year old.
1679	Maximilian II rules Bavaria as Elector until 1726.
1685	Birth year of J. S. Bach, George Frederick Handel and Domenico Scarlatti.
1687	Newton writes *Principia Mathematica*.
1689	Hamburg opens first opera house in Germany.
1697	Augustus the Strong (1670–1733), Electoral Duke of Saxony, becomes Augustus II, King of Poland.
1701–14	War of Spanish Succession.
1701	Frederick, Elector of Brandenburg, becomes King *in* Prussia.
1705	Both J. S. Bach and Handel go to hear Buxtehude play the organ at Lubeck. Handel's first opera, *Almira*, is given at Hamburg.
1708	George Louis, Duke of Brunswick-Luneburg, becomes Elector of Hanover.
1710	Johann Friedrich Böttger discovers Chinese secret of making porcelain at Meissen.
1712	Maurice de Saxe, aged 12, starts his military career.
1713	Frederick William I (1688–1740) becomes King *in* Prussia.
1714	Elector George Louis of Hanover becomes King of England.
1716	Lady Mary Wortley Montagu in Hanover. Death of Leibniz.
1719	David Hume produces his *Treatise on Human Understanding*. Johann Philipp Franz von Schönborn becomes Bishop of Würzburg.
1721	Christian Wolff (1679–1554) dismissed by Frederick William I from his professorship at Halle.
1726	Maurice de Saxe (1696–1750) establishes his claim to the Duchy of Courland with a loan from Adriana Lecouvreur.
1730	Duke Eberhard's chateau at Ludwigsburg largely finished.
1733	Augustus II becomes Elector of Saxony and King, as Augustus III (1734), of Poland. Charles Eugene (1726–93) succeeds Eberhard as Duke of Württemberg.

1734	J. S. Bach's *Mass in B Minor* first performed at coronation of Augustus III of Poland.
1737	George II, King of England and Elector of Hanover, founds Göttingen University.
1738	Carl Philipp Emanuel Bach, born 1714, enters service of Frederick the Great (until 1768).
	Execution of Jew Süss (Oppenheimer, born 1698) in Württemberg.
1740	Frederick II 'The Great' (1712–86) becomes King *of* Prussia.
1741	Dresden opens its opera house.
1742	Publication of Edward Young's *Night Thoughts*.
1743	Moses Mendelssohn (1729–86) enters Berlin as a poor Jew.
1745	Maximilian III becomes Elector of Bavaria (till 1777).
1746	Augustus II of Saxony acquires picture collection of Maria Theresa of Austria.
1747	Carl Philipp Emanuel Bach appointed court composer by Frederick the Great.
1748	Friedrich Gottlieb Klopstock (1724–1803) produces the first three cantos of *The Messiah*.
1749	Birth of Goethe.
1750–2	Tiepolo family fresco residence in Würzburg.
1756–63	Seven Years War begins with Frederick the Great's invasion of Saxony.
1759	Voltaire writes *Candide*.
	Birth of Schiller.
1760	Casanova visits friends in Stuttgart, Württemberg.
1761	Haydn in service of Prince Esterhazy in Hungary.
1762–6	Christoph Wieland (1733–1813) translates 22 plays of Shakespeare.
1764	Boswell tours Germany.
	Winckelmann writes his *History of the Art of Antiquity*.
	Boswell visits Berlin.
1766	Gotthold Lessing (1729–81) writes *Laoköon*.
1767	Margrave of Baden abolishes torture.
	Moses Mendelssohn writes *Phaidon*.
1769	Alexander von Humboldt born (died 1859).
1770	Immanuel Kant (1724–1804) becomes Professor of Logic and Metaphysics at Königsburg.
1772	Dr Charles Burney tours Germany investigating music and musicians.
	Duchess of Weimar appoints Christoph Wieland (1713–1833) tutor to her children.
1773	Gottfried August Bürger (1747–94) publishes *Lenore* (*Leonora*).
	Goethe (1749–1842) writes *Götz of Berlichingen*.
	Haydn composes *L'Infedelta Delusa*, the first of four operas for Prince Esterhazy.
1774	Goethe writes *The Sorrows of Young Werther*.
	Christoph Willibald Gluck (1714–87) presents *Iphigénie en Aulide* in Paris.

1775	Charles Augustus assumes majority as Duke of Weimar and invites Goethe to join him.
1776	Goethe secures Johann Gottfried Herder (1744–1803) a post in Weimar.
	Friedrich Maximilian Klinger (1752–1831) writes the first of his *sturm und drang* plays.
1777	Charles Theodore, Elector Palatine, becomes Elector of Bavaria (until 1796).
	Goethe starts *Wilhelm Meister*, first part finished in 1796.
1778	Mozart in Mannheim hoping to be commissioned to write an opera.
1779–1800	Friedrich von Hardenberg aka Novalis (1772–1801) publishes his *Hymn to the Night*.
1779	Lessing writes *Nathan the Wise*.
1780	Joseph II succeeds Maria Theresa as ruler of the Austrian dominions.
1781	Friedrich Schiller (1759–1805) writes *The Robbers*.
1785	Rudolf Erich Raspe (1737–94) in London publishes *Baron Munchausen's Narrative of Marvellous Tales and Campaigns in Russia*.
	Casanova 'retires' to Bohemia as librarian to Count von Waldstein.
1786–8	Goethe visits Italy.
1786	John Moore visits Germany.
1787	Christian Schubart (1739–91) released from Württemberg prison at instance of Frederick the Great.
	Schiller writes most of *Don Carlos* in Dresden.
1792	Wilhelm von Humboldt (1767–1835) seeks to define the limits of state education.
1793	Death of Charles Eugene of Württemberg.
1794	Ann Radcliffe writes *The Mysteries of Udolpho*.
1796	Wordsworth and Coleridge visit Germany.
1797	Goethe visiting Württemberg is shocked by Ducal extravagance.
	Goethe publishes *Hermann and Dorothea*.
	Friedrich Schelling (1775–1854) produces *Ideen zu einer Philosophie der Natur* and becomes 'father of *Naturphilosophie*'.
1798	August Wilhelm Schlegel (1767–1845) begins translating Shakespeare in Jena.
	Samuel Taylor Coleridge (1772–1834) produces *The Rime of the Ancient Mariner*.
1799	Schiller writes *Wallenstein*.
	Walter Scott translates Goethe's *Götz von Berlichingen*.
1800	Coleridge translates Schiller's *Wallenstein*.
1803	Adalbert von Chamisso (1781–1838) founds *The Berlin Museum Almanack*.
1805	Death of Schiller.
1806	Francis II resigns the title Holy Roman Emperor and becomes Francis I of Austria.
	Frederick Augustus III, Elector of Saxony, becomes King Frederick Augustus I.

Elector Maximilian IV becomes King of Bavaria and Elector. Frederick becomes King of Württemberg.

Napoleon defeats Prussia at Jena.

1807   Jerome Bonaparte (1784–1860) created King of Westphalia [former Confederation of the Rhine (1806)].

Alexander Humboldt (1769–1850) publishes in Paris his *Voyage to the Southern Region of the New Continent* made in 1799–1804.

1808   Goethe meets Napoleon at Erfurt.

Karl Wilhelm Friedrich Schlegel (1772–1829) publishes *On the Language and Wisdom of India*.

Goethe publishes *Faust* part 1 (part 2 published in 1832).

1809   Prince Metternich (1773–1859) becomes Austrian Foreign Minister.

Wilhelm Humboldt heads Department for Church and Education in Berlin.

1810   Four Viennese painters (Johann Friedrich Overbeck 1789–1869, Peter von Cornelius et al.) establish the Nazarene artistic community in Rome.

Heinrich Wilhelm von Kleist (1771–1811) produces *The Marquise of O*.

E. T. A. Hoffmann reviews Beethoven's 5th symphony.

1812–15   The Brothers Grimm write their *Fairy Tales (Kinder und Hausmarchen)*.

1812   la Motte Fouqué (1777–1843) writes *Undine*.

1813   Mme de Staël writes *De l'Allemagne*.

William Wordsworth writes *The Excursion*.

August Wilhelm Schlegel: *Lectures on Dramatic Art and Literature*.

Friedrich Schlegel: *History of Ancient & Modern Literature*.

S. T. Coleridge writes *Christabel* (published 1816).

Goethe publishes his *Italian Journey*.

E. T. A. Hoffmann (1776–1822) writes *The Sandman*.

Georg Wilhelm Friedrich Hegel publishes his *Encyclopaedia of Philosophical Sciences*.

Franz Schubert composes *Death and the Maiden*.

Samuel Prout (1783–1852) begins to tour Europe to record the picturesque features of its architecture.

Birth of Richard Wagner.

1814   Hanover becomes a kingdom.

Hoffmann writes the opera *Undine*.

1816   Byron takes a trip down the Rhine.

1818   Karl Marx born in Prussian Rhineland.

Caspar David Friedrich (1774–1840) paints *The Wanderer above the Mists*.

1819   Assassination of August Friedrich von Kotzebue (born 1761) by a Jena student.

1820   Heinrich von Kleist (1777–1811) writes *The Prince of Homburg*.

Goethe writes *Wilhelm Meister*.

1821   Alexander Humboldt produces his account of his Russian expedition: *Voyage Round the World*.

Thomas Carlyle (1795–1831) translates *Wilhelm Meister*.

1823	Carl Maria von Weber (1786–1826) presents *Euryanthe* in Dresden.
	Karl Friedrich Schinkel (1781–1841) paints *A Gothic Temple by Water*.
1825	Ludwig I (1786–1868) becomes King of Bavaria.
1826	Felix Mendelssohn (1808–1847) composes the overture to *A Midsummer Night's Dream*.
1827	Walter Scott publishes his *Life of Napoleon Buonaparte*.
	Julius Hare (1795–1855) translates Niebuhr's *History of Rome*.
1829	Walter Scott publishes *Anne of Geierstein*.
	Prince Otto of Bavaria elected King of Greece.
	Goethe's *Conversations with Eckermann* appears.
1830	Thackeray in Weimar.
1832	Thomas Carlyle writes *Sartor Resartus*.
	Goethe publishes *Faust* part 2 and dies.
1833	Coleridge assembles *Table Talk*.
	Wagner writes *Die Feen* (*The Fairies*).
1834	Wilhelm von Humboldt: *On the Diversity of Human Language Construction*.
	Wagner's *Rienzi* performed in Dresden.
	Charles Eastlake (1793–1865) translates Goethe's *Theory of Colours*.
	Donizetti produces *Maria Stuarda* at Naples.
1837	Princess Victoria succeeds William IV as Queen of England.
1840	Carlyle writes *Heroes and Hero Worship*.
	Ruskin writes volume 1 of *Modern Painters*.
1841	Prince Albert appoints a commission for the fresco decoration of the British Houses of Parliament.
1842	Thackeray's *The Fitzboodle Papers* appear in *Fraser's Magazine*.
1844	Thackeray writes *Barry Lyndon*.
1845	Wagner writes *Tännhauser*.
1846	Lola Montes (1821–61) meets Ludwig I of Bavaria in Munich.
	Felix Mendelssohn produces *Elijah* in Birmingham.
1848	Young artists meet at house of John Millais to found the Pre-Raphaelite Brotherhood.
1850	Franz Liszt mounts Wagner's *Lohengrin* at Weimar.
1851	Otto von Bismarck, a member of the Frankfurt Diet, concludes that Prussia must assume the leadership of Germany.
1855	George Lewes produces his *Life of Goethe*.
1858–65	Carlyle writes *Frederick the Great*.
1862	Christina Rossetti produces *Goblin Market*.
1863	Edouard Manet paints *Le Déjeuner sur l'Herbe*.
1864	Ferdinand Lassalle (1825–64) meets Helene von Dönniges and is mortally wounded in a duel with her fiancé.
1865	First performance of Wagner's *Tristan und Isolde*, in Munich.
1868	Wagner's *Die Meistersinger von Nürnberg* presented in Munich.
1880	George Meredith writes *The Tragic Comedians*.

Jacques Offenbach (1819–80) starts but does not finish *The Tales of Hoffmann*.

1882   Wagner's last opera, *Parsifal*, is staged at Bayreuth.

1894   Anthony Hope writes *The Prisoner of Zenda*.

Notes

Introduction

1 Berlin, Isaiah, 'Georges Sorel', in C. Abramsky (ed.), *Essays in Honour of E. H. Carr* (London, 1974), p. 21.

2 Ashton, Rosemary, *Thomas & Jane Carlyle, Portrait of a Marriage* (London, 2003), p. 195. The coinage may be attributed to Leigh Hunt.

Chapter 1

1 Thackeray, W. M., *Vanity Fair* (London, 1847–8), chapters 62–3.

2 A brass wind instrument developed from the serpent, a S-shaped instrument making a deep bass sound and much in use in the eighteenth and nineteenth centuries in English, and German, church bands.

3 Thackeray, W. M., *Vanity Fair*, chapter 63.

4 There was a ceremony redolent of Pumpernickel during Queen Elizabeth II's visit to Brazil in 1969, when a suitcase full of minor Brazilian orders arrived at the British embassy in Rio de Janeiro from the Brazilian foreign affairs ministry. British staff could not accept any of them, which were delightedly pillaged by the non-British members of the embassy establishment.

5 Thackeray, W. M., 'The Fitzboodle Papers' (1842–3), in *Burlesques* (London: Thomas Nelson, 1907), pp. 452–81.

6 Goethe, Johann Wolfgang von, *Conversations with Eckermann*, translated by Wallace Wood (New York, 1901), pp. 218–19. Entry for 5 July 1827.

7 Thackeray's letter to his mother, quoted in D. J. Taylor, *Thackeray* (London, 1999), p. 81.

8 Letter to George Lewes, 28 April 1855, in W. M. Thackeray, *Essays, Reviews etc* (London: Thomas Nelson, 1904), pp. 407–10.

9 Thackeray, *The Fitzboodle Papers*, p. 471.

10 *Ibid.*, p. 474.

11 Burney, Charles, *The Present State of Music in Germany, the Netherlands and United Provinces* (London, 1773 [facsimile reprint, London: Travis & Emery, 2008]) vol. ii, p. 100, ii, p. 8.

12 Boswell, James, *On the Grand Tour: Germany and Switzerland, 1764* (London: Frederick Pottle, 1953), pp. 9, 48, 69. Entries for 13 and 24 June, 4 and 24 August 1764.

13 Moore, John, *A View of Society and Manners in France, Switzerland and Germany*, 1786, vol. 2 (Montana US, no date), p. 16.

14 Wilson, Frances, *The Ballad of Dorothy Wordsworth* (London, 2008), pp. 91–3.

Chapter 2

1 Friedrich, *The Age of the Baroque, 1610–1660* (New York, 1952), p. 195. The worst affected states were Bohemia, Württemberg, Saxony and minor principalities in Thuringia.

2 Moore, *A View of Society and Manners in France, Switzerland and Germany, 1786*, pp. 42, 121, 140–4, 150. Dukes were sovereigns and every son of a Duke was a prince, 'although he had as many as old King Priam'.

3 Boyle, Nicholas, *Goethe, The Poet and the Age*, vol. 1 *The Poetry of Desire, 1749–1790* (Oxford, 1991), p. 9. The Imperial knights claimed sovereign rights over about 200,000 citizens. A higher figure (350,000) is in Tim Blanning, *The Pursuit of Glory: Europe 1648–1815* (London, 2007), p. 278.

4 Blanning, *The Pursuit of Glory: Europe 1648–1815*, pp. 276–8. A degree of check on autocracy was exercised, far from democratically, by the existence of time-honoured Estates – in most of the larger principalities – and of city councils, rural magistratures and ecclesiastical chapters.

5 Burney, *The Present State of Music in Germany, the Netherlands and United Provinces*, vol. i, p. 73; C. H. Glover, *Dr Charles Burney's Continental Travels, 1770 to 1772* (London, 1927), p. 163.

6 Blanning, *The Pursuit of Glory: Europe 1648–1815*, p. 87. The number of Huguenot migrants was enhanced later in the century when the French invaded the Palatinate in 1689, causing another displacement of population. Immigrants with skills were given special privileges, like exemption from military service. States enhanced their economic power by selective immigration, caused both by religious intolerance and by economic hardship. By 1720 every fifth citizen in Berlin was either a Huguenot or of Huguenot origin.

7 Gay, Peter, *The Enlightenment: an Interpretation* (London, 1966), p. 150.

8 Carlyle, Thomas, 'Goethe's Works', in *Critical & Miscellaneous Essays*, vol. 3 (Boston: Brown & Taggart, 20 and 29 Cornhill, 1860), p. 197.

9 Carlyle, Thomas, 'State of German Literature' (1827), in *Critical & Miscellaneous Essays*, vol. 1 (Boston: Brown & Taggart, 20 and 29 Cornhill, 1860), p. 30. Not all potentates however were admirers of French culture. Frederick II's father, Frederick William I, was bitterly opposed, on Germanic principle, to his son's French 'fopperies, flutings, cockatoo fashions of hair'. Thomas Carlyle, *The History of Frederick II of Prussia called Frederick the Great* (London: Chapman and Hall, 1892), 2, book 4, chapter 12, p. 67.

10 Voltaire, F. M. Arouet, *Candide* (London and Paris, 1759 [Novel Library ed., London, 1947]), chapter 1.

11 Being generally well-disposed to France he became, first, Elector of Baden in a Napoleonic reorganisation of the Rhineland in 1803, and then, when Francis II suppressed the title of Holy Roman Emperor, Grand-Duke.

12 Carlyle, 'German Literature', p. 48; 'Count Cagliostro', pp. 379–82, in *Essays*, vol. 3.

13 *'L'Allemagne fourmille de princes, ducs, don't les trois-quarts n'ont pas un esprit sain.'* The Comte de Manteufel, quoted by Adrien Fauchier-Magnan, *Les Petites Cours d'Allemagne au XVIII Siècle* (Paris, 1947), p. 43.

14 Quoted in H. H. Herwig, *Hammer or Anvil, Modern Germany 1648 to the Present* (Lexington, 1994), p. 1.

15 Moore, *A View of Society and Manners in France, Switzerland and Germany, 1786*, p. 40.

16 Fauchier-Magnan, *Les Petites Cours d'Allemagne au XVIII Siècle,* p. 98.

17 Burney, *The Present State of Music in Germany, the Netherlands and United Provinces*, vol. i, p. 103; Glover, *Dr Charles Burney's Continental Travels, 1770 to 1772*, p. 116.

18 Mauch, Christof (ed.), *Nature in German History* (New York/Oxford, 2004), p. 3.

19 Moore, *A View of Society and Manners in France, Switzerland and Germany, 1786*, p. 30.

20 Glover, *Dr Charles Burney's Continental Travels, 1770 to 1772*, p. 211.

21 Thackeray, *Barry Lyndon*, chapters 6 and 7.

22 Moore, *A View of Society and Manners in France, Switzerland and Germany, 1786*, p. 42.

23 Quoted in Fauchier-Magnan, *Les Petites Cours d'Allemagne au XVIII Siècle*, p. 98.

24 Fauchier-Magnan, *Les Petites Cours d'Allemagne au XVIII Siècle*, p. 48.

25 Boswell, *On the Grand Tour: Germany and Switzerland, 1764*, 4 September 1764.

26 The *staatssicherheit*, State Security Service of the former German Democratic Republic, was not as efficient in deterring defection as Frederick's military system of firing a gun to mark a desertion and mobilising the population to hunt the deserter down.

27 Moore, *A View of Society and Manners in France, Switzerland and Germany*, 1786, pp. 121, 140–3, 144, 150.

28 Boswell, *On the Grand Tour: Germany and Switzerland, 1764*, p. 66, 20 August 1764.

29 Moore, *A View of Society and Manners in France, Switzerland and Germany, 1786*, pp. 76–7.

30 Giuseppe Balsamo (1743–95) liked to be known as Cagliostro. Goethe, who was a genuine scientist, disapproved of such genuine fraudsters and was not above deceiving Cagliostro's mother, Felicità Balsamo, whom he found in Palermo living in poverty. He claimed to know her son, promising her that he was alive and well and at liberty in France. He offered to take her blessings and a letter to him. He did not admit to being a friend, only that all Europe knew Cagliostro, but as he had left his family in penury he decided that it would be too much trouble to take a letter which the charlatan might not wish to receive; he also thought he might pay off the debt for which Cagliostro had fled Palermo and which hung over his family, but thought better of it. A man less confessional by habit might have kept this little episode untold. *Italienische Reise (Italian Journey),* diary entry, Palermo, 13–14 April 1787. In 1791 Goethe wrote a cruel comedy about Cagliostro and the Diamond Necklace Affair, which he called *The Great Coptha (Der Grosse Coptha)*.

31   The titles of Joseph II, for example, were over 40 in number, from Roman Emperor
      and King of Hungary to Prince of Here and Lord of There, Duke of This and
      Archduke of That. Blanning, *The Pursuit of Glory: Europe 1648–1815*, p. 28, lists
      many of them, quoting one description of the empire as a 'centripetal agglutination
      of bewilderingly heterogeneous elements'.

32   Senesino (1685–1758), was, as his name implied, a Sienese who created 17 of
      Handel's leading operatic roles after joining his orchestra in London in 1720.

33   A one-act *serenata* performed in 1766 after a piece by Metastasio. A royal wedding
      is to take place and Parnassus is at sixes and sevens over how to celebrate it suitably.
      The four archduchesses are reprimanded by Apollo for their indecision, but at
      length he declares that he is confident that they will eventually produce something
      worthy of the occasion.

34   Burney, *The Present State of Music in Germany, the Netherlands and United Provinces*, vol.
      i, p. 177.

35   *Ibid.*, pp. 205, 327–8; Glover, *Dr Charles Burney's Continental Travels, 1770 to 1772*,
      pp. 161–2.

36   Thackeray, W. M., 'George the First', in *The Four Georges*, (London: Everyman
      edition, 1857) p. 294.

37   Thackeray, W. M., 'George the Second', in *The Four Georges*, p. 350.

38   Montagu, Lady Mary Wortley, *Letters* (London: Everyman edition, 1909), p. 84:
      letter of 1 December (old style) 1716.

39   Thackeray, 'George the First', in *The Four Georges*, p. 296.

40   Carlyle, 'The Prinzenraub', in *Essays*, vol. 4, p. 489.

41   Goethe's salary as a Privy Councillor in Weimar was 1,200 thalers and this did not
      rise markedly for the rest of his life.

42   Locke, John, *An Essay Concerning Human Understanding* (London, 1690 [Everyman
      ed., 1947), book 4, chapter 19, section 4, p. 340.

43   Carlyle, 'Goethe's Works', in *Essays*, vol. 3, pp. 193–4.

Chapter 3

1   Eckermann, Johann Peter, *Conversations with Goethe*, trans. by Wallace Wood (New
      York, 1901) p. 195. Entry for 11 April 1827, records Goethe as quoting Lessing
      differently: 'If God would give him truth, he would decline the gift, and prefer the
      labour of seeking for it himself.'

2   Gay, *The Enlightenment: an Interpretation*, p. 21. Kant defined Enlightenment as
      mankind's exit from its self-incurred immaturity. MacCulloch, p. 803.

3   MacCulloch, pp. 740–1. The University of Halle emerged in 1694 from a medical-
      charitable endowment of an orphanage, medical clinic, schools for poor children
      and teacher training, and a printing press, designed to ensure that all children should
      learn to read the Bible and a practical skill. The institution too had a mission to
      convert the Jews of Eastern Europe as preparation for the End of Time. It became
      the powerhouse of north European Pietism.

4   Berlin, Isaiah, *The Magus of the North: J. G. Hamann & the Origins of Modern Irrationalism* (New York, 1993), p. 5.

5   Boyle, Nicholas, *Goethe, The Poet and the Age*, vol. 2, *The Poetry of Desire, 1749–1790* (Oxford, 1991), p. 41.

6   Preface to 2nd (1787) edition of Kant, Immanuel, *Critique of Pure Reason* (London Everyman ed., 1948 [1787]), p. 18.

7   Stark, W., 'Literature & Thought: The Romantic Tendency', in *The New Cambridge Modern History*, vol. viii (1965), p. 79.

8   Carlyle, 'German Literature', *Essays*, vol. i, p. 78.

9   Goethe, *Conversations with Eckermann*, p. 196, entry for 11 April 1827.

10 Carlyle, *Schiller*, p. 86. Goethe's sentence, p. 185, comes from his account of his friendship with Schiller.

11 Carlyle, *Life of Friedrich Schiller* (London, 1893), p. 87, quoting Goethe.

12 The name *sturm und drang* derived from a tragedy of that name by Friedrich Klinger (1752–1831) in 1760, which seemed to epitomise the movement. Klinger was a childhood friend of Goethe's, who helped him through university. He wrote throughout his life, first as a theatre director, later as a soldier in Austrian, then Russian service. His plays were deeply tinged with pessimism from the hard struggle of his growing up without a father who died when he was a child. He married a natural child of the Empress Catherine and her grandson, Alexander I, put him in charge of the University of Dorpat in 1803, where he expounded the ideas that had led to storm and stress.

13 Gay, *The Enlightenment: an Interpretation*, p. 5.

14 Quoted by Sarah Symmons in an essay on Winckelmann in *The Listener* of 19 October 1972.

15 Carlyle, 'German Literature', *Essays*, vol. i, p. 51. No edition of Lessing's work was available in English in the land of Carlyle's readers.

16 Gay, *The Enlightenment: an Interpretation*, p. 113.

17 Blunt, Wilfred, *On Wings of Song, a Biography of Felix Mendelssohn* (London, 1974), p. 14.

18 Frederick never allowed either Lessing or Mendelssohn to be nominated to the Academy, partly from distrust of their theology but partly because he wished its members to be Prussians. Johann van der Zanden, 'Prussia and the Enlightenment', in P. G. Dwyer, *The Rise of Prussia 1700–1830* (Harlow, 2000).

19 Burke, Edmond 'Reflections on the Revolution in France', p. 127, in vol. 8 of *The Writings and Speeches of Edmund Burke* (Oxford, 1979).

20 Berlin, *The Magus of the North: J. G. Hamann & the Origins of Modern Irrationalism*. Paraphrasing J. G. Hamann, p. 113.

Chapter 4

1   Carlyle, *Essays*, vol. 1, p. 454. Appendix; Preface and Introduction to the book called 'German Romance'.

2   In 1809, as part of Napoleonic adjustments in Germany Charles-Augustus became Duke of Saxe-Weimar Eisenach and in 1815 he was elevated to Grand-Duke after the fall of Napoleon Bonaparte.

3   Lewes, George Henry, *The Life of Goethe* (London: Everyman edition, 1908), pp. 196–7.

4   Lewes, *The Life of Goethe*, p. 207.

5   *Ibid.*, p. 217.

6   See chapter 15.

7   Goethe, *Conversations with Eckermann,* p. 119, entry for 27 April 1825.

8   Carlyle, 'Goethe', *Essays,* vol. 1, p. 465.

9   Lewes, *The Life of Goethe*, p. 441. Some virtual Weimar dramas adapted well to opera: Gounod's *Faust*, Verdi's *Don Carlos*, Donizetti's *Mary Stuart* and Rossini's *William Tell,* after plays by Goethe and Schiller, were performed there, the lyric imperative to produce a hummable tune and show-stopping arias or ensembles giving them the dramatic edge they lacked under Goethe's rather unimaginative direction.

10 The second part, exploring the possibilities of redemption, followed 24 years later.

11 Coleridge, Samuel Taylor, *Table Talk, Specimens* (London: HNC, 1835), vol. ii, p. 114. Lewes, *The Life of Goethe*, p. 483.

12 Burney, *The Present State of Music in Germany, the Netherlands and United Provinces*, vol. ii, p. 248.

13 Lewes, *The Life of Goethe*, p. 486.

14 *Ibid.*, p. 530, quoting from Luden's *Rückbliche in Mein Leben*, p. 113 et seq.

15 Carlyle, 'German Literature', *Essays,* vol. i, p. 49.

16 Gay, 'The German Enlightenment', in *The Age of Enlightenment* (Netherlands, 1966), p. 147.

17 Lewes, *The Life of Goethe*, p. 53.

18 Goethe, *Conversations with Eckermann*, pp. 128–9, entry for 20 April 1825, wrote that 'love of truth in conflict with error induced him to make his pure light shine even into [the] the darkness' of Newton's 'great error, highly injurious to the human mind'. It led him to spend many hours producing his theory of colours, which is of some interest to art historians.

19 Carlyle, quoting Goethe in 'Goethe's Works', *Essays,* vol. 3, p. 190.

20 Lewes, *The Life of Goethe*, p. 136.

21 Carlyle, 'Goethe's Works', in *Essays,* vol. 3, p. 199. William Morris, reading Carlyle's translation of *Wilhelm Meister* in 1869, found it heavy going but acknowledged its genius. The mutual attraction of a married couple for two other people was not, given the strict marriage conventions about the sanctity of marriage, a comfortable theme for Victorian readers, many of whom, like Morris, experienced it in their own marriages. Fiona MacCarthy, *William Morris, A Life for Our Times* (London, 1994), p. 236.

22 Carlyle, Preface and Introduction to 'German Romance', in *Essays,* vol. 1, p. 456.

23 Boyle, vol. 1, p. 30.

24 Carlyle, 'Goethe's Works', in *Essays*, vol. 3, p. 191.

25 Quoted by Tim Blanning, *The Romantic Revolution* (London, 2010), p. 98.

26 George Lewes, *The Life of Goethe*, p. 109, saw in Götz, otherwise a lawless freebooter, a touch of Robin Hood chivalry as 'he was found on the side of the weak and persecuted. To his strong arm the persecuted looked for protection.' Winckelmann had converted himself to Grecian realities in the Dresden gallery and, after service with cardinal Albani in Rome, had made himself champion of all that was Greek, noble and beautiful – indeed the only true beauty – in art.

27 Goethe believed that the reputation of Tasso the poet was annihilated by comparison with Byron. 'With a single line of *Don Juan* one could poison the whole of *Gerusalemme Liberata*', Goethe, *Conversations with Eckermann*, p. 75, entry for 18 May 1824.

28 Boyle, vol. 1, p. 25.

29 Blanning, *The Romantic Revolution*, p. 62.

30 Carlyle, 'Goethe's Works', in *Essays*, vol. 3, p. 197.

31 Burney, *The Present State of Music in Germany, the Netherlands and United Provinces*, vol. ii, p. 248.

32 Berlin, *The Magus of the North: J. G. Hamann & the Origins of Modern Irrationalism*, pp. 2, 19.

33 Carlyle, Thomas, 'The Landed', book 4, chapter 6, in *Past and Present* (Collins Classic edition, 1843), p. 313.

34 Robertson, J. G., 'Literature in Germany', in *Cambridge Modern History*, vol. 10 (Cambridge, 1907), p. 386.

Chapter 5

1 Carlyle, Thomas, *Life of Friedrich Schiller (1825) and Life of John Sterling (1851)* (London, 1893), p. 12.

2 *Ibid.*, reproduces the manifesto on p. 176.

3 Fauchier-Magnan, *Les Petites Cours d'Allemagne au XVIII Siècle*, p. 227. Goethe, years later thought it was the duke himself that said these words. Goethe, *Conversations with Eckermann*, p. 158, entry for 17 January 1827.

4 Quoted in Nancy Mitford, *Frederick the Great* (London, 1970), p. 287.

5 Carlyle, *Life of Friedrich Schiller (1825) and Life of John Sterling (1851)*, p. 161, reproduces a letter dated 2 May 1788, to his Mannheim patron, Wolfgang Dalberg, director of the theatre that put on *The Robbers*.

6 Carlyle gives a critical analysis of these plays in his *Life of Schiller*; *Don Carlos*, pp. 52–64 (of this play he wrote that Schiller's genius was 'impetuous, exuberant, majestic; and a heavenly fire gleams through all his creations. He transports to a holier and higher world.' p. 64); *Wallenstein*, pp. 101–82, *Mary Stuart*, pp. 118–21, *Joan of Arc* (*The Maid of Orleans*), pp. 121–32 and *William Tell*, pp. 135–45. For Coleridge's treatment of *Wallenstein* and *Mary Stuart*, see chapter 10.

7 Verdi *I Masnadieri* (*The Robbers*), *Luisa Miller* (*Kabale und Liebe* [*Intrigue and Love*]), *Giovanna d'Arco*, and *Don Carlos*; Donizetti *Mary Stuart* and Rossini *William Tell*.

8   Carlyle quoting *Uber die Aesthetische Erziehung des Menschen*, in 'German Literature', *Essays*, vol. i, p. 62.

9   Carlyle, *Life of Friedrich Schiller (1825) and Life of John Sterling (1851)*, p. 18.

10 Praz, Mario, *The Romantic Agony* (Oxford: Collins paper edition, 1932 [1960]), p. 77.

11 Schiller, Friedrich von, *The Robbers* and *Wallenstein*, translated by F. J. Lamport (Harmondsworth: Penguin Books, 1979), act 5, scene 2, p. 159.

12 Lamport, F. J., p. 10. The play was *Clavigo*.

13 Carlyle, *Life of Friedrich Schiller (1825) and Life of John Sterling (1851)*, p. 18.

14 Carlyle, 'To Madeira', chapter 5, *Life of Friedrich Schiller (1825) and Life of John Sterling (1851)*. Sterling to Carlyle, 16 November 1837.

15 See chapter 1: *Fitzboodle in Pumpernickel*.

16 Lockhart, John Gibson, *The Life of Sir Walter Scott* (London: Everyman edition, 1906), p. 315.

17 Boyle, vol. 1, pp. 5–7.

18 Burney, *The Present State of Music in Germany, the Netherlands and United Provinces*, vol. i, p. 196.

19 Carlyle, 'German Literature', *Essays*, vol. 1, p. 41. In the original *Hansel & Gretel* story it was the natural parents who decided that there was not enough food for the family and to lose the children in the forest to starve or be eaten by wild animals. The savagery of this was too strong and the mother was transmogrified by the Grimms into a stepmother who might be more guilty of such unnatural behaviour. By the time Humperdinck composed his opera in 1893 for Weimar both parents had been acquitted of unnatural designs. They had been careless, and were reunited after the witch's death in a happy family. Julian Johnson, 'Kindergarten Wagner – for Grown Ups', pp. 105–8, programme note for the Glyndebourne Festival, 2010.

20 In Terry Gilliam's film, *The Brothers Grimm* (2005), the evil and enchanted forest assumes the characteristic of the treacherous scenario of the later sagas of Hogwarts, the school for warlocks invented by J. K. Rowling. She marries the eighteenth century world of sinister fantasy to the contemporary world of cars and trains. The triumph of good over evil is left as ambivalent in her stories as in those of the Brothers Grimm.

21 Fates meted out in *Snowdrop, The Three Dwarfs* and *Mother Holle* (Grimm, Jacob & Wilhelm, *The Complete Fairy Tales*, translated by Jack Zipps (London, 2002), pp. 119–22) in Andrew Lang (ed.), *The Red Fairy Book* (New York, 1966 edition), pp. 339, 245, 306 respectively. The fate of *Cinderella*, Grimm, pp. 106–14. See also Marina Warner, *From the Beast to the Blonde* (London, 1994), p. 211.

22 Warner, *From the Beast to the Blonde*, p. 41.

23 Goethe, *Conversations with Eckermann*, pp. 340–1, entry for 17 March 1830.

24 Berlin, *The Magus of the North: J. G. Hamann & the Origins of Modern Irrationalism*, pp. 27–8.

25 Roberts, John M., *The Mythology of the Secret Societies* (London, paperback edition, 1972 [2008]), pp. 52–3.

26 *Ibid.*, p. 114.

27 *Ibid.*, pp. 121–4.

28 *Ibid.*, pp. 132–49.

29 *Ibid.*, p. 148.

30 Joseph-Marie, Comte de Maistre, 'The Saint Petersburg Dialogues (Les Soirées de St Petersburg)', 1821, Eleventh Dialogue, in *Works* edited by J. Lively (London, 1965). Illuminism was an omnium gatherum term for sects that wished to upset the status quo, and included in their time levellers, Jacobins, radicals, *carbonari,* independents and liberals, some of whom were freemasons, but most were not. Roberts, *The Mythology of the Secret Societies*, p. 317.

31 Berlin, *The Magus of the North: J. G. Hamann & the Origins of Modern Irrationalism*, pp. 29–30.

32 The expression 'natural society' was used by William Vaughan in a broadcast on BBC Radio Three for the *Deutsche Romantik* season.

33 Mauch, *Nature in German History*, p. 5.

34 See chapter 17.

35 Lewes, *The Life of Goethe*, p. 100.

36 Robertson, 'Literature in Germany', in *Cambridge Modern History*, vol. 10, pp. 395–8, for a tentative and essentially neutral discussion of the definitions of German Romanticism.

37 Blanning, *The Romantic Revolution*, pp. 151–4. Friedrich Klopstock wrote a trilogy in praise of Hermann in 1769 (*Hermann's Battle*), 1784 (*Hermann and the Priests*) and in 1787 (*Hermann's Death*), in which, in Blanning's words, Germans showed all the virtues of 'modesty, chastity, piety, humanity, morality and devotion to justice, duty and self-sacrifice'.

38 Goethe, *Conversations with Eckermann*, p. 129, entry for 15 October 1825.

Chapter 6

1 Thackeray, W. M., 'George the First', in *The Four Georges*, p. 301.

2 Montagu, *Letters*, letter to Lady Rich, Hanover, 1 December (OS) 1716, p. 84.

3 Burney, *The Present State of Music in Germany, the Netherlands and United Provinces*, vol. i, p. 79; Coleridge, 'Cologne', in William B. Scott (ed.), *The Poetical Works of Samuel Taylor Coleridge* (London: George Routledge & Son, no date), p. 376.

4 Thackeray, 'George the First', in *The Four Georges*, p. 303, lists them by function. In 2005 there were about 300 palace servants at Buckingham Palace.

5 Carlyle, Thomas, *The History of Frederick II of Prussia called Frederick the Great*, vol. ii, book 5, chapter 1, p. 85.

6 Thackeray, 'George the First', in *The Four Georges*, p. 306.

7 Carlyle, *The History of Frederick the Great*, vol. i, book 1, chapter 3, p. 36; Thackeray, in *The Four Georges*, p. 309, believed his body was burned by his assassins.

8 Thackeray, 'George the first', in *The Four Georges*, pp. 306–9.

9 Voltaire, F. M. Arouet, *The History of Charles XII* (1731), in translation of Winifred Todhunter (London: Everyman edition), pp. 74–5.

10 Carlyle, *The History of Frederick II of Prussia called Frederick the Great*, vol. 2, book 6, chapter 3, p. 219, put the number of progeny at 354.

11 The incident with Mme Orzelska is in Carlyle, *The History of Frederick II of Prussia called Frederick the Great*, vol. ii, book 6, chapter 3, pp. 217–20. Another account by the Crown Princess of Prussia Wilhelmina stated that the lady was 'in the condition of our First Parents … more beautiful than they paint Venus and the Graces'. Carlyle claimed that the future Frederick the Great was charmed by the sight of this 'gay young baggage' who later enjoyed the sexual favours of her half-brother and her father, pp. 219–20.

12 A novel about Maria Aurora by Pierre Benoit (*Koenigsmark*), 1918, was made into a film in 1935 by Maurice Tourneur with Pierre Fresnay and Elissa Landi – 'splendid Ruritanian trash', according to one viewer. A. E. W. Mason's picaresque novel about Philipp Königsmark was published in 1938.

13 Carlyle, *The History of Frederick II of Prussia called Frederick the Great*, vol. iii, book 6, chapter 3, pp. 230–1.

14 *Ibid.*, vol. x, book 21, chapter 4, p. 9.

15 Blanning, *The Pursuit of Glory*, pp. 454–5.

16 Burney, *The Present State of Music in Germany, the Netherlands and United Provinces*, vol. ii, p. 60.

17 This insight was that of George Lewes, *The Life of Goethe*, p. 203.

18 The factory also produced Saxonware portrayals of Lotte and Werther from Goethe's *The Sorrows of Young Werther*.

19 They were the portrait of a man in a black beret (1657), known popularly as *Portrait of a Rabbi*, and *Portrait of a Man in a Hat Decorated with Pearls* (1667).

20 Reputed to be a gift from the monks of St Sixtus's priory in Piacenza, Raphael had painted it originally for the della Rovere family, and it may have been intended for the tomb of the della Rovere Pope, Julius II. St Sixtus was the family's patron saint.

21 Burney, *The Present State of Music in Germany, the Netherlands and United Provinces*, vol. ii, p. 58; Glover, *Dr Charles Burney's Continental Travels, 1770 to 1772*, p. 192.

22 Carlyle, *The History of Frederick II of Prussia called Frederick the Great*, vol. ii, book 5, chapter 5, p. 42–3.

23 The treatment of his wife and son, the future Frederick II, amounted to a form of hereditary madness, a disorder called generically porphyria, which afflicted members of the royal houses of Scotland, Hanover and Prussia. The most extreme sufferer was George III of England. There was some physical justification for the remark that Germany 'swarms with princes, and dukes, of whom three quarters aren't quite right in the head'. See chapter 2, note 13.

24 Archbishop Firmiani started pogroms against conscientious, Bible-reading Protestants in 1727. In all some 900–1,000 of them were forced to emigrate to the Protestant north.

25 Konigsburg was transferred to Russia in 1945 and rechristened Kaliningrad in memory of an editor of *Pravda* who was also President of the USSR.

26 Blanning, *The Pursuit of Glory*, p. 454.

27 Quoted in Gerhard Ritter, *Frederick the Great*, translated by Peter Paret (London, 1968), p. 19. Frederick William's absolutism was tempered by the diversity of his territories and by local opposition from the nobility to his centralising ambitions. Dwyer, *The Rise of Prussia 1700-1830*, p. 4.

28 From Frederick's political testament, quoted by Dwyer, *The Rise of Prussia 1700-1830*, p. 16. Expansion of territory was at the time almost a shibboleth among continental powers and a practice among colonial.

29 Palmer, R. R., 'Social and Psychological Foundations of the Revolutionary Era', in *New Cambridge Modern History (NCMH)*, vol. viii (Cambridge, 1965), p. 434.

30 Van der Zande, Johann, 'Prussia and the Enlightenment', in Dwyer, *The Rise of Prussia 1700-1830*, p. 95.

31 Wangermann, E., 'Habsburg Possessions and Germany', in *New Cambridge Modern History*, vol. viii, pp. 297–8.

Chapter 7

1 Montesquieu, *Voyage fait en 1728–9*, quoted in Fauchier-Magnan, *Les Petites Cours d'Allemagne au XVIII Siècle*, p. 68.

2 Fauchier-Magnan, *Les Petites Cours d'Allemagne au XVIII Siècle*, p. 130.

3 Carlyle, *The History of Frederick II of Prussia called Frederick the Great*, vol. ii, book 7, chapter 6, p. 450.

4 Fauchier-Magnan, *Les Petites Cours d'Allemagne au XVIII Siècle*, pp. 124–43; Klaus Merten, *The Residence Castle, Ludwigsburg* (Tubingen, 1989), passim.

5 Carlyle, *The History of Frederick II of Prussia called Frederick the Great*, vol. ii, book 7, chapter 6, p. 430.

6 Elon, Amos, *The Pity of it All: A Portrait of German Jews, 1743–1933* (London, 2003), p. 28.

7 Fauchier-Magnan, *Les Petites Cours d'Allemagne au XVIII Siècle*, p. 200.

8 *Ibid.*, p. 202.

9 *Ibid.*, p. 212.

10 Casanova, Giacomo, *History of My Life*, vol. 6, pp. 67–8.

11 Boswell, *On the Grand Tour: Germany and Switzerland, 1764*, p. 137.

12 Burney, *The Present State of Music in Germany, the Netherlands and United Provinces*, vol. i, p. 105.

13 Fauchier-Magnan, *Les Petites Cours d'Allemagne au XVIII Siècle*, p. 216.

14 *Ibid.*, on Daniel Christian Schubart, pp. 220–1. Some of his poems were set to music by Franz Schubert.

15 Carlyle, *Life of Friedrich Schiller (1825) and Life of John Sterling (1851)*, pp. 164–70; Appendix 1 Daniel Christian Schubart. His account introduced the free-thinking organist and journalist to English readers. Schubart's association with Schiller seems to have been confined to the one visit to him in prison with the draft of *The Robbers*. But even Carlyle admitted he was an *ignis fatuus* with scarcely any moral worth,

but he had poetic gifts and was an early student of the old German *Volkslied* which underpinned German Romanticism. Some of Schubart's poems were about the Wandering or Eternal Jew, an enduring myth of Europe that appealed to German Romantics.

16 Fauchier-Magnan, *Les Petites Cours d'Allemagne au XVIII Siècle*, p. 220.

17 *Ibid.*, p. 229.

18 Carlyle, *Life of Friedrich Schiller (1825) and Life of John Sterling (1851)*, p. 170.

19 Glover, *Dr Charles Burney's Continental Travels, 1770 to 1772*, pp. 114–15.

20 Fauchier-Magnan, *Les Petites Cours d'Allemagne au XVIII Siècle*, p. 235, quoting Goethe's *Journal* of 1 September 1797.

21 *Ibid.*, p. 242, quoting Karl-August in a letter to Goethe.

Chapter 8

1 He had, in fact, far fewer, even as few as five. Sire, H. J. A., *The Knights of Malta* (London, 1994), p. 189.

2 Cavaliero, Roderick, *Italia Romantica* (London, 2005), pp. 144–7, 171. Sire, pp. 188–9. The Polish Priory was created by the Tsar to accommodate the Catholic nobility he had acquired as subjects at the partitions of Poland.

3 Bourke, John, *Baroque Churches of Central Europe* (London, 1958 [1978 paper edition]), p. 36.

4 Hitchcock, H. R., *Rococo Architecture in Southern Germany* (London, 1968), p. 5. 'Family teams, usually teams of brothers as in the case of Dominikus and Johann Baptist Zimmermann or Cosmas Damian and Egid Quirin Asam, were responsible for much of the finest early and mid-eighteenth century church architecture and decoration in south Germany. Septs of architects, stuccoers and sculptors – if not so much of painters – especially those with Italian names who originated in the Swiss Grigioni had long been prominent in the south [and] upper Bavaria.' Also Blanning, *The Pursuit of Glory*, pp. 458–9.

5 Hitchcock, *Rococo Architecture in Southern Germany*, pp. 1–17.

6 *Ibid.*, pp. 44–7. St George, emerging on his horse from the high altar in the monastic church of Weltenburg (Assam brothers, 1721) piercing a writhing dragon on one side while he contemplates the athletic virgin he has saved on the other, is a marvellously cinematic version of spectator art, resembling the work of Bernini in Rome, who put spectators into their family boxes to view the event he was carving in the Cornaro Chapel of Santa Maria della Vittoria, and the Altieri Chapel in San Francesco a Ripa.

7 Bourke, *Baroque Churches of Central Europe*, p. 56.

8 Johann Balthasar Neumann (*floreat* 1711–53) was trained as an artillery engineer, but instead made his name for the design of the Würzburg palace and the church of the Fourteen Holy Helpers, at Bad Staffelstein, Bamberg in Bavaria. These became the prime exemplars of the special German amalgam of architecture and art known as the 'Würzbug rococo'.

9   Lukas von Hildebrandt (*floreat* 1695–1745) was born of a Genoese mother and German father. Italian trained, he became a principal designer of palaces and churches in Vienna that combined the Italian and German taste of the day. He was, perhaps, a more skilful decorator than an architect – he had his rivals among these – but for interior and exterior decorative detail he became an arbiter of Imperial taste.

10 Bachmann, Erich and Burkard von Roda, *Residenz Würzburg* (Munich, 1989), p. 12.

11 Building and decoration were carried on under successive Bishops until the Bishopric was stripped of its independence in 1802, when Napoleon tinkered with the political map of south Germany to give him a cordon of friendly client states against the threat from rival Austria. The Prince-Bishopric was added to the Electorate of Bavaria and his *Residenz* became an alternative home for the King whom Napoleon had created in 1806. No longer could the Church compete for magnificence with the secular princes of Pumpernickel.

Chapter 9

1   Burney, *The Present State of Music in Germany, the Netherlands and United Provinces*, vol. i, pp. 96–7.

2   Boswell, *On the Grand Tour: Germany and Switzerland, 1764*, p. 56. Entry for 12 August 1764.

3   Gay, *The Age of the Enlightenment*, p. 123. He first experienced problems with the Pietist pastor in Mühlhausen.

4   Blunt, *On Wings of Song, a Biography of Felix Mendelssohn*, p. 84.

5   Montagu, *Letters*, p. 86: letter to the Countess of Mar, Blankenburg, 17 December (O.S.) 1716.

6   Addison, Joseph, *Remarks on Several Parts of Italy* (London, 1705).

7   Hogwood, Christopher, *Handel* (London, 1984), pp. 46–7.

8   Thackeray, 'George I', in *The Four Georges*, p. 303.

9   Hampson, Norman, *The Enlightenment* (Harmondsworth, 1968), p. 60. In 1716 the elector of Saxony employed in Dresden alone an orchestra of 65 players, 20 French singers and 60 French dancers as well as a theatre company. Some of his ministers employed musical ensembles of their own.

10 Burney, *The Present State of Music in Germany, the Netherlands and United Provinces*, vol. ii, p. 233.

11 Johann Joachim Quantz, born 1697, the son of a Hanoverian blacksmith, perfected his flute-playing in Dresden under Augustus II of Poland, and joined Frederick's service in 1740. He died in 1773 leaving 300 flute concerti and a handbook in English on flute-playing.

12 Burney, *The Present State of Music in Germany, the Netherlands and United Provinces*, vol. ii, pp. 245, 270; Glover, *Dr Charles Burney's Continental Travels, 1770 to 1772*, pp. 236–8.

13 Anderson, Emily, *The Letters of Mozart & His Family* (London, 1989), p. 891: Mozart to Haydn, Vienna, 1 September 1785. During his 1760 visit to London, Mozart was also influenced by Johann Christoph Friedrich Bach's operatic compositions.

14 Burney, *The Present State of Music in Germany, the Netherlands and United Provinces*, vol. ii, pp. 11–12, 21; Glover, *Dr Charles Burney's Continental Travels, 1770 to 1772*, pp. 180–1.

15 Hogwood, Christopher, *Handel*, p. 203, quoting Dr Burney.

16 Burney, *The Present State of Music in Germany, the Netherlands and United Provinces*, vol. i, pp. 288–90; Glover, *Dr Charles Burney's Continental Travels, 1770 to 1772*, pp. 168–9.

17 Boswell, *On the Grand Tour: Germany and Switzerland, 1764*, p. 166. Letter to John Johnston, 7 November 1764.

18 Anderson, *The Letters of Mozart & His Family*, p. 362. Wolfgang Mozart to his father, 9 July 1778.

19 Burney, *The Present State of Music in Germany, the Netherlands and United Provinces*, vol. i, p. 93; Glover, *Dr Charles Burney's Continental Travels, 1770 to 1772*, p. 110.

20 Anderson, *The Letters of Mozart & His Family*, pp. 355–6, 370. Letters to his father, 4 & 13 November, 1777. Johann Christian, the youngest son of Johann Sebastian and pupil of his brother Carl Philipp Emanuel, came to London in 1762 and became court musician to Queen Charlotte. Mozart met him there in 1764 and claimed that his music influenced Mozart's own. George Joseph Vogler, born the son of a violin-maker in Würzburg, early entered the service of the Elector Charles Theodore of the Palatine, who sent him to Italy for his musical formation. When he returned to Mannheim he set up his first music school and developed techniques for playing keyboard instruments. His subsequent reputation may not have wholly justified Mozart's criticisms; when Charles Theodore moved to Munich, Vogler set off on his own becoming a peripatetic performer and instructor finally settling in Hesse-Darmstadt with a reputation as a brilliant performer and much-esteemed teacher of both Carl Maria von Weber and Meyerbeer.

21 *Ibid.*, pp. 448, 469. Letters to his father, 17 January & 7 February 1778.

22 *Ibid.*, p. 506. Letter to his father, 7 March 1778.

23 Blanning, *The Pursuit of Glory*, p. 484.

24 Sternfield, F. W., 'Music, Art & Architecture', in *New Cambridge Modern History*, vol. viii (Cambridge, 1965), p. 90.

25 Goethe, *Conversations with Eckermann*, p. 117, entry for 20 April 1925.

26 Warrack, John, 'In Search of Grand Opera', programme notes for a performance of *Euryanthe* at Glyndebourne in 2002, p. 93.

Chapter 10

1 Robinson Crusoe was, christened Kreutzmaer, in 1632, while the Hanseatic Free Imperial City was beleaguered by Swedes and Imperialists during the Thirty Years War. Defoe published *Robinson Crusoe* in 1719; the allusion to his German parentage, made only in the first chapter, was more perhaps in tribute to Robinson's stout Protestant origins from a stoutly Protestant city, than to the fact that England had lately acquired her monarch thence.

2 Emet-Ullah, born 1725, converted to Christianity and married Denis-Daniel de Froment in 1763.

3 Boswell, *On the Grand Tour: Germany and Switzerland, 1764*, p. 14.

4 *Ibid.*, p. 116. Entry for 1 October 1764.

5 Boswell, James, *On the Grand Tour, Germany and Switzerland*, p. 166. Letter to John Johnstone, 7 November 1764.

6 Holmes, Richard, *Coleridge: Early Visions* (London, 1989), pp. 196–7.

7 Willey, Basil, *Samuel Taylor Coleridge* (London, 1972), p. 57, quoting a letter from Coleridge to Thomas Poole of 4 May 1796.

8 See, chapter 5, for the influence of old German ballads on Coleridge during his stay there.

9 Carlyle, *Life of Friedrich Schiller (1875) and Life of John Sterling (1851)*, p. 323.

10 Holmes, *Coleridge: Early Visions*, p. 236.

11 Coleridge, Samuel Taylor, *Biographia Literaria* (London: Everyman edition, 1817), chapter 9, p. 76.

12 *Ibid.*, chapter 9, p. 76.

13 *Ibid.*, chapter 9, passim.

14 William Bell Scott (1811–90) was referring to *Biographia Literaria* in his introductory memoir to *The Poetical Works* (no date). Scott was himself a minor poet and critic, friend of Rossetti and Swinburne, until he offended the Rossettis in his memoirs. Willey, *Samuel Taylor Coleridge*, pp. 86–9, tries to elucidate how Coleridge interpreted Kant. As the 'noumenal world', of God, was beyond human minds, then the 'phenomenal world', accessible through human moral experience, must be the basis of religion and ethics. Having locked God in a cloud of unknowing, Coleridge found his way to accepting Christianity.

15 Carlyle, *Works*, vol. 2, p. 52, quoted by Mark Cumming, *The Carlyle Encyclopedia* (Cranbury, New Jersey: Associated University Presses, 2004), p. 101.

16 Carlyle, *Life of Friedrich Schiller (1825) and Life of John Sterling (1851)*, p. 91.

17 Coleridge, to the author of *The Robbers*, in Quiller-Couch (ed.), *Poems* (Oxford, 1907), sonnet XV.

18 Holmes, Richard, *Coleridge: Darker Reflections* (London, 1998), p. 508.

19 Carlyle, *Life of Friedrich Schiller (1825) and Life of John Sterling (1851)*, p. 111.

20 *Ibid.*, p. 105.

21 Wedgwood, C. V., *The Thirty Years War* (London, 1944), pp. 346, 359.

22 Carlyle, *Life of Friedrich Schiller (1825) and Life of John Sterling (1851)*, p. 120.

23 The quotations are not Coleridge's but taken from act 3 of Peter Oswald's translation, performed at the National Theatre in London, 2005, pp. 60–5. The term *'vil bastarda'* is actually used by Donizetti's librettist, Giuseppe Bardari, not Schiller, at this climactic moment. Bardari (1817–61) was discouraged by the vicissitudes of his libretto with the censor (he was only 17) and wrote no others, concentrating on his law studies, rising to be prefect of the Bourbon Naples police. He sided with Garibaldi, and wrote the farewell proclamation of the ousted king,

Francis II. He was appointed a councillor of the Naples financial court by the provisional government but died, aged 44, before he could proceed higher.

24 Donizetti had great trouble with his opera, *Maria Stuarda,* based on Schiller's play. Commissioned by the San Carlo opera house in Naples in 1834, he could not obtain the librettist he wanted. The one he eventually chose removed all the ambiguities of Schiller's plot. The singers of both queenly parts so identified themselves with the score that they traded the insults between queens as their personal insults between prima donnas. Both meant the vituperation they hurled at each other in song, so that the dress rehearsal was almost too dramatic. The management then woke up to the fact that the opera was about the death of queens, and in very bad language too. The Queen of Naples was at that time notably pious, and was said to have been shocked by the passions displayed at the dress rehearsal (which, unreliable sources claimed, she had uncharacteristically attended) and, as the music had already been rehearsed, it was decided to present the opera with a different title and a completely new text. Donizetti received, as a result, a very poor reception for this, his 46th opera, and he was little better served in Milan. When it opened eventually at La Scala in 1835, Mary Stuart, sung by the celebrated Maria Malibran, was in poor voice. After its first performance the censors, who had already passed the script, demanded changes, particularly the removal of the words *vil bastarda*, and for subsequent performances, the first act was followed by two acts of Rossini's Otello, with Malibran metamorphosing from Mary Stuart to Desdemona. Finally, in 1865, *Maria Stuarda* was performed as originally intended at San Carlo but it was nearly 100 years before it was performed again, in Donizetti's hometown of Bergamo.

Schiller's play and Donizetti's opera were both surprising ventures into English history. Donizetti's librettist was pretty faithful to Schiller's text and Schiller, having been at one time Professor of History at Jena, was considered to know his subject. For his part Donizetti's grasp of English history and topography was shaky – *Emilia di Liverpool* was set in a Liverpool just a short journey from London – and the bel canto tradition was not to explore the strength and weaknesses of the human personality but the powers – and often the weaknesses – of the human voice. In choosing Schiller as his author, Donizetti made of Mary Stuart a more exciting and complex heroine than his other controversially historical leading lady, Lucrezia Borgia. Schiller's play having received the accolade of Shakespearean, one cannot be left unmoved, either dramatically or musically, by the fate of the enigmatic queen, heroine of numberless Romantic novels, plays and films since.

25 Lamb, Charles, *Letters*, vol. 1 (Everyman edition 1909), p. 11, 10 June 1798.

26 Carlyle, *Life of Friedrich Schiller (1825) and Life of John Sterling (1851)*, p. 122–3.

27 Gamer, Michael, *Romanticism & the Gothic* (Cambridge, 2000), p. 77.

28 *Ibid.*, p. 78, quoting *The Monthly Mirror* 4 (1797), p. 356.

29 *Ibid.*, p. 129, quoting *The Monthly Review* (1798).

30 Lamb to Coleridge 5 July 1796, *Letters*, vol. 1, p. 32, referring to the ballad's publication in *The Monthly Review*.

31   For Coleridge on Radcliffe, Cavaliero, *Italia Romantica*, p. 47; on witchcraft, Gamer, *Romanticism & the Gothic*, p. 77, quoting Coleridge's review of *The Monk* in *The Critical Review* series 19 (1797), p. 197.

32   *Sturm und drang* marks the music of Verdi's *I Masnadieri* (*The Banditti*). Verdi had begun work on the opera he was to base on Schiller's *The Robbers* before he had finished Macbeth and his mind was still full of Shakespearean echoes of evil and dark conspiracy and the triumph of spiritual liberation. He had a distinguished librettist, the poet and translator, Andrea Maffei, who had already translated Schiller's *Mary Stuart*, *The Maid of Orleans* and *William Tell*, as well as other German poets, including Goethe's *Faust*. In reducing Schiller's long and convoluted interior musings, both of Karl and Franz Moor, to the musical monologues that Verdi enjoyed, Maffei showed much skill, though he reduced the plot to a rather conventional drama to be superseded by the intricacy and psychological insight of Verdi's later works.

I *Masnadieri* was presented at Her Majesty's Theatre in July 1847. It starred the hugely popular Jenny Lind, the diminutive 'Swedish nightingale', as Amalia. Verdi was at the rostrum, conducting one of his own operas for the first time there; the gala premiere was attended by Queen Victoria herself. It was a great and glorious occasion to mark this musical tribute to a great dramatist, whose near countryman, Prince Albert of Saxe-Coburg Gotha, had been born not two score miles from Weimar. The performance, however, did not herald the entry of a new Romantic opera into the regular repertoire. The reception was mixed, though Verdi's appearance was greeted with applause lasting a quarter of an hour, while throughout the performance there was 'clapping, shouts, recalls and repetitions'. Verdi recognised that if it had not actually caused a furore, it had gone down well enough to prompt him to return the next year to write and present another opera. He never did. Not everyone was enthusiastic. One critic (J. F. Chorley of *The Athenaeum*) thought it the worst opera ever to be presented at Her Majesty's Theatre and the Queen herself, sighing for her beloved Mendelssohn, found the music very noisy and trivial (Budden, Julian, *Verdi* (London, 1987), pp. 42–4).

The trouble may have been with the part of Amalia. One unkind critic believes that the unexpected death of Amalia – when instead of accepting her offer to join his robber band, Karl stabs her to prevent her doing anything so ignoble – was Schiller's way of disposing of a character whose personality he did not seem able to develop in the prescribed *sturm und drang* manner. Verdi had asked for Jenny Lind to sing the role but the decoration that he gave her music did not suit her voice. The cause may also lie in Maffei's reduction of the original play to a stand-up melodrama.

Chapter 11

1   Burney, *The Present State of Music in Germany, the Netherlands and United Provinces*, vol. ii, p. 61. The Elector of Saxony 'has manifested himself to be susceptible of the tender feelings of humanity, by the abolition of racks and tortures to which criminals were exposed'.

2 Sansculotte: 'without trousers'. Goethe, *Conversations with Eckermann*, p. 147, entry for 3 January 1827.

3 Esdaile, Charles, *Napoleon's Wars: An International History 1803–1815* (London, 2007), pp. 168–9, argues that man for man the French soldiers were not markedly better than the soldiers of other continental armies, whose officers were hardy and battle trained. What gave France the edge was the new French officer who had risen fast under the new regime, and was not held back by caste or tradition from taking risks and going out to win.

4 Shelley P. B., *A Defence of Poetry* written in 1821 and first published in 1840.

5 Bruford, W. H., 'German Constitutional and Social Development, 1795–1830', in *New Cambridge Modern History*, vol. 9 (Cambridge, 1965), p. 393.

6 Goethe, *Conversations with Eckermann*, p. 266, entry for 3 October 1828.

7 MacFarlane, C., *The Lives & Exploits of Banditti and Robbers* (London, 1839), pp. 261–2. The Jews may only have been made to take off shoes and stockings, and then forced to find them from a mingled heap. But the casual if not fatal cruelty is prophetic of the Nazi treatment of Jews at the time of *kristalnacht*.

8 Lewes, *The Life of Goethe*, p. 515.

9 *Ibid.*, p. 516.

10 *Ibid.*, p. 517.

11 Goethe, *Conversations with Eckermann*, p. 120, entry for 27 April 1825.

12 Quoted in Hampson, *The Enlightenment*, p. 49.

13 Goethe, *Conversations with Eckermann*, p. 247, entry for 11 March 1828.

14 Fisher, H. A. L., *Napoleon* (London, 1912), p. 144. Carlyle, 'German Literature', *Essays*, vol. i, p. 78. For *Werther* in Egypt, see M. Hulse, in his introduction to the 1989 Penguin edition of Gothe, *The Sorrows of Young Werther* (1989), p. 16.

15 Dalberg remained one of the three Princes of the Church who were dispossessed but not eliminated. The other two were, surprisingly, the Grand Master of the Knights of Malta, who had incorporated the Priory of Brandenburg, Protestantised but retained at the Reformation, into the Catholic order. Its lands otherwise lay in suspension following the loss of Malta, and the German Grand Master, Ferdinand von Hompesch, lived in hope of a Napoleonic restoration to the island. Napoleon seems to have kept the Order in existence as a bargaining counter for a settlement of the future of Malta that would have kept both Britain and Russia out of the island. Hompesch died in 1805, by which time the prospect of any return of the Knights to Malta had receded. The other survivor was the Grand Master of the Teutonic Knights, deprived of lands but, after 1809, kept titularly alive in Austria. Anachronistic survivals were typical of the unreconstructed Germany. The Abbey of Riddingshausen had been secularised by the reformers but the 'Abbot' continued as a private individual, drawing a revenue well into the eighteenth century. Jerusalem, son of the 'Abbot', was an acquaintance of Goethe's whose motiveless suicide was said to have been the model for Werther's. Lewes, *The Life of Goethe*, pp. 125, 139.

16 Blanning, *The Pursuit of Glory*, pp. 637–40.

17 Lloyd, E. M., 'The Third Coalition, 1806–7', chapter x in *The Cambridge Modern History*, vol. ix (Cambridge, 1907), p. 281.

18 Esdaile, *Napoleon's Wars: An International History 1803–1815*, pp. 429–32. Raymond Horricks, *In Flight with the Eagle* (Tunbridge Wells, 1988), pp. 44–5. Jerome rallied to his brother during The Hundred Days and fought bravely at Waterloo, retiring once more into exile. Louis-Philippe allowed him to return and made him a Governor of Les Invalides where his brother's remains rested, and he became life President of the Senate. His second son was Prince Napoleon, 'Plon-Plon', cousin of Napoleon III.

19 Las Cases, Emmanuel de, *Souvenirs de Napoléon Ier* (Paris, 1935), p. 73.

20 *Ibid.*, p. 157.

21 Paradoxically, Napoleon may have become a villain, and a tyrant to be deposed but he was also a hero, who had stridden, as Goethe believed, across the ancient shibboleths of Europe. Any artist who also strode across the narrow limitations of art was introduced into a pantheon of titans, presided over by the ex-Emperor. Byron, Beethoven, Rossini, Paganini and Liszt were elevated to it by public acclaim. Blanning, *The Romantic Revolution*, pp. 102–7.

22 In fact Prussia was in arrears with the payments until they were cancelled in the general downfall of Napoleon, because the other social reforms, especially the educational, proved so expensive.

23 Staël, Germaine de, *De l'Allemagne*, vol. iii (Paris, 1814), p. 344, quoting Novalis. 'All the force and all the finest part of human existence are necessary to understand.' Blake's *Auguries of Innocence* was written probably in 1803. Novalis died in 1801.

24 Carlyle, 'Novalis', in *Essays*, vol. 2, p. 131.

25 Jean Paul Richter, quoted in Carlyle, 'Novalis' in *Essays*, vol. ii, p. 133, a remarkable premonition of the depressing message of films like Irvin Kershner's *Star Wars* (1980).

Chapter 12

1 Blanning, *The Pursuit of Glory*, p. 502. Goethe actually mentions 20 universities, and though there had been 14 new creations between 1648–1798, including Halle (1694) and Göttingen (1737), some of the 40 were more like gymnasia or high schools, which Goethe may not have ranked as proper universities. Hampson, *The Enlightenment*, p. 60, calculates that at the beginning of the eighteenth century there were 37 universities in the Holy Roman Empire and five in German-speaking lands outside the empire, three alone in Saxony with its population of only two million.

2 Goethe, *Conversations with Eckermann*, pp. 267–8, entry for 23 October 1828.

3 Brose, Eric Dom, *German History, 1789–1871* (Oxford/New York, 1997), p. 1.

4 Berlin was an exception. Its population grew from 20,000 in 1688 to 70,000 in 1740, augmented by immigration from other states, especially Protestants, and from the countryside. Hampson, *The Enlightenment*, p. 63.

5 Brose, *German History, 1789–1871*, p. 4, quoting Christian Wilhelm Dohm in 1781.

6 Carlyle, 'Goethe', in *Essays*, vol. iii, p. 31.

7 There was even in Buda, Hungary, a Turkish pasha at the end of the seventeenth century who had managed to keep a harem and a private slave market to keep him supplied with vital necessities. Hampson, *The Enlightenment*, p. 61.

8 Pollard, A. F., 'The German Federation 1815–40', in *Cambridge Modern History*, vol. 10 (Cambridge, 1907) chapter 11, p. 343.

9 King of Bavaria, Duke of Franconia, Duke in Swabia and Count Palatine of the Rhine, the latter title last enjoyed by Charles I's nephew, Rupert.

10 Pollard, 'The German Federation 1815–40', vol. 10, chap. 20, p. 363.

11 *Ibid.*, p. 340.

12 Gay, *The Enlightenment; an Interpretation,* p. 364–5.

13 Carlyle contemptuously called Kotzebue and his fellow dramatists 'intellectual Jacobins' and believed they had brought German theatre into contempt in England. *Schiller, The Robbers and Wallenstein*, p. 30. Jane Austen would no doubt have been shocked at his assassination. It was in *Mansfield Park* that the Bertrams had decided to put on, in Sir Thomas's absence and in its translation by Mrs Inchbald, Kotzebue's *Das Kind der Liebe* (1798), a play of seduction and reparation, in which the youthful Baron Wildenheim had seduced Agatha, and reduced her to poverty as a result. He is persuaded later in life with the help of a *deus ex caelis*, a pastor, to marry her and allow the marriage of his daughter to the youthful aspirant to her hand rather than to the wealthy Count Cassell. The part was to be played by Mr Rushworth. Edmund Bertram thought it 'exceedingly unfit for private representation', and was sure his parents would disapprove. He was right. Austen, *Mansfield Park*, chapter 15.

14 Pollard, 'The German Federation 1815–40', p. 357. Speech to the staff of the Laibach Lyceum.

15 The Yiddish-speaking population of eighteenth- and nineteenth-century Germany numbered several million, the population of a reasonably sized state. The nations of the German confederacy were paradoxically their virtual homeland. They were a nation without a nation and so had no national dreams like Czechs, Slovaks, Ruthenians, Croats, Serbs and Poles. The fatal logic of Nazi Germany was to decide that, as they belonged nowhere, they might as well be eliminated. It was the fatal cul de sac of nationalism.

Chapter 13

1 Byron, George Gordon, Lord, *Childe Harold*, Canto the Third, 1816, stanza 48, lines 1–4.

2 The 'Romantic Rhine' with its Drachenfels, its Lorelei, its Mouse Tower, its Pfalz, Bacharach, Kembs, had been the subject of countless poems and songs (at least 400 in ten years) and paintings. It was then, not the industrialised highway of today but a lazy waterway of 'sinewy curves, oxbows, braids and thousands of islands ... of unpredictable flow and underwater cliffs so dangerous that it spawned a legend of

a siren'. Mark Cioc, 'The Political Ecology of the Rhine', apud Mauch, *Nature in German History*, pp. 34–5.

3 Byron, *Childe Harold*, Canto the Third, stanzas 48, 56–7, 60.

4 Byron, George Gordon, Lord, 'So Late into the Night', in L. A. Marchand (ed.), vol. 5 of *Letters & Journals, 1816–7* (London, 1976), pp. 76–7, Letter to Hobhouse, Carlsruhe, 16 May 1816.

5 Goethe, *Conversations with Eckermann,* entry for 19 October 1823 (New York and London, 1901), p. 24.

6 Shelley, Mary, in Betty T. Bennett (ed.), *The Letters of Mary Wollstonecraft Shelley*, vol. 3 (John Hopkins UP, 1988), p. 37: letter to Claire Claremont, 16 August 1842. Mary Shelley felt similarly about the common or garden Italians. She shared many of the English middle-class opinions of foreigners of her generation.

7 Arnim, Elizabeth von, *Elizabeth in Rügen* (London, 1904), pp. 61–2.

8 Clay, Jean, *Le Romanticisme* (Paris, 1980) (English translation, Oxford, 1981), p. 71, quoting the French naturalist, Horace Bénédict de Saussure, who had first climbed Mont Blanc in 1787 at the age of 47, and who published his observations on the mineralogy, geology, the weather and vegetation in *Voyages dans les Alpes* in four volumes from 1779–96.

9 Mauch, *Nature in German History*, p. 5.

10 Johnson, Edgar, *Sir Walter Scott, the Great Unknown, 1771–1821*, vol. i, (London, 1970), p. 129.

11 Lockhart, *The Life of Sir Walter Scott*, p. 89.

12 Goethe, *Conversations with Eckermann*, p. 228, entry for 25 July 1827. Eckermann had to translate the missive, dated Edinburgh 9 July 1827, as Goethe found the handwriting illegible. It warned Goethe that he would shortly receive a copy of Scott's life of Napoleon.

13 Carlyle, 'Preface ... to "German Romance"', in *Essays*, vol. 1, p. 455.

14 For *I Masnadieri* see chapter 10, note 28.

15 Johnson, *Sir Walter Scott, the Great Unknown, 1771–1821*, vol. i, pp. 129, 159. Scott translated Maier's *Fust von Stromberg*, Iffland's *Die Mündel*, Schiller's *The Conspiracy of Fiesco*, von Babo's *Otto von Wittelsbach*, as well as *Götz* and when he had finished *Götz*, he embarked on Lessing's *Emilia Galotti*.

16 The letter, dated 9 July 1827, is carried in Goethe, *Conversations with Eckermann*, pp. 227–30, entry for 25 July 1827.

17 Lockhart, *The Life of Sir Walter Scott*, pp. 541–2, quoted Goethe's praise of Scott, which had appeared in *Kunst und Altherthum*. Lockhart also reckoned that Scott's *Life of Napoleon Buonaparte* would have been contained in 13 or 14 volumes if produced in novel form.

18 Goethe, *Conversations with Eckermann,* p. 267, 3 October 1828; p. 359, 9 March 1831. In 1828 Goethe was reading *The Fair Maid of Perth* (1820), in 1831 *Rob Roy* (1817).

19 Lewes, *The Life of Goethe*, p. 113.

20 Scott, *The Journal*, pp. 315–16.

21 Lockhart, *The Life of Sir Walter Scott*, p. 627.

22 Johnson, *Sir Walter Scott, the Great Unknown, 1771–1821*, vol. ii, p. 1084. Lockhart, *The Life of Sir Walter Scott*, pp. 570–1, reports that the initial reception at a reading of the novel, as the manuscript sheets came from his pen, was highly appreciative of the 'felicity with which he had divined the peculiar character and outdone, by the force of his imagination, all the efforts of a thousand actual tourists'.

23 Scott added an introduction and footnotes (numbers 6 and 10) to *Anne of Geierstein* after it was finished, to incorporate the researches of the Jewish Christian convert lawyer, Francis Palgrave, into the byways of Gothic history. The so-called Vehmic Tribunals had a certain legitimacy and, if as ruthless as Inquisitorial courts, they were equally punctilious in their procedures. They were established by the Emperor Charles IV in 1332, and the Archbishop of Cologne was their Grand Master who by decree of Pope Boniface II was permitted to exercise jurisdiction of both life and death. Goethe featured the secret tribunal in his *Götz von Berlighingen* and Scott himself had written about it in his early drama *The House of Aspen*, adapted from Veit Wener's *Das Heilige Vehme*.

24 Scott, *Anne of Geierstein*, chapter 25.

25 Scott, *The Journal,* pp. 573, 621, entries for 16 January, 27 April 1829.

26 *Ibid.,* p. 573, entry for 26 January 1827.

27 Johnson*, Sir Walter Scott, the Great Unknown, 1771–1821*, vol. ii, p. 1207.

28 Carlyle, 'Sir Walter Scott', in *Essays*, vol. 4, pp. 221–2.

29 Holmes, *Coleridge: Darker Reflections*, pp. 275–80, picks his way delicately through the mystery why Coleridge was so defensive, even mendacious, about plagiarism.

30 *Ibid.*, p. 553.

31 Froude, J. A., *The Earl of Beaconsfield*, (London, 1980 [Everyman ed., 1914]), pp. 23–4. The opaque question of 'favourite master' was kicked out of touch by a German Jew, born in 1818 in the Rhineland territory given to Prussia at the Congress of Vienna. Karl Marx rejected metaphysics for socio-political pragmatism owing parentage to Hegel; such metaphysics as he believed in were the iron laws of economics, which England was teaching the world. With no missionary, civilising power her driving force was a commitment to commerce, creating and satisfying wants. She merely ensured that the society with which she traded was advanced enough to understand that it had wants England could satisfy. Marx, surveying the laws of her progress from the safe perspective of Berlin, reflected the intellectual primacy of the Prussian capital that was emerging from under the shadow of Pumpernickel Weimar; if he owed any debt to metaphysics it was his belief that man by following his laws would progress towards the fabled millennium.

32 Blake, Robert, *Disraeli* (London, 1966 [University paperback ed., 1969]), p. 34, asserts that Disraeli's claim to have written 88,000 words in four months while beset by the business of his law firm does not stand up to scrutiny and that for the most part *Vivian Grey* was written in 1826, when he was a year older.

33 Disraeli, *Vivian Grey*, book 5, chapter 2. Disraeli visited Germany twice, on a short visit to the Rhineland with his father before writing the first part of *Vivian Grey* and

for a longer period, for his health, before completing part two. When he took three years off, travelling Europe after its publication, he did not include Germany.

34　*Ibid.*, book 5, chapter 8.

35　Stephanie Nettall, introduction to *Vivian Grey*, p. xii.

36　Disraeli, *Vivian Grey*, book 5, chapter 1.

37　*Ibid.*, book 7, chapter 2.

38　Judgment of the American Film Institute's Top Ten, 17 June 2008.

Chapter 14

1　Hadden, J. Cuthbert, *Composers in Love & Marriage* (London, 1913), p. 142.

2　*Die Hermannschlact (Hermann's Battle)*, was intended to rouse German resistance to the conqueror and humiliator, but in it Hermann is prompted to ruthless action, pretending that Romans had performed the atrocities his own men were now encouraged to do; a tactic used by latter-day Germans to justify their invasion of Poland in 1939. Blanning, *The Romantic Revolution*, p. 154.

3　Christiansen, Rupert, *Romantic Affinities, Portraits from an Age, 1780–1830* (London, 1988), p. 78, quoting Kleist's letter of 1802 to his sister. G. Witkowski, *German Drama of the Nineteenth Century* (New York, 1909), pp. 21–2.

4　Hans Werner Henze's opera, *The Prince of Homburg*, was premiered in Hamburg in 1960, but Kleist's Elector of Brandenburg, instead of promising to teach the prince 'what military discipline and obedience are' promises, in the words of the librettist, to teach him 'freedom and honour.'

5　Carlyle, 'ETW Hoffmann', in *Essays*, vol. 1, p. 434.

6　Hoffmann, Ernst Theodor (Amadeus), *'Allgemeine Musikalische Zeitung, July 1810'*, in H. C. Robbins Landon, *Beethoven, a Documentary Study* (London, 1970), pp. 219–20.

7　Warrack, John, *Carl Maria von Weber* (London, 2008), p. 210, describes how Weber was impressed by it and could have benefited from Hoffmann's literary skills in writing *Die Freischütz*.

8　*Ritter Gluck* (1809), appeared in *Fantasiestücke in Callots Manier* (1814). The other collections were *Nachstücke* (1817) which included *The Sandman*; and *Die Serapionsbruder* (1819) in which appeared *Councillor Krespel, Doge and Dogaressa*, and *Mlle de Scudery*.

9　Dent, Edward, *Mozart's Operas* (London, 1913), p. 179: *Don Juan, eine fabelhaftige Begebenheit (Don Juan, a fabled happening)*. Also Christiansen, *Romantic Affinities, Portraits from an Age, 1780–1830*, p. 159. The foreboding of the eternal appears in Hoffmann's critique of Beethoven. See note 6 above.

10　Gosse, Edmund (ed.), 'Introduction', in F. H. K. La Motte-Fouqué, *Undine, Sintram and His Companions, Aslauga's Knight, The Two Captains* (Oxford: Worlds Classics, no date), p.vii.

11　Coleridge, *Table Talk, Specimens*, p. 92.

12　Gosse, 'Introduction', to *Undine*, p. xvi.

13 Characteristics which formed the basis of *Aslauga's Knight* and *The Two Captains*, the first translated by Carlyle, the second by P. E. Matheson, translator of Epictetus.

14 Harding, James, 'The Mozart of the Champs Elysées', in Russell Brown (ed.), *Offenbach, 1819–1880, a Tribute* (London, 1980).

15 They are *Der Sandman* (*The Sandman*), *Rath Krespel* (*Councillor Krespel*) and *Das Verlorene Spiegelbild* (*The Lost Reflection*).

16 Newman, Ernest, *Wagner Nights* (London, 1949 [1988 reprint]), pp. 59–67.

17 The difficult singing given to this love-struck virgin compels the singer to be usually of a more mature and often robust age. As she is a foil to the eternal, and therefore an ageless Goddess of Love, the contest is still usually performed as one between matrons.

18 La Motte-Fouqué, *Undine, Sintram and His Companions*, chapter 1, p. 185.

19 Wagner repeats the formula in Senta's passion for the Dutchman, Sieglinde's incest, Siegfried's passion for an elderly Valkyrie, Elsa's for the dream-knight who comes to her rescue towed by a swan, Tristan's for Isolde. They are the result of ignorance, or deceit, or a dream, or a potion, or just reading too much fiction.

Chapter 15

1 Blanning, *The Romantic Revolution*, p. 102, quoting E. T. A. Hoffman.

2 Blunt, *On Wings of Song, a Biography of Felix Mendelssohn*, pp. 270, 90.

3 Allderidge, Patricia, *The Late Richard Dadd, 1817–1886* (London: Tate Gallery, 1974), pp. 59–61.

4 Blunt, *On Wings of Song, a Biography of Felix Mendelssohn*, pp. 251, 257.

5 Similar pique from rejection, unopened, of some pieces on which he wanted the maestro's comments nearly estranged Brahms from Schumann, but Brahms could not bear the separation that an enduring rift would have entailed from Clara. None of Wagner's paramours were known to Mendelssohn.

6 Sabor, Rudolph, *The Real Wagner* (London, 1987 [paperback edition, 1989]), p. 257, quoting *The Morning Post* of 13 March, and p. 160 quoting *The Times* of 13 May 1855.

7 *Die Feen*. Carlo Gozzi (1720–1806) proved a happy mine for opera. Apart from Wagner's, there is Puccini's *Turandot* – from a Schiller translation – and Prokofiev's *Love of Three Oranges*.

8 It had been given by Wagner to Ludwig II and it was then given to Hitler by the Bavarians when he became Chancellor.

9 Shaw, Bernard, *The Perfect Wagnerite*, 3rd ed. (London 1963), p. 136.

10 *Das Liebesverbot* was not performed until 1923 and revived by the BBC in Wagner's centenary year in 1983.

11 Barker, John, quoting Wagner, Introduction to first recording of *Rienzi* by the Dresden State Opera, EMI 1976, p. 3.

12 Sabor, *The Real Wagner*, p. 90, quoting Wagner in a letter to Franz Liszt, 18 April 1851.

13 Blunt, *On Wings of Song, a Biography of Felix Mendelssohn*, pp. 183, 255. Shaw as a young music critic was anxious to displace one Victorian idol by another.

14   Sabor, *The Real Wagner*, pp. 267–8, quoting Richard to Minna Wagner, 12 June 1855; p. 270, *Sunday Times* review of 6 May 1855.

15   *Ibid.*, p. 270, quoting a letter of 22 October 1845.

16   *Ibid.*, p. 265, Wagner on the English, letter to Otto Wesendonck 21 March 1855.

17   Actually Wagner took more from the Icelandic *Volsunga Saga* than from anything German, apart from its gods. Its Germanness, which annoyed William Morris, was essentially rather Wagnerian than Icelandic, which Ludwig recognised.

18   William Morris's *The Story of Sigurd the Volsung and the Fall of the Nibelungs* appeared in 1876, a year before Wagner produced his complete *The Ring of the Nibelungs* at Bayreuth. Morris based his poem on the Icelandic saga and was anything but enthusiastic about Wagner's version, the music of which appeared to him 'as an artist and non-musical man perfectly abhominable (sic)'. He thought 'the idea of a sandy-haired German tenor tweedledeeing over the unspeakable woes of Sigurd, which even the simplest words are not typical enough to express', nothing short of desecration. And to show Fafnir as a pantomime dragon, 'puffing steam and showing his red danger-signal like a railway engine', infuriated him. MacCarthy, *William Morris, A Life for Our Times*, p. 372, quoting letters to Henry Buxton Forman, 12 November 1873, and to Aglaia Coronio.

19   Lambert, Constant, quoting Ernest Newman in *Music Ho!*, London 1934, p. 316.

20   Shaw, *The Perfect Wagnerite*, p. 76.

21   Sabor, *The Real Wagner*, p. 293. Ludwig to Wagner, 5 May 1864.

22   *Ibid.*, pp. 291–2. Wagner to Frau Wille, 4 May 1864.

23   Blunt, Wilfred, *The Dream King, Ludwig II of Bavaria* (London, 1970), p. 108.

24   *Ibid.*, chapter 9 passim.

25   *Ibid.*, quoting Ludwig to Wagner on 13 May 1868. An epitaph to Ludwig appears in Isak Dinesens, 'The Invincible Slave Owner', in *Winter's Tales* (London, 1942), p. 65. 'Ludwig ... the swan hermit ... *"seul roi de ce siècle, salut!"* ... To me his solitude at Neuschwanstein is exquisite and majestic, sublime. He cannot live in Munich. He cannot breathe the air polluted by the crowd, nor bear the rank smell of it. He cannot enjoy art in the presence of the profane ... At Neuschwanstein, high above the common world, the King is happy. In that mountain air and silence, he wanders, dreams and meditates, there he feels near God.'

26   Newman's translation, *Wagner Nights*, p. 413.

27   Cosima Wagner on 25 February 1881 quotes Wagner: 'As if anything comes of reason ... Only religion and art can educate a nation.' Cosima Wagner, *Diaries 1878–1883*, edited by M. Gregor-Dellin and D. Mack (London, 1980), p. 631.

28   From Wagner's Sketch of 1848, translated by Newman, *Wagner Nights*, p. 415.

Chapter 16

1   See Roberts-Jones, Philippe, *Beyond Time and Place: Non-Realist Painting in the 19th Century* (Oxford, 1978), pp. 156–7.

2   Jameson, Anna, *Visits and Sketches at Home and Abroad*, vol. ii (London, 1834), p. 144.

3 Quoted in Roberts-Jones, *Beyond Time and Place: Non-Realist Painting in the 19th Century*, p. 116.

4 Schlegel quoted in Vaughan, William et al., *Caspar David Friedrich, 1774–1840* (London: Tate Gallery, 1972), p. 135.

5 Quoted in Roberts-Jones, *Beyond Time and Place: Non-Realist Painting in the 19th Century*, p. 39. The quotation is on p. 118.

6 Quoted in Vaughan, *Caspar David Friedrich, 1774–1840*, p. 44.

7 Clay, *Le Romanticisme*, p. 108.

8 Friedrich's love of mists was expressed in his belief that 'a landscape swathed in mist appears vaster and more sublime; it stimulates the imagination and increases expectancy, like a girl wearing a veil.' Quoted in Roberts-Jones, *Beyond Time and Place: Non-Realist Painting in the 19th Century*, p. 39.

9 Parshall, Linda, in 'Landscape as History: Pückler-Muskau, the "Green Prince" of Germany', apud Mauch, *Nature in German History*, p. 48, locates the resemblance in Hoffmann's *Fantasiestücke in Callots Manier*.

10 *Theorie der Gartenkunst* by Christian Cay Lorenz Hirschfeld (1742–92).

11 Parshall, 'Landscape as History: Pückler-Muskau, the 'Green Prince' of Germany', p. 50.

12 For the Byronic comparison see Parshall, 'Landscape as History: Pückler-Muskau, the 'Green Prince' of Germany', pp. 55–6, and source note 29 on p. 70.

13 'Whoever loves the German forest also loves an orderly political system ... he also loves the German *Heimat* out of the depths his soul.' Konrad Adenauer, German Chancellor in 1953. Sandra Chaney, 'For Nation & Prosperity, Health and a Green Environment', apud Mauch, *Nature in German History*, p. 98.

14 Roberts-Jones, *Beyond Time and Place: Non-Realist Painting in the 19th Century*, p. 92.

15 *Ibid.*, p. 42.

16 Ruskin, John, *Modern Painters*, vol. 1 (London: Everyman edition, 1843), p. 105.

17 Ruskin, John, *Praeterita, The Autobiography* (Oxford, 1989), pp. 65, 69, 100, 387.

18 Ruskin, *Modern Painters*, vol. 1, p. 104.

19 Prominent among the founding members of the fraternity was Johann Friedrich Overbeck (1789–1869), born in Lubeck and trained in Vienna where he became enthusiastic about the work of Giotto and his contemporaries. Reacting violently against the neo-classicism of Winckelmann, he founded the Brotherhood, and finding his views generally uncongenial to the arts establishment of Vienna the 'brothers' moved to Rome. The nucleus consisted of Franz Pfor (1788–1812), Peter von Cornelius (1783–1867), Schnorr von Carolsfeld (1794–1853) and Wilhelm Schadow (1788–1862). They painted frescoes as an act of obeisance to the great age of fresco art, particularly scenes from the life of Joseph in Egypt for Mendelssohn's uncle, consul-general Bartholdy; they decorated the *casino* of the Palazzo Massimo with scenes from Tasso. Overbeck remained domiciled in Rome until his death, painting grand subjects, like *The Adoration of the Magi*, *Germany and Italy* and *The Triumph of Religion over the Arts*. Cornelius also executed fresco commissions from Ludwig I in Munich.

20 Winter, Emma L., 'German Fresco Painting and the New Houses of Parliament at Westminster 1834–51', *The Historical Journal*, 47, 2 (Cambridge, 2004), p. 300, quoting Cornelius, who joined the brotherhood in 1812.

21 Blunt, *On Wings of Song, a Biography of Felix Mendelssohn*, p. 128.

22 Winter, 'German Fresco Painting and the New Houses of Parliament at Westminster 1834–51', p. 293, quoting *The Athenaeum* of 10 September 1842.

23 *Ibid.*, p. 302.

24 *Ibid.*, p. 301–2. The painter was Julius Schnorr. Jameson's *Visits and Sketches at Home and Abroad*, vol. i, p. 300.

25 *Ibid.*, p. 309.

26 *Ibid.*, pp. 319–20, quoting *Punch* in September 1845, and *Pointon's life of William Dyce* (Oxford, 1979), p. 89.

27 Bowness, Alan (ed.), *The Pre-Raphaelites* (London: Tate Gallery/Penguin Books, 1984), p. 1, quoting William Michael Rossetti.

28 *Ibid.*, p. 1, quoting Holman Hunt, *Pre-Raphaelitism and the Pre-Raphaelite Brotherhood*, vol. i (1905), p. 87.

29 Dickens, Charles, *Household Words (1850–9)*, 15 June 1850.

30 This was despite his painting for the Free Exhibition of 1848 of 'The First Translation of the Bible'. The subject was suitably Reformist but the style damned it. Bowness, *The Pre-Raphaelites*, pp. 14–15.

Chapter 17

1 The best source for Raspe's life is Carswell, John, *The Prospector; being the Life and Times of Rudolph Eric Raspe, 1737–1794* (London, 1950).

2 Scott, Sir Walter, *The Antiquary* (Edinburgh, 1816), chapter 24.

3 This incident is not in Raspe's collection, but Mme de Staël may have made it up or remembered it from another collection of the exploits of the eponymous Baron Münchhausen.

4 Herold, J. Christopher, *Mistress to an Age: The Life of Madame de Staël* (London, 1959), pp. 255, 259.

5 *Ibid.*, p. 256.

6 Lewes, *The Life of Goethe*, p. 458.

7 Staël, de, Germaine, *De l'Allemagne*, vol. iii (Paris, 1814), p. 29.

8 Herold, *Mistress to an Age: The Life of Madame de Staël*, p. 263.

9 Goethe, quoted by de Staël in *De l'Allemagne*, vol. iii, p. 151.

10 Staël, Germaine de, *De l'Allemagne*, vol. iii, p. 561.

11 *Ibid.*, vol. iii, p. 561.

12 *Ibid.*, vol. iii, pp. 62, 87.

13 *Ibid.*, vol. iii, p. 583.

14 Schlegel is also believed to have invented the word, in his articles for *The Athenaeum*, which may have emerged simultaneously from their prolonged and profound conversations.

15 Lewes, *The Life of Goethe*, p. 81.

16 Hare, Augustus, *Memorials of a Quiet Life*, vol. i (London, 1884), p. 149.

17 *Ibid.*, vol. i, p. 195.

18 *Ibid.*, vol. i, pp. 201–2.

19 *Ibid.*, vol. i, pp. 205–6, which contains Leigh Hunt's poem to the Dashwood family home, quoted in part here.

20 *Ibid.*, vol. i, p. 497. Julius to Augustus W. Hare, 15 October 1833.

21 *Ibid.*, vol. i, p. 429. Julius to Maria Hare, 4 April 1833.

22 Carlyle, *Life of Friedrich Schiller (1825) and Life of John Sterling (1851)*, chapter viii, pp. 235–6.

23 Carlyle, *Essays*, vol. 1, p. 63.

24 *Ibid.*, vol. 2, p. 255 reproduces his 1831 review of *Correspondence between Schiller and Goethe, 1794–1805* (Stuttgart, 1828–9).

25 Carlyle to Thomas Murray and Jane Baillie Welsh, *Letters*, vol. iii, pp. 139 and 199 quoted in Cumming, *The Carlyle Encyclopedia*, p. 97.

26 Carlyle, Thomas, *Reminiscences*, ed. J. A. Froude (New York, 1881), p. 289.

27 Johann-Paul Friedrich Richter (1763–1825) was a prolific man of letters, trained as a theologian, which study he abandoned for the world of fiction. In 1798 he settled in Weimar, but the supernatural and grotesque in his work did not commend itself either to Goethe or to Schiller, and he was never among their intimates. He is said to have had a vision of his own death, and he adopted the name Jean Paul in honour of Rousseau whom he greatly admired. Carlyle translated two of his 'life fictions' and wrote two appreciations of his work, and translated his review of Germaine de Staël's *De l'Allemagne*. Carlyle admired his style: 'Titanian, deep, strong, tumultuous, shining with a thousand hues, fused from a thousand elements, and winding in labyrinthine mazes.' Carlyle, 'Jean Paul Friedrich Richter', in *Essays*, vol. 1, p. 117. Like his own indeed.

28 Letter to Jane Baillie Welsh, in *Letters*, vol. iii, p. 233, quoted by Robert Morrison, apud Cumming, *The Carlyle Encyclopedia*, p. 117.

29 Carlyle, 'German Literature', *Essays*, vol. i, p. 62, quoting Schiller's treatise on the Aesthetic Education of Man.

30 Carlyle, *Life of Friedrich Schiller (1825) and Life of John Sterling (1851)*, Schiller, part 3, p. 80.

31 Carlyle, Thomas, 'The Hero as Priest' in *Heroes and Hero-worship* (New York,1893), p. 137.

32 Quotations from Thomas Carlyle, *Heroes and Hero-Worship, and The Heroic in History* (London, 1893), pp. 150, 152, 217, 269.

33 Carlyle, *The History of Frederick II of Prussia called Frederick the Great*, vol. i, book 1, chapter 1, p. 9.

34 Carlyle, 'Schiller', in *Essays*, vol. 2, pp. 292–3, quoting a letter to Goethe. Schiller admitted that Christianity was the only aesthetic religion, representing a moral Beauty or Incarnation of the Holy, requiring a Free Inclination not Kant's Imperative

to determine correct human behaviour. Carlyle (p. 294) could not decide whether this meant that Schiller was 'no healthy poetic nature'.

35   Carlyle, *Life of Friedrich Schiller (1825) and Life of John Sterling (1851)*, Schiller, part 3, p. 151.

36   Sorensen, David R., 'Goethe's Significance to Carlyle', in Mark Cumming (ed.), *The Carlyle Encyclopedia*, p. 301.

37   *Ibid.*, p. 202.

38   Quotation in T. Peter Park, 'Germany', in Cumming (ed.), *The Carlyle Encyclopedia*, p. 190.

39   Carlyle, *The History of Frederick II of Prussia called Frederick the Great*, vol. ii, book 6, chapter 2, pp. 203–4. Carlyle was using as his source the *Posthumous Historical Memoirs* of Nathanial Wraxall (1751–1831) published in London, in 1836.

40   Steinweis, Alan, *Hitler and Carlyle's 'Historical Greatness'*, *History Today*, vol. 15 (6) (London, 1995), p. 37. The essay argues for and against a causal identity of Carlyle's views and the development of the ideology of Nazi Germany.

41   Carlyle, *The History of Frederick II of Prussia called Frederick the Great*, vol. i, book 1, chapter 1, pp. 8, 11–12.

42   *Ibid.*, vol. i, book 1, chapter 1, p. 10.

43   Ashton, Rosemary, *G. H. Lewes: An Unconventional Victorian* (Oxford, 1991 [Pimlico edition 2009]), p. 115.

44   The dedication to Lewes's *The Life of Goethe*.

45   See chapter 1.

46   Ashton, *G. H. Lewes: An Unconventional Victorian*, p. 137 quoting Margaret Fuller from her *Life* in 1852.

47   *Ibid.*, p. 166.

Chapter 18

1   Meredith, George, *The Adventures of Harry Richmond*, chapter 15.

2   Goethe, *Conversations with Eckermann*, pp. 227–9, entry for 12 March 1828. On the other hand (p. 307, 1 September 1829) he could not help imputing their opposition to the slave trade, not to philanthropy but to a practical conclusion that it no longer benefited the English, so must be ended.

3   Keynes, *Two Memoires*, quoted by Timothy Rogers, *Rupert Brooke* (London, 1971), pp. 23–4.

4   *A Man of Mark*, published privately, remarkable only as a presage of what was to come.

5   The British Council, in writing its financial handbook as a guide for the management of its overseas offices, set its representation in Ruritania, with its capital at Strelsau and regional directorate in Zenda.

6   Meredith, *The Adventures of Harry Richmond*, chapter 15.

7   Perhaps not unacknowledged. Elie Halévy made this claim for him.

8   Meredith, George, *The Tragic Comedians* (London, 1904), pp. 156–7.

9   Eliza Parsons (1739–1811) wrote 19 novels to support herself and her indigent family. Her two Gothic German novels are resolutely anti-Catholic.

10 Rated the strangest and most 'thrilling' of the Gothic genre.

11 Francis Lathom (1774–1832), son of an East India Company trader, was a prolific Gothic novelist. *The Midnight Bell* summoned villainous Roman Catholic monks to their nefarious meeting, thus placing it firmly in the generally anti-Catholic ranks of the Gothic novel.

12 *Orphan of the Rhine* is really a Franco-Italian Gothic novel opening in Switzerland with some action set in the Upper Rhine.

13 Heavily criticised in its time for its lurid accounts of sex, violence and barbarism.

14 *Clermont*, by the prolific Irish born novelist, Regina M. Roche (1764–1845) was twice mentioned by Jane Austen (in *Emma* and in *Northanger Abbey*), and was her only truly Gothic novel but not set in Germany. Roche at one time rivalled Ann Radcliffe in popularity.

15 Hale, Terry (ed.), 'Introduction' in *Tales of the Dead, The Ghost Stories of the Villa Diodati* (Chislehurst, 1992), p. 9.

16 *Ibid.*, p. 18.

17 Shelley, Mary, *The Journals, 1814–44*, edited by Feldman & Scott-Kilvert (Baltimore: John Hopkins University Press, 1987). Entry for 18 August 1816.

18 Alexander Humboldt was inspired by Georg Forster (1714–94), who had accompanied Captain Cook to the South Seas on his second voyage, becoming a respected authority on Polynesia and member of the Royal Society of London, and a distinguished member of the Hanoverian university at Göttingen.

19 Goethe, *Conversations with Eckermann*, p. 64, entry for 14 April 1824.

20 *Ibid.*, p. 81, entry for 3 December 1824.

21 *Ibid.*, p. 128, entry for 11 June 1825.

22 *Ibid.*, pp. 211, 208, entries for 6 May and 3 May 1827.

23 This chivalry was the theme of Jean Renoir's 1937 anti-war film, *La Grande Illusion*, in which Captain the Baron von Rauffenstein tells his aristocratic prisoner the French aviator, the Comte de Boildieu: 'I do not know who is going to win this war (1914–18). Whatever it is it will be the end of the Rauffensteins and the Boildieus.'

Bibliography

Abramsky, C. (ed.), *Essays in Honour of E.H. Carr* (London, 1974).

Addison, Joseph, *Remarks on Several Parts of Italy* (London, 1705).

Allderidge, Patricia, *The Late Richard Dadd, 1817–1886* (London: Tate Gallery, 1974).

Anderson, Emily, *The Letters of Mozart & His Family* (London, 1989).

Arnim, *Elizabeth & Her German Garden* (London, 1898).

———, *Elizabeth in Rügen* (London, 1904).

———, *The Solitary Summer* (London, 1989).

Ashton, Rosemary, *Thomas & Jane Carlyle, Portrait of a Marriage* (London, 2003).

———, *G. H. Lewes: An Unconventional Victorian* (Oxford, 1991 [Pimlico edition 2009]).

Bachmann, Erich and Burkard von Roda, *Residenz Würzburg* (Munich, 1989).

Bedford, Sybille, *A Legacy* (London, 1966 [Penguin paper edition, 1956])

Berlin, Isaiah, *The Magus of the North: J. G. Hamann & the Origins of Modern Irrationalism* (New York, 1993).

Blake, Robert, *Disraeli* (London, 1966 [University Paperback edition, 1969]).

Blanning, Tim, *The Pursuit of Glory: Europe 1648–1815* (London, 2007).

———, *The Romantic Revolution* (London, 2010).

Blunt, Wilfred, *The Dream King, Ludwig II of Bavaria* (London, 1970).

———, *On Wings of Song, a Biography of Felix Mendelssohn* (London, 1974).

———, *The Pre-Raphaelite Tragedy* (London, 1942 [1975 paper edition]).

Boswell, James, *On the Grand Tour, Germany and Switzerland, 1764*, edited by Frederick Pottle (London, 1953).

Bourke, John, *Baroque Churches of Central Europe* (London, 1958 [1978 paper edition]).

Bowness, Alan (ed.), *The Pre-Raphaelites* (London: Tate Gallery/Penguin Books, 1984).

Boyle, Nicholas, *Goethe, The Poet and the Age*, vol. 1, *The Poetry of Desire, 1749–1790.* (Oxford, 1991).

———, *Goethe, The Poet and the Age*, vol. 2, *The Age of Renunciation, 1790–1832.* (Oxford, 2000).

Brose, Eric Dom, *German History, 1789–1871* (Oxford/New York, 1997).

Bruford, W. H., 'German Constitutional and Social Development, 1795–1830', in *New Cambridge Modern History*, vol. 9 (Cambridge, 1965), pp. 367–94.

Budden, Julian, *Verdi* (London, 1987).

Burke, Edmund, 'Reflections on the Revolution in France', in vol. viii of *Writings and Speeches of E. B.* (Oxford, 1979)

Burney, Charles, *The Present State of Music in Germany, the Netherlands and United Provinces* (London, 1773 [facsimile reprint, London: Travis & Emery, 2008]).

Byron, George Gordon, Lord, *Childe Harold*, cantos 1 and 2 (1812), 3 (1816) and 4 (1818).

————, 'So Late into the Night', in L. A. Marchand (ed.), vol. 5 of *Letters & Journals, 1816–7* (London, 1976).

Carlyle, Thomas, *Sartor Resartus, The Life and Opinions of Herr Teufelsdröckh*, originally published in *Fraser's* Magazine 1833–4, and then in book form by Archibald MacMechan (ed.) (Boston: Ginn and Company, 1896).

————, *Past and Present* (London: Collins Classic edition, 1843).

————, *Critical & Miscellaneous Essays*, 4 vols (Boston: Brown & Taggart, 20 and 29 Cornhill, 1860).

————, *Reminiscences*, ed. J. A. Froude (New York, 1881).

————, *The History of Frederick II of Prussia called Frederick the Great*, 10 vols (London: Chapman and Hall, 1892).

————, *Life of Friedrich Schiller (1825) and Life of John Sterling (1851)* (London, 1893).

————, *Heroes and Hero-Worship, and The Heroic in History* (London, 1893).

————, *The Carlyle Encyclopedia*, edited by Mark Cumming (Cranbury, New Jersey: Associated University Presses, 2004).

Carswell, John, *The Prospector; being the Life and Times of Rudolph Eric Raspe, 1737–1794* (London, 1950).

Casanova, Giacomo, *History of My Life*, vol. 6, translated by W. R. Trask (London, 1968).

Cavaliero, Roderick, *Italia Romantica* (London, 2005).

Christiansen, Rupert, *Romantic Affinities, Portraits from an Age, 1780–1830* (London, 1988).

Clay, Jean, *Romanticism* (Oxford, 1981), originally *Le Romanticisme* (Paris,1980).

Coleridge, Samuel Taylor, *Table Talk, Specimens* (London: HNC, 1835).

————, *Biographia Literaria* (London, 1817 [Everyman edition, 1906]).

————, *The Poetical Works of Samuel Taylor Coleridge* (London: George Routledge & Son, no date), See also *Scott, William B.*

Cumming, Mark (ed.), *The Carlyle Encyclopedia* (Cranbury, New Jersey: Associated University Presses, 2004).

Dent, Edward, *Mozart's Operas* (London, 1913).

Disraeli, Benjamin, *Vivian Grey*. Introduction by Stephanie Nettall (London: First Novel Library Cassel, 1968 [1826–7]).

Dwyer, P. G., *The Rise of Prussia 1700–1830* (Harlow, 2000).

Eckermann, Johann Peter, *Conversations with Goethe*, translated by Wallace Wood (New York, 1901).

Elon, Amos, *The Pity of it All: A Portrait of German Jews, 1743–1933* (London, 2003).

Esdaile, Charles, *Napoleon's Wars: An International History 1803–1815* (London, 2007).

Fauchier-Magnan, Adrien, *Les Petites Cours d'Allemagne au XVIII Siècle* (Paris, 1947).

Fisher, H. A. L., *Napoleon* (London, 1912).

Froude, J. A, *The Earl of Beaconsfield* (London, 1890 [Everyman ed., 1914]).

Gamer, Michael, *Romanticism & the Gothic* (Cambridge, 2000).

Gay, Peter, *The Enlightenment; an Interpretation* (London, 1966).

——, *The Age of the Enlightenment* (Netherlands, 1966).

Glover, C. H., *Dr Charles Burney's Continental Travels, 1770 to 1772* (London, 1927).

Goethe, Johann Wolfgang von, *Götz von Berlichingen* (1773).

——, *Der Grosse Coptha (The Great Coptha)* (Weimar, 1791).

——, *Italienische Reise (Italian Journey)* (Leipzig, 1817).

——, *Zur Farbenlehre* (1810 [translated by Charles Eastlake as *The Theory of Colours*, London 1840])

——, *Conversations with Eckermann*, translated by Wallace Wood (New York, 1901).

——, *The Sorrows of Young Werther, (Die Lieden des Jungen Werther, 1774)*, translated by M. Hulse (Harmondsworth: Penguin Books, 1989).

Gosse, Edmund, see la Motte-Fouqué.

Grimm, Jacob & Wilhelm, *The Complete Fairy Tales*, translated by Jack Zipps (London, 2002).

Hadden, J. Cuthbert, *Composers in Love & Marriage* (London, 1913).

Hale, Terry (ed.), *Tales of the Dead, The Ghost Stories of the Villa Diodati* (Chislehurst, 1992).

Hampson, Norman, *The Enlightenment* (Harmondsworth, 1968).

Harding, James, 'The Mozart of the Champs Elysées', in Russell Brown (ed.), *Offenbach, 1819–1880, a Tribute* (London, 1980).

Hare, Augustus, *Memorials of a Quiet Life*, vol. i (London, 1884).

Hawkins (Hope), Anthony, *The Prisoner of Zenda* (London, 1894).

Herold, J. Christopher, *Mistress to an Age: The Life of Madame de Staël* (London, 1959).

Herwig, H. H., *Hammer or Anvil, Modern Germany 1648 to the Present* (Lexington, 1994).

Hitchcock, H. R., *Rococo Architecture in Southern Germany* (London, 1968).

Hirschfield, Christian Cay Lorenz, *Theorie der Gardenkunst*, five volumes from 1779–1785, edited and translated by Linda Parshall as *The Theory of Garden Design* (Pennsylvania, 2001).

Hoffman, Ernst Theodor (Amadeus), *Tales*, translated by R. J. Hollingdale (Harmondsworth: Penguin Classics, 1982).

Hogwood, Christopher, *Handel* (London, 1988).

Holmes, Richard, *Coleridge: Early Visions* (London, 1989).

——, *Coleridge: Darker Reflections* (London, 1998).

Horricks, Raymond, *In Flight with the Eagle* (Tunbridge Wells, 1988).

Jameson, Anna, *Visits and Sketches at Home and Abroad*, two vols (London, 1834).

Johnson, Edgar, *Sir Walter Scott, the Great Unknown, 1771–1821*, vols i and ii, (London, 1970).

Joseph-Marie, Comte de Maistre, 'The Saint Petersburg Dialogues (Les Soirées de St Petersburg)', 1821 in *Works* ed. J. Lively (London, 1963).

Kant, Immanuel, *Critique of Pure Reason* (London, Everyman ed., 1948 [1787])

Kleist, Heinrich von, *The Marquise of O and Other Stories*, translated by D. Luke & N. Reeves (Harmondsworth: Penguin Books, 1978).

La Motte-Fouqué, F. H. K., *Undine, Sintram and His Companions, Aslauga's Knight, The Two Captains*, edited by Edmund Gosse (Oxford: World's Classics, no date).

Lamb, Charles, *Letters,* vol. 1 (London: Everyman edition, 1909).

Lambert, Constant, *Music Ho!* (London, 1934).

Lamport, F. J. (ed. and trans.), *Schiller's The Robbers and Wallenstein* (Harmondsworth: Penguin Books, 1979).

Lang, Andrew (ed.), *The Red Fairy Book* (New York, 1966 edition).

Las Cases, Emmanuel de, *Souvenirs de Napoléon Ier* (Paris, 1935).

Lessing, Gotthold, *Laoköon, or The Limits of Poetry and Painting* (Leipzig 1766), (translated into English 1853).

Lewes, George Henry, *The Life of Goethe* (London: Everyman edition, 1908).

Lloyd, E. M., 'The Third Coalition, 1806–7', chapter x in *The Cambridge Modern History*, vol. ix (Cambridge, 1907).

Locke, John, *An Essay Concerning Human Understanding* (London, 1690 [Everyman edition, 1947]).

Lockhart, John Gibson, *The Life of Sir Walter Scott* (London: Everyman edition, 1906).

MacCarthy, Fiona, *William Morris, A Life for Our Times* (London, 1994).

MacCulloch, Diarmaid, *A History of Christianity* (London, 2009).

MacFarlane, C., *The Lives & Exploits of Banditti and Robbers* (London, 1839).

Mason, A. E. W., *Konigsmark* (London, 1938)

Mauch, Christof (ed.), *Nature in German History* (New York/Oxford, 2004).

Meredith, George, *The Adventures of Harry Richmond* (London, 1871 [Mickleham 1924 edition]).

———, *The Tragic Comedians* (London, 1880).

Merten, Klaus, *The Residence Castle, Ludwigsburg* (Tubingen, 1989).

Mitford, Nancy, *Frederick the Great* (London, 1970).

Montagu, Lady Mary Wortley, *Letters* (London: Everyman edition, 1909).

Moore, John, *A View of Society and Manners in France, Switzerland and Germany, 1786*, vol. 2 (Montana, no date).

Newman, Ernest, *Wagner Nights* (London, 1949 [1988 reprint]).

Nugent, Thomas, *The Grand Tour* (London, 1756).

Palmer, R. R., 'Social and Psychological Foundations of the Revolutionary Era', in *New Cambridge Modern History*, vol. viii (Cambridge, 1965), pp. 421–47.

Park, T. Peter, 'Germany', in Cumming (ed.), *The Carlyle Encyclopedia* (Cranbury, New Jersey: Associated University Presses, 2004). p. 190.

Pollard, A. F., 'The German Federation 1815–40', in *Cambridge Modern History*, vol. 10 (Cambridge, 1907), pp. 340–82.

Praz, Mario, *The Romantic Agony* (Oxford: Collins, 1932 [paper edition, 1960]).

Quiller-Couch, A. T. (ed.), *Oxford Book of English Poems* (Oxford, 1907).

Raspe, Rudolf Eric, *Narrative of his Marvellous Travels and Campaigns in Russia* (London, 1785). The 1865 edition, *The Adventures of Baron Munchausen*, illustrated by Gustav Doré, was produced in a paper edition (New York, 2005).

Ritter, Gerhard, *Frederick the Great*, translated by Peter Paret (London, 1968).

Robbins Landon, H. C., *Beethoven, a Documentary Study* (London, 1970).

Roberts, John M., *The Mythology of the Secret Societies* (London, 1972 [paperback edition, 2008]).

Roberts-Jones, Philippe, *Beyond Time and Place: Non-Realist Painting in the 19th Century* (Oxford, 1978).

Robertson, J. G., 'Literature in Germany', in *Cambridge Modern History*, vol. 10 (Cambridge, 1907), pp. 383–412.

Rogers, Timothy, *Rupert Brooke* (London, 1971).

Ruskin, John, *Modern Painters*, vol. 1 (London: Everyman edition, 1843).

Sabor, Rudolph, *The Real Wagner* (London, 1987 [paperback edition, 1989]).

Schiller, Friedrich Yvon, *Maria Stuart*, first performed in Weimar in 1800.

———, *The Antiquary* (Edinburgh, 1816).

———, *Life of Napoleon Buonaparte* (Edinburgh, 1827)

———, *Die Jungfrau von Orleans* (1801, translated into English as The Maid of Orleans, 1835).

———, *The Age of the Baroque, 1610–1660* (New York, 1952).

———, *The Robbers* and *Wallenstein*, translated by F. J. Lamport (Harmondsworth, Penguin Books, 1979).

———, *Mary Stuart*, translated by Peter Oswald (London, 2006).

Scott, Walter, *Anne of Geierstein* (Edinburgh, 1829).

———, *The Journal*, edited by W. E. K. Anderson (Edinburgh, 1998 edition).

Scott, William B. (ed.), *The Poetical Works of Samuel Taylor Coleridge* (London: George Routledge & Son, no date), contains Coleridge's translation of Schiller's *Wallenstein*.

Shaw, Bernard, *The Perfect Wagnerite*, 3rd edition (London, 1963).

Shelley, Mary, *The Journals, 1814–44*, edited by Feldman & Scott-Kilvert (Baltimore: John Hopkins University Press, 1987).

———, *The Letters of Mary Wollstonecraft Shelley*, vol. 3, edited by Betty T. Bennett (Baltimore: John Hopkins University Press, 1988).

Sire, H. J. A., *The Knights of Malta* (London, 1994).

Sorensen, David R., 'Goethe's Significance to Carlyle', in Mark Cumming (ed.), *The Carlyle Encyclopedia* (Cranbury, New Jersey: Associated University Presses, 2004).

Stäel, Germaine de, *De l'Allemagne*, 3 vols (Paris, 1814).

Stark, W., 'Literature & Thought: The Romantic Tendency', in *The New Cambridge Modern History*, vol. viii (Cambridge, 1965), pp. 55–80.

Steinweis, Alan, *Hitler and Carlyle's 'Historical Greatness'*, *History Today*, vol. 15 (6), (London, 1995), pp. 33–8.

Sterne, Laurence, *A Sentimental Journey through France and Italy* (London, 1768).

Sternfield, F. W., 'Music, Art & Architecture', in *New Cambridge Modern History*, vol. viii (Cambridge, 1965), pp. 81–96.

Taylor, D. J., *Thackeray* (London, 1999).

Thackeray, W. M., *The Luck of Barry Lyndon* (London, 1844).

———, *Vanity Fair* (London, 1847–8).

———, *The Rose and the Ring* (London, 1855).

————, *The Four Georges* (London: Everyman edition, 1857).

————, *Essays, Reviews etc* (London: Thomas Nelson, 1904).

————, 'The Fitzboodle Papers' (1842–3), in *Burlesques*, (London: Thomas Nelson, 1907).

Van der Zande, Johann, *Prussia and the Enlightenment* apud P. G. Dwyer, *The Rise of Prussia 1700–1830* (Harlow, 2000).

Vaughan, William et al., *Caspar David Friedrich, 1774–1840* (London: Tate Gallery, 1972).

Voltaire, F. M. Arouet, *The History of Charles XII,* 1731, in translation of Winifred Todhunter (London: Everyman edition, 1908).

————, Voltaire, F. M. Arouet, *Candide,* (London and Paris, 1759 [Novel Library ed., London 1947])

Wagner, Cosima, *Diaries 1878–1883*, edited by M. Gregor-Dellin and D. Mack (London, 1980).

Wangermann, E., 'Habsburg Possessions and Germany', in *New Cambridge Modern History*, vol. viii, (Cambridge, 1965), pp. 279–305.

Warner, Marina, *From the Beast to the Blonde* (London, 1994).

Warrack, John, *Carl Maria von Weber* (London, 1968).

Wedgwood, C. V., *The Thirty Years War* (London, 1944).

Willey, Basil, *Samuel Taylor Coleridge* (London, 1972).

Wilson, Frances, *The Ballad of Dorothy Wordsworth* (London, 2008).

Winckelmann, Johann Joachim, *Geschichte der Kunst des Alterthums* (Leipzig, 1762) (translated in 1764 as *History of the Art of Antiquity*).

Winter, Emma L., 'German Fresco Painting and the New Houses of Parliament at Westminster 1834–51', *The Historical Journal*, 47, 2 (Cambridge, 2004), pp. 291–329.

Witkowski, G., *German Drama of the Nineteenth Century* (New York, 1909).

Index

Adolph, Joh., Duke of Saxe Weissenfels, 130–1
Adventures of Harry Richmond (Meredith), 8, 13, 103, 207, 320–1
Albert Saxe-Coburg, Prince Consort, 9, 40, 252, 282–5
Alexander I of Russia, 165–6, 170, 177, 199, 202
Allemagne de l' (de Staël), 84, 296, 305
Almira (Handel), 132
Amalia, Duchess of Weimar, 56, 68
America, 111, 184–7; Declaration of Independence, 45, 76; South A., 186, 290
Anne of Geierstein (Scott), 8, 76, 214–17
Antiquary, The (Scott), 291–2
Arnim, Elizabeth von, 10, 209, 313
Aslauger's Knight (La Motte Fouqué), 297, 302
Assam brothers, 346n
Augustus (the Strong), II of Poland and I Elector of Saxony, 30, 32, 34, 90–5, 98, 131, 230
Augustus, Frederick, II of Saxony and III of Poland, 94, 96–8
Augustus, Frederick, III of Saxony and I King of Saxony, 98–9
Austen, Jane, 63, 321, 351–2n, 364n
Austria, 2, 24, 69, 83, 100–1, 104, 111, 115, 133, 183, 261, 266; France's main rival, 4, 9, 35–6; French revolutionary wars, 164–9, 172; post war Imperial Austria, 191–4, 199–204; and southern states of Germany, 119–21; visit by Dr Burney, 37–8

Bach, family, 6; Carl Philipp Emanuel, 129, 131, 134–5, 140–2, 145; Joh. Christian, 128, 140, 348n; Joh. Sebastian, 9, 11, 67, 97, 128–30, 135, 137, 141–2, 249, 251–2
Baden, 29, 31, 65, 108, 119, 164, 173, 190, 193, 198–9

Balsamo, Joseph (see Cagliostro)
Baltic, 46, 54, 99–100, 272
Bamberg, 123, 231, 233
Barry Lyndon (Thackeray), 13, 17, 31, 314
Bavaria, 9, 24, 30, 58, 80–1, 87, 97, 99, 119–22, 128, 137, 164, 170, 173, 179, 190, 193–8, 259–60, 265, 267, 282, 285, 295
Bayreuth, 110–11, 266, 269
Bedford, Sibylle, 119, 314
Beethoven, Ludwig van, 7, 9, 71, 128–9, 139, 141–3, 231–2, 248, 255, 295, 353n
Bellotto, Bernardo, 95, 97
Berlin, 7, 9–10, 28, 50, 52–3, 83–4, 110–11, 131–5, 141, 143, 145, 175, 183–4, 193, 290, 294–5, 297, 311, 318; Academy of Sciences, 41, 53, 100–2, 230–1, 233–6; as intellectual capital of Germany, 247–8, 275–7 (see also Schinkel); power-house of German revival, 54
Bismarck, Otto von, 205, 239, 266, 308, 314, 319
Blake, William, 181, 272
Blucher, G. L. von, 179, 247
Blumenbach, Joh. Friedrich, 150–1, 324
Bodmer, Jacob, 65
Bohemia, 24, 93, 103, 137, 139
Bonaparte (see Napoleon), Jerome, 76, 174–6, 190, 193, 238, 314, 353n; Scott's *Life of Napoleon Buonaparte*, 212–13
Boswell, James, 1, 7, 20, 34, 113, 128, 164, 166, 323
Böttger, Johann Friedrich, 35, 96
Brandenburg, 10, 24, 30, 46, 87, 99, 100–1, 223, 225, 235, 275, 310
Brown, Ford Madox, 285
Brucker, Joh. Jacob, 201–2
Brunswick, 31, 40, 128, 131, 174, 193; Duke of, 51, 60, 87–8, 205, 236

Buckler, Hannes, 168–9, 212
Burke, Edmund, 54
Bürger, Gottfried August, 84, 211, 281, 291, 321
Burgundy, 8, 120, 214–16, 287 (see also Charles V of, 9)
Burney, Dr Charles, 7, 19–20, 27, 31–2, 37, 66, 75, 88, 98, 112, 114, 116, 127, 134–5, 137–40
Buxtehude, Dietrich, 127, 129–31
Byron, George Gordon, 8, 17, 62, 64, 167, 207–10, 214, 218–21, 248, 287, 305, 322, 325, 353n

Cagliostro, 30, 35, 95, 337n
Calzabigi, Ranieri de, 138
Carlyle, Thomas, 1, on Coleridge, 304; enthusiasm for Germany, 5–6, 8–9, 29–31, 48–9, 51, 71, 76, 96, 115, 173, 216–17, 287, 289, 297, 301–8, 314–15, 326; Frederick the Great, 307–10; on Goethe, 59–60, 308–9; on Heroes, 306–7; on Hoffmann, 230; and Lewes' Life of Goethe, 311–12; Life of Schiller, 305–6, 341n, 345n; on Werther, 62–3, 217
Casanova, Giacomo, 5, 30–2, 34, 95, 97, 110, 112, 117
Cezy, Wilhelmina von, 143–59 (see also Euryanthe)
Chamisso, Louis (Adalbert) de, 236–7
Charles XII of Sweden, 90–1, 94
Charles Augustus of Weimar, 7, 56–60, 70, 74, 108, 186–7, 278
Charles Augustus III of Württemberg, 116
Charles Eugene of Württemberg, 69–70, 73, 81, 110–17, 198, 219
Charles Frederick of Baden, 29
Charles Theodore, Elector of Bavaria, 120, 195; Elector Palatine, 140, 348n
Coleridge, S. T., 4, 5–6, 8, 20–1, 48, 71, 84–5, 88, 211, 281, 279, 297, 300–4, 308, 314–15, 324–5, 349n; London lectures, 218–20 (see also Wallenstein; Rime of the Ancient Mariner)
Cologne, 13, 24, 103, 122, 209, 247
Colloredo, Archbishop, 131, 140
Confederation of the Rhine (see Rhine)
Cornelius, Peter von, 282–4 (see also Nazarenes)
Courland, Duchy of, 91–3, 97

Dadd, Richard, 252
Dalberg, Otto von, 173, 352n
Darwin, Charles, 186, 324
Denmark, 65, 128, 143, 193
De Quincey, Thomas, 304, 314
Digby, Jane, 195–6
Disraeli, Benjamin, 8–9, 52, 69, 87, 200, 220–2, 283, 308, 356–7n (see also Vivian Grey)
Don Carlos (Schiller), 60, 71, 95
Don Giovanni (Mozart) 234, 240, 244
Donizetti, Gaetano, 349–50n
Dousterswivel (see The Antiquary)
Dresden, 10, 28, 57, 67, 90, 93–8, 131, 134, 141, 143, 200, 225, 255, 257, 260, 271–3, 283

Eastlake, Charles, 281, 283–4
Eberhard IV, of Württemberg, 104–7, 244
Eckermann, J. P., 188, 213, 325–6
Eliot, George (Marian Evans), 6, 19, 57, 311–12, 319
Elizabeth/Matilda (Tannhäuser), 241–4, 259
England, 64, 87, 111, 116, 123, 133, 166, 188, 208–9, 229; conflict with Napoleon, 170, 176–8; cultural influence, 273, 276, 279; emergence as European power, 2–4, 6; E. freemasonry, 79–80; home of experiment and empiricism, 41–2, 61; image of Germany, 321; imagination baffled by Goethe, 74; influence on German thought, 44, 46, 50–1; interest in Germany, 8, 15, 20, 24–5, 38–9; and Mendelssohn, 251–3; a natural society, 82; school of fresco painting, 283–6
Enlightenment, The, 5, 43, 64, 79, 82, 84, 181
Erfurt, 81, 94, 128, 170
Esterházy, family, 37, 250, 266; Prince Paul Anton, 141–3
Essay Concerning Understanding (Hume) 52
Eugene, Prince of Savoy, 35, 91, 106, 108
Euryanthe (Weber), 19, 144, 254

Fairies, 252–4 (see also Dadd, Richard; Feen, Die (Wagner))
Faust (Goethe), 60, 74, 214, 249, 255, 279, 308, 350n
Feen, Die (Wagner) 254
Fichte, Joh. Gottlieb, 6, 181, 220, 236, 266, 292, 294–5, 303

Fitzboodle, George, 3, 8, 15–16, 32; *The F. Papers* (Thackeray), 15–18

Florence, 37, 132, 282; F. of the Elbe (see Dresden)

France, 1, 3–9, 15, 24, 33–5, 45, 56, 104–5, 111, 117, 119, 122, 190, 226–9, 231, 239, 248, 259, 264, 266; French baroque, 76; Bourbon F., 210, 212; cultural hegemony, 3, 25, 28, 50, 127, 163, 277–8, 281; freemasonry, 79–80; influence of French classicism, 66–7; lodestar of south Germany, 314; and Maurice de Saxe, 91–2; music and opera, 128–9, 131–2, 136, 145; revolutionary and Napoleonic Wars, 74, 84, 121, 163–179, 187–8, 198, 273, 352n

Francis I of Austria/Francis II, Holy Roman Emperor, 174, 199–203

Frankenstein (Mary Shelley), 44, 322–5

Frankfurt, 20, 56, 83, 128, 173, 183, 193, 197, 200–1, 205, 293

Frederick I of Prussia, 90, 99

Frederick II the Great, 5, 33, 35, 58, 64, 70, 90, 92, 99, 110, 114–15, 117, 120, 164, 179, 275, 327, 346n; Carlyle on, 307, 309–10 (see also Carlyle's *Life of*); enthusiasm for France, 7, 9–11, 25, 27, 31–4, 54; and Moses Mendelssohn, 53; as musical patron, 128–9, 131, 134–5, 145; Napoleon's view of, 174–5; as ruler of Prussia, 101–2; sparks Seven Years War, 36

Frederick Eugene, Duke of Württemberg, 117, 197

Frederick William of Prussia, I, 27, 31, 45–6, 100, 107; II, 79; III, 10, 179–80, 184–5, 189, 191, 203, 233, 247

Freemasonry, 79–81

Freischütz, Die (Weber), 144–5, 232

Friedrich, Caspar David, 10, 271–6, 279–80, 282, 313

Friedrich, Prinz von Homburg (Kleist), 227; (Henze), 357n

Friedrich I, Emperor of Germany, 314

George (Louis) elector of Hanover and King of England, I, 38–9, 40, 88–90, 133, 309; II, 39, 92, 208, 289; III, 4, 284, 289, 344n

Germany, absolutism, 29; ambiguities and unification, 8, 192; Anglo-G. rivalry, 315; appetite for the mysterious, 5–6, 79–81; baroque style, 105–6, 122–3; Carlyle on, 5,

49; Carlyle's view of, 307–10; Coleridge's opinion of, 20; Confederation, 199–200; culture, 3, 7–8, 67; and de Staël, 292; deep cloud of melancholy, 63; discovery of Shakespeare, 51; drama, 71, 226; empire of the air, 1, 3–4, 10; encyclopaedism, 81; enlightenment, 164; fading of idealism, 177; fiction and stories, 10, 29; folk songs and ballades, 67, 211; forests, 6, 31, 276; France intellectually challenged, 297; French influence, 29, 50; French revolutionary and Napoleonic wars, 88, 208–9; Hapsburg led Germany *reich* 'infamous', 201; hunting, 34–5, 57, 106; idealism, 220; Imperial G., 325; interest in Middle Ages, 188, 244; land of romantic fantasy, 76, 210; language, 2, 4, 28, 66, 94, 182, 211; little courts governance, 4–6, 10, 33, 87; looking to its past, 85; love, 5, 267; military passions, 31, 33; music, 10, 28, 127–132, 137, 248–50, 314; mystics, 3, 66, 84; nationalism, 6, 10, 61, 191, 199; and nature, 9, 67, 19; opera, 21, 61, 131, 133–4, 143, 232–3; other images, 75–6; palaces, 2, 6, 39, 103, 122–3; philosophy, 4, 42, 79; poetry, 5, 10, 50, 65; princes and electors, 2–4, 24–5, 30; recovers from Thirty Years War, 23–4; religion, 25–7, 45–51; renaissance, 3, 10, 41; respect for church and state, 166; status after Waterloo, 190–4; the volk, 67, 74; trade, 20; travel, 20; universities, 9, 48

Getty, John Paul, 93

Gilbert, W. S., 18, 55, 254

Gluck, Christoph Willibald, 37, 128, 134, 137–9, 142–3, 145, 232, 234

Goebbels, Joseph, 247, 310

Goethe, Joh. Wolfgang von, 5, 6, 9, 11, 33, 54, 64, 66–8, 81, 85, 115–16, 184, 186–9, 226, 232, 238, 244, 247, 255, 300–1, 305; admires Bach, 129, 141, 144; his anglophilia, 4; attitude to France, 166–7, 171–2; attitude to reform, 163–4; designs park for Weimar, 276–7; encounter with Thackeray, 18–19; and G. language, 21; on German places of learning, 353n; on German religion, 27, 33, 42; Germans on the English, 315, 325–6; the *Goethezeit*, 323–6; and Kant, 48–9, 56–61; Lewes's Life, 311–12, 315; meets Napoleon, 7, 59,

74, 171–2, 351–2n; and Mendelssohn, 249–50, 278; and Mme de Staël, 7; nature and reason, 6, 41–2, 8–11, 17; on Newton, 340n; Ottilia von, 21 post-Napoleonic vision, 180–2, 186–9; and Schiller, 70–1, 778–9; and *Sorrows of Werther*, 5, 10, 57, 62–3, 292–8; theory of colour, 279–81; view of German histories, 220; and Walter Scott, 211–14; in Weimar, 56–61, 73–4; on women, 208–9 (see also, *Hermann and Dorothea*; *Götz von Berlichingen*; *Sorrows of Young Werther, The*)

Göttingen, university, 4, 21, 83, 183, 202, 220, 289, 325, 324, 353n

Götz von Berlichingen (Goethe), 57, 62–4, 207–8, 211–15, 217, 281, 326, 341n, 356n

Gray, Thomas, 82

Grävenitz, Christina Wilhelmina, 104–8, 112–13, 196–7, 244

Greece, Kingdom of, 6, 26, 78, 77–8, 195; appreciation of beauty, 326; G. Classicism, 50, 64–6; influence on Ludwig I, 195, 275

Grimm brothers, 6, 188, 221, 232, 238, 272, 281, 314, 342n; Jacob, 75–6, 78, 289; Wilhelm, 77, 176, *The Fairy Tales* (*Kinder und Hausmarchen*), 75–8, 85

Gustavus Adolphus, King of Sweden, 89, 94

Halle, 27, 43, 130, 161, 185, 235–6, 338n

Hamburg, 28, 51, 65, 90, 128, 131–2, 135, 143, 192, 211, 248

Handel, George Frederick, 6, 122, 130–3, 136–9, 257, 250–1

Hanover, 2, 4, 24, 30, 38–40, 83, 87–9, 91, 93, 133, 141, 128, 130–3, 135–9, 131–2, 174, 193, 208, 289

Hardenberg, George Frederick (see Novalis)

Hare, Julius, 297–301, Georgiana Hare-Naylor, 298

Haydn, Joseph, 7, 37, 135, 139, 141–2, 231–2, 249–50, 266, 316, 324

Haydon, Benjamin Robert, 279, 281, 284

Hegel, G. W. F., 266, 318, 356n

Herder J. G., 6, 17, 56, 58, 61, 66–7, 70–1, 81, 163, 181, 191, 219, 298

Herman und Dorothea (Goethe), 187

Hesse, 76, 183, 205; Hesse-Cassel, 30, 32, 45, 75–7, 174, 183, 289

Hildebrandt, Lucas von, 124, 347n

Hitler, Adolph, 264, 268, 310

Hoffmann, E. T. A., 10, 41, 143, 229–235, 237–45, 272, 276–7, 281, 295, 314, 316, 326; *Tales of Hoffmann, The*, 239–40, 245, 320 (see also *Undine*)

Hohenheim, Francisca de, 113, 115–17; palace of, 116

Hohenzollerns, The, 95, 99, 101, 131, 35, 190, 193, 266, 313, 326–7

Holy Roman Empire, 2, 23–4, 64, 87, 97, 108, 120, 124, 165, 190, 193; Napoleon dissolves, 173–4, 178, 302, 326–7

Hope, Anthony, 8–9, 223, 316–18

Hubert, St, 34, 106, 221

Humboldt, Alexander von, 183, 185–6, 247, 290, 318, 324, 364n; William von, 183–5, 218, 247

Hume, David, 5, 42, 47–9, 52, 315

Hunt, Holman, 125–7; James Leigh, 299–300, 311

Illuminati, Illuminists, 6, 81–2, 95

Iphigenia in Tauris (Gluck / Goethe), 64, 79, 175

Italy, 3–4, 6, 10, 19, 21, 36, 38, 198, 204, 212–13; music and opera, 28, 128–9, 133–4, 136, 145, 249, 274, 280–1

Jameson, Anna, 274, 279, 284

Jena, battle of, 170, 176, 179, 225, 231, 237, 247, 310; university, 44, 58, 65, 84, 94, 181, 201–2, 218, 220

Jesus, 51, 53; Society of Jesuits, 36, 41, 80, 120–1, 196–7

Jews, 51–4, 80, 108–10, 168, 295, 268, 310, 352n, 354n; Jew Süss (see Oppenheimer); Wagner on Judaism, 256 (see also Lassalle)

Johnson, Samuel, 4, 323

Joseph, Emperor of Austria, I, 97; II, 36, 200–1, 338n

Kant, Immanuel, 1, 4–6, 43, 46–9, 48–50, 53–4, 66–8, 80–1, 163, 173, 209, 211, 220, 229–30, 243, 296–7, 303, 308, 315–16, 325–6; 'categoric imperatives' 47; his theory of knowledge, 47

Karlschule, 114

Keith, George, 20

Kleist, Heinrich von, 9, 10, 225–9, 271–2, 326 (see also *Marquise d'O*; Henriette Vogel)

Klopstock, Friedrich Gottlieb, 65–7, 68–9, 74, 191, 211, 229, 250, 323 (see also *Die Messia*)

Knights, 76, 85; imperial K.s, 29, 166, 173; of Malta, 33, 79, 89, 120–1, 202, 352n; Templars, 51–2, 80; Teutonic K.s, 46, 99, 191, 236, 273, 352n

Königsburg, 46–8, 100, 141, 172, 229–30, 255

Königsmark, Maria Aurora, 90–2; Philip, 89–90

Kosegarten, Ludwig Theobul, 273–4

Kotzebue, August Friedrich, 17, 202–3, 354n

La Gardela, 112–13

La Motte Fouqué, Friedrich de, 10, 231–2, 235–7, 223–4, 281, 297, 302, 326 (see also *Undine*; *Auslager's Knight*; *Sintram*)

Lady of the Lake (Scott), 212, 218

Lamb, Charles, 300

Laökoon (Lessing), 50–1, 304

Lassalle, Ferdinand, 318–20 (see also *Tragic Comedians, The* (Meredith))

Leibniz, 40–1, 43–4, 53, 99, 102, 220, 278, 296

Lecouvreur, Adriana, 91, 93, 357n

Leipzig, 65, 128–9, 231, 251–4; battle, 238, 277; university, 55, 166, 181

Leopold of Austria, I, 36; Leopold II, 36–7, 199

Lessing, Gotthold, 6, 43, 50–4, 58, 63, 84, 102, 136, 163, 166, 219, 297, 304

Lewes, George, 18, 57, 75, 84, 311–12

Lewis, Mathew ('Monk'), 218, 322

Liszt, Franz, 6, 257–8, 263, 353n

Locke, John, 41–2, 46–8

Lockhart, John Gibson, 154, 355–6n

Lohengrin (Wagner), 85, 145, 258, 260–1, 264–9

London, 41; art scene, 284; music in, 247–57

Louis XI, 214; XIV, 2, 24–5, 29, 31, 35, 87, 103–4, 112–13, 164–5, 168, 264, 267; XV, 4, 92, 164, 171, 267; XVI, 60, 97, 165, 194

Louisburg (Ludwigsburg), 69–70, 103, 106–9, 114–16

Ludwig, King of Bavaria I, 9, 194–7, 258, 275, 282–4; Ludwig II, 58, 145, 258–267, 359n (see also Wagner, Montez)

Luther, Martin, 2, 57, 62, 94, 123, 182, 298, Lutherans, 25–6, 28, 58, 64, 66, 84, 89,

123, 132, 202, 220, 227, 238, 244, 268, 273, 299, 327

Macpherson, James, 67 (see Ossian)

Maid of Orleans (Schiller), 71, 187, 350n

Mainz, 24, 29, 123, 169, 173, 200, 239

Maistre, Joseph de, 81

Malta (see Knights of)

Manfred (Byron), 207, 210, 275

Mansfield Park (J. Austen), 351–2n

Mannheim, 70–1, 103, 115, 139–41, 198

Marburg, 75–6

Maria Theresa of Austria, 7, 36–7, 98, 101, 137, 290

Marlborough, Duke of, 2, 35, 38, 91, 104, 122, 164, 208

Marmion (Scott), 212, 218

Marquise d'O… (Kleist), 225, 227

Martius, Fred. Philip von, 186, 324 (see also Spix G. B.)

Mary Stuart (Schiller), 71, 187, 226, 244, 350n

Marx, Karl, 266, 356n

Masnadieri I (Verdi), 351n

Matilda (see Tannhäuser, Elizabeth)

Matthew Passion, The (Bach J. S.), 129, 249

Maximilian Elector of Bavaria, I, 194, II, 119, 166, 265–6, III, 119

Meissen, 96

Meistersinger von Nürnberg, Die (Wagner), 123, 262, 267

Mendelssohn, Abraham, 54, 248; Felix, 9, 41, 52, 54, 130, 143–4, 239, 247–58, 278, 282–3, 287–8, 314, 351n; Moses, 9, 52–4, 189, 248, 326

Meredith, George, 8–9, 13, 103, 207, 223, 317–20 (see also *Adventures of Harry Richmond*, *Tragic Comedians, The*)

Messiah, The (Handel), 253; *Messia Die* (Klopstok), 65–6, 229

Metastasio, Pietro, 136–9, 143, 338n

Metternich, Prince C. W. L., 10, 74, 183, 193, 199–204, 222

Meyerbeer, Giacomo, 240, 348n

Midsummer Nights Dream, A (Shakespeare/ Mendelssohn), 249, 252–3

Milton, John, 50, 65, 284

Minnesingers, 85, 123, 182, 241–2, 244, 258, 326

Montagu, Lady Mary Wortley, 39, 88

Montez, Lola, 9, 195–7, 222, 258, 260–1, 265

Moore, George Edward, 315–16; Thomas, 325
More, John, 7, 31, 34
Moreau, Jean, 117, 169
Morris, William, 340n, 359n
Mozart, Wolfgang A., 7, 37, 128, 131, 135–6, 139–40, 142–3, 145, 231–2, 234, 249, 275, 316, 326, 348n (see also *Zauberflöte, Die*)
Munchäusen Baron von, 290–2, 296; For *Travels of Baron M.* (see Raspe, R. E.)
Munich, 9, 28, 37, 103, 143, 195–6, 258, 260, 262, 265–6, 283–4, 295

Napoleon Bonaparte, 4, 9, 59, 60, 92, 96, 99, 163–5, 183, 189, 191, 195, 198, 201, 204, 208, 213, 221, 116, 229, 231, 237–8, 248, 275–7, 281, 293, 296, 306–7, 310–12, 314; as a 'hero', 353; changes balance of power, 166–9; deconstructs Holy Roman Empire, 172–4; designs for future, 177–8; effect on Germany, 7; and Goethe, 7, 59–60, 74, 171–2, 351–2; meets Goethe, 171–2; N. wars, 19; Napoleonic system, 190–1; Napoleon III, 230; and Prussia, 178–82; escapes from Elba, 93
Nathan the Wise (Lessing), 51–2
Nature, 42; acquires a personality, 323–4; back to N., 59–6; 'Christ's Bible', 273–4; composed of volcanoes and moonlight, 84; in C. D. Friedrich, 273; laws of, 46–7, 54; *natur philosophie*, 210, 219–20, 278; and reason, 43–4 (see also Puckler-Muskau)
Nazarenes, The, 282–7
Neumann, Balthazar, 123–5, 346n
Neuschwanstein, 262–5, 267, 359n
Newton, Isaac, 42, 44, 62, 315
Nibelungen (see *Ring des N., Der*)
Nietzsche, Friedrich, 74
Night Thoughts (Young), 65, 323
Novalis, also Hardenberg, George Frederick von, 180–2, 188, 272, 295

Offenbach, Jacques, 233, 239–40, 245
One-State conferences; Boston (2009), xiv–xv, 7; Haifa (2008) (2010), 8; London (2007), 6–7; Madrid (2007), 6; York University (2009), 7–8
Oppenheimer, Jew Süss, 108–10
Orzelska, Marie, 90, 344n
Ossian, 63–4, 67, 250, 272, 274

Ottoman Empire, 35–6, 38, 120–1, 173, 178, 192, 199, 204, 290
Overbeck, Joh. Friedrich, 282, 286, 360n (see also Nazarenes)

Palatinate, The, 24, 38, 103, 119–20, 123, 127, 139, 168, 198, 200
Paracelsus, Theophrastus, 6, 35, 116, 182, 238
Paris, 7, 75, 83, 101–2, 117, 136, 138–9, 144–5, 148, 171, 178, 196, 205, 233, 239–40, 247, 255–6, 275–6, 287, 292, 312, 314; Peace of, 183
Parliament, Houses of, 271–5
Parsifal (Wagner), 242
Pedestrianising, 152–3, 323
Pergolesi, G. B., 136, 142
Phaidon (M Mendelssohn), 53
Piccolomini, The (see *Wallenstein*)
Pietism, pietists, 6, 27, 44, 46, 49, 64–5, 68, 82, 167, 202, 230, 327
Poland, 30, 32, 34, 90–4, 97–9, 177, 191–2, 199, 204, 230, 236, 275, 277
Pomerania, 10, 84, 230, 234, 273–4, 279, 302, 313
Potsdam, 7, 31, 227, 235, 326
Pre-Raphaelite Brotherhood, 285–7
Prince of Homburg (Henze), 352n
Prisoner of Zenda, The (Hope), 316–18
Prout, Samuel, 279–82, 285
Prussia, by Boswell, 148, 164; defeated at Jena, 170, 172–4, 178–9; emergence of, 7–10, 20–1; home of the 'Hoffmen', 225, 227, 230–1, 233, 235–9; kingdom of, 3–4, 43, 46, 50, 52, 66, 87, 99, 111–12, 129, 131, 166, 174, 176, 248, 275–7, 302, 315; military, 31, 36, 40; P.'s rebirth, 183, 189–90, 193–4, 201, 203, 205; post-Jena, 178–82, 288; and de Staël, 294; under Frederick the Great, 24–7, 31, 54, 69, 90, 99–102, 262; victory at Rossbach, 310, 315, 326–7; visited by Dr Burney, 134–5 (see also Brandenburg)
Puckler-Muskau, Prince Hermann, 276–8 (see also Nature)
Pumpernickel, bread, 3, 93, 164; Duchy of Kalbsbraten-P., 3, 14–19; P. states and as synonym for the German collective, 3, 8–11, 21, 29, 38, 40, 43, 46, 34, 39, 41, 55–7, 60, 67, 71, 74, 77, 88–9, 99–101, 117, 120–2,

125, 127, 132, 134, 139, 141–2, 145, 162, 172–3, 176, 178–9, 188, 191, 193–4, 197, 199, 205, 210, 218, 221, 253, 257, 263, 267, 288, 307, 309, 313–14, 316–17, 326

Radcliffe, Ann, 82, 161–2, 215, 321
Raphael Sanzio, 98, 282, 344n
Raspe, Rudolph Eric, 289–92
Renoir, Jean, 364n
Rhine, 2, 4, 8–9, 13, 35, 38, 56, 119, 165–6, 168–70, 174, 165–6, 168–70, 174, 207–15, 221, 226, 276, 280, 354n;
   The Confederation of the, 170, 173–4, 177;
   The Legend of the R. (Thackeray), 19;
   Rhine-maidens (*Der Ring des Nibelungen*), 258, 262, 268
Richardson, Samuel, 62, 68, 82
Richter, Joh. Paul, 1, 3, 304–5, 355n, 362n
Rienzi (Wagner), 254–6
Rime of the Ancient Mariner, The (Coleridge), 84, 150, 324
Ring des Nibelungen, Der (Wagner), 257–60, 262–3, 268, 284
Robbers, The / Die Rauber, (Schiller), 70–2, 115, 154, 161, 198, 211, 213, 306, 352n
Robinson Crusoe, 142, 147, 348n
Romantic (ism), art and aesthetic, 272–6, 287–8; elixir of, 3; essential ingredients of R., 296–7; European, 3–4; R. Fantasies, 321–2; R. fiction, 98; German R., 41, 82–4, 182; image of man, 167, 187–8; R. kingdom of Pumpernickel, 326–7; make believe, 8; R. music, 68, 145, 231–2, 245, 248, 288; nobility, 212; origin of R., 78–9; R. Scotland, 250; a sickness, 188; R. zeitgeist, 275
Rome, 2, 6, 26, 98, 218, 243, 275, 281
Rose and the Ring, The (Thackeray), 17
Rossbach, battle of, 35, 175, 310
Rousseau, J. J., 48–9, 63, 81, 117, 136, 164, 214, 210
Ruritania, 8, 190, 316–17, 363n
Ruskin, John, 279–81, 285–6
Russia, 71, 165, 173, 176–8, 180, 183, 192, 195, 200, 204, 231, 277, 240

Salzburg, 100, 128, 131, 140
Sand, George, 92–3, 196
Sartor Resartus (Carlyle), 5, 289, 306, 309
Saxe, Maurice de, 32, 90–3, 97, 196, 208

Saxe-Gotha, 94; Saxe-Weissenfels, 130–1, 129; Saxe-Wittenberg, 94 (see also Saxe-Weimar)
Saxony, 10, 21, 24, 30, 32, 34–5, 50, 58, 65, 71, 85, 90–9, 150, 152, 164, 166, 179–80, 191, 193, 200, 202, 205, 212, 220, 247, 258, 271, 275–6, 290, 294, 324; becomes a Kingdom, 173, 177; porcelain, 95–6, 267
Scarlatti, Domenico, 128, 133
Schelling, Friedrich Wilhelm von, 153, 181, 219–20
Schiller, Friedrich, 5, 8–9, 17, 54, 56, 59–60, 67, 69–73, 78–9, 95, 115–16, 149, 151, 154–62, 165–7, 186–8, 191, 211, 213, 218, 220, 226, 229, 236, 244, 250, 255, 265, 293–4, 297–8, 305–6, 308, 325, 349–51n, 362n (see also *Maid of Orleans*; *Mary Stuart*; *Wallenstein*)
Schinkel, Karl Friedrich, 10, 275–6
Schlegel, Frederick, 78, 83, 144, 181; August, 83, 181, 218, 236, 295–6, 300, 361n
Schönbrunn, Count J. P. F. von, 110, 123–4
Schubart, Daniel Christian, 114–15, 345–6n
Schubert, Franz, 8, 145, 248, 288, 326
Schumann, Robert and Clara, 41, 114–15, 225, 234–6, 248, 257, 288, 358n
Scotland, 4, 6, 38, 148, 214, 250, 274, 315, 323; 'Scottish' masonry, 79
Scott, Sir Walter, 4, 8, 17, 19, 51, 53, 60, 74, 76, 80, 155, 161, 211–19, 236, 238, 250, 278, 287, 291–308, 291, 325, 356n; Harriet, 212; William Bell, 153, 349n (see also *Anne of Geierstein*; *Antiquary, The*)
Seven Years War, The, 23–4, 33, 35, 56, 96, 98, 111, 117, 307
Shakespeare, William, 4–5, 8–9, 56, 58, 64, 66–8, 70–1, 73, 83–4, 144, 152, 154–8, 161, 171, 182, 211, 249, 255, 284, 295, 297, 300
Shaw, Bernard, 234, 257–8, 287
Shelley, Mary, 44, 161, 209, 322, 324–5; Percy Bysshe, 67, 74, 287
Shudder Novel, The, 161, 321
Sintram (La Motte Fouqué), 297–9
Sorrows of Young Werther, The, 5, 17, 57–9, 62–4, 78, 172, 211, 217, 227, 229, 244, 249, 292, 312, 352n (see also Goethe)
Spain, 3, 35, 104, 119, 122
Spix, J. B. von, 186, 324

Staël, Germaine de, 4, 7, 60, 84, 181, 210, 237, 237, 278, 289, 292–6, 300, 303, 305
Stamitz, Joh. (Stamic Jan), 135, 139, 141–2
Sterling, John, 74, 300–1
Stettin (Szczecin), 21, 84, 100
Strasbourg, 54, 208
Sturm und Drang, 48–9, 62, 64, 71, 73–4, 83–4, 162, 187–8, 226, 229, 248, 278, 288, 339n, 351n
Stuttgart, 67, 69, 103, 106, 111–16
Sweden, Swedes, 2, 8, 89–91, 100, 104, 155–6, 236
Sweiten, Gottfried, 141–2
Switzerland, 4, 151, 176, 197, 209–15, 226, 257

Tannhäuser (Wagner), 85, 233, 240–5, 257, 263–7
Telemann, Georg Philip, 128, 135
Teutonic (See Knights)
Thackeray, W. M., 3, 8, 13, 15, 17–19, 31–2, 28–40, 60, 74, 87–9, 298, 311, 314, 326
Thirty Years War, 23–4, 41, 94, 104, 119, 128, 130, 188, 192
Thomasius, Christian, 43–4
Tiepolo, Giambattista and Domenico, 124–5
Tragic Comedians, The (Meredith), 318–20
Tristan und Isolde (Wagner), 182, 241, 257, 259–60, 267, 269, 320
Turner J. M. W., 271–2, 279, 285

Undine (Hoffmann, La Motte-Fouqué), 143, 231–9, 244, 254, 316

Vanity Fair (Thackeray), 4, 13–15, 17
Venice, 131, 133, 161, 233, 254
Venusberg (see Tannhäuser), 263
Verdi, Giuseppe, 351n
Versailles, 29–30, 39, 101, 113, 123, 142, 264, 267
Victoria, Queen, 9, 40, 88, 95, 101, 203, 218, 253, 257, 281, 285–7
Vienna, 28, 36–8, 41, 98, 104–5, 108, 115, 122, 124, 128–9, 131, 137–9, 141, 143, 145, 183–5, 193, 200, 253, 257, 295, 311; Congress of, 76, 88, 184, 194, 275
Vivian Grey (Disraeli), 8, 220–3
Vogel, Henriette, 227, 229 (see also Kleist)
Vogler, Abbé, 140, 348n
Voltaire, 7, 29, 43, 68, 90, 102, 164, 166, 171, 202, 210, 213, 292, 307

Wagner, Richard, 7, 9, 41, 58, 85, 123, 139, 145, 229, 233, 240–5, 247–8, 253–69, 275, 288, 302, 314, 319, 358–9n; Cosima W., 260–2, 267, 359n (see also Feen, Die; Lohengrin; Meistersinger, Die; Parsifal; Tannhäuser; Tristan and Isolde)
Wallenstein, Albrecht Wenzel, Duke of Friedland, 156–7; Coleridge's translation, 154–7; The Wallenstein Plays (Schiller), 60, 71, 116, 187, 217, 226, 306
Walpole, Horace, 82, 89
Warsaw, 94, 97, 134, 231–2
Waterloo, Battle of, 7, 13, 16, 179, 247
Weber, Aloisa, 140; Costanze, 143; Karl Maria von, 41, 143–5, 232, 240, 254, 316, 348n (see also Die Freischütz; Euryanthe)
Weimar, 5, 8, 12, 17–18, 21, 41, 55, 57–9, 60, 67–8, 69–71, 74, 116, 128, 125, 141, 145, 155, 158–60, 170–2, 186, 193, 207, 213, 226, 236, 247–50; Saxe-W., 33, 75, 166, 194, 201, 275, 278, 293–5, 298, 311–12, 326
Weishaupt, Adam, 80
Wesley, Charles, 252; Samuel, 129
Westphalia, 1, 7, 76, 174–6, 179, 190, 192, 196, 208, 215, 239; Peace of, 23
White, Gilbert, 323
Wieland, Christoph Martin, 58, 67–8, 70–81, 149, 292, 298
Wilhelm Meister (Goethe), 73, 187, 293, 304–5
William Tell (Schiller), 71, 210, 255–6, 265, 351n
Winckelmann, Johann Joachim, 50–1, 64–5, 98, 106, 188, 341n, 360n
Wittelsbachs, The, 120, 195, 265
Wolff, Caspar, 210; Christian, 27, 44–6, 82, 153
Wordsworth, Dorothy and William, 20–1, 149–61, William, 211, 219–20, 287, 303–4, 314, 324
Württemberg, 32, 34, 69, 81, 98, 103–5, 108, 110–12, 114, 117, 170–1, 175–6, 190, 193–4, 198, 219, 244
Würzburg, 123–5, 254, 349n

Young, Edward, 65, 82, 323

Zimmermann brothers, 346n
Zauberflöte, Die (Mozart), 142–4